CORPORATE RESPONSIBILITY

This book is dedicated to my late mother, Elenora M. Argenti,
who taught me what responsibility is really all about.

CORPORATE RESPONSIBILITY

Paul A. Argenti
The Tuck School of Business at Dartmouth College

Los Angeles | London | New Delhi
Singapore | Washington DC

Los Angeles | London | New Delhi
Singapore | Washington DC

FOR INFORMATION:

SAGE Publications, Inc.
2455 Teller Road
Thousand Oaks, California 91320
E-mail: order@sagepub.com

SAGE Publications Ltd.
1 Oliver's Yard
55 City Road
London EC1Y 1SP
United Kingdom

SAGE Publications India Pvt. Ltd.
B 1/I 1 Mohan Cooperative Industrial Area
Mathura Road, New Delhi 110 044
India

SAGE Publications Asia-Pacific Pte. Ltd.
3 Church Street
#10-04 Samsung Hub
Singapore 049483

Copyright © 2016 by SAGE Publications, Inc.

Printed in the United States of America.

ISBN 978-1-4833-8310-1

This book is printed on acid-free paper.

Acquisitions Editor: Maggie Stanley
eLearning Editor: Katie Bierach
Editorial Assistant: Nicole Mangona
Production Editor: Bennie Clark Allen
Copy Editor: Rachel Keith
Typesetter: C&M Digitals (P) Ltd.
Proofreader: Rae-Ann Goodwin
Indexer: Robie Grant
Cover Designer: Gail Buschman
Marketing Manager: Liz Thornton

15 16 17 18 19 10 9 8 7 6 5 4 3 2 1

BRIEF CONTENTS

DETAILED CONTENTS

A test bank, PowerPoint slides, and teaching notes for the cases are available on the password-protected instructor resource site at study.sagepub.com/argenti.

PREFACE

This book stems from a decade of researching, teaching, and developing the field of study referred to throughout this text as *corporate responsibility*, or "CR." Although the term itself is not new, the notion of it as a field of study for business schools as well as a function of management is more recent. In this introduction, I would like to talk more about why I became interested in this topic, what the book is all about, and why I think everyone needs to know more about this important and emerging discipline.

WHY CORPORATE RESPONSIBILITY?

I first became interested in corporate responsibility as an outgrowth of my career-long interest in corporate communication.[1] In writing a case in cooperation with Starbucks focusing on their decision to sell fair trade coffee, I realized that many of the nongovernmental organizations (NGOs) attacking corporations were really looking at whether corporations were conducting their business and working with their value chain responsibly. My first article on this topic[2] was presented at a conference hosted by *California Management Review* and Boston University that included professors working in the area of corporate responsibility from management, strategy, and communications. I immediately saw a corollary to my earlier work focusing on reputation. Here was an emerging area of study that crossed disciplines, was important to management, and, unlike the area of reputation, had as its focus making the world a better place.

The next year, I developed an elective in Corporate Responsibility here at the Tuck School that initially relied on the work of colleagues at other schools and from other disciplines. The course was an immediate success with the MBA students, and a new area for me to work on after two decades of research primarily focused on corporate communication. I started to write cases for the course (most of which appear in this textbook), attend conferences, read the latest research, and meet with executives in the area, and soon became passionate about developing material to fuel the class. After feeling the same frustration that I had felt decades earlier around finding material for my Corporate Communication class, I realized that there was no text that could serve as the focus of my new course.

That led me to a proposal for this book with SAGE. The result of over two years of work appears in this text.

WHAT IS THIS BOOK ABOUT?

Chapter 1, "An Introduction to Corporate Responsibility," serves as an introduction to the topic and includes a definition of the field as well as an argument for the importance of CR across fields and disciplines. In Chapter 1, we take a deep dive into the development of corporate responsibility since its inception. We argue that CR should be integrated fully into a company's business strategy to ensure success in today's global and transparent environment.

The Starbucks case in Chapter 1 explains their decision to sell fair trade coffee and the culture of responsibility that comes hand in hand with that decision.

Chapter 2, "The Business Case for CR," explains why I believe a properly carried out corporate responsibility strategy makes *both* financial and moral sense. When awareness levels of environmental and social impact are considered, risk and cost are minimized. A well-executed CR strategy also leads to a stronger reputation, contributing to consumer spending and loyalty. CR is becoming imperative for companies that hope to remain competitive and currently relevant, but it is also important for retaining the attention of all stakeholders in a company, including executive leadership and board members, consumers, and governmental bodies.

The Unilever case outlines the drastic sustainability efforts of a consumer goods company that seeks to double sales and halve its environmental impact by 2020.

Chapter 3, "Environmental Responsibility," describes the most familiar aspect of CR. An environmentally responsible company will hypothetically deliver for current stakeholders, while ensuring its existence for future stakeholders. In this chapter, we see how environmental responsibility has evolved over the past 50 years, why consumers should be wary of "greenwashing" as well as other sustainability/environmental ranking systems, and how a focus on sustainability is synonymous with innovation going into the next 50 years.

The Wal-Mart case explains how Wal-Mart has pursued a proactive sustainability approach since the fall of 2005, and the challenges it has faced in keeping prices affordable while maintaining sustainability and environmental awareness.

Chapter 4, "The Corporation's Responsibility to Society: Human Rights and Labor Issues," examines the corporation's responsibility to its employees and the communities surrounding its operations. I explain that socially responsible business practices are not taken on because of regulation but rather because of the company's interest in acting responsibly. Social responsibility includes awareness of sexual and racial discrimination, labor issues (especially in corporations with international labor), and the health and safety of employees.

The Shell case describes two crises that the company faced as a result of its environmental and social impact, both at home and abroad.

Chapter 5, "The Corporation's Responsibility to Consumers," explains how and why corporations are responsible to consumers: in their treatment of the surrounding community, but also in their products' long-term health effects. I use the example of the food industry and the rapid increase in obesity over the past 50 years to illustrate this point, and make a similar argument for the healthcare and pharmaceutical industries.

The McDonald's case explores the various corporate social responsibility efforts that the company has pursued and delves into the motivation behind these decisions. Is McDonald's actually interested in consumer health and safety or just trying to increase profits?

Chapter 6, "Responsible Corporate Governance," explains corporate governance's role under the umbrella of corporate responsibility. The governance of a company's operational practices and risk management, aimed to benefit its shareholders, has altered since the early 20th century. Through an investigation of corporate governance practices in crisis situations, I explain why this field will continue to adjust to a changing business world: one that focuses on corporate responsibility as part of the general business strategy.

The New York Stock Exchange executive compensation case examines the controversy surrounding executive compensation for the former chief executive and chairman of the NYSE, Richard Grasso. The case focuses on the sticky circumstances that can arise when a CEO also serves as chairman of the board of directors.

Chapter 7, "Corporate Ethics," analyzes the integration of ethics into corporate culture, the history and evolution of business ethics, how to create and maintain a valuable code of ethics for a corporation, and how ethics should trickle down from the top in corporate decision-making. I argue that ethics education should begin in schools but should remain an ongoing process within companies.

The case in Chapter 7 focuses on a moral dilemma that a young MBA faces on the job as she is set to release a new product that may cause cancer.

Chapter 8, "Corporate Philanthropy," looks at the motivations behind and critiques of corporate philanthropy, the root of today's field of CR. Motivations for corporate philanthropy are relatively obvious, including the public relations and employee retention benefits associated with it. However, critics often argue that corporate philanthropy programs are just a distraction from whatever negatives the company seeks to conceal. I argue that when a CP program is managed wisely, it can boost both social impact and the bottom-line contribution of the company.

The Goldman Sachs corporate philanthropy case examines the firm's strategic, yet philanthropic, decision to invest in small businesses after the 2008 financial crisis.

Chapter 9, "Communicating Corporate Responsibility," serves as an explanation for the importance of communicating CR efforts to stakeholders. Communication is a necessary portion of CR because it completes the circle of restoration of trust in business and creation of a positive corporate reputation. While I outline a strategic approach to CR communications efforts, including the necessity of authenticity, consistency, and transparency, I also take a closer look at the impact of technology in particular on communication strategy.

The FIJI Water case in Chapter 9 looks at FIJI's decision to join the Carbon Disclosure Project in 2005 and its other environmental initiatives since that time. It looks into the communication of these efforts and FIJI's positioning of itself as a "green" corporation.

Chapter 10, "Implementing a CR Strategy," teaches you just that: how to execute and deliver on a strong CR strategy within a corporation. I describe a number of approaches that are currently being implemented, and then make my own argument for the best approach. This includes maintaining a strong definition of CR within the corporation, figuring out a strategy to rally employees behind this strategy, partnering with external parties that will help get the job done, and creating a robust system to measure progress and performance along the way.

The Timberland case explains how Jeff Swartz, former CEO of Timberland, reacted to the economic downturn in 2008. He saw it as an opportunity to increase sales while maintaining current corporate social responsibility, or "CSR," efforts and creating a socially responsible supply chain.

WHY IS CORPORATE RESPONSIBILITY SO IMPORTANT TODAY?

The responsibility of business has always been important to most of the corporation's key stakeholders, but it has become much more important to everyone in this century. Why?

First, most people, particularly in the United States, do not trust business to act responsibly. Polls show that most Americans felt that business did a good job of balancing profit and the public interest in the late 1960s; today, the number of people who feel that way has dropped to the lowest levels in history. Only about 10% of people would answer that question positively. This is the result of several crises since the turn of the century involving companies like Enron, Toyota, and BP.

Second, as a result of government downsizing in the 1980s, people expect business and the free enterprise system to answer questions that were once the exclusive purview of government. Perhaps this was an unintended consequence of eliminating big government, but it is now a given that we expect companies to pick up some of that slack.

Third, our deeper understanding and depth of knowledge about the inner workings of companies has given us greater insight into their business practices. Thanks to social media, the rise of NGOs, and more extensive reporting from traditional media, we know how much executives are paid, what their labor practices are like in developing nations, and how often they bribe local governments to create opportunities in new markets.

Fourth, and perhaps most important of all, corporations have realized that developing a culture of "doing the right thing" is actually good for business. Research by prominent scholars like Michael Porter[3] shows that companies focused on making the world a better place are more likely to be great companies for the long term.

This book describes not only what is happening in the area of corporate responsibility, but also what companies can and should do to cultivate responsible behavior in all their practices. By seeing corporate responsibility as a much broader and strategic topic than just having a greater focus on the environment, corporations will be able to face the coming decades with strategies and tools that few companies in the world have at their fingertips.

I am quite sure that the current interest in this topic is not a passing fancy or a flavor of the month. Indeed, responsible corporations are now looking for ways to differentiate themselves from other companies that are not in tune with the times. Once companies realize that responsible behavior is both what stakeholders now demand of their corporations and a way to differentiate themselves in the marketplace, we have the makings of a successful discipline and functional area.

I hope you enjoy reading about this emerging area of study as much as I have enjoyed learning about and developing material for this book.

NOTES

1. Argenti, P. A. (2013). *Corporate communication* (6th ed.). New York, NY: McGraw-Hill.
2. Argenti, P. A. (2004, Fall). Collaborating with activists: How Starbucks works with NGOs. *California Management Review, 47*(1), 91–114.
3. Kramer, M. R., & Porter, M. E. (2011, January/February). Creating shared value. *Harvard Business Review.*

ACKNOWLEDGMENTS

Without the help and support of the Tuck School at Dartmouth, I could not have written or conducted research for this book. Over the last decade, I have been given funds to write cases and conduct research as well as sabbatical time to work on the material in this book. I am particularly grateful to my colleagues and friends Paul Danos, Matt Slaughter, and Bob Hansen for their many years of support that are only now starting to pay dividends.

Many executives have influenced my thinking about corporate responsibility as well, but none as much as the amazing Dailah Nihot at ING. Dailah is the first executive I met who really understood the power of corporate responsibility to make a difference in how an organization does business and then realizes the benefit of that approach. Over many meetings and visits between the Netherlands and the U.S., Dailah taught me more than what I read in books or articles.

I am indebted as well to the hundreds of students I have taught at the Tuck School in my Corporate Responsibility course over the last seven years. They have tested and challenged these ideas in their fertile minds, which gave me the inspiration necessary to come up with new ways to think about corporate responsibility.

Many researchers have also helped me with this project over the last two years, but I am particularly grateful to my incredible project manager and senior research associate, Kathleen O'Leary, for making this book come to life; without Kat, there would be no first edition of *Corporate Responsibility*. I also want to thank Nicole Bertucci for working so diligently to get the book ready for its final review over the past summer; Nicole turned this from a good book to a great one. I would also like to thank my daughter, Lauren Argenti, and Sara Glazer for working on the proposal and outline that ultimately turned into a real book. Their work over two and a half months started this project off on the right path.

Several former students here at Tuck also contributed significantly to this book, especially Dafna Eshet, JJ Gantt, Kellie Ciofalo, Lauren Hirsch, and Taylor Cornwall. Georgia Aarons, who has been with me for several years on so many projects as my researcher, also put her talents to work on this book. And Jessica Osgood, my tireless assistant, contributed hours to making sure I stuck to deadlines and got the right drafts of chapters in to the right publisher, all the while cleaning up the mess we left behind.

My thanks also go to the staff of SAGE Publications: Maggie Stanley, Katie Bierach, Nicole Mangona, Rachel Keith, and Bennie Clark Allen. This book was improved because of the advice and suggestions that reviewers have offered. These individuals include Benedict Uzochukwu, Virginia State University; Yezdi H. Godiwalla, University of Wisconsin–Whitewater; Holly Ott, Shippensburg University; Ellis Jones, Holy Cross College; Stephanie Jue, University of Texas at Austin; David W. Jordan, Slippery Rock University; Noema Santos, State College of Florida; Fidaa Shehada, Centennial College; Michelle Katchuck, University of Hawaii; Joseph Youchison, Benedictine University; Stephen Castle, Coventry University; and Edward Murphy, Northeastern University.

Finally, I would like to thank my wife, Jennifer Kaye Argenti, for giving me the time, space, and support necessary to take a bunch of crazy ideas and turn them into a book. She is my biggest fan; I couldn't do what I do without her.

Paul A. Argenti
Hanover, New Hampshire
2014

The author would like to receive any comments or questions as well as corrections and suggestions for future editions of this text. Please email comments directly to: paul.argenti@dartmouth.edu.

ABOUT THE AUTHOR

Professor Paul A. Argenti has taught management, corporate responsibility, and corporate communication, starting in 1977 at the Harvard Business School, from 1979 to 1981 at the Columbia Business School, and since 1981 as a faculty member at Dartmouth's Tuck School of Business. He has also taught as a visiting professor at the International University of Japan, the Helsinki School of Economics, Erasmus University in the Netherlands, London Business School, and Singapore Management University. He currently serves as faculty director for Tuck's Leadership and Strategic Impact Program, its Brand and Reputation programs, and its executive programs for Novartis, Hitachi, and SCTE.

The seventh edition of Professor Argenti's textbook, *Corporate Communication*, will be published in 2015. Argenti also coauthored (with Courtney Barnes) *Digital Strategies for Powerful Corporate Communication*, published in 2009. Some of his other books include *Strategic Corporate Communication*, published in 2007; *The Power of Corporate Communication* (coauthored with UCLA's Janis Forman); and *The Fast Forward MBA Pocket Reference* (several editions). Professor Argenti has written and edited numerous articles for academic publications and practitioner journals, such as *Harvard Business Review*, *California Management Review*, and *Sloan Management Review*. Professor Argenti also blogs regularly for publications such as *Harvard Business Review*, the *Washington Post*, and *U.S. News & World Report*, and appears frequently on radio (NPR, APM) and television (CNBC, Fox Business), commenting on topics related to communications, reputation, and corporate responsibility.

Professor Argenti is a Fulbright Scholar and a winner of the Pathfinder Award in 2007 from the Institute for Public Relations for the excellence of his research over a long career. The Ethisphere Institute also listed him as one of the most influential people in business ethics in 2014. He serves on the board of trustees for the Arthur W. Page Society and the Ethisphere Institute. He has also served on advisory boards to CEOs globally for a variety of companies. Finally, he has consulted and run training programs for executives at hundreds of companies over the last three decades, including General Electric, ING, Mitsui, Novartis, and Morgan Stanley. You can follow Professor Argenti on twitter at www.twitter .com/paulargenti.

SAGE was founded in 1965 by Sara Miller McCune to support the dissemination of usable knowledge by publishing innovative and high-quality research and teaching content. Today, we publish more than 850 journals, including those of more than 300 learned societies, more than 800 new books per year, and a growing range of library products including archives, data, case studies, reports, conference highlights, and video. SAGE remains majority-owned by our founder, and after Sara's lifetime will become owned by a charitable trust that secures our continued independence.

Los Angeles | London | New Delhi | Singapore | Washington DC

PART I

WHAT AND WHY

Chapter 1

AN INTRODUCTION TO CORPORATE RESPONSIBILITY

Corporate responsibility (CR) is the manifestation of a corporation's social and environmental obligations to its constituencies and greater society. CR is increasingly being used by constituencies ranging from the general public to investors to analyze and critique modern-day corporate behavior.

When did society's expectations of corporations shift to include responsible and accountable behavior in addition to profit-making? As recently as two decades ago, the general public viewed such "do-gooding" as the primary domain of non-profit organizations and Good Samaritans. At the time, many considered businesses to be purely self-interested entities. Positioned in a corner directly opposite charities, the purpose of a corporation was profit maximization, with any efforts to give back to the community being limited to check-writing and philanthropy at an arm's length. Milton Friedman, a University of Chicago economist, embodied the belief that businesses should be strictly economic while governments and non-profits should handle social and environmental issues. In the 1970s, Friedman's doctrines became famous through his *New York Times Magazine* article "The Social Responsibility of Business Is to Increase its Profits," in which he declared:

> What does it mean to say that "business" has responsibilities? Only people can have responsibilities. A corporation is an artificial person and in this sense may have artificial responsibilities, but "business" as a whole cannot be said to have responsibilities, even in this vague sense.[1]

In the 1970s, society began to more actively question the means by which corporations generate profits, acknowledging for the first time that corporate practices and society's well-being are closely linked.[2] Corporations became more environmentally aware once large-scale disasters such as Union Carbide's chemical leak in Bhopal, India, in 1984 and the Exxon Valdez oil spill in 1989 sparked widespread uproar about the irresponsibility of big business.[3] In the 1990s, a series of exposés in the mainstream media revealed to many consumers for the first time the "sweatshop" labor conditions and child labor used in garment and footwear supply chains by companies such as Nike and the Kathie Lee line of clothing sold at Wal-Mart. These exposés led to consumer outrage and boycotts, which prompted corporations to adopt codes of conduct to protect workers' rights.

Today, companies are becoming increasingly aware of the effect that their operations have in their many communities and beyond. We see companies forging into unprecedented territory by tackling issues ranging from income inequality and global pandemics to climate change and access to clean water—issues previously considered to be unrelated to their organizational mission. They are implementing community programs and partnerships with nongovernmental organizations (NGOs) and, most innovatively, are adapting their own business models to be more responsible and sustainable. In this millennium, the for-profit and nonprofit sectors are no longer at odds; instead, the once-distinct lines between them are blurring.

The 2012 Edelman goodpurpose® study found that 87% of global consumers felt that "business needs to place at least equal weight on society's interests as on business interests," while only 28% believed that business was performing well in addressing societal issues. In improving CR efforts to bring them more in line with consumer expectations, corporations have an opportunity to increase profits: 73% of consumers surveyed by Edelman stated that they would switch brands if a different brand of similar quality supported a good cause.[4]

It's unsurprising, then, that many global executives today view corporate responsibility as critical to their business strategy and operations. The 2014 Pricewaterhouse Coopers Global CEO Survey revealed that over three-quarters of CEOs believe that satisfying wider societal needs and protecting the interests of future generations is vital to their business.[5] A 2013 KPMG study found that "over half of reporting companies worldwide now include CR information in their annual financial reports. This is a striking rise since 2011 (when only 20 percent did so) and 2008 (only 9 percent)." This trend shows that today's leaders understand the importance of CR and demonstrates the value and resources they are investing in CR initiatives.[6]

WHAT IS CORPORATE RESPONSIBILITY?

Corporate responsibility, *corporate social responsibility*, *corporate citizenship*, *sustainability*, and even *conscious capitalism* are some of the terms used in the news media and corporate marketing efforts as companies jockey to win the trust and loyalty of constituents around the world.[7] The acronym *ESG*, which stands for "environmental, social, and governance," is also used to describe corporate responsibility initiatives. The term *triple bottom line*, popularized in 1994 by John Elkington, founder of British consulting firm SustainAbility, is also used in corporate responsibility conversations and refers to "profit, people, and planet."

Corporate responsibility describes an organization's respect for society's interests, as demonstrated by its taking ownership of the effect its activities have on key constituencies, including customers, employees, shareholders, communities, and the environment, in all parts of its operations. In short, CR prompts a corporation to look beyond its traditional bottom line (economic profit or loss) to consider the greater social implications of its business.

This accountability often extends beyond baseline compliance with existing regulations to encompass voluntary and proactive efforts to improve the quality of life for employees and their families, as well as for the local community and society at large. A responsible company makes a concerted attempt to reduce the negative social and environmental footprint of its operations through a thoughtfully developed strategy implemented over the long term and not merely through temporary, stopgap measures such as monetary contributions to charitable causes.[8] For example, ExxonMobil's donation of $250 million over 32 years to sponsor Masterpiece Theatre qualifies as philanthropy, but it cannot be categorized as CR, as it makes no effort to mitigate the lasting impact of the company's operations.

In contrast, Starbucks' efforts to minimize the negative effects of its coffee supply chain and retail operations by purchasing beans from fair trade growers and paying its employees wages higher than industry averages serve as cornerstones of its CR strategy.[9] Many times, a company's corporate responsibility efforts involve donations of time and expertise as opposed to cash. However, *Corporate Responsibility Magazine* observed in 2010 that the days of "checkbook philanthropy" are over and noted that contributions of in-kind products, services, and experience represented greater than 65% of corporate contributions. Additionally, 64% of global consumers felt that it was no longer enough for a company to donate only money. Instead, consumers felt that companies must incorporate good works into the fabric of their business.[10]

In shaping a CR strategy, a corporation ideally acknowledges and integrates the full spectrum of constituencies' "extra-financial" concerns—social, environmental, governance, and others—into its strategy and operations. The Global Reporting Initiative (GRI), an organization that promotes sustainability reporting as a tool to help organizations become more sustainable and help with sustainable development, describes five interdependent capital asset classes: financial, human, natural, social, and technological. *The Economist* has described CR as "part of what businesses need to do to keep up with (or, if possible, stay slightly ahead of) society's fast-changing expectations."[11] Developing an authentic CR strategy signals a corporation's intent to look beyond short-term financial returns and focus on long-term success and sustainability by managing those expectations. This consideration often requires the executives of public companies to fight prevailing pressures to achieve strong quarterly results at the expense of longer-term, often less tangible benefits.[12]

Despite these challenges, Harvard Business School guru Michael Porter and consultant Mark Kramer argue that CR is a strategy that, if implemented thoughtfully and thoroughly, can enhance a corporation's competitiveness. They analyze the interdependence of a company and society by using the same tools used to analyze overall competitive positioning and strategy development. In this way, CR can be used strategically to set an "affirmative [CR] agenda that produces maximum social benefit as well as gains for the business."[13] A CR strategy should not be reactive but should proactively identify the social consequences of a company's entire value chain—the full spectrum, including all the activities it engages in when doing business—to pinpoint potential problems and opportunities wherever business and society intersect.[14]

In 2013, 90% of the 250 largest global companies said they used their reports on CR to highlight environmental and social changes that could affect their firm and their key stakeholders, and 70% of these companies noted that these changes have created opportunities for the innovation of new products and services.[15] KPMG has identified the two principle drivers of increased value from corporate responsibility as cost-savings and improved reputation.[16] A recent IBM survey found that 87% of executives were focusing on CR activities that would help them to improve efficiency, and 69% were focusing on CR activities that would help with new ideas for revenue generation.[17]

To help companies with strong corporate responsibility platforms gain more credibility and recognition, an American nonprofit, B Lab, has created the B Corp certification, with the "B" standing for "Benefit."[18] B Corps are companies that meet "rigorous and independent standards of social and environmental performance, accountability, and transparency." Companies can apply for B Corp status much in the same way that companies can apply to certifying bodies to achieve fair trade, organic, or LEED certification. As of 2014, B Lab reported that over 1,000 companies in over 30 countries had become B Corps. These companies represent 60 industries and include investment groups and construction firms. Consumer product companies such as King Arthur Flour, Dansko, Method, Seventh Generation, Ben & Jerry's, and Patagonia have achieved B Corp status. B Lab has made significant progress since 2012, when there were only 502 certified B Corp companies. However, in 2012, the 502 companies had a combined revenue of only

$2.5 billion, which demonstrates that the largest Fortune 500 companies are not yet part of this movement.[19]

On its website, B Lab lists the following reasons that companies may want to become a B Corp: "Differentiate your brand, maintain mission, save money [particularly via partnerships and discounts negotiated for members by B Lab], generate press, attract investors, improve and benchmark performance, and build a movement."[20]

In addition to providing its own certification, B Lab has taken its mission a step further and is working with state governments to legitimize the B corporation as a legal incorporation option. Similar to the C corporation, S corporation, LLC, and LLP, B corporation status reflects the organizational structure of a company as well as the tax laws that affect it. As of July 2014, 25 states had passed legislation recognizing B corporations, including New York, California, Massachusetts, Delaware, Illinois, and Washington, DC. B Lab is pursuing this agenda because it believes that "current corporate law makes it difficult for businesses to consider employee, community, and environmental interests when making decisions."[21]

With more states reviewing B corporation legislation and with consumers agitating for more corporate responsibility, it seems increasingly likely that corporations that do not make an effort to carve out their own CR niche will be left trailing their competition.

THE 21ST CENTURY'S CR SURGE

Corporations are becoming increasingly aware that as they look out for society's best interests, they are actually looking out for their own interests too, particularly in the long run. As Charles Handy notes, "business needs a sustainable planet for its own survival, for few companies are short-term entities; they want to do business again and again, over decades."[22] Businesses do not exist in a vacuum—they inevitably intersect with society and are mutually dependent for their survival. As *Financial Times* assistant editor Michael Skapinker argues:

> Companies cannot thrive in collapsing societies. Without political stability, the future of business is grim. Even in the most stable countries, companies need the community's approval to function. Opinion can turn against them fast: witness European consumers' distaste for genetically modified food, or the attacks on pharmaceutical companies over the pricing of AIDS drugs in Africa.[23]

This argument includes corporations' need for an environmentally stable context in which to operate. Pressing environmental and social issues today—from climate change to income inequality—pose serious threats to "business-as-usual" operations. Sal Palmisano, former chairman of the board and former CEO of IBM, describes the new expectations corporations must meet to survive in light of these risks:

> All businesses today face a new reality. Businesses now operate in an environment in which long-term societal concerns—in areas from diversity to equal opportunity, the environment and workforce policies—have been raised to the same level of public expectation as accounting practices and financial performances.[24]

Corporations slow to adapt to this new reality pay a price. An often cited example is Wal-Mart's 2004 discovery of a report prepared by McKinsey & Company—and subsequently made public by walmartwatch.com, a public education campaign devoted to challenging Wal-Mart to become a better corporate citizen—stating that up to 8% of Wal-Mart consumers surveyed in 2004 had ceased shopping at the chain because of its reputation, which at the time included a perceived CR deficit.[25] Wal-Mart's then CEO, Lee Scott, reacted with this comment: "We thought we could sit in Bentonville, take care of customers, take care of associates—and the world would leave us alone. It doesn't work that way anymore."[26] In a published statement, Scott also admitted that Wal-Mart had been caught off-guard by its entanglement in social and environmental issues:

> To be honest, most of us at Wal-Mart have been so busy minding the store that the way our critics have tried to turn us into a political symbol has taken us by surprise. But one thing we've learned from our critics is that Wal-Mart's size and industry leadership mean that people expect more from us. They're right to, and when it comes to playing our part we intend to deliver.[27]

People today are expecting more. *The Economist* has described CR as "a do-gooding sideshow" that has now turned mainstream.[28] When IBM surveyed 1,700 global CEOs, they found that 72% of CEOs believe that they must improve their firm's understanding of individual customer needs and their firm's response time to market needs. Nearly half of all CEOs surveyed also believe they need to increase transparency, corporate accountability, and their firms' social and environmental responsibilities.[29] In today's world of heightened awareness of climate change, human rights, and scarcer resources, a corporation's "extra-financial" behavior—how well it treats its stakeholders and the world in which it operates—contributes greatly to its trustworthiness. Trust is not an abstract notion; it can have a significant impact on a company's bottom line. The Trust Barometer, published by the international public relations firm Edelman, revealed that 73% of people have refused to buy the products or use the services of a corporation they do not trust.[30]

Large corporations started the new millennium on a precarious note, the effects of which still linger today. Enron and WorldCom's respective scandals shocked the world and undermined the average person's trust in the motives and operations of big business. Enron's now famous *Code of Ethics*—last published in July 2000, prior to the company's downfall—described such fundamental values as respect, integrity, communication, and excellence. Belief in the altruistic motives of big business subsequently crashed; by 2002, a *Businessweek*/Harris survey reported that 79% believed that "most corporate executives put their own personal interests ahead of employees and shareholders."[31] Over a decade later, the general public still demonstrates low levels of faith in corporations. In June 2014, Gallup reported that only 21% of Americans say they have a "great deal" or "quite a lot" of confidence in big business, compared to 74% for the military.[32]

At the same time, widespread Internet access (an estimated 2.4 billion people were online as of June 2012[33]) has redefined the notion of transparency for corporations. The Internet and social media platforms such as Twitter and Facebook now serve as powerful forums for like-minded people to educate and organize themselves. Individuals also now have a powerful tool for spreading once-proprietary company information. It is easier than ever for constituents to monitor companies and to criticize them for everything from human rights violations that take place in a distant corner of a company's supply chain to carbon emissions that are in excess of local regulatory limitations. Even traditional media is benefiting from the Internet when reporting on corporate responsibility issues. In 2010, *Corporate Responsibility Magazine* published a "black list" of the 30 companies that it rated worst in terms of transparency regarding their corporate responsibility practices, making a point of noting that the 30 black-list companies had underperformed both the S&P 500 and the magazine's list of "100 Top Corporate Citizens" based on three-year total return. This controversial list became fodder for many online blogs and websites, ultimately reaching a much wider audience than the magazine edition alone.

Further attention is being paid to corporations' CR efforts through a proliferation of socially responsible indices and rankings, such as the "Best in Social Responsibility" category on *Fortune*'s World's Most Admired Companies list. In 2009, *Newsweek* began publishing its annual Green Rankings to evaluate corporate responsibility initiatives. Many corporations today vie for inclusion on widely admired indices, including the FTSE4Good Index—an index created by benchmarking company FTSE and designed specifically to help measure the performance of companies meeting globally recognized corporate responsibility standards.[34] Another index of such companies is the Dow Jones Sustainability World Index, which designates the top 10% of 2,500 companies worldwide according to long-term economic, environmental, and social sustainability criteria.[35]

These communication channels and points of engagement directly influence constituencies' impressions of a corporation. A corporation lacking a CR strategy and a clear execution plan for its CR strategy runs the risk of losing control of its reputation in today's highly networked and highly scrutinized business environment.

THE UPSIDE OF CR

Although CR is taking center stage thanks to a business environment of proliferating risks, adopting a socially responsible strategy can offer a compelling upside to corporations. Contrary to Friedman's claims, responsible business practices do not necessarily undermine a corporation's profit motive. In fact, many CEOs today describe acting responsibly as pragmatic—it makes good business sense. A well-executed CR strategy can translate into an array of benefits, including attracting and retaining customers, identifying and managing reputational risks, attracting the best-quality employees, and reducing costs.[36] Wal-Mart—the top company on the Fortune 100, driven by a fierce cost-cutting mantra—explains the value of CR from a strategic perspective. In former CEO Lee Scott's words:

> By thinking about sustainability from our standpoint, it is really about how do you take the cost out, which is waste, whether it's through recycling, through less energy use in the store, through construction techniques we're using, through the supply chain. All of those things are simply the creation of waste.[37]

Cutting costs allows Wal-Mart to charge even lower prices, which supports its mission of helping customers to "Save Money. Live better." General Electric (GE) has also achieved significant cost savings through eco-friendly action, such as investing in alternative energy technologies in 2002 when oil was priced at $25 per barrel. In 2011, with oil prices six times higher and rising, GE was reaping the benefits of the demand it predicted nine years before.[38]

The scale and nature of the benefits from CR activities for an organization can vary depending on the business and are often difficult to quantify, though increased efforts are being made to link CR initiatives directly to financial performance.[39] In the meantime, a strong case exists that CR makes good business sense and positively affects the bottom line.

Reputation Risk Management

Managing reputational risk is a central part of any robust corporate strategy. As Berkshire Hathaway CEO Warren Buffett once famously noted, "It takes 20 years to build a reputation and five minutes to ruin it. If you think about that, you'll do things differently." Corruption scandals or environmental accidents can devastate a carefully honed corporate reputation in a matter of days. These events can also draw unwanted attention from regulators, courts, governments, and media. Building a genuine culture of "doing the right thing" within a corporation—the foundation of any genuine CR strategy—can help offset these risks.

Brand Differentiation

In crowded marketplaces, companies strive for a unique selling proposition that can separate them from the competition in consumers' minds. Corporate responsibility can help build customer loyalty based on distinctive ethical values. Several major brands, such as Stonyfield, Seventh Generation, TOMS shoes, and The Body Shop, are built on such ethical values. GE CEO Jeffrey Immelt emphasized the importance of brand differentiation by staying ahead of issues and evolving with ever-changing constituency concerns:

> When society changes its mind, you better be in front of it and not behind it, and [sustainability] is an issue on which society has changed its mind. As CEO, my job is to get out in front of it because if you're not out in front of it, you're going to get [plowed] under.[40]

Talent Attraction and Retention

As we will discuss in more detail later in the chapter, a CR program can aid in employee recruitment and retention. It can also help improve the image of a company among employees, particularly when they become involved through fundraising activities, community volunteering, or helping to shape the company's CR strategy itself. Using these tactics to strengthen goodwill and trust among present and future employees can translate into reduced costs and greater worker productivity.[41] In 2010, an estimated 34% of employees said they would take a pay cut to work for a socially responsible firm.[42]

Once a company decides to implement corporate responsibility practices, it should be sure to communicate them to its employees and other key constituencies to maximize the return on its efforts. That same 2010 study found that a full 53% of employees were not sure if their company had any CR practices in place.

License to Operate

Corporations want to avoid interference in their business through taxation or regulations. By taking substantive voluntary steps, they may be able to persuade governments and the wider public that they are taking current issues like health and safety, diversity, and the environment seriously and thus avoid intervention. Expenses today can result in future cost-savings or increased revenue streams from new, socially responsible products and services. Consider DuPont, which has saved more than $2 billion from energy use reductions since 1990—an upfront investment that, years later, continues to pay dividends.[43]

CR Critics

Despite mounting evidence in support of CR's benefits, followers of Milton Friedman and others continue to argue that there is no place for social responsibility in business. These critics rail against CR as detracting from a corporation's commercial purpose and effectiveness, thereby inhibiting free markets. In this view, responsibility and profitability constitute a zero-sum game; corporations are for-profit institutions whose primary purpose is profit, and they lose competitiveness through altruistic, profit-diminishing behavior.[44] Some critics claim that CR is little more than a public relations strategy, in which companies cherry-pick their good activities to showcase and ignore the others, creating an inaccurate image of a socially or environmentally responsible company. Others contest that CR programs are often undertaken in an effort to distract the public from the ethical questions posed by their core operations. In general, however, constituencies are increasingly calling for more corporate responsibility and demanding that companies rise to the occasion.

RESPONSIBILITY INSIDE AND OUT: EMPLOYEE INVOLVEMENT IN CR

Employees play an essential role as brand ambassadors for a corporation. This is especially true in the implementation of a CR strategy. The next generation of corporate leaders is actively searching for responsible practices in corporate track records as they recruit and pick a place to start their careers.

In 2011, *Harvard Business Review* shared research findings that 88.3% of MBA graduates from top programs would take a pay cut to work for an ethically responsible company and would be willing to forgo an average of $8,087 in compensation.[45] Top business schools around the world are offering a greater number of corporate responsibility, values-based leadership, and sustainable enterprise courses and programs, addressing business students' desire not just to work hard but to do some good at the same time.[46] Net Impact, an association of more than 40,000 business professionals working to improve corporate responsibility, reports that 98% of the top 50 MBA programs have active chapters.[47]

Once a corporation has attracted top talent, engaging those employees from all levels of the organization in a company's CR efforts is imperative. Employees are often the primary spokespeople for a corporation, responsible for much word-of-mouth information shared and impressions formed. Furthermore, making employees central to a CR strategy can boost employee goodwill and morale, decrease turnover, and increase operational efficiencies by encouraging employees to identify opportunities for sustainability and cost-savings.[48] Many corporations are missing out on this upside: though more than three-quarters of executives say corporate citizenship fits their companies' traditions and values, only 36% report talking to their employees about corporate citizenship.[49]

IBM serves as an example of a company successfully engaging its employees in CR issues, as it hosts regular brainstorming sessions focusing on corporate responsibility and sustainability. It often refers to its now-famous, and still largest, first "InnovationJam" held in 2006.[50] During this InnovationJam, more than 150,000 IBM employees, family members, clients, and partners in 104 countries joined in on an online conversation on IBM's global intranet. Driven primarily by IBM employees, more than 46,000 observations and ideas were posted on how to translate IBM's technologies into economic and broader societal value. IBM allocated $100 million to explore 10 promising business opportunities suggested, including creating access to branchless banking for the underprivileged masses around the world and working with utility companies to increase power grid and infrastructure efficiency.[51]

Stanley Litow, IBM's vice president of corporate citizenship and corporate affairs and president of IBM's Foundation, further explains IBM's approach to corporate responsibility:

> In the *Harvard Business Review*, Rosabeth M. Kanter described the IBM approach as going from "spare change to real change." With the spare change approach, the company makes X amount of dollars and they give their spare change back to the community, with the goal being generosity. But with the real change approach, you take what is most valuable to the company—in our case, our innovation technology, and the skill and talent of our people—and contribute it into the community. The real change approach is strategic, it's a systemic part of the way we operate as a company, and that is the case for tie-in to business strategy. In the end, it's even more generous to do it that way.[52]

Strong evidence exists that the general public now views genuinely responsible behavior as starting inside the four walls of an organization. As FleishmanHillard posted on its website following the 2011 Fortune Green Brainstorming Conference, "a company cannot meet its sustainability or reputation goals without a smart strategy that incorporates employees."[53] After conducting research with FleishmanHillard, the National Consumers League reports that 76% of American consumers agree that for a company to be socially responsible, it should prioritize salary and wage increases for employees over making charitable contributions.[54] Observers credit Google's workplace environment for its strong social responsibility reputation, because the company does not traditionally score in the top five for its environmental or community cause involvement on the major rankings.[55] As Robert Fronk of Harris Interactive explains, "corporate responsibility, in the minds of consumers, starts with your own employees first."[56]

Corporations have an excellent opportunity to differentiate themselves based on such internally responsible behavior. There is a sharp contrast today between executive talk and action pertaining to the treatment of employees. While four out of five senior executives "see the importance of valuing employees and treating them well," only half of companies surveyed offer health insurance to employees, and less than one-third provide either training or career development to low-wage employees.[57]

BUILDING A VALUES-BASED CULTURE

A critical element of valuing employees is codifying corporate beliefs—including those pertaining to employees and other constituencies—in a set of corporate values for each employee to embody. A clear and prominent set of values or code of ethics instilled in employees should ideally serve as a navigational compass for everyday work activities. Employees who live and breathe their company's values are far less likely to engage in legal or ethical breaches. A strong, values-based culture can also contribute to an organization's competitive edge, increasing employee pride, loyalty, and willingness to go the extra mile for the sake of the corporation's mission.[58] Former IBM chairman Thomas J. Watson described the importance of corporate values and strong employee faith in them this way:

> Consider any great organization—one that has lasted over the years—and I think you will find that it owes its resiliency, not to its form of organization or administrative skills, but to the power of what we call beliefs and the appeal these beliefs have for its people. This, then, is my thesis: I firmly believe that any organization, in order to survive and achieve success, must have a sound set of beliefs on which it premises all its policies and actions. Next, I believe that the most important single factor in corporate success is faithful adherence to those beliefs. And finally, I believe that, if an organization is to meet the challenges of a changing world, it must be prepared to change everything about itself except those beliefs as it moves through corporate life.[59]

For a values-based corporate culture to take root and thrive, the tone must be set from the top. Warren Buffett, CEO of Berkshire Hathaway and noted philanthropist, is adamant about this, taking an active role in clearly communicating his ethical expectations to his employees. Using blunt, everyday language—and analogies that any employee can easily identify with—he explicitly states intolerance for ethical wrongdoing, citing it as more important than profits. Most important, Buffett creates a clear connection between the individual actions of employees and corporate culture, in turn shaping the organization's overall reputation. Buffett emphasized this personal accountability in a now legendary September 2006 memo to Berkshire Hathaway employees (see Figure 1.1):

> Your attitude on such matters, expressed by behavior as well as words, will be the most important factor in how the culture of your business develops. And culture, more than rule books, determines how an organization behaves. Thanks for your help on this. Berkshire's reputation is in your hands.[60]

Research underscores the enormous impact corporate leaders have on the atmosphere of a workplace and the values and behavior encouraged within it. Deloitte has found that 75% of employees identify either their senior or middle management as the primary source of pressure they feel to compromise the standards of their organizations.[61] In 2010, Deloitte found that 31% of employees believed that their colleagues were more likely to behave unethically as a result of the challenging economic conditions.

Ensuring that employees are striking a healthy balance in their lives is another important piece of building an ethical culture. Deloitte's Ethics & Workplace Survey also found that an overwhelming 91% of employed adults polled claimed they were more likely to behave ethically in the workplace when they maintained a good work–life balance.[62] A positive working environment reduces stress and frustration levels, thereby diminishing the likelihood of cutting corners to meet unrealistic demands. It is disturbing to consider research by the corporate trend-tracking service DYG SCAN pointing to a pattern of employees no longer believing in employer loyalty, concern, and personal commitment.[63] Investing in employees to foster a sense of mutual accountability and encouraging the free airing of issues without fear of reprimand or retaliation can go a long way toward strengthening an ethical culture.[64] Taking another step to provide employees with resources—such as ethics training to prepare them for dilemmas or a hotline to call if one occurs—can be critical to keeping a corporate culture aligned with the strong values that must underpin all successful corporate citizenship efforts.

Figure 1.1 Berkshire memorandum

Memorandum

To: Berkshire Hathaway Managers ("The All-Stars")

From: Warren E. Buffett

Date: September 27, 2006

The five most dangerous words in business may be "Everybody else is doing it." A lot of banks and insurance companies have suffered earnings disasters after relying on that rationale.

Even worse have been the consequences from using that phrase to justify the morality of proposed actions. More than 100 companies so far have been drawn into the stock option backdating scandal and the number is sure to go higher. My guess is that a great many of the people involved would not have behaved in the manner they did except for the fact that they felt others were doing so as well. The same goes for all of the accounting gimmicks to manipulate earnings—and deceive investors—that has [*sic*] taken place in recent years. You would have been happy to have as an executor of your will or your son-in-law most of the people who engaged in these ill-conceived activities. But somewhere along the line they picked up the notion—perhaps suggested to them by their auditor or consultant—that a number of well-respected managers were engaging in such practices and therefore it must be OK to do so. It's a seductive argument. But it couldn't be more wrong. In fact, every time you hear the phrase "Everybody else is doing it" it should raise a huge red flag. Why would somebody offer such a rationale for an act if there were a good reason available? Clearly the advocate harbors at least a small doubt about the act if he utilizes this verbal crutch. So, at Berkshire, let's start with what is legal, but always go on to what we would feel comfortable about being printed on the front page of our local paper, and never proceed forward simply on the basis of the fact that other people are doing it.

A final note: Somebody is doing something today at Berkshire that you and I would be unhappy about if we knew of it. That's inevitable: We now employ well over 200,000 people and the chances of that number getting through the day without any bad behavior occurring is nil. But we can have a huge effect in minimizing such activities by jumping on anything immediately when there is the slightest odor of impropriety. Your attitude on such matters, expressed by behavior as well as words, will be the most important factor in how the culture of your business develops. And culture, more than rule books, determines how an organization behaves. Thanks for your help on this. Berkshire's reputation is in your hands.

Source: Full text of Warren Buffett's memorandum. FT.com. http://www.ft.com/cms/s/0/48312832-57d4-11db-be9f-0000779e2340.html#axzz21NuYXyCz. Accessed 7/12/2014.

THE EVOLUTION OF CR

As discussed earlier in the chapter, the past couple of decades have seen a shift in societal expectations of corporate behavior. In adapting to these changing expectations, companies have shifted their approach to corporate responsibility from viewing CR initiatives as an obligation to embracing CR as an important component of business strategy. Accordingly, companies have adjusted their CR operations to suit a more visionary approach. Some of the ways they have demonstrated this change in thinking include making long-term commitments to specific social issues and initiatives, providing more than monetary support to causes, sourcing funds from business units as well as philanthropic budgets, and forming strategic alliances—and doing all of this in a way that advances business goals.[65] Table 1.1 outlines the differences between a first- or second-generation CR program and a third-generation CR program, with a first- or second-generation program engaging all stakeholders but being structured as a separate division, and a third-generation program being woven into the fabric of the company, its culture, and guiding business principles.

How did this change come about? While CR has been a major topic of discussion for only the past couple of decades, its origins date back to much earlier. One early example of CR is the 1830 boycott of slave-produced goods led by the National Negro Convention, which spurred shifts in corporate behavior across the

Table 1.1 Strategic shifts between first- and second-generation CR and third-generation CR, according to Dave Stangis, president of the Campbell Soup Foundation

First- and Second-Generation CR Strategies	Third-Generation CR Strategies
• Risk management or mitigation • Commitment to reporting • Environmental, health, and safety measures • Annual performance targets • Community relations strategy • Transparency surrounding workplace and ethics • CSR and sustainability governance • Materiality assessment • Stakeholder engagement • Branding and marketplace programs	• Integrated into culture • Integrated into innovation cycle • Integrated into recruitment and leadership development • Integrated into performance management and compensation • Differentiating and identifiable to employees, customers, suppliers, and consumers • Integral to mission, values, and strategies • Provide operational focus • Leverage unique strengths

Source: Net Impact Issues in Depth call with Dave Stangis, president of the Campbell Soup Foundation, June 28, 2010.

United States.[66] More recently, a 1950s U.S. Supreme Court decision removed legal restrictions and unwritten codes which up to that point had restricted or limited corporate contributions and involvement in social issues, paving the way for companies to rethink their approach to corporate responsibility. Consequently, by the 1960s, most companies felt pressure to demonstrate social responsibility and had established foundations and giving programs.

In the decades following the Supreme Court's actions, other events have resulted in increased corporate scrutiny and greater importance of CR initiatives. The Rainforest Action Network established its influence as an NGO by orchestrating a 1987 boycott of Burger King for importing beef from countries where rainforests are destroyed to provide pasture for cattle.[67] Burger King's sales subsequently declined by 12%, prompting the company to cancel $35 million worth of beef contracts in Central America and announce an end to rainforest beef imports.[68]

A milestone in the world of corporate responsibility was the 1989 Exxon Valdez oil spill, an event which called into question the philanthropic approach seen in the 1970s and 1980s, in which companies gave money to social issues irrespective of such issues' relationship to corporate missions. Rather than funneling its corporate giving into preventative measures against such disasters, Exxon's philanthropic efforts had revolved around Masterpiece Theatre—a noble cause, but not one related to Exxon's core business or its corporate mission.

In the 1990s, new models arose suggesting that not only should a company's philanthropic arm support philanthropic initiatives but also that business units should provide support for philanthropic activities with corporate resources such as expertise.[69] Similar to the 19th-century boycott and the Burger King incident discussed above, Shell faced consequences in the mid-1990s stemming from its 1995 decision to dispose of an oil storage platform that it no longer needed, the Brent Spar, by sinking it in the Atlantic Ocean. Environmental NGO Greenpeace staged protests, using vivid and emotional language, prompting a widespread boycott of Shell stations in northern Europe, with sales volumes in Germany dropping up to 40% in June 1995.[70] As seen from the examples above, NGOs have played a tremendous role in bringing corporate errors in judgment to the attention of the public.

In the 21st century, increased globalization of business as well as major advancements in information technology have increased corporate accountability.[71] As companies focus on organizing and prioritizing their CR efforts, they are increasingly connecting with other organizations to develop guidelines and standards. As of June 2014, over 12,000 businesses in 145 countries around the world had signaled their commitment to sustainability of human and environmental resources by participating in the United Nations Global Compact, which was launched in July 2000 and is the largest sustainability/corporate responsibility policy initiative in the world.

To help guide companies in their corporate responsibility efforts, the United Nations Global Compact drew upon several diplomatic human rights and sustainability documents when crafting its list of "Ten Principles" (see Figure 1.2). Companies can use this list to guide their corporate responsibility initiatives.[72]

According to the UN, the Global Compact offers a unique strategic platform for participants to advance their commitment to sustainability and corporate citizenship. Structured as a public–private initiative, the Global Compact is a policy framework for the development, implementation, and disclosure of sustainability principles and practices, offering participants a wide spectrum of specialized workstreams, management tools and resources, and topical programs and projects. The purpose of the Global Compact is to advance sustainable business models and markets, with the goal of contributing to the initiative's overarching mission of helping to build a more sustainable and inclusive global economy.[73]

Figure 1.2   The United Nations Global Compact: Ten principles

Human Rights

Principle 1: Businesses should support and respect the protection of internationally proclaimed human rights; and
Principle 2: make sure that they are not complicit in human rights abuses.

Labour

Principle 3: Businesses should uphold the freedom of association and the effective recognition of the right to collective bargaining;
Principle 4: the elimination of all forms of forced and compulsory labour;
Principle 5: the effective abolition of child labour; and
Principle 6: the elimination of discrimination in respect of employment and occupation.

Environment

Principle 7: Businesses should support a precautionary approach to environmental challenges;
Principle 8: undertake initiatives to promote greater environmental responsibility; and
Principle 9: encourage the development and diffusion of environmentally friendly technologies.

Anti-Corruption

Principle 10: Businesses should work against corruption in all its forms, including extortion and bribery.

Source: "United Nations Global Compact," http://www.unglobalcompact.org. (Accessed 7/13/14).

Unlike the old view of corporate responsibility, in which companies largely engaged in hands-off philanthropic activities unrelated to their core businesses, the new approach to CR hinges on the idea that a corporation's social initiatives should be in line with overall corporate objectives. Increasingly, companies aim both to do well and to do good, selecting strategic areas of CR focus that fit with their corporate values.[74] Some ways that corporations have integrated CR into their overall strategy include identifying issues related to their core products and markets, seeking out issues that offer opportunities to meet marketing objectives, and identifying the issues most important to their constituencies, including the community, customers, and employees.[75] Corporations have also become increasingly visionary in their approach to CR, looking at longer-term commitments to social programs. Meanwhile, the development of corporate responsibility as a core strategy has manifested itself in myriad ways, including in-kind contributions of a company's products, volunteering employee time, and integrating CR initiatives into departments beyond the CR niche.[76] Indeed, at the 2011 Net Impact Conference, an overarching theme was the ultimate goal of doing away with CR departments, with even CR professionals stating their vision for the elimination of distinct CR arms and the incorporation of CR functions into primary business units and CR principles into companies' core strategies.

Why should corporations embrace CR's infiltration of traditional departments? In his book *Social Innovation, Inc.*, Jason Saul explains that organizations that have failed to realize the business potential of CR initiatives are leaving money on the table. He identifies the unrealized market potential as "social arbitrage," noting that:

> Embracing the business potential of issues like the environment, education, health care, hunger relief, discrimination, and economic development could earn companies tens of billions of dollars, open up new markets, attract new customers, prompt new innovations, and dramatically lower costs.[77]

CR has undergone a shift from pure philanthropy to a strategy embedded in a company's values involving action. There is a difference between doing good and doing less bad, and good CR policy should result in positive returns for a company.[78]

Beyond the monetary benefits of effective CR policy, corporations have come to understand CR as a means of enhancing corporate reputation. To hedge against reputational risk, Seventh Generation co-founder Jeffrey Hollender emphasizes the importance of transparency about a company's weaknesses as well as communicating where it has done well in CR, citing the need for corporations to embrace their faults and try to improve upon them to move forward. He states that being an authentically good company means building every aspect of your business strategy around responsibility.[79]

Effective CR strategy must come from the top of an organization. The results of the 2012 Global Chief Executive Officer Study, conducted by IBM and including 1,700 business leaders, offer some key insights, suggesting that CEOs must find a balance between control and openness to be successful. CEOs that focus on ethics and values, build a collaborative environment, and define a purpose and mission for their firms will have the most successful workforce.[80] The world is changing rapidly and increasing in complexity at a pace faster than that at which companies are able to adapt. To keep up, leaders must empower their employees through the values of their company, engage customers as individuals, and promote innovation through a variety of partnerships.[81]

Because of technological advances, the world is not only becoming increasingly complex but also increasingly connected. It is no surprise that the IBM study identifies communication with consumers as a key component of creating a successful corporate strategy, and the same is true of CR. Businesses must take stakeholders into account with every decision that is made, "uncover patterns and answer questions they never thought to ask."[82] As globalization continues and grows stronger, many CEOs believe that the business world will be increasingly influenced by governmental bodies.

In a rapidly changing world, business has taken on a new role in society. Business plays a larger role because of unprecedented levels of disparity between economic situations in different countries.[83] With weakened governments and a stronger private sector but no one in control, CR has the potential to become the most important issue of the modern era.[84] The nature of governance is changing, with national governments having less power because of globalization. There is no governance at the global level. Governments must pick their battles and are unable to deal with every social issue that arises. For this reason, CR has immense potential to be a response to globalization.[85] While the problems that CR addresses are not all the result of globalization, globalization makes things faster, larger, and more visible, and therefore has increased the pressure on corporations to behave responsibly. Globalization, therefore, has created a new interdependence between corporations and governments.[86]

HOW TO THINK ABOUT CR: FRAMEWORKS AND IMPLEMENTATION

According to Jeffrey Hollender, co-founder of Seventh Generation, CR must be holistic and systemic. It must be embedded into strategic planning as a key driver.[87] Three frameworks have emerged as the dominant way to organize and categorize the broad array of issues related to corporate responsibility.

Three Key Frameworks

Triple bottom line. The triple bottom line framework incorporates the addition of social and environmental values into the traditional economic measures of a corporation or organization's success.[88] The triple bottom line concept looks beyond profits to incorporate the impact of a company's behavior on people and the planet.

In advocating the triple bottom line approach, John Elkington argued that a corporation should account for its impact beyond the traditional financial profit-and-loss bottom line.[89] A corporation should also measure the bottom line of its "people account"—in other words, corporations must assess how socially responsible they have been throughout their operations. Additionally, a corporation should look at its "planet account," analyzing its efforts to be environmentally responsible. The triple bottom line framework looks at the whole picture of corporate behavior, assessing a corporation's financial, social, and environmental performance, with the idea that a corporation must look at all three Ps to fully account for the cost of doing business.[90]

Responsive vs. strategic CR. In developing the responsive vs. strategic CR framework, Michael Porter and Mark Kramer identified three ways in which businesses are involved in society. The first is *generic social issues*, which are important to society but neither are significantly affected by a company's operations nor influence a company's long-term competitiveness. The second is *value chain social impact*, which includes issues affected by the company in its ordinary course of business. The third is *social dimensions of competitive context*, which are factors in the environment that affect underlying drivers of competitiveness where a company operates.[91] How companies approach these three elements constitutes *responsive CSR* vs. *strategic CSR* (see Figure 1.3).

Responsive CSR includes corporate behaviors such as being a good corporate citizen, paying attention to evolving social concerns of stakeholders, and mitigating existing or anticipated risks from business activities. An example of responsive CR is GE's program in which it "adopts" underperforming high schools near several major U.S. facilities. This program creates goodwill in the immediate communities in which GE operates, improves the company's governmental relations, and contributes to employee pride. At the same time, it is incidental to GE's business, and the effects of the program in terms of recruitment and retention are small.

Strategic CSR, on the other hand, moves beyond good corporate citizenship and risk mitigation, seeking instead to identify strategic CR initiatives with sizable social and business benefits. Unlike responsive CR, strategic CR creates the

Figure 1.3 A strategic approach to CSR

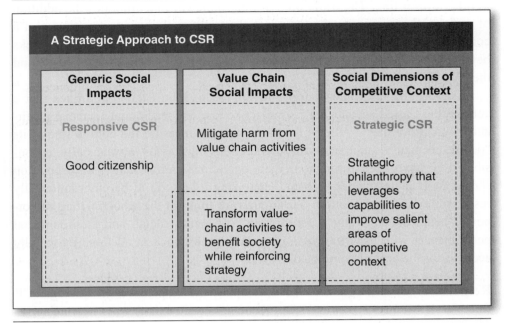

Source: Porter, M. E., & Kramer, M. R. (2006, December). "Strategy and society: The link between competitive advantage and corporate responsibility." *Harvard Business Review.* https://hbr.org/2006/12/strategy-and-society-the-link-between-competitive-advantage-and-corporate-social-responsibility.

opportunity for shared value. An example of strategic CR in practice is the launch of the Toyota Prius. In introducing the Prius to the market, Toyota had a competitive business advantage by offering the first hybrid engine mass-produced worldwide while touting the environmental benefits from fewer emissions and less reliance on gasoline.[92]

ESG. The ESG framework takes into account environmental, social, and governance issues and is a catchall term for criteria used in socially responsible investing. According to Peter Kinder, former president of KLD Research and Analytics:

> ESG came largely from the institutional side, which has been uncomfortable with terms like "socially" and "responsible." They wanted an acronym that stripped away the moral aspects of what we do and made it a function of data and information.[93]

Investment firms and their decision-makers apply ESG criteria in their own way. KLD looks at the following in thinking about ESG:

- *Environmental*: climate change, product/services (beneficial vs. harmful), operations and management
- *Social*: community involvement, diversity, employee relations, human rights, products (i.e., benefits to the economically disadvantaged)
- *Governance*: reporting, structure

Goldman Sachs takes a slightly different approach to the same set of concerns:[94]

- *Environmental:* inputs (energy/water); outputs (climate change, emissions, waste)
- *Social:* leadership (accountability, reporting, development); employees (diversity, training, labor relations); customers (product safety, responsible marketing); communities (human rights, social investments, transparency)
- *Governance:* transparency, independence, compensation, shareholder rights

This book will look at corporate responsibility through the lens of all three frameworks, starting with the business case for CR, and will then examine environmental, social, and governance issues that affect businesses today.

HOW TO THINK ABOUT CR: FRAMEWORKS AND IMPLEMENTATION

With a record number of companies devoting significant budgets and human capital to CR efforts, there is more CR chatter to compete with, which makes it difficult to differentiate a company as responsible. By July 2008, an article in *Environmental Leader* had dubbed this effect "green fatigue" or "green noise."[95] In this environment, responsibility is no longer an option; it is a necessary condition that a corporation must meet to maintain positive relationships with its constituents and ensure its ongoing survival. The following list of key takeaways can ensure that a thoughtful communication strategy is properly integrated to fuel the success of a corporation's CR program.

1. It Starts on the Inside

Throughout the chapter, we have emphasized the importance of engaging employees in a CR strategy. Wal-Mart cites employee engagement in its CR efforts as a critical part of its green plan's success. Each employee is encouraged to make voluntary changes in his or her life to make a positive individual contribution to the environment—from using compact fluorescent lights to riding a bike to work—which helps employees rally more personally around Wal-Mart's corporate environmental efforts and share those messages in-store with consumers.[96] At Wal-Mart Canada, vice presidents drew from the lower ranks of the company's 75,000-employee pool (as of 2008; the employee pool is about 91,500 as of February 2014)[97] to pull together 14 "Sustainability Value Networks," teams that submit proposals and action plans on topics including greenhouse gas reduction and operational waste reduction.[98] Ensuring that a CR strategy resonates strongly with employees can help drive greater efficiencies and positive feelings of ownership and membership in a company that stands for something greater than profits alone.

2. Collaborate With Friends and Foes

The old adage holds true in CR communications: Keep your friends close and your enemies even closer. The continued influence of NGOs presents an opportunity for corporations to forge partnerships to defend against attacks and build credibility with the millions of consumers who hold these cause-driven organizations in high regard. McDonald's, for example, worked closely with the Environmental Defense Fund in the early 1990s to change from plastic and foam packaging to paper through a collaborative effort.

3. Present the Bad With the Good

The importance of transparency cannot be overstated in the implementation of a CR strategy. Companies that do not disclose or downplay the negative attributes or effects of their operations do so at their own peril. Given the sophistication and vigilance of NGOs and the accessibility of the Internet today, a company's constituents will likely find out the truth whether or not the company proactively tells them.

Being transparent means being clear in CR communication and not clouding realities with vague or verbose prose. Admitting mistakes and missteps is the first, and perhaps most crucial, step to correcting them. Constituents will be more forgiving and trustful of a company that openly discusses its challenges in implementing CR initiatives than they will be of companies that attempt to mask or misrepresent shortcomings. Clarity also means using metrics and quantifying CR efforts wherever possible and, just as important, explaining the methodology. Constituencies will appreciate and engage with a company's CR strategy only if they are able to understand what it is and how the results are being measured.

4. Stay One Step Ahead of Antagonists

Corporations should keep a finger on the pulse of influencers, critics, and all constituents to gauge existing opinions and spot potential trouble brewing well in advance of a CR crisis erupting. This monitoring will enable a company to tell its own story and maintain a strong grasp on its reputation. In the words of Mary Jane Klocke, former director of North American Shareholder Marketing at BP:

Engagement raises brand awareness, offers valuable insights and perspectives from key stakeholders and gives us avenues of influence and opportunity to get the facts out rather than have the [socially responsible investment or SRI] community receive its information from the media or other third parties.[99]

5. Match Rhetoric With Action

Constituencies today have little patience for self-aggrandizing corporations that inaccurately inflate their CR efforts or do not deliver on promises made. The greater the number of corporations that vie to win approval through CR efforts, the more savvy and discerning constituencies will be in separating hollow rhetoric from bona fide results. Companies should also be careful to never express complacency in their efforts to be responsible. Just as the business environment—and a corporation's intersection with social, environmental, and governance issues—is constantly in flux, a CR strategy must also be continually reshaped.[100] David Douglas, former vice president of eco-responsibility at Sun Microsystems, explains:

A big mistake is to send the message that your company believes it has done all it can do. There is always room for improvement when it comes to developing business practices that create social and business value. To indicate otherwise brings the credibility of your company's entire [CR] program into question.[101]

CONCLUSION

Corporate responsibility is increasing in importance because of increased globalization and complexity, as well as the ease of the spread of information facilitated by technological advancements. Corporations must seek to define the role of CR in their businesses and move to the third-generation understanding of CR, which is integrated into a company's strategy and culture and based on the notion of doing good to do well.

NOTES

1. Friedman, M. (1970, September 13). "The social responsibility of business is to increase its profits." *New York Times Magazine.*

2. Margolis, J. D., & Walsh, J. P. (2001). *People and profits? The search for a link between a company's social and financial performance.* London, UK: Lawrence Erlbaum.

3. Franklin, D. (2008, January 17). "Just good business." *The Economist.*

4. Edelman. (2012). "2012 Edelman goodpurpose study." Retrieved July 13, 2014, from http://purpose.edelman.com

5. PricewaterhouseCoopers. (2014). "17th annual global CEO survey." Retrieved July 13, 2014, from http://www.pwc.com/gx/en/ceo-survey/2014/key-findings/purpose.jhtml

6. KPMG International. (2013). "The KPMG survey of corporate responsibility reporting 2013." Retrieved July 13, 2014, from http://www.kpmg.com/Global/en/IssuesAndInsights/ ArticlesPublications/corporate-responsibility/Documents/kpmg-survey-of-corporate-responsibility -reporting-2013.pdf

7. "Conscious capitalism: Now creed is good." (2000, May 4). *BBC News.*

8. Columbia Business School. (2008, April 16). "The ROI of CSR" [Q&A with Geoffrey Heal]. *Ideas at Work.* Retrieved from http://www8.gsb.columbia.edu/ideas-at-work/publication/613/ the-roi-of-csr

9. Ibid.

10. Litow, S. (n.d.) "From spare change to real change." *Corporate Responsibility Magazine.* Retrieved March 13, 2015, from http://www.thecro.com/content/spare-change-real-change

11. "Do it right." (2008, January 17). *The Economist,* Special Report: Corporate Social Responsibility.

12. Mintzberg, H., Simons, R., & Basu, K. (2002, Fall). "Beyond selfishness." *MIT Sloan Management Review, 44*(1).

13. Porter, M. E., & Kramer, M. R. (2006, December). "Strategy and society: The link between competitive advantage and corporate social responsibility." *Harvard Business Review.* Retrieved March 1, 2015, from https://hbr.org/2006/12/strategy-and-society-the-link-between -competitive-advantage-and-corporate-social-responsibility

14. Ibid.

15. KPMG International, "KPMG survey of corporate responsibility reporting 2013."

16. Ibid.

17. Pohle, G., & Hittner, J. "Attaining sustainable growth through corporate social responsibility." IBM Institute for Business Value. Retrieved March 13, 2015, from http://www-935.ibm .com/services/us/gbs/bus/pdf/gbe03019-usen-02.pdf

18. http://www.bcorporation.net/ (accessed July 25, 2014).

19. Ibid.

20. Ibid.

21. Ibid.

22. Handy, C. (2002, December). "What's a business for?" *Harvard Business Review.*

23. Skapinker, M. (2008, February 12). "Corporate responsibility is not quite dead." *Financial Times.*

24. Yankelovich, D. (2006). *Profit with honor: The new stage of market capitalism* (p. 9). New Haven, CT: Yale University Press.

25. Gunther, M. (2006, August 7). "The green machine." *Fortune.*

26. "The debate over doing good." (2005, August 15). *BusinessWeek.*

27. Yankelovich, *Profit with honor*, p. 10.

28. Franklin, "Just good business."

29. IBM Institute for Business Value. (2012). "Leading through connections: Insights from the IBM Global CEO Study." Retrieved July 13, 2014, from http://www-935.ibm.com/services/ us/en/c-suite/ceostudy2012

30. "Edelman Trust Barometer 2011." Retrieved July 13, 2014, from http://www.edelman.com

31. Yankelovich, *Profit with honor*, p. 24.

32. Gallup Poll. (2014, June 5–8)."Confidence in institutions." Retrieved July 13, 2014, from http://www.gallup.com/poll/1597/confidence-institutions.aspx

33. Internet World Stats. (2012, June 30). "Internet usage and world population statistics." Retrieved July 13, 2014, from http://www.internetworldstats.com

34. FTSE. (n.d.). "FTSE4Good Index series." Retrieved July 13, 2014, from http://www.ftse .com/Indices/FTSE4Good_Index_Series/index.jsp

35. Dow Jones Sustainability Indices, http://www.sustainability-index.com (accessed July 13, 2014).

36. Argenti, P. A. (2012, October 1). *Corporate communication* (6th ed.). McGraw Hill Higher Education.

37. Murray, A. (2008, March 24). "Waste not." *Wall Street Journal.*

38. Witzel, M. (2008, July 2). "A case for more sustainability." *Financial Times.*

39. Argenti, *Corporate communication.*

40. Ibid.

41. Ibid.

42. Ibid.

43. Porter & Kramer, "Strategy and society."

44. Argenti, *Corporate communication.*

45. "New MBAs would sacrifice pay for ethics." *Harvard Business Review*'s *The Daily Stat.* Retrieved July 13, 2014.

46. Strom, S. (2007, May 6). "Make money, save the world." *New York Times.*

47. Net Impact. (n.d.). "2012–2013 annual report." Retrieved July 13, 2014, from https:// netimpact.org/sites/default/files/documents/2013-annual-report.pdf

48. McDonald, G. (2007, November/December). "In-house climate change: Use communication to engage employees in environmental initiatives (the Green Revolution)." *Communication World.*

49. Boston College Center for Corporate Citizenship. (2007, December). "Status of corporate citizenship 2007: Time to get real: Closing the gap between rhetoric and reality." Retrieved from http://bcccc.net/index.cfm?fuseaction=document.showDocumentByID&DocumentID=1172

50. IBM Jam Events, http://www.collaborationjam.com/ (accessed July 13, 2014).

51. Ibid.

52. "From spare change to real change: An interview with Stanley Litow." (2010, April). *LEADERS.* Retrieved July 13, 2014, from http://www.leadersmag.com/issues/2010.2_Apr/ Making%20a%20Difference/Litow.html

53. "Trends in corporate sustainability." (2011, April 6). *Fleishman-Hillard blog.* Retrieved 2011 from http://fleishmanhillard.com/2011/04/reputation-management/trends-in-corporate-sustainability

54. "Worker's rights: Social responsibility all about worker welfare, survey says." Retrieved 2011 from http://www.nclnet.org/social_responsibility_all_about_worker_welfare_survey_says

55. Harris Interactive. (n.d.). "The annual RQ 2007–2008." Author.

56. Ibid.

57. Boston College Center for Corporate Citizenship, "Status of corporate citizenship 2007."

58. Aguilar, F. J. (1992). *General managers in action: Policies and strategies* (2nd ed.). Oxford, UK: Oxford University Press.

59. Ibid.

60. "Full text of Warren Buffett's memorandum." *Financial Times.* Retrieved July 12, 2014, from http://www.ft.com/cms/s/0/48312832-57d4-11db-be9f-0000779e2340.html#axzz21NuYXyCz

61. Ethics Resource Center. (2005). "National Business Ethics Survey: How employees view ethics in their organization, 1994–2005." Author.

62. Allen, S. (2007, June 11). "Creating a culture of values." *Forbes.*

63. Yankelovich, *Profit with honor*, p. 43.

64. Gebler, D. (2005, September). "Is your culture a risk factor?" Working Values Ltd.

65. Smith, C. (1994, May/June). "The new corporate philanthropy." *Harvard Business Review*, pp. 105–107. As quoted in Kotler, P., & Lee, N. (2005). *Corporate social responsibility: Doing the most good for your company and your cause* (p. 7). Hoboken, NJ: John Wiley.

66. Hickman, L. (2005, October 4). "Should I support a consumer boycott?" *The Guardian* (UK).

67. Rainforest Action Network, http://www.ran.org (accessed July 13, 2014).

68. Ibid.

69. Ibid., p. 8.

70. Baron, D. P. (2003, August). "Facing-off in public." *Stanford Business.*

71. "Values, trust and reputation in an increasingly complex world." (2010, June 28). *Irving Wladawsky-Berger* (blog). Retrieved July 13, 2014, from http://blog.irvingwb.com/blog/2010/06/values-trust-and-reputation-in-an-increasingly-complex-world.html#more

72. United Nations Global Compact, http://www.unglobalcompact.org (accessed July 13, 2014).

73. United Nations Global Compact. (n.d.). "The ten principles." Retrieved March 1, 2015, from https://www.unglobalcompact.org/AboutTheGC/TheTenPrinciples/index.html

74. Kotler & Lee, *Corporate social responsibility*, p. 9.

75. Ibid.

76. Ibid.

77. Saul, J. (2010, September 2). *Social innovation, Inc.: 5 strategies for driving business growth through social change* (p. 1). Hoboken, NJ: John Wiley.

78. Savitz, A., & Weber, K. (2006). *The triple bottom line.* San Francisco, CA: John Wiley.

79. Net Impact Issues in Depth call ("The responsibility revolution") with Jeffrey Hollender, June 16, 2010.

80. IBM Institute for Business Value. (2012). "Leading through connections: Insights from the IBM Global CEO Study." Retrieved July 13, 2014, from http://www-935.ibm.com/services/us/en/c-suite/ceostudy2012

81. Ibid.

82. Ibid.

83. Blowfield, M., & Murray, A. (2011). *Corporate responsibility* (p. 81). New York, NY: Oxford University Press.

84. Ibid., p. 107.

85. Ibid., p. 107.

86. Ibid., p. 107.

87. Net Impact Issues in Depth call ("The responsibility revolution") with Jeffrey Hollender, June 16, 2010.

88. Elkington, J. (1997). "Cannibals with forks: The triple bottom line of 21st century business." Oxford, UK: Capstone.

89. "Idea: Triple bottom line." *The Economist.* Retrieved July 13, 2014, from http://www.economist.com/node/14301663

90. Ibid.

91. Porter & Kramer, "Strategy and society," p. 6.

92. Ibid., pp. 7–10.

93. Drucker, D. (2009, October). "From SRI to ESG." *Financial Planning,* p. 74.

94. Forrest, S. (2006, June). "Goldman Sachs ESG: Integrating ESG into investment research." Global Investment Research, AHC Group June 2006 Shareholder Value Workshop, slide 4.

95. Davis, V. (2008, July 10). "Are consumers falling off the green wagon and should we care?" *Environmental Leader.*

96. Dias, D. (2008, July/August). "Giant steps." *Financial Post Business* (Canada).

97. Walmart, http://corporate.walmart.com/our-story/locations/canada (accessed July 12, 2014).

98. Ibid.

99. Glaser, G. (2007). "Lessons learned in promoting CSR." Corporate Responsibility Officer.

100. Porter & Kramer, "Strategy and society."

101. Glaser, "Lessons learned in promoting CSR."

STARBUCKS COFFEE COMPANY

On an overcast February afternoon in 2000, Starbucks CEO Orin Smith gazed out his office window in Seattle and contemplated what had just occurred at his company's annual shareholder meeting. In prior years, the meeting had always been a fun, all-day affair where shareholders from around the country gathered to celebrate the company's success. This year, however, Smith and other senior Starbucks executives heard an earful from the activist group Global Exchange. A human rights organization dedicated to promoting environmental, political, and social justice around the world, Global Exchange criticized Starbucks for profiting at farmers' expense by paying low prices and not buying "fair trade" coffee beans. Not only did the activists disrupt the company's annual meeting to the point that the convention hall security police asked the activists to leave, but they also threatened a national boycott if the company refused to sell and promote fair trade coffee. Although Smith strongly disagreed with using the shareholders meeting as a public forum, he knew there was a strong likelihood his company could face serious reprisals if it did not address the issues raised by Global Exchange.

FAIR TRADE

Fair trade began after World War II as religiously affiliated, nonprofit organizations purchased handmade products for resale from European producers. Fair trade coffees were coffees purchased directly from cooperatives of small farmers at a guaranteed floor price. Fair trade coffee focused on the worker's economic sustainability by attempting to cut out or limit middlemen and providing much-needed credit to small farmers so that they could end their poverty cycle. Licensing organizations in individual importing countries certified fair trade coffee from farmers listed on the Fair Trade Registry. Consequently, there were a host of different certifying agencies, and fair trade coffee accounted for a different market share in each country.[1]

By the late 1990s, the fair trade movement had gained a foothold in the United States, and in early 1999, TransFair USA, a third-party certification agency, launched its Fair Trade Certified coffee label. During that summer, Global Exchange began a campaign to educate consumers and the media about labor conditions in the coffee industry, focusing on getting the message out to specialty coffee consumers. Although the activists were successful in educating pockets of consumers, they knew their effectiveness was limited unless they directed blame for the farmers' woes. Global Exchange decided to take an anti-corporation stance and focused their attention on the most visible brand in specialty coffee: Starbucks.

Source: This case was sponsored by the Allwin Initiative for Corporate Citizenship and prepared by Alison Stanley, T'02, under the direction of Professor Paul A. Argenti, with the cooperation of Starbucks Coffee Company.

Starbucks Coffee Company had grown from a small, regional business into the undisputed leader in the specialty coffee industry by buying only the best-quality coffee and providing an unmatched store experience. The company's coffee buyers had built long-standing relationships with farmers and believed it paid the highest prices in the industry for top-quality beans. Adopting the fair trade model would cause serious concerns for Starbucks, as fair trade paid a floor price of $1.26 regardless of bean quality. Starbucks coffee buyers had to admit that while they paid high prices, they didn't always know whether farmers got their fair share. It was virtually impossible to track the flow of money from the importers and exporters back through the supply chain to the individual farmer. By dealing only with cooperatives, TransFair USA bypassed most of these problems and added value by producing financial transparency. Yet being a socially responsive corporation was a key tenet of Starbucks' mission statement. The intent of fair trade advocates to raise small-farmer incomes was consistent with the company's values. Treating partners (Starbucks employees), customers, and suppliers with dignity and respect was essential to the company. In fact, it came as a shock to many at Starbucks that activist groups were criticizing their company for unfair practices. As he watched the sky darken outside his window, Orin Smith asked himself just how socially responsive his company could be without affecting the fundamental business practices that had been the foundation of its great success.

STARBUCKS CULTURE

In 1990, Starbucks' senior executive team had drafted a mission statement laying out the guiding principles behind the company. The team hoped that the principles included in this mission statement would help partners gauge the appropriateness of their decisions and actions. As Orin Smith explained, "Those guidelines are part of our culture, and we try to live by them every day."[2] After drafting the mission statement, the executive team asked all Starbucks partners to review and comment on the document. Based on their feedback, the final statement (see Exhibit 1.1) put "people first and profits last."[3] In fact, the number one guiding principle in Starbucks' mission statement was to "provide a great work environment and treat each other with respect and dignity."[4]

Going forward, Starbucks did three things to keep the mission and guiding principles alive: First, it provided all new partners with a copy of the mission statement and comment cards during orientation. Second, when making presentations, Starbucks leadership continually related decisions back to the appropriate guiding principle or principles they supported. And third, the company developed a "Mission Review" system through which any partner could comment on a decision or action relative to its consistency with one of the six principles. The partner most knowledgeable on the comment had to respond directly to such a submission within two weeks or, if the comment was anonymous, the response appeared in a monthly report.[5] As a result of this continual emphasis, the guiding principles and their underlying values had become the cornerstones of a very strong culture.

After buying Starbucks, Howard Schultz had worked to develop a benefits program that would attract top people who were eager to work for the company and committed to excellence. One of Schultz's key philosophies was to "treat people like family, and they will be loyal and give their all." Accordingly, Starbucks paid more than the going wage in the restaurant and retail industries, granted stock options to both full- and part-time partners in proportion to their level of base pay, and offered health benefits for both full- and part-time partners.[6] In return, Starbucks had a partner turnover rate of 60% compared to the restaurant industry average of 200%.[7] Furthermore, when asked by outside agencies, 82% of the partners reported being "very satisfied" and 15% as being "satisfied" with their jobs. While such a high satisfaction rate could be found in many small, privately held companies, it was virtually unheard of for a large, publicly traded corporation of over 55,000 employees.[8] All of this had fostered a strong culture that employed a predominately young and educated workforce who were extremely proud to work for Starbucks. Their pride came from working for a very visible and successful company that tried to act in accordance with their shared values. According to Smith, "it's extremely valuable to have people proud to work for Starbucks, and we make decisions that are consistent with what our partners expect of us."[9]

CORPORATE RESPONSIBILITY AT STARBUCKS

Just as treating partners well was one of the pillars of Starbucks' culture, so was contributing positively to the communities it served and to the environment.[10] Starbucks had made this commitment not only because it was the right thing to do, but also because its workforce was aware and concerned with global environmental and poverty issues. In addition to sustaining and growing its business, Starbucks supported causes "in both the communities where Starbucks stores were located and the countries where Starbucks coffee was grown."[11]

On the local level, store managers were granted discretion to donate to local causes and provide coffee for local fundraisers. One Seattle store donated more than $500,000 to Zion Preparatory Academy, an African-American school for inner-city youth.[12] In 1998, Starbucks and Erwin "Magic" Johnson's company, Johnson Development Corporation, formed a joint partnership and created the Urban Coffee Opportunities. Subsequently, 28 stores opened in urban communities, providing new employment and revitalization opportunities in several U.S. cities.[13]

Internationally, in 1991, Starbucks began contributing to CARE, a worldwide relief and development foundation, as a way to give back to coffee-origin countries. By 1995,

Starbucks was CARE's largest corporate donor, pledging more than $100,000 a year and specifying that its support go to coffee-producing countries.[14] The company's donations helped with projects like clean-water systems, health and sanitation training, and literacy efforts.[15] Over the years, Starbucks has contributed more than $1.8 million to CARE.[16]

In 1998, Starbucks partnered with Conservation International (CI), a nonprofit organization that helped promote biodiversity in coffee-growing regions, to support producers of shade-grown coffee. The coffee came from cooperatives in Chiapas, Mexico, and was introduced as a limited edition in 1999. The cooperatives' land bordered the El Triunfo Biosphere Reserve, an area designated by CI as one of the 25 "hot spots" that were home to over half the world's known plants and animals.[17] Since 1999, Starbucks had funded seasonal promotions of the coffee every year, with the hope of adding it to its lineup of year-round offerings. The partnership had proven positive for both the environment and the Mexican farmers. Shade acreage increased by 220%, while farmers received a price premium of 65% above the market price and increased exports by 50%. Since the beginning of the partnership, Starbucks had made loan guarantees that helped provide over $750,000 in loans to farmers.[18] This financial support enabled these farmers to nearly double their income.

In 1992, Starbucks developed an environmental mission statement to articulate more clearly how the company interacted with its environment, eventually creating an Environmental Affairs team tasked with developing environmentally responsible policies and minimizing the company's "footprint."[19] Additionally, Starbucks actively used environmental purchasing guidelines, reducing waste through recycling and energy conservation and continually educating partners through the company's "Green Team" initiatives. In 1994, Starbucks hired Sue Mecklenburg as the first director of environmental affairs.

Although Starbucks had supported responsible business practices virtually since its inception, as the company itself had grown, so had the importance of defending its image. It was Mecklenburg who developed the idea of using paper sleeves instead of double cupping.[20] At the end of 1999, Starbucks created a Corporate Social Responsibility department, and Dave Olsen was named the department's first senior vice president. According to Sue Mecklenburg, "Dave really is the heart and soul of the company and is acknowledged by others as a leader. By having Dave be the first Corporate Responsibility SVP, the department had instant credibility within the company."[21] Between 1994 and 2001, Starbucks' CSR department grew from only one person to 14.

THE ECONOMICS OF COFFEE

After oil, coffee is the second most traded commodity on worldwide markets. Coffee is grown in more than 80 tropical and subtropical countries, employs an estimated 20 million rural farmers, and is the principal source of foreign exchange in many countries.[22]

In 2001, coffee farmers and plantations produced 15.5 billion pounds of coffee while the world market bought only 13 billion pounds. Overproduction was not unusual in the coffee industry and was one of the major reasons why historically prices had traveled a boom-to-bust cycle.

From Bean to Export

Coffee beans begin at the farm on coffee trees. After trees are planted, it takes between one and three years for the trees to bear coffee "cherries," which typically contain two beans. Each tree produces 2,000 to 4,000 beans a year—approximately one pound of roasted coffee. However, yields alternate with a good crop one year and a poor crop the next.

Farm sizes range from 5 acres (traditional farms) to large plantations covering thousands of acres. Farming and harvesting methods differ greatly between traditional and large coffee farms. Traditional farms, called *fincas* in Latin America, usually have many non-coffee trees that shade the coffee plants from the glaring tropical sun. These farms are integrated agricultural systems that provide additional crops, protection from soil erosion, and homes to insects that act as natural pest control. Farmers on these smaller plots handpick cherries when it's time to harvest the trees. In contrast, large coffee plantations, *fazendas* (estates) in Brazil, use little to no shade, plant trees more densely in rows, and harvest the cherries mechanically.

By 2001, between 50% and 70% of the global coffee supply was coming from small-scale farms.[23] These small producers usually did not own the *beneficios* (mills) that were used to process the product from cherry to bean. While some did operate as part of a cooperative that collectively owned the mills, not all small-scale farmers had this option. Often mills were owned and operated by the large farms, and consequently small farmers had little leverage when negotiating prices with these much larger owners. Coffee must be processed, and it was common for small farmers to accept a considerably lower price to be able to get their coffee to market. Often, these small producers had difficulties financing their operations throughout the year and would sell their crop to middlemen known as "coyotes" prior to harvest to receive a cash advance. These middlemen provided small farmers with credit at high interest rates in exchange for bringing their beans to market. Small-scale farmers were often caught in a perpetual cycle of poverty: small production levels limited their access to cash, which in turn hindered their potential for increasing output. For many producing countries, coffee was tightly connected to the social and political power structures that had existed for hundreds of years.[24]

From Export to Cup

The coffee export process varied greatly depending on country of origin and buyer. In some countries, beans were exported through government coffee boards, while other countries used private exporters only. After they were shipped to the import country, coffee beans were visually inspected and taste-tested for quality through a process called "cupping." After passing inspection, coffee was stored in warehouses until it was shipped to roasters. Large roasters often had their own coffee buyers and procured green beans directly from producers. Large roasters also stockpiled green coffee at the import warehouses to help decrease their exposure to market conditions. Conversely, smaller roasters bought coffee from independent brokers and importers who might have amassed beans at warehouses and thus were exposed to a much larger risk of price fluctuations.

After roasters buy green coffee, the beans are shipped to roasting facilities where the beans are roasted until they receive their characteristic color and aroma and then cooled. Once the beans are cooled, roasters blend beans from different countries to balance the flavors and strengths. Roasters then package, market, and distribute coffee through a variety of methods.

FAIR TRADE COFFEE

In 1997, an umbrella group called the Fairtrade Labelling Organizations International (FLO) was formed to coordinate the monitoring and certification processes for fair trade coffee. There were 277 cooperatives from 24 countries representing 550,000 farmers that produced coffee on the Fair Trade Registry in 2001.[25] FLO estimated that in 2000, farmers produced 165 million pounds of coffee, but only 29.1 million were actually sold as fair trade coffee, with a retail value of $393 million.[26]

Four main criteria for fair trade coffee greatly affected the number of farmers this system could influence. The criteria were that roasters and importers:

- Must purchase directly from small farmers who cultivated less than 3 hectares of land. These farmers had to be organized into democratically run cooperatives.
- Must pay a guaranteed price of $1.26 for arabica, $1.06 for robusta, and $1.41 for organic beans. If the market price was above these levels, farmers received a $.05 premium over market.
- Must offer farmers advanced financing to help cover costs.
- Must develop long-term relationships with cooperatives.

Unlike organic certification, roasters and importers signed a licensing agreement to sell fair trade beans with the fair trade certification agency. The licensing fee paid for some of the certification and monitoring costs.[27] Thus, roasters and importers paid a floor price and a licensing fee for fair trade beans.

On the whole, fair trade coffee was a small fraction of the overall coffee market in 2001 in both producing and consuming countries. An estimated 75% of coffee farmers worldwide are smallholder farmers who harvest approximately 1,000 to 3,000 pounds of coffee a year.[28] Farmers working with fair trade cooperatives are typically such smallholder farmers. However, many smallholder farmers could not join cooperatives due to such factors as their isolated location. And without a cooperative, individual farmers could never amass the quantity necessary to export directly to consuming countries.[29] The 165 million pounds produced in 2001 was 1.2% of the total global output and influenced only 2.2% of the farmers and workers in coffee-producing countries. This model effectively ignored the plight of workers on large coffee estates.[30] However, coffee insiders said there was a long backlog of cooperatives asking for certification but that FLO was hesitant to add more farmers since much of the fair trade coffee was not bought at fair trade prices.[31] Although consumer knowledge of fair trade coffee had continued to grow in the 1990s, purchasing patterns did not always reflect this. European countries developed fair trade labels well before the United States and Canada, but fair trade coffee market share had flattened out by 2001. Holland, which introduced the fair trade label in 1988, had a 2.7% fair trade market share and was one of the higher percentages in Europe.[32] Adoption was somewhat sporadic and depended greatly on consumer sentiment. In 1992, Germany, France, and Switzerland all adopted the label but had a 1%, 0.1%, and 3% market share, respectively, in 2001.[33]

STARBUCKS AND FAIR TRADE COFFEE

For Starbucks, the real issues were brand and consumer proposition. Starbucks hesitated to sign a fair trade license, not wanting to commit until it had carefully weighed all the implications.[34] According to Starbucks executives, their chief concern with fair trade coffee was finding top-quality beans from cooperatives that had not demonstrated an ability to produce quality beans to Starbucks standards. From earlier cupping analyses, Starbucks had little evidence that fair trade coffee met its quality standards. Starbucks was beginning to move toward purchasing more of its coffee through direct relationships with exporters or farmers and negotiated a price based on quality. The company was willing to pay higher prices for great-quality beans and had developed long-term contracts with many of its suppliers.

Mary Williams, senior vice president of the Coffee department, was known throughout the coffee industry as a "tough cupper" who would not settle for anything less than top-quality beans. She explained:

The relationships I have with farmers were built over the last 20 years. It's taken some of them years before I would use their beans consistently and pay them $1.26 or more. Now I was being asked to use another farmer who I didn't know and pay him the same price without the same quality standards?[35]

On average, farmers sent samples and met with Starbucks coffee buyers at their farms for at least two years before Starbucks accepted their beans. In weighing the fair trade coffee issue, Williams had secondary concerns with how the farmers she worked with would react when they discovered that other farmers received the same price without being held to Starbucks quality standards. This was not a trivial issue, because it was more expensive to grow high-quality beans. Further, Williams feared that the smaller cooperatives would not be able to guarantee that they could take back a low-quality shipment and replace it based on Starbucks' volume and quality needs.

Starbucks was also concerned about its brand exposure if the quality of fair trade coffee turned out to be very different from the rest of its whole-bean coffee line. Coffee quality was a critical component of the Starbucks brand, and if it was compromised the value of the brand could be seriously diminished. "Honestly, we didn't want to put our brand at risk," said Tom Ehlers, vice president of the Whole Bean department. "This was an uncharted category, and as marketers we were concerned about endorsing a product that didn't meet our quality standards."[36] The Whole Bean department would face several challenges in introducing fair trade coffee to 3,200 stores in the U.S. First, it would have to come up with a good story for fair trade coffee. As Tim Kern, Whole Bean product manager, explained:

> A lot of our business is about the romance of coffee—where it comes from and how to make it come alive for the customer. We weren't really sure where fair trade beans would be coming from because of the quality.[37]

In addition to confirming the marketing message and being able to communicate it effectively to both employees and customers, Kern wasn't sure Starbucks could change its product offerings as quickly as outsiders thought the company could. "It's not that easy to make changes to over 3,000 stores. We have a calendar set with coffee promotions and it takes time to create new materials and distribute them to all of our stores."[38]

And how would fair trade coffee be priced? Starbucks coffee was a high-margin business, but if the company were to charge a premium for fair trade, how would customers perceive this? While pricing was a secondary issue to consider, it was not a reason for Starbucks to abandon fair trade coffee. Orin Smith recalled:

> In fact, a number of people believed that the sale of low-quality fair trade coffee undermined their entire business proposition with customers: Starbucks and other specialty coffee companies had persuaded customers to pay high prices for quality coffee. This enabled roasters to pay the highest prices in the industry to coffee sellers.[39]

If quality were reduced, specialty coffee would be no different than mass-market coffee and the consumer would be unwilling to pay premium prices. This would destroy the industry's ability to pay price premiums to producers. According to Smith:

The best way to improve the standard of living for farmers is to expand the specialty coffee industry by persuading more consumers to buy quality coffee. While some consumers are persuaded to pay premium prices to help farmers, most are not willing to pay high prices regardless of quality.[40]

THE FAIR TRADE DECISION

Starbucks defined being a socially responsible corporation "as conducting our business in ways that produce social, environmental and economic benefits to the communities in which we operate."[41] Not only were consumers demanding more than just a "product," but also employees were increasingly electing to work for companies with strong values. In a 1999 survey by Cone Communications, 62% of respondents said they would switch brands or retailers to support causes they cared about.[42] Another survey conducted in 2001 showed that 75% to 80% of consumers were likely to reward companies for being "good corporate citizens," while 20% said they'd punish those who weren't.[43] The company cared about being a responsible corporation for a variety of reasons: increasing employee satisfaction, maintaining quality supply sources, obtaining a competitive advantage through a strong reputation, and increasing shareholder value.[44]

As he looked out over the busy port in Seattle's South of Downtown district, Orin Smith pondered all these issues. At 5 p.m., he was to meet with his executive team to hear their concerns and issues before making his decision.

Although offering fair trade coffee was a good objective and consistent with the company's aims of being a socially responsible organization, Smith knew he could not base his decision on this factor alone. He drummed his fingers on the desk and asked himself how Starbucks could support fair trade coffee given that the company had limited resources, a strong image to protect, and shareholders who were willing to support causes only so much.

Case Questions

1. What are the key corporate responsibility issues for Starbucks?

2. How does the Global Exchange situation present an opportunity for Starbucks to create shared value?

3. How should Starbucks' culture and mission statement (see Exhibit 1.1) inform the company's approach to corporate responsibility?

Exhibit 1.1 Starbucks Mission Statement

Establish Starbucks as the premier purveyor of the finest coffee in the world while maintaining our uncompromising principles as we grow. The following six guiding principles will help us measure the appropriateness of our decisions:

1. Provide a great work environment and treat each other with respect and dignity.
2. Embrace diversity as an essential component in the way we do business.
3. Apply the highest standards of excellence to the purchasing, roasting and fresh delivery of our coffee.
4. Develop enthusiastically satisfied customers all the time.
5. Contribute positively to our communities and our environment.
6. Recognize that profitability is essential to our future success.

Source: Porter, M. E., & Kramer, M. R. (2006, December). "Strategy and society: The link between competitive advantage and corporate responsibility." *Harvard Business Review.* Retrieved March 1, 2015, from https://hbr.org/2006/12/strategy-and-society-the-link-between-competitive-advantage-and-corporate-social-responsibility.

NOTES

1. Rice, P., & McLean, J. (1999, October 15). "Sustainable coffee at the crossroads" (p. 78). White paper for the Consumer's Choice Council.
2. Interview with Orin Smith, Starbucks CEO, July 25, 2002.
3. Schultz, H. (1997). *Pour your heart into it* (p. 131). New York, NY: Hyperion.
4. Schultz, *Pour your heart into it*, p. 139.
5. Smith interview; Schultz, *Pour your heart into it*, p. 132.
6. Schultz, *Pour your heart into it*, pp. 125–137.
7. Pendergrast, M. (1999). *Uncommon grounds: The history of coffee and how it transformed our world* (p. 374). New York, NY: Basic Books.
8. Smith interview.
9. Ibid.
10. Schultz, *Pour your heart into it*, pp. 139, 293.
11. Ibid., pp. 139, 293.
12. Ibid., p. 281.
13. Starbucks Coffee Company. (February 2002). "Corporate social responsibility FY01 annual report" (p. 14). Author.
14. Pendergrast, *Uncommon grounds*, p. 375.
15. Schultz, *Pour your heart into it*, pp. 295–296.

16. Starbucks Coffee Company, "Corporate social responsibility FY01 annual report," p. 5.

17. McClure, R. (1999, August 3). "Starbucks soon to have it made in the shade." *Seattle-Post Intelligencer*, p. 2.

18. Packard, B. (2001, January 16). "Sustainability practices presentation." National Recycling Coalition Conference.

19. Starbucks Coffee Company, "Corporate social responsibility FY01 annual report," p. 8.

20. Schultz, *Pour your heart into it*, pp. 303–304.

21. Interview with Sue Mecklenburg, "Starbucks VP business practices," July 25, 2002.

22. Dicum, G., & Luttinger, N. (1999). *The coffee book: Anatomy of an industry from crop to the last drop* (p. 38). New York, NY: New Press.

23. This percentage varies depending on how small-scale farms are defined. In one source, small-scale farms are those occupying less than 5 acres (50%); in another, they occupy less than 10 acres (70%).

24. Dicum & Luttinger, *The coffee book*, pp. 44–47, 58–65.

25. "Spilling the beans on the coffee trade" (pp. 20–21). (2002, March). Fairtrade Foundation.

26. Giovannucci, D. (2001, May). "Sustainable coffee survey of the North American specialty coffee industry" (p. 24). The two main certifying agencies for shade-grown coffee are the Smithsonian Migratory Bird Center and Eco-OK. When asked in the SCAA survey, several responded with various certifiers who in fact are not recognized as certifying agencies.

27. Rice & McLean, "Sustainable coffee at the crossroads," p. 55.

28. Ibid., p. 56.

29. Interview with Paul Rice, executive director of TransFair USA, August 9, 2002.

30. Rice & McLean, "Sustainable coffee at the crossroads," p. 56.

31. Rice interview.

32. Krier, J.-M. (2001, January). "Fair trade in Europe 2001" (p. 15). European Fair Trade Association.

33. Ibid., pp. 27, 30, 55.

34. Smith interview.

35. Interview with Mary Williams, senior vice president of the Starbucks Coffee Department, July 24, 2002.

36. Interview with Tom Ehlers, vice president of the Starbucks Whole Bean department, July 25, 2002.

37. Interview with Tim Kern, product manager of the Starbucks Whole Bean department, July 25, 2002.

38. Kern interview.

39. Smith interview.

40. Ibid.

41. Starbucks Coffee Company, "Corporate social responsibility FY01 annual report," p. 3.

42. Rice & McLean, "Sustainable coffee at the crossroads," p. 34.

43. Maitland, A. (2002, March 11). "Bitter taste of success." *Financial Times*, p. 2.

44. Packard, "Sustainability practices presentation."

Chapter 2

THE BUSINESS CASE FOR CR

As seen in Chapter 1, the modern concept of corporate responsibility evolved from the responses of NGOs and other interested parties to social and environmental errors made by corporations. Since CR's beginnings, however, corporations have discovered that behaving in socially, ethically, and environmentally responsible ways can often contribute to a company's financial bottom line.

WHAT IS THE "BUSINESS CASE" FOR CORPORATE RESPONSIBILITY?

But why does CR have to make good financial sense—that is, why does CR need to result in profit? Isn't it enough for a corporation's CR activities to contribute to the other two Ps of Elkington's triple bottom line framework—people and planet? While this is a nice idea in theory, there are many stakeholders in a corporation who need to see the quantifiable return on investment of CR activities. These stakeholders include parties such as board members, top executives, and shareholders, who are obviously concerned about CR's bottom-line impact, but there are also additional parties with incentives to see CR efforts as a component of a company's financial success.[1]

Social activists are primarily invested in the success of CR programs because of their intrinsic value—that is, their contribution to social and environmental issues. But activists also want CR to succeed economically, because its financial sustainability is its best chance of being incorporated into an organization's long-term strategic plans.

As is evident from the results of the Edelman goodpurpose® study, consumers also have a stake in seeing that companies continue with their CR initiatives, as they prefer to put their financial support behind brands that give back.[2] Only product offerings that make good business sense will remain part of corporations' brand portfolios, so consumers have a vested interest in seeing socially responsible brands succeed. Even governmental bodies are interested in the relationship between CR and financial performance, as they pay close attention to the evolving conversation about whether corporations are better positioned to produce social and environmental benefits cost-effectively.[3]

There are two approaches to evaluating the business case for CR. The narrow view, or "business-case model," looks only at the specific benefits of CR that have a clear impact on a firm's financial performance.[4] A second, broad view, the "syncretic model," looks not only at the link between CR activities and financial performance, but instead expands its scope to include both direct and indirect relationships between CR and firm performance. The syncretic model encompasses more information than the business-case model, as it allows a firm to identify and exploit opportunities that exist outside the business-case model's purview. This broad view of CR's impact on business activities becomes increasingly relevant in today's changing world, as it moves beyond mere financial performance to recognize the interdependence between business and society.[5]

Blowfield and Murray state that making the business case for corporate responsibility "has become the Holy Grail," explaining that demonstrating the positive correlation between CR and financial performance is a means of legitimizing the former in the eyes of mainstream business.[6] In doing so, CR stakeholders will greatly increase the likelihood that corporate responsibility practices will be adopted in individual corporations as well as on a wider societal scale.

The 2010 Corporate Social Responsibility Branding Survey by Penn Schoen Berland reported that social responsibility remained important to consumers despite the recession, with more than 75% of consumers reporting that corporate responsibility is important for each tested industry.[7] Echoing the Edelman goodpurpose® study, the CSR Branding Survey's results also indicated that social responsibility remained a differentiator for products and brands. Whereas the Edelman study found that 73% of consumers would switch brands if a competing brand supported a good cause, 55% of respondents in the CSR Branding Survey reported that they were more likely to choose a product that supported a certain cause when choosing between otherwise similar products. Despite the economic recession, meanwhile, some consumers were willing to pay more for products with added social benefits, with 38% of respondents planning to spend the same or more on products or services from socially responsible companies, compared to their spending in 2009.[8]

In a 2011 *Harvard Business Review* article titled "Creating Shared Value," Michael Porter and Mark Kramer introduced a new framework for thinking about the business case for corporate responsibility. Porter and Kramer define shared value as "policies and operating practices that enhance the competitiveness of a company while simultaneously advancing the economic and social conditions in the communities in which it operates."[9] Shared value creation is the means by which these practices identify the connections between societal and economic progress and turn them into opportunities for global growth.[10] Porter and Kramer outline three key ways that corporations can create shared value opportunities:[11]

1. Reconceiving products and markets

Demand for products and services that meet societal needs is growing, and companies can begin their approach to this type of shared value creation by looking at the societal needs, benefits, and issues that are currently or potentially created through their business activities.[12] Corporations must continue to evaluate opportunities for shared value creation through product and service innovation, as they will continue to evolve as the world changes and societal needs change with it. GE's Ecomagination line of clean-tech products is an example of how corporations can use product development to create shared value. Since the launch of Ecomagination in 2005, Ecomagination revenue has increased to $160 billion.[13]

2. Redefining productivity in the value chain

The relationship between productivity and shared value arises because social and environmental issues can lead to economic costs in a corporation's value chain. In addressing societal issues such as natural resource usage, health and safety, and working conditions, firms also have an opportunity to innovate new ways of operating that will benefit not only society but the bottom line.[14] In 2009, Wal-Mart dealt with both the economic and environmental costs of excess packaging and greenhouse gas emissions by streamlining its packaging and cutting its total trucking routes by 100 million miles, an effort that saved the company $200 million even with an increase in product shipments.[15] See Figure 2.1 for the relationship between company productivity and attention to social and environmental issues.

3. Enabling local cluster development

This method of shared value creation relies on understanding that corporations do not exist in a vacuum—that is, a company's success is affected not only by its internal operations, but also by surrounding companies and infrastructure. Porter and Kramer explain that a firm's productivity and innovation are affected by clusters, which they define as "geographic concentrations of firms, related businesses, suppliers, service providers, and logistical infrastructure in a particular field."[16]

Nestle enabled cluster development through its Nespresso line, building agricultural, technical, financial, and logistical firms and capabilities in its different

Figure 2.1 How addressing social and environmental issues benefits company productivity

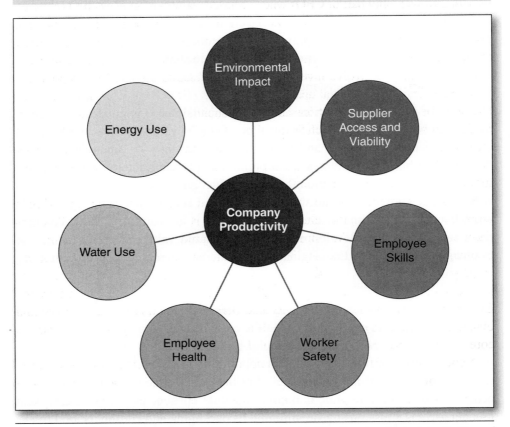

Source: Porter, M. E., & Kramer, M. R. (2011, January/February). "Creating shared value" (p. 6). *Harvard Business Review.* Retrieved from https://hbr.org/2011/01/the-big-idea-creating-shared-value.

coffee regions, which engendered efficiency and increased the quality of local production. Nestle helped regional farmers gain access to necessary inputs and finance better production facilities. The company also provided additional training on growing techniques and partnered with the Rainforest Alliance to teach more-sustainable practices. Beyond the social and environmental benefits of these efforts, Nestle improved its productivity.[17]

PERCEIVED BARRIERS TO CORPORATE RESPONSIBILITY

Despite the myriad stakeholders interested in seeing proof of CR success, measurement and communication of CR results have proven challenging. Surveys of corporate leaders routinely report that CEOs believe environmental, social, and governance performance is becoming increasingly important to their business.[18] Despite these beliefs, however, only half of CEOs whose companies engage in CR activities understand the importance of communicating their sustainability strategies to investors. Meanwhile, companies identify short-term thinking among such investors as a major obstacle to improving their performance on environmental, social, and governance issues. By failing to involve investors in the conversation around CR, corporations limit the potential for financial upside from CR activities. Meanwhile, investors may not be as resistant to conversations about CR initiatives as corporate leaders believe. Studies show that 56% of chief financial officers (CFOs) and investors believe CR creates value for business, but 51% of CR professionals don't know if CR creates value for business.[19] Better CR measurement and reporting is therefore crucial to the future success of CR programs.

Why don't corporations have better reporting mechanisms in place? One simple answer is that gathering the data needed to support assertions about the business value of CR and justify investments in CR programs can be very difficult. The narrow, business-case view of CR, often the tack embraced by corporations, emphasizes linking CR initiatives to visible bottom-line results, but even with metrics in place, it can be difficult to demonstrate the direct connection between CR programs and their attendant financial benefits.[20] As a result, executives and investors are in danger of viewing CR programs as separate from a company's core business and unrelated to its shareholder value.

A counterargument to this narrow view of corporate responsibility has arisen in the form of the corporate social performance (CSP) model, created by Donna Wood in 1991. The CSP view is more in line with the syncretic model's approach to evaluating CR.

CSP is an umbrella term that includes both descriptive and normative aspects and incorporates all facets of firm success related to corporate responsibility initiatives.[21]

A key question in evaluating the business benefits of corporate responsibility is how to define CR in the first place. Who makes the distinction between what is and is not corporate responsibility? According to Blowfield and Murray, what constitutes CR should be the domain of governmental bodies, with the business case for corporate responsibility ultimately becoming the political case.[22] Government can and in some cases may need to influence what constitutes the business case for CR.[23]

Starbucks is one company that has done an excellent job of communicating its CR results to its constituents. Each year, the corporation releases a scorecard with its CR goals compared with year-end results.[24] This document accompanies a longer Year in Review report that breaks Starbucks' CR progress down into categories such as environmental stewardship, community, ethical sourcing, and farmer support. The company's transparency around its CR initiatives makes it easy to track achievements and shortfalls—and to understand how Starbucks incorporates CR into all areas of its business as a strategic imperative.[25]

Instead of reinforcing an environment in which corporations must seek out opportunities to profit from CR, there must be a shift toward creating markets in which responsible practices are rewarded.[26] Under the current system, consumers have limited ability to support companies who are committed to CR activities, because such organizations have limited power in the marketplace. As demonstrated by the studies cited earlier in the chapter, consumers actively seek out companies and brands that incorporate CR initiatives into their missions. Policymakers have an opportunity to enable such brands to deliver on such consumer expectations and desires, thereby empowering consumers with more information from companies. One way to do so would be to create a CSR label on consumer packaged goods to distinguish companies with good CR practices from those without.[27] As consumers become increasingly educated about corporations' environmental, social, and governance (ESG) impact, companies will face increasing pressure to improve upon their metrics for the ESG impact of their business practices.

This philosophy is in diametric opposition to Milton Friedman's view of the relationship between business and society. In a seminal *New York Times Magazine* article titled "A Friedman Doctrine: The Social Responsibility of Business Is to Increase Its Profits," University of Chicago economist Friedman espoused his belief that businesses should focus strictly on profit maximization.[28] Friedman challenged the notion that corporations are capable of having responsibilities in the same way that individuals do and stated that the only purpose of business is to use its resources and engage in activities designed to increase its profits. Instead of encouraging corporations to create a positive impact on society, Friedman exhorts them to focus instead on operating within the rules of a free enterprise property system, "engag[ing] in open and free competition without deception or fraud."[29]

While Friedman's angle suggests that profit maximization and social responsibility are competing interests, the truth is that in practice, corporate responsibility often encompasses activities that can be justified on grounds beyond the traditional do-gooding CR rationale.[30] For example, a shipping company's efforts to reduce its consumption of cardboard by reengineering its packaging delivers positive results on both business and social fronts: reducing cardboard consumption has a positive impact on the environment but may also save the company considerable amounts of money, allowing it to increase its profit margins. Outside quantifiable savings, companies known for their responsible business practices may have an easier time attracting desirable employees whose interests align with their CR initiatives.[31]

Given such obvious examples of how effective corporate responsibility creates good business, why isn't there more credence given to the "doing well by doing good" rationale for CR? One answer is that corporate responsibility is a victim of its own success. In other words, when CR-related initiatives such as those discussed above are demonstrated to positively impact an industry's financial bottom line, these initiatives cease to be associated with CR in and of itself and are instead viewed as rational profit maximization. The end result is that many CR successes are attributed not to corporate responsibility programs but instead viewed as evidence of the ability of free markets to address CR issues.[32]

How can CR professionals counter this viewpoint? Here, the triple bottom line framework comes in handy. Beyond taking into account the obvious financial costs, efficient resource allocation depends on prices that reflect a holistic cost-accounting method, incorporating environmental, social, and economic costs. Dunkin' Brands, the parent company of Dunkin' Donuts and Baskin Robbins, includes an Issues Assessment Grid in its CSR report to look at the intersection of stakeholder interests and business interests.[33] The list of stakeholder interests was compiled using input from Ceres, a nonprofit organization that advocates sustainability leadership. In doing so, Dunkin' Brands is taking steps to evaluate the effect of its business practices on the surrounding world. Without considering the impact of doing business on areas beyond finance, the invisible hand of the market may steer in the wrong direction. In this way, the increasing role of CR in business presents an opportunity to make markets more efficient.[34]

MODELS CREATED TO CATEGORIZE THE BENEFITS OF CR INITIATIVES

There are many potential upsides to business from corporate responsibility efforts. The benefits of corporate responsibility initiatives can be categorized in the following ways:

1. CR can minimize risk and cost

In making the business case for CR, it is essential to establish a relationship between key aspects of sustainability and widely recognized business principles.[35] In *Management Models for Corporate Social Responsibility*, Jan Jonker and Marco de Witt identify three main pillars to use in creating the business case for CR: (1) *natural capital*, or the natural resources that human beings consider "valuable, vulnerable, scarce, fragile, or irreplaceable enough to justify investments in monitoring"; (2) *economic capital*, or produced assets that can be assigned monetary value; and (3) *social equity*, a concept that includes the "trust, norms and networks that people can draw upon to solve common problems."[36] The authors emphasize the importance of viewing sustainability as a direction for a corporation to take, rather than as a destination.[37] For sustainability to function as a tool of corporate transformation, its leaders must see sustainability as a strategic opportunity for value creation.[38]

Jonker and de Witt also identify four levers that corporations can use to derive short-, medium-, and long-term value from their corporate responsibility initiatives: (1) *cost leverage*, or the ways in which sustainability can be used to increase cost savings; (2) *risk reduction*, which includes the management of both long-term and short-term risk; (3) *options creation*, or a corporation's ability to develop new operational methods, identify untapped market opportunities, and deliver on emerging stakeholder values; and (4) *stakeholder preference*, which is cultivated by developing stronger relationships with stakeholders. These levers are important because they align the goals of CR programs with established business management principles.[39] More information about each lever is included in Table 2.1.

According to John Zinkin and Paul Thompson in *Investors Digest*, corporate responsibility can mitigate a corporation's risk of damaging or losing its license to operate, or its ability to exist, do business, and earn a profit.[40] Beyond regulatory bodies, which have the ability to rescind a business's legal ability to operate, there are several other types of stakeholders who can affect an organization's license to operate. Consumers directly affect a company's license to operate by choosing not to purchase its products. While the decision of consumers not to buy a company's products may be driven by dissatisfaction with product quality or competitiveness, it can also be driven by dissatisfaction with the company's attention to social or environmental issues. Consumer boycotts of socially undesirable corporations have forced such corporations to change their business practices.

Employees are possibly more powerful, as they can leave a company if they feel that the company does not pay or treat its employees fairly, or because of dissatisfaction with a company's socially undesirable activities. Employees can also create a situation in which it is expensive to recruit and train talent if they feel ashamed to be associated with a company because of its irresponsible behavior.

Investors have obvious influence in that they can withdraw funds and backing from corporations that do not meet CR requirements. With the rise of socially responsible investors, certain funds may not be eligible to invest in corporations that do not satisfy such requirements. All these stakeholders have the capacity to affect a corporation's license to operate in different ways from regulators, who can pass legislation to limit a company's freedom to operate.

Table 2.1   Jonker and de Witt's four levers

Lever	Definition	Operational Benefits	Example
Cost leverage	Using sustainable improvement to maximize cost savings	• Fewer disruptions and delays • Reduced dependency on and usage of raw materials • Reduced waste • Lowered insurance premiums • Decreased energy usage • Improvements to operational efficiency	Reduced packaging both lessens the strain on resources and saves money on shipping supplies
Risk reduction	Managing both long-term and short-term risks	• Fewer operational disruptions • Less risk of prosecution and penalties • Less customer and regulatory retaliation • Fewer supply chain disruptions • Better management of business risk • Fewer risks to license to operate	Ensuring the safety of workers along a company's supply chain reduces the risk of facility shutdowns
Options creation	Developing new operational methods, identifying opportunities in untapped markets, and delivering on new stakeholder values	• Development of competitive advantage • New operational methods • Increased access to new market opportunities • Opportunity to influence regulation • Increased barriers to entry for competitors	Using compliance with environmental regulation serves as an opportunity for innovation
Stakeholder preference	Building stronger relationships with stakeholders to increase stakeholder preference	• Enhanced relationships with stakeholders • Opportunities to work with best supply chain and business partners • Ability to attract resources, people, and investment to the company • Increased employee retention, morale, and motivation • Improved corporate reputation • Ease of regulatory approval	Suppliers can be empowered by providing additional training or using corporate clout to ensure access to resources

Source: Adapted from Jonker, J., & de Witte, M. (2006). *Management models for corporate social responsibility* (p. 329). Springer.

2. CR increases reputation and leads to increased sales and better human capital

Managing reputational risk is an integral part of corporate strategy. As Berkshire Hathaway CEO Warren Buffett once famously noted, "it takes 20 years to build a reputation and five minutes to ruin it. If you think about that, you'll do things differently." Corruption scandals (such as the one at Enron) or environmental accidents (such as BP's 2010 Deepwater Horizon oil spill) can devastate a carefully honed corporate reputation in a matter of days. These events can also draw unwanted attention from regulators, courts, governments, and media. Building a genuine culture of "doing the right thing" within a corporation—critical to effective CR strategy—can help offset these risks. See Figure 2.2 for a list of the global business drivers as reported by G250 companies, the top 250 companies listed in the Fortune Global 500 ranking, as identified in the KPMG International Survey of Corporate Responsibility Reporting 2011.

To determine how corporate responsibility might affect a corporation's reputation, it is essential to identify the measures of business performance on which CR

Figure 2.2 Reputation and ethical considerations top the list of global business reporting drivers for G250 companies

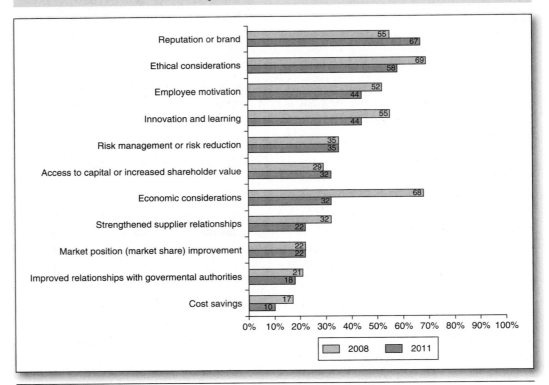

Source: KPMG International Survey of Corporate Responsibility Reporting 2011, p. 19.

might have an impact.[41] A study undertaken by SustainAbility in 2001 and 2002 looked at areas including shareholder value, revenue, operational efficiency, access to capital, customer attraction, brand value and reputation, human capital, risk management, innovation, and license to operate.[42] Based on the results of the study, the most significant CR dimensions are eco-efficiency, working conditions, and environmental products.[43] The study also indicates that the areas of business performance in which CR has the greatest impact are brand value and recognition, risk management, and license to operate.[44]

Three types of business-case arguments for corporate responsibility grow out of this analysis.[45] The first is the role of CR as a means of avoiding financial loss. The second is CR as a driver of tangible financial gains. The third is the idea of CR as an important component of a corporation's strategic approach to long-term business performance. Research from BSR (Business for Social Responsibility), a nonprofit that promotes social responsibility in businesses, identifies a series of financial bottom-line benefits that result when a corporation fully integrates its CR initiatives into its overall business operations and strategy, citing increases in both dollar sales and market share, strengthened brand positioning, enhanced corporate image, improved recruitment and retention of employees, decreased operating costs, and increased appeal to investors and financial analysts.[46]

3. CR is a strategic imperative and benefits the business overall

In Chapter 1, we looked at the Porter/Kramer framework separating responsive CSR from strategic CSR. Strategic CSR is how corporations leverage their contributions to society to create shared value, as described earlier in this chapter. Instead of looking at business and societal interests as competing goals, shared value creation explores and seeks to expand the connections between societal and economic progress. In short, strategic CSR is good business.

Porter and Kramer point out that value creation is a concept that has been long recognized in business but that, in the past, businesses have failed to consider a value perspective in their approach to societal issues.[47] Applied to business, assessing value means looking at profit results—that is, revenues earned from customers minus the costs incurred in earning these revenues.[48] The strategic CSR approach applies the principle of value creation to CR programs, asserting that both economic and social progress should be addressed according to value principles. Similar to how calculating profits requires a corporation to look not only at gains but also at costs, a value creation approach to CR looks at benefits relative to costs, rather than just benefits alone.[49]

Approaching CR programs from a strategic, value-oriented approach is essential to demonstrate the business benefits of CR to constituents. Companies are becoming increasingly aware that they must appear socially responsible to remain productive, competitive, and relevant.[50] The ways in which a company relates to its workers, communities, and the market can contribute to its ability to sustain long-term business success.[51]

A 2009 McKinsey survey found that CR represents an opportunity for long-term contribution to shareholder value.[52] As discovered in the KPMG International Survey of Corporate Responsibility Reporting, one-third of the largest companies in the world report opportunities to grow their market share and reduce costs through their CR program. With an increased emphasis on innovation and learning as key drivers for reporting, the corporate understanding of CR has shifted from seeing it as a moral imperative to recognizing it as a critical business issue.[53]

Cisco is one company with a robust commitment to strategic CSR. Its Networking Academy educates hundreds of thousands of students worldwide in the skills needed to build, design, and maintain networks. The program not only assists students by improving their career prospects, but also fills the global demand for workers with these skill sets. It is no accident that the skills Cisco pays for students to develop are skills the company needs in its employees. In operating 10,000 academies in 165 countries, Cisco's Networking Academy enables its students to achieve industry-recognized certifications, positioning them for entry-level information and communication technology careers—and creates the type of loyalty that benefits the company as former students become employees.[54]

Another example of the strategic CSR framework advocated by Porter and Kramer is seen in the Starbucks case included in Chapter 1. Starbucks has incorporated corporate responsibility into its core business, turning what was initially a CR blunder into a crucial piece of its strategic plan. Wal-Mart also has incorporated sustainability into its operations as a matter of strategic necessity rather than mere social good.

Beyond enhancing corporate reputation, ESG programs can create value in other ways, including contributing to business growth, improving a corporation's return on capital, mitigating risk, and improving the quality of a company's management.[55]

How, specifically, does effective CR contribute to organizational growth? CR enables companies to expand into new markets. As seen in the Cisco example, some companies are able to reach far beyond their home countries through their CR initiatives. Not only does a program like Cisco's create potential future employees in countries around the world, but it also creates consumer loyalty in local communities worldwide through its demonstration of a commitment to educating and empowering a nation's people. CR also forces companies to get creative in their product offerings in order to deliver satisfactory products to socially minded consumers.[56] This spurs new product development and leads to innovation.

Aside from growth opportunities into new markets internationally, CR represents an opportunity to enter untapped market segments in countries where an organization already does business. For example, Telefónica has developed new products and services geared toward customers over 60, a program that has both met a social need and enabled the company to target new customers in what was previously an underrepresented segment.[57] CR can also help corporations increase their market share by identifying synergistic projects to invest in and exploit for benefits from partner organizations. For example, Coca-Cola developed more environmentally friendly, energy-efficient coolers for retailers, which saved the retailers money in energy costs; as a result, Coke is better positioned than its competition to negotiate for space in stores.[58]

CR also offers returns on capital through increased operational efficiency. For example, a Novo Nordisk initiative to reduce carbon emissions eliminated 20,000 tons of CO_2, with the company using the savings to invest in a supplier's premium price for wind power. As of 2014, all of Novo Nordisk's activities in Denmark are powered by green energy.[59] CR can also contribute to workforce efficiency. For example, Best Buy created the Women's Leadership Forum to reduce its employee turnover rate among women, with favorable results. Not only did the company reduce female employee turnover, but it also increased its sales to female consumers.[60]

CR initiatives can also aid in risk mitigation. Corporations can limit regulatory risk by working with policymakers to develop business policies that contribute to social good. By courting public support, companies can avoid potential backlashes over perceived CR shortcomings in operations. For example, Coca-Cola put resources behind quantifying risks and developing plans to mitigate risks around water usage. This proactive approach has helped the company avoid backlash over water usage.[61]

Another way CR can head off risk is through supply chain adjustments. For example, Nestle's Creating Shared Value strategy allows the company to work with farmers and agricultural communities to ensure access to necessary raw materials. Nestle secures this access by investing in these communities through infrastructure improvements, training programs for local farmers, and paying fair-market prices directly to the producers rather than involving middlemen. This program not only helps the communities where Nestle operates but also helps to ensure Nestle's access to elements along its supply chain when shortages occur.[62]

Management quality is also positively affected by CR programs. For example, leadership development programs might send executives to work on pro bono projects with NGOs, entrepreneurs, or governments in emerging markets. The result is that emerging markets benefit from the executives' expertise, while executives benefit from increased cultural competency, global awareness, and commitment to the company. Another way in which management quality benefits from CR is through enhanced adaptability. For example, Cargill maintains a presence in

Zimbabwe despite difficult political and economic conditions. There, Cargill pays employees in food parcels and fuel vouchers instead of in Zimbabwean dollars, as Zimbabwe's currency is incredibly volatile.

Management also benefits from taking the long-term, strategic view required to fulfill many CR initiatives. Novo Nordisk manages to a triple bottom line. In addition to its previously discussed environmental program, the company invests in programs designed to help people, making investments to prevent, diagnose, and treat diabetes and build up related health care infrastructure. It has also used its investments to strengthen the company's position in mature markets and to develop business in new ones.[63]

The *ICCA* [Institute for Corporate Culture] *Handbook on Corporate Social Responsibility* breaks down the business case for CR into economic drivers and managerial drivers.[64] Economic drivers include increasing shareholder value and creating competitive advantage. Managerial drivers are organized around balancing stakeholder interests. The stakeholder theory of the firm, introduced by Edward Freeman, states that a firm needs to pay attention to all stakeholders, not just shareholders. In his 1984 book *Strategic Management: A Stakeholder Approach*, Freeman stated:

> Rather than being simply agents of shareholders, management must take the rights and interest of all legitimate stakeholders into account. While they still have a fiduciary responsibility to look after shareholders' interests, managers must balance this with the competing interests of other stakeholders for the long-term survival of the corporation, rather than just maximizing the interests of just one group at a time.[65]

Differences between the traditional managerial model and the stakeholder model can be seen in Figures 2.3 and 2.4.

Freeman's stakeholder view of the firm is especially relevant today, as evidenced by a recent spate of articles and books that have called into question what is now seen as an overstated influence of shareholder value in guiding business decisions. In *The New York Times*, Joe Nocera looks at the consequences of the narrow focus on shareholder value in business culture, namely, the pressure on chief executives to boost short-term earnings at the expense of long-term value creation.[66]

Meanwhile, a piece by Justin Fox and Jay W. Lorsch in *Harvard Business Review* asks "What Good Are Shareholders?" and looks at the three areas in which shareholders contribute to a firm—money, information, and discipline—identifying the issues that limit the value of shareholder participation in each sphere.[67] Fox and Lorsch state that while providing money to a firm seems to be the most straightforward role of shareholders, the reality of how shareholder money translates to power over firm decision-making is much more complex. In situations where corporations

Figure 2.3 Traditional managerial model of the firm

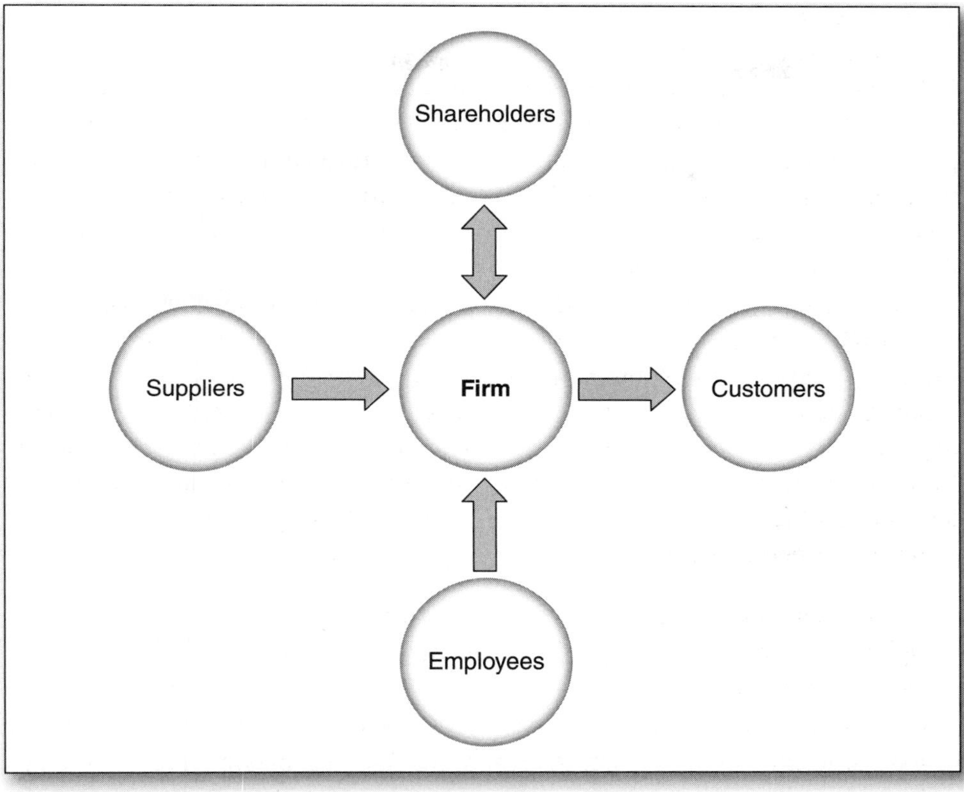

Source: Adapted from Freeman, E. (1984). *Strategic management: A stakeholder approach.* Cambridge, UK: Cambridge University Press.

cannot operate without capital from equity investors, such investors are often rewarded with increased influence in the form of board seats or veto power over managerial decisions.[68] At the same time, Fox and Lorsch point out that such situations do not represent the typical shareholder–corporation relationship, in which the funding role is primarily filled by the overall stock market rather than by shareholders alone. As they explain:

> The market provides liquidity. Having shares that can easily be bought and sold, with prices that all can see, reassures lenders and business partners. It enables mergers. It allows early investors and employees to sell company shares and exercise options. It gives investors who come forward when cash is sorely needed a way to realize gains on their investments later. It greases the wheels of capitalism.[69]

Figure 2.4 Stakeholder model

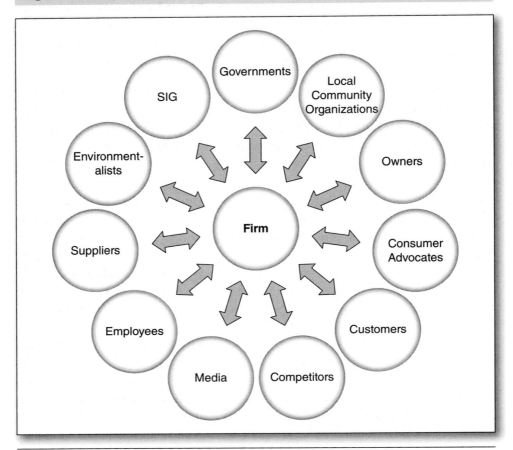

Source: Adapted from Freeman, E. (1984). *Strategic management: A stakeholder approach.* Cambridge, UK: Cambridge University Press.

The downside of this is that increases in stock issuance over the past few decades have destroyed value and decreased liquidity.

The flow of information from shareholders to corporations is also a complicated issue. While shareholders communicate with companies through stock prices, they also do so through actual conversations in meetings and conference calls. But what could be an opportunity for managers to glean valuable insights from investors is often prevented from reaching its full potential. Fox and Lorsch note that the Regulation Fair Disclosure, adopted by the Securities and Exchange Commission in 2000, requires all substantive corporate disclosures to be released immediately to the public, making both managers and shareholders reluctant to share information.[70] As a result:

Communication between managers and the investor community now takes place mostly during the conference calls that follow the release of quarterly earnings. The participants in these calls are a mix of actual investors and analysts from brokerages and independent research firms. In our experience, analysts ask most of the questions, and they tend toward the superficial and the short term.[71]

Discipline is yet another complicated issue, as it highlights the conflict between managerial and shareholder interests. A 1976 academic article by Michael C. Jensen and William H. Meckling identified shareholders as "principals" and managers as "agents" and argued that if an agent owns the business, there is no conflict; however, with their ownership percentage, agents are more inclined to act on their own behalf than in a way that benefits the firm's principals.[72] Thus, Jensen and Meckling defined the primary challenge of corporate governance as preventing agents from taking advantage of principals. Jensen explains the singular focus on protecting shareholder interests (vs. looking at the interests of the various stakeholders; see Figure 2.4) as follows: "Since it is logically impossible to maximize in more than one dimension, purposeful behavior requires a single valued objective function."[73]

Jensen would have advocated not maximizing shareholder value, however, but maximizing enterprise value (which includes both a company's equity and its debt). But, as Fox and Lorsch explain, "shareholders and debt holders often have different interests and priorities, so shareholder value became the shorthand goal that executives, investors, academics, and others latched on to."[74] The problem is that without the existence of a major shareholder with real power in an organization, shareholders are limited in their ability to keep managers in check, having only two real options at their disposal: selling shares and casting votes.[75] Each has its own limitations: the former simply isn't possible in some cases, such as index funds that are unable to sell certain stocks; meanwhile, short-term investors are not positioned to use votes to guide firms in the right direction.

The issues discussed in each of the areas limit the effectiveness of shareholders in positively influencing firm activity, and they lack a short-term solution. Until these issues are resolved, the role of shareholders in a corporation is insufficient to justify the strong emphasis on shareholder value in business culture.

CREATING VALUE THROUGH CORPORATE RESPONSIBILITY

According to the results of a global survey by McKinsey, more than 80% of both CFOs and investment professionals believe that having high-performing ESG programs can be a proxy for how effectively a business is managed.[76] Two-thirds of CEOs and three-quarters of investment professionals included in the study agree that environmental, social, and governance activities create value for shareholders in normal economic times.[77] CFOs (79%), investment professionals (75%), and CSR professionals (79%) agree that corporate reputation or brand equity is the most important way these programs create value; however, the members of these three groups disagree on how much value is created. A quarter do not know what effect, if any, these activities have on shareholder value or on what activities are the most important, when asked to consider the following: compliance/transparency; changing business processes; investment in social issues; creating new revenue streams; and charitable giving.[78]

How can corporations close the gap between CR potential and reality? Porter and Kramer's shared value creation framework is a good place to start, as the relationship between CSR and creating shared value (CSV) in many ways reflects the relationship between traditional corporate responsibility approaches and the emerging perspective that corporate responsibility must be integrated into all aspects of a company's operations. Porter and Kramer identify several ways in which CSR differs from CSV, explaining that while a CSR approach defines value as simply doing good (similar to corporations' traditional philanthropic approach to social issues), the CSV approach looks at economic and societal benefits relative to cost (see Table 2.2).[79]

THE BUSINESS CASE FOR SUSTAINABILITY

Sustainable business is a subset of corporate responsibility that has garnered increasing attention in the past few years, and one that Rice University professor

Table 2.2 CSR vs. CSV

CSR	CSV
Value = doing good	Value = economic and societal benefits relative to cost
Citizenship, philanthropy, sustainability	Joint company and community value creation
Discretionary or in response to external pressure (reactive)	Integral to competing (proactive)
Separate from profit maximization	Integral to profit maximization
Agenda is determined by external reporting and personal preferences	Agenda is company-specific and internally generated
Impact is limited by corporate footprint and CSR budget	Realigns the entire company budget

Source: Adapted from Porter, M. E., & Kramer, M. R. (2011, January/February). "Creating shared value." *Harvard Business Review*, p. 16. Retrieved from https://hbr.org/2011/01/the-big-idea-creating-shared-value.

and sustainability expert Marc J. Epstein argues not only demands urgent attention from corporations but also presents opportunities for tangible payoffs.[80] Sustainability is an urgent matter because government regulations will increasingly require attention to sustainable business procedures in the near future, and because sustainability can bolster a corporation's community relations, helping it secure licenses to operate and engendering loyalty and trust among community constituents. Sustainability is a means of hedging against future risk and an opportunity to strengthen existing business relationships.[81]

Epstein identifies several types of payoffs associated with sustainability. Perhaps most essential to articulate, given skepticism of the economic value of CR programs, are the financial rewards. Attention to sustainability leads to reduced operating costs, increased revenues, lower administrative and capital costs, and stock market premiums.[82] Beyond economics, corporations that devote attention to sustainability stand to benefit from improved customer relations through increased customer satisfaction, product innovation, and market share, along with an improved corporate reputation and the opportunity to capitalize on new markets.

Operationally, sustainability presents a variety of opportunities for improvement. Emphasis on sustainability in operations can result in process innovation, productivity gains, reduced cycle times, improved resource yields, and waste minimization.[83] Additionally, there are organizational benefits from CR, such as increased employee satisfaction, better relationships with other stakeholders, the potential for reduction in regulatory intervention, lower risk, and an increase in learning.

Writing in *Harvard Business Review*, Ram Nidumolu, C. K. Prahalad, and M. R. Rangaswami explain that corporate leaders conduct business in a way that suggests that they must choose between the social benefits and financial costs of developing sustainable products. Executives seem to subscribe to the traditional view that social and financial gains are competing interests. But as Nidumolu et al. explain, this is not the case: "Our research shows that sustainability is a mother lode of organizational and technological innovations that yield both bottom-line and top-line returns."[84] Identifying sustainability as a long-term strategic goal now will allow companies to get ahead of the competition, as it will continue to be a crucial part of product development.[85]

But how can top leaders be convinced that sustainability makes sense not just from a social perspective, but from a business perspective as well? Nidumolu et al. describe the process of becoming sustainable as having five stages, each with its own challenges:[86]

1. Viewing compliance as opportunity

The firm must adjust its perspective on corporate compliance, viewing it as an opportunity for innovation.[87] For example, in the 1990s, HP realized that lead usage would be subject to regulation in the future, so the company developed alternatives, positioning HP as a front-runner when regulation came into effect.

2. Making value chains sustainable

The company must increase efficiencies throughout its value chain, identifying and developing sustainable sources of raw materials and components, increasing its reliance on clean energy, and coming up with innovative uses for returned products. FedEx replaced older aircraft used for shipping with Boeing 757s, reducing its aircraft fuel consumption by 36% while increasing its shipping capacity by 20%.[88]

3. Designing sustainable products and services

The company can also develop sustainable product and service offerings by introducing new techniques to its product development process and developing eco-friendly packaging. For example, Clorox introduced its Green Works line of nonsynthetic household cleaners in early 2008. By the end of the same year, it had grown the U.S. natural cleaners market by 100% and gained a 40% share of the market, valued at $200 million.[89]

4. Developing new business models

Here, a firm must come up with novel ways of delivering and capturing value, such as inventing new delivery technologies that change value chain relationships, creating monetization models around services rather than products, and devising business models that combine digital and physical infrastructures.[90] For example, a California start-up, Calera, is using carbon dioxide from industrial emissions to create cement through a process intended to mimic the one by which coral produces shells and reefs from the calcium and magnesium contained in seawater. Calera's technology removes harmful emissions, while the company's business model is built on giving the product away free and charging polluters a fee for removing carbon dioxide.[91]

5. Creating next-practice platforms

Finally, the company must question the logic behind business today through the lens of sustainability, building business platforms that will allow customers and suppliers to manage energy in a different way, developing products that can be created without the need for water consumption, and designing technologies that make it possible to use energy produced as a by-product.[92]

Nidumolu et al. identify two key factors that signal success in creating sustainability initiatives. First, commitment to sustainability must start at the top of an organization. When a company's executive leadership articulates a focus on sustainability, change will happen quickly. Second, beyond top leadership, the people within the organization matter. Three-quarters of workforce entrants in the United States consider social responsibility and commitment to environmental issues to be important criteria when selecting employers.[93] Not only are employees committed to these issues more likely to contribute to a corporate environment in which CR initiatives are successful, but corporations are likely to find that delivering on employee expectations about corporate responsibility creates an environment in which it is easier to attract and retain talent.

STRUCTURE OF CR FUNCTION

Corporate responsibility is a relatively new functional area, and its role and structure within organizations continues to evolve. According to BSR's report on designing a CSR structure:

> The ultimate goal of a CSR management system is to successfully integrate corporate responsibility concerns—social, environmental and economic—into a company's values, culture, operations and business decisions at all levels of the organization, which can help create better management practices overall.[94]

BSR advocates an approach to designing a CSR structure that can be broken into nine steps, as seen in Figure 2.5. We will look at this process in more depth in Chapter 10.

It is important to remember that CR programs, like other business areas, should be tailored to company culture and industry specifics. As seen in the sidebar, corporations in certain industries must contend with industry-specific hot-button CR issues (see Table 2.3) and must ensure that these issues are included in their CR initiatives. The structure of a CSR department should depend on a corporation's CR needs and goals. In designing a senior leadership structure for its CR program, a corporation can choose to pursue either a centralized or decentralized management structure. The former involves a single head of the CSR department who is responsible for the design, development, and coordination of CSR activities within the company.[95] The latter incorporates CR into different business units, with several departmental leaders being assigned responsibility for CR activities in their respective departments.[96] On the lower-management and specialized staff level, corporations have a variety of options: (1) containing these staff members within a separate CSR department; (2) creating a series of separate specialized CSR departments; (3) placing staff members within existing business units, reporting to decentralized upper managers; (4) creating CSR groups within geographic regions; or (5) organizing CSR management and staff by skill set.[97]

Figure 2.5   Nine steps to designing a CSR structure

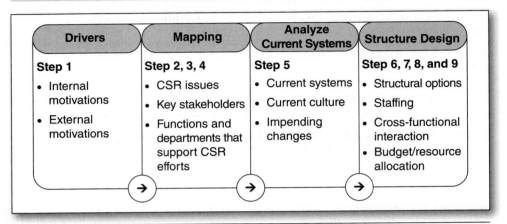

Source: Adapted from Business for Social Responsibility. (2002). "Designing a CSR structure: A step-by-step guide including leadership examples and decision-making tools." Retrieved July 15, 2014, from http://research .dnv.com/csr/PW_Tools/PWD/1/00/L/1-00-L-2001-01-0/lib2001/Designing%20a%20CSR%20Structure%20 %28fra%20BSR%29.pdf.

Table 2.3   Hot-button CR issues to address, by industry

- **Agriculture** – Biodiversity, genetically modified organisms (GMOs), work conditions, wages
- **Apparel** – Human rights, labor conditions, use of subcontractors, wages
- **Automotive** – Climate change, product safety
- **Extractives** – Bribery, indigenous communities, land use
- **Financial Services** – Red-lining, predatory lending
- **Pharmaceuticals** – Patent access, animal testing, bioethics
- **Technology** – Digital divide, product take-back, privacy

Source: Adapted from Business for Social Responsibility. (2002). "Designing a CSR structure: A step-by-step guide including leadership examples and decision-making tools." Retrieved July 15, 2014, from http://research .dnv.com/csr/PW_Tools/PWD/1/00/L/1-00-L-2001-01-0/lib2001/Designing%20a%20CSR%20Structure%20 %28fra%20BSR%29.pdf.

In recent years, much of the conversation among CSR professionals has turned to the goal of eliminating isolated CSR departments within organizations, as it is believed that for corporate responsibility to truly become an integrated part of a corporation's long-term strategy, CR responsibilities must exist within every arm of an organization. As Unilever's chief marketing officer, Keith Weed, told *Marketing Magazine* in late 2011, "We don't have a CSR department—if you have a CSR department, then it's an add-on."[98] As this line of thinking becomes increasingly popular among corporate executives—and the economic bottom-line value of CR programs is increasingly understood and valued in the business world—separate CSR departments are likely to inch toward obsolescence.

CONCLUSION

The business case for corporate responsibility is not just about creating economic value for shareholders. Corporate responsibility initiatives need to be undertaken in line with the stakeholder theory of the corporation, considering the effect on various interested parties including board members, executive leadership, shareholders, customers, and governmental bodies, among others.

NOTES

1. Carroll, A., & Shabana, K. (2010). "The business case for corporate social responsibility: A review of concepts, research and practice." *International Journal of Management Reviews, 12*(1), 85–105. Retrieved from http://onlinelibrary.wiley.com/doi/10.1111/j.1468-2370.2009.00275.x/pdf

2. goodpurpose, http://purpose.edelman.com/ (accessed July 15, 2014).

3. Carroll & Shabana, "The business case for corporate social responsibility," p. 92.

4. Ibid.

5. Ibid, p. 93.

6. Blowfield, M., & Murray, A. (2011). *Corporate responsibility* (2nd ed., p. 151). New York, NY: Oxford University Press.

7. Penn Schoen Berland. (2010). "Corporate social responsibility branding survey." Retrieved July 15, 2014, from http://www.slideshare.net/BMGlobalNews/csr-branding-survey-2010-final

8. Ibid.

9. Porter, M. E., & Kramer, M. R. (2011, January/February). "Creating shared value." *Harvard Business Review*, p. 6. Retrieved from https://hbr.org/2011/01/the-big-idea-creating-shared-value

10. Ibid.

11. Ibid, p. 5.

12. Ibid, p. 8.

13. Frodl, D. (2015). "Ecomagination overview." GE 2013 Global Impact. Retrieved July 15, 2014, from http://www.ge.com/globalimpact2013/#/ecomagination

14. Ibid., pp. 8–9.

15. Ibid., p. 9.

16. Ibid., p. 12.

17. Ibid., p. 13.

18. Grayson, D. (2009, November). "Sustainability and business success." *Governance, 192,* 5.

19. Saul, J. (2010). *Social innovation, Inc.: 5 strategies for driving business growth through social change* (pp. 151–152). Jossey-Bass.

20. Bonini, S., Koller, T., & Mirvis, P. (2009). "Valuing social responsibility programs." *McKinsey Quarterly, 4,* 65.

21. Carroll & Shabana, "The business case for corporate social responsibility."

22. Blowfield & Murray, *Corporate responsibility*, pp. 155–156.

23. Ibid., pp. 155–156.

24. "Starbucks global responsibility report: Goals and progress 2013." (n.d.). Retrieved July 5, 2014, from http://www.starbucks.com/responsibility/global-report

25. Ibid.

26. Zadeck, S., Sabapathy, J., Dossing, H., & Swift, T. (2003). "Responsible competitiveness: Corporate responsibility clusters in action" (p. 1). London, UK: Accountability.

27. Carroll & Shabana, "The business case for corporate social responsibility," p. 100.

28. Friedman, M. (1970, September 13). "A Friedman doctrine: The social responsibility of business is to increase its profits." *New York Times Magazine.*

29. Ibid.

30. Blowfield & Murray, *Corporate responsibility*, p. 290.

31. "New trends redefine doing well by doing good." (2008). *Guide to best practices in corporate social responsibility* (Vol. 2). *PR News.*

32. Blowfield, M., & Murray, A. (2008). *Corporate responsibility: A critical introduction* (p. 150). New York, NY: Oxford University Press.

33. "Dunkin' Brands 2012 corporate social responsibility report." Retrieved July 15, 2014, from http://www.dunkinbrands.com/internal_redirect/cms.ipressroom.com.s3.amazonaws.com/226/files/201411/2012%20CSR%20Report%20Online%20Design%20-%20FINAL%2006.28.13.pdf

34. Ibid., p. 151.

35. Jonker, J., & de Witte, M. (2006). *Management models for corporate social responsibility* (p. 327). Springer.

36. Ibid., pp. 327–328.

37. Ibid., p. 328.

38. Ibid., p. 328.

39. Ibid., pp. 328–329.

40. Zinkin, J., & Thompson, P. (2003, May 16). "Why corporate social responsibility matters." *Investors Digest.*

41. Blowfield & Murray, *Corporate responsibility* (2nd ed.), pp. 151–152.

42. Ibid., p. 157.

43. Ibid., p. 157

44. Ibid., p. 157.

45. Ibid., p. 159.

46. Kotler, P., & Lee, N. (2005). *Corporate social responsibility: Doing the most good for your company and your cause* (pp. 10–11). Hoboken, NJ: John Wiley.

47. Porter & Kramer, "Creating shared value," p. 6.

48. Ibid.

49. Ibid.

50. "What is corporate social responsibility? 8 questions and answers" (p. 3). (2002, July). USAID Catalyst Consortium.

51. Ibid.

52. Bonini, S., Brun, N., & Rosenthal, M. (2009). "McKinsey Global Survey results: Valuing corporate social responsibility" (Exhibit 5). *McKinsey Quarterly.*

53. "The KPMG survey of corporate responsibility reporting 2013." (2013). KPMG International. Retrieved July 15, 2014, from http://www.kpmg.com/Global/en/IssuesAndInsights/ArticlesPublications/corporate-responsibility/Documents/kpmg-survey-of-corporate-responsibility-reporting-2013.pdf

54. Cisco Networking Academy, http://www.cisco.com/web/learning/netacad/index.html (accessed July 15, 2014).

55. Bonini, S., Koller, T., & Mirvis, P. (2009). "Valuing social responsibility programs." *McKinsey Quarterly, 4,* 66.

56. Ibid.

57. Ibid., p. 67.

58. Ibid., pp. 67–68.

59. Andreasen, T. R., & Larsen, B. H. "A business partnership: Driving sustainability: How to save energy and increase profit while investing in renewable energy." (n.d.). Retrieved July 15, 2014, from http://www.novonordisk.com/content/dam/Denmark/HQ/Sustainability/documents/13%2011%2026_Partnership_Sustainability-04-pages.pdf

60. Bonini et al., "Valuing social responsibility programs," p. 69.

61. Ibid., p. 70.

62. Ibid., p. 70.

63. Ibid., p. 71.

64. Hennigfeld, J., Pohl, M., & Tolhurst, N. (Eds.). (2006). *ICCA handbook on corporate social responsibility.* Hoboken, NJ: John Wiley.

65. Freeman, E. (1984). *Strategic management: A stakeholder approach.* Cambridge, UK: Cambridge University Press.

66. Nocera, J. (2012, August 10). "Down with shareholder value." *New York Times.* Retrieved July 15, 2014, from http://www.nytimes.com/2012/08/11/opinion/nocera-down-with-shareholder-value.html

67. Fox, J., & Lorsch, J. W. (2012, July/August). "What good are shareholders?" *Harvard Business Review.* Retrieved July 15, 2014, from http://hbr.org/2012/07/what-good-are-shareholders/

68. Ibid.

69. Ibid.

70. Ibid.

71. Ibid.

72. Ibid.

73. Ibid.

74. Ibid.

75. Ibid.

76. Bonini et al., "McKinsey Global Survey results," p. 5.

77. Ibid., p. 2.

78. Ibid., pp. 2–4.

79. Porter & Kramer, "Creating shared value," p. 16.

80. Epstein, M. (2008). *Making sustainability work* (pp. 21–22). Greenleaf.

81. Ibid.

82. Ibid., pp. 251–252.

83. Ibid.

84. Nidumolu, R., Prahalad, C. K., & Rangaswami, M. R. (2009, September). "Why sustainability is now the key driver of innovation" (pp. 57–58). *Harvard Business Review.*

85. Ibid.

86. Ibid.

87. Ibid., p. 60.

88. Ibid., p. 60.

89. Ibid., p. 63.

90. Ibid., p. 60.

91. Ibid., pp. 63–34.

92. Ibid., p. 61.

93. Ibid., p. 64.

94. Business for Social Responsibility. (2002). "Designing a CSR structure: A step-by-step guide including leadership examples and decision-making tools." Retrieved July 15, 2014, from http://research.dnv.com/csr/PW_Tools/PWD/1/00/L/1-00-L-2001-01-0/lib2001/Designing%20a%20CSR%20Structure%20%28fra%20BSR%29.pdf

95. Ibid.

96. Ibid.

97. Ibid.

98. Chapman, M. (2011, November 29). "CSR departments are redundant, says Unilever's Weed." *Marketing Magazine.* Retrieved July 15, 2014, from http://www.marketingmagazine.co.uk/news/1106701/CSR-departments-redundant-says-Unilevers-Weed

UNILEVER'S SUSTAINABLE LIVING PLAN: REVOLUTIONIZING SUSTAINABILITY ON A GLOBAL SCALE

How to grow sustainably is the biggest challenge facing companies everywhere. The great challenge of the 21st century is to provide good standards of living for 7 billion people without depleting the earth's resources or running up massive levels of public debt. To achieve this, government and business alike will need to find new models of growth which are in both environmental and economic balance.

—Paul Polman, CEO, Unilever[1]

"Business has to decide what role it wants to play. Does it sit on the sidelines waiting for governments to take action or does it get on the pitch and start addressing these issues?"[2] This question was posed by Unilever CEO Paul Polman in a message to the public upon the release of the company's new Sustainable Living Plan. Unilever announced in November 2010 a new plan to double revenues while halving its environmental impact by 2020. Proponents of the plan immediately lauded it as a game changer for global business,[3] while others were critical of the plan for its potential to be incompatible with shareholder value creation.[4] Regardless of their position, most commentators saw the plan as a dramatic shift in how a global business approached the issue of corporate responsibility, and more specifically, environmental sustainability.

Polman conveyed the dramatic shift with the following statement:

In Unilever we believe that business must be part of the solution. And it will have to recognize that the needs of citizens and communities carry the same weight as the demands of shareholders. We believe that in the future this will become the only acceptable model of business. If people feel that the system is unjust and does not work for them, they will rebel against it. And if we continue to consume key inputs like water, food, land and energy without thought as to their long-term sustainability, then none of us will prosper.[5]

Was Unilever's Sustainable Living Plan a game changer for global business or just another example of a company using greenwashing to improve its corporate reputation and drive awareness of its products?

Source: Unilever Sustainable Living Plan Progress Report, 2011.

UNILEVER

Founded in January 1930 by Antonius Johannes Jurgens, Samuel van den Bergh, and William Hulme Lever, Unilever was a multinational consumer goods company with a product portfolio that included cleaning agents, personal care products, foods, and beverages. With its products being sold in over 190 countries and 2 billion customers using one of its products on any given day, Unilever by 2012 was the second largest consumer goods company in the world, ranking behind only Procter & Gamble.[6] Additionally, Unilever was the world's largest producer of ice cream.[7] Unilever was a dual-listed public company comprising Unilever N.V. in Rotterdam, Netherlands, and Unilever PLC in London, United Kingdom. Both companies operated as a single entity with the same directors and executive management team.

Unilever owned more than 400 brands and categorized them into four major categories: Homecare, Personal Care, Food, and Beverages. According to the company, 12 of the 400 brands generated sales in excess of €1 billion per year. In 2012, the company announced that Dove had become the company's first €3 billion Personal Care brand based on 2011 sales.[8] The company's other brands included Axe, Ben & Jerry's, Bertolli, Hellman's, Lipton, Omo/Surf, Pond's, St. Ives, TRESemmé, VO5, and Vaseline.

Unilever had a truly global footprint, with operations and factories on every continent except Antarctica. Additionally, the company had established research laboratories in the United States, England, the Netherlands, China, and India. As of 2012, the company employed 171,000 people worldwide.

In 2004, Unilever unveiled a new logo intended to convey how the company's brands add "vitality to life." Designed by Wolff Olins, the logo formed the letter "U" out of 24 icons that each represented one of the company's brands or one of its corporate values. Unilever affirmed on its website that the company is "driven by strong set of values." The company's stated mission was as follows:

> We work to create a better future every day. We help people feel good, look good, and get more out of life with brands and services that are good for them and good for others. We inspire people to take small, everyday actions that can add up to a big difference for the world. We will develop new ways of doing business with the aim of doubling the size of our company while reducing our environmental impact.[9]

OVERVIEW OF THE SUSTAINABLE LIVING PLAN

In November 2010, Unilever announced its Sustainable Living Plan, an ambitious plan to double sales while halving the environmental impact of its products by 2020. The plan was bold in both its scope and detail. Jonathan Porritt, founder of Forum for the Future, called the plan upon its release a "game changer for the way that global companies behave."[10] The plan was the result of an intensive two-year environmental audit by Unilever that included data-gathering on the environmental impact caused by the use of its products. For over 10 years, Unilever had already made intensive efforts to reduce the environmental footprint of its manufacturing, processing, and transporting operations. But Unilever realized that the environmental footprint of its own operations was dwarfed by the environmental impact caused by the actual use of its products by consumers. As such, Unilever set out a rigorous plan to collect data on the environmental impact of its products, brand by brand. After two years, the company compiled the data and created a new plan for growing sustainably that addressed growing concerns about the environmental impact of global companies. According to chief executive Paul Polman:

> In Unilever we believe that business must be part of the solution. But to be so, business will have to change. It will have to get off the treadmill of quarterly reporting and operate for the long term. It will have to see itself as part of society, not separate from it. And it will have to recognize that the needs of citizens and communities carry the same weight as the demands of shareholders.[11]

Additionally, Polman stated candidly that the company's new Sustainable Living Plan was in direct response to the failures of capitalism. While Polman credited capitalism with lifting millions out of poverty, enabling a second agricultural revolution, and modernizing the world through digital technology, he also stated that capitalism had failed in other equally important arenas, including environmental sustainability. In a message on Unilever's website, Polman wrote:

> But capitalism is not a panacea. For those things which we find hard to put a price on—biodiversity, carbon, natural capital—the market has failed us. As a result we live in a world where temperatures are rising, natural resources are being depleted, species loss is accelerating and the gap between rich and poor is increasing. This is completely unsustainable.[12]

Additionally, Santiago Gowland, vice president of brand and corporate responsibility at Unilever, stated in an interview in *The Guardian* that "the structure of our financial capitals and the inability to capture businesses' externalities" is the biggest challenge to creating a more sustainable world. Unilever took a bold step by creating a Sustainable Living Plan that reflected the company's belief that "growth and sustainability go hand in hand."[13]

Unilever was bold in setting a scope for the Living Sustainability Plan that included the company's entire value chain. The new plan included not only its own waste, water use, and greenhouse gas emissions, but also the environmental impact of its suppliers and consumers. Regarding the inclusion of consumers in its sustainability plan, Unilever commented that "more than two thirds of greenhouse emissions and half the water in Unilever products' lifecycle come from consumer use so this is a commitment on an unprecedented scale." Further, Unilever stated:

> What makes our Plan different is that it applies right across the value chain. We are taking responsibility not just for our own direct operations but for our suppliers, distributors and—crucially—for how our consumers use our brands.[14]

The new plan involved not only adjusting the formulas or packaging of its products, but also altering the way the company engaged with its customers. For example, to achieve specific targets, the plan required Unilever to educate its customers to adjust the way consumers had historically used the company's products.

Unilever was bold in the detail of the plan by including approximately 60 specific targets to be achieved by 2020. The company also committed to tracking its progress against the 60 targets with plans to release an annual Sustainability Progress Report. At a high level, CEO Paul Polman detailed the three primary outcomes of the plan:

- Help more than a billion people improve their health and well-being
- Halve the environmental footprint of Unilever products
- Allow Unilever to source 100% of its agricultural raw materials sustainably

These broad objectives would be realized by achieving the 60 detailed targets set forth in the plan.

In addition to setting a broad scope and detailed objective, the plan also included new partnerships to encourage cross-sector change. CEO Paul Polman stated, "But if we achieve our sustainability targets and no one follows, we will have failed."[15] Accordingly, Unilever established partnerships with the Consumer Goods Forum, the World Economic Forum, the World Business Council for Sustainable Development, other NGOs, and several governments.

PROGRESS AS OF APRIL 2012

In April 2012, Unilever released its first progress report for its Sustainable Living Plan. Unilever announced its most significant accomplishment in the update: the company had reached its sustainable palm oil target three years ahead of schedule. Having achieved the goal three years ahead of schedule, the company announced a new goal to buy 100% of its palm oil from certified traceable sources by 2020. To achieve this goal, Unilever had engaged in negotiations with the Indonesian government to invest over €100 million in a plant to help achieve the new target. Additionally, the plan detailed the firm's performance against its targets in three broad categories:

1. Areas where the company was making genuinely good progress

2. Areas where the company had to consider carefully how to achieve its targets but was ready to scale up

3. Areas the company was finding especially challenging and would need to work with partners to achieve its targets.

See Exhibit 2.1 for details on Unilever's Sustainable Living Plan and its progress.

In September 2012, Unilever attained first place for the 14th consecutive year on the Dow Jones Sustainability Index in the food and beverage sector. Unilever's sustainability index was 86%, significantly higher than the average score of 46% for other food and beverage sector companies.[16] Upon release of the results, Gail Klintworth, chief sustainability officer at the time, stated:

> This is a great testament to the hard work and dedication of our people at Unilever who are working every day to help us achieve our ambition of doubling the size of our business while reducing our environmental impact and increasing our positive social impact in the world.[17]

Yet, with all the positive response to Unilever's sustainability efforts, critics questioned whether the efforts hurt shareholder value creation. In the face of such critics, CEO Paul Polman had a short retort: "If you don't like it, go somewhere else."[18] The world will wait and see whether or not investors and customers go somewhere else, or if Unilever can successfully achieve its daunting sustainability mission.

Case Questions

1. How is Unilever's dedication to sustainability reflected in the company's mission statement? In your opinion, has the company succeeded in incorporating sustainability into the company's DNA?

2. In your opinion, is Unilever's plan too aggressive and detailed? Is the company setting itself up for failure if objectives are not met as detailed?

3. What is your reaction to CEO Paul Polman's response to critics "If you don't like it, go somewhere else"? Should a CEO of a publicly traded company be so bold in his reaction to investors and shareholders?

4. What are your thoughts on CEO Paul Polman's opinion that capitalism has failed the world with respect to biodiversity, carbon, and natural resources? Is it the role of a business in a capitalist market to address these negative market externalities?

5. How would you rate Unilever's progress against its plan? See Exhibit 2.1 for details on Unilever's progress.

Exhibit 2.1   Unilever Sustainability Plan

Summary
Of Progress: 2011

KEY
- ◐ achieved
- ● on-plan
- ● off-plan
- ⊘ missed target

IMPROVING HEALTH AND WELL-BEING

We estimate that we helped 135 million people take action to improve their health and well-being

HEALTH AND HYGIENE

We have reached 100 million people with our hand-washing, oral care and self-esteem programmes, and a further 35 million with safe drinking water.

- Reduce diarrhoeal and respiratory disease through handwashing
- Improve oral health
- Improve self-esteem
- Provide safe drinking water

NUTRITION

We increased the proportion of our portfolio that meets the highest nutritional standards from 22% in 2010 to 25% in 2011.

- ⊘ Improve heart health
- Reduce salt levels
- Saturated fat:
  - Reduce saturated fat
  - Increase essential fatty acids
  - Remove trans fat
- Reduce sugar
- Reduce calories
- Provide healthy eating information

REDUCING ENVIRONMENTAL IMPACT

An interim sample of 2010 data shows that our environmental footprint has remained broadly unchanged.*

GREENHOUSE GASES

Our greenhouse gas (GHG) footprint has remained broadly unchanged.*

- Reduce GHG from skin cleansing and hair washing
- Reduce GHG from washing clothes:
  - Concentration
  - Reformulation
  - Consumer behavior
- Reduce GHG from manufacturing:
  - CO_2 from energy
  - Renewable energy
  - New factories
- Reduce GHG from transport
- Reduce GHG from refrigeration

WATER

Our water footprint has remained broadly unchanged.*

- Reduce water use in agriculture
- Reduce water use in the laundry process:
  - Easy rinse products
  - Detergents that use less water
- Reduce water use in skin cleaning and hair washing
- Reduce water use in manufacturing process:
  - Reduce abstraction
  - New factories

WASTE

Our waste footprint has remained broadly unchanged.*

- Reduce packaging:
  - Reuse packaging
- Recycle packaging:
  - Increase recycling and recovery rates
  - Increase recycled content
- Reduce waste from manufacturing:
  - Reduce total waste
  - New factories
  - Tackle sachet waste
  - Eliminate PVC

ENHANCING LIVELIHOODS

We do not yet have a robust methodology for measuring improvements in livelihoods. In 2012 we will work to develop one.

SUSTAINABLE SOURCING

Sustainably sourced agricultural raw materials increased from 14% in 2010 to 24% in 2011.

- Palm oil
- Paper and board
- Soy beans and soy oil
- Tea
- Fruit
- Vegetables
- Cocoa
- Sugar
- Sunflower oil
- Rapeseed oil
- Dairy
- Fairtrade Ben & Jerry's
- Cage-free eggs

BETTER LIVELIHOODS

We revised our smallholder farmers target. We engaged with 45,000 small-scale distributors.

- Smallholder farmers
- Small-scale distributors

PEOPLE

- Reduce workplace injuries and accidents
- Improve employee health and nutrition
- Reduce employee travel
- Reduce energy consumption in our offices
- Reduce office waste:
  - Recycle, reuse, recover
  - Reduce paper consumption
  - Eliminate paper in processes
- Increase sustainable sourcing of office materials

* Throughout this document our environmental targets are expressed on a 'per consumer use' basis. This means a single use, portion, or serving of a product. We have taken a lifecycle approach with a baseline of 2008.

Source: Unilever Sustainable Living Plan Progress Report, 2011, pp. 8–9.

NOTES

1. "Our approach to sustainability." (n.d.). Unilever. Retrieved September 17, 2012, from http://www.unilever.com/sustainable-living/ourapproach/messageceo/

2. Ibid.

3. "Unilever's trailblazing environmental plan." (n.d.). *The Guardian.* Retrieved September 17, 2012, from http://www.guardian.co.uk/sustainable-business/blog/unilever-sustainable -agriculture-plan

4. "Unilever wants short, soapy showers and long-term investors." (2012, July 5). *Bloomberg News.* Retrieved September 17, 2012, from http://mobile.bloomberg.com/news/2012-07-05/unilever -wants-short-soapy-showers-and-long-term-investors?category=

5. "Our approach to sustainability," Unilever.

6. Boyle, M. (2012, July 26). "Unilever reports faster sales growth than analysts estimated." *Bloomberg Business.* Retrieved September 17, 2012, from http://www.bloomberg.com/news/2012 -07-26/unilever-second-quarter-sales-growth-beats-analysts-estimates.html

7. Boyle, M. (2012, August 5). "Fat is back as Unilever Magnum bites Nestle Skinny Cow: Retail." Bloomberg Business. Retrieved September 17, 2012, from http://www.bloomberg.com/ news/2012-08-05/fat-is-back-as-unilever-magnum-bites-nestle-skinny-cow-retail.html

8. Sterling, T. (2012, July 26). "Unilever grows sales in spite of EU slowdown." *Boston.com.* Retrieved September 17, 2012, from http://articles.boston.com/2012-07-26/business/32872124_1_ chief-executive-paul-polman-weaker-euro-commodity-costs

9. "Annual report and accounts." (n.d.). Unilever. Retrieved September 17, 2012, from http:// www.unilever.com/investorrelations/annual_reports/AnnualReportandAccounts2011/

10. "Unilever's trailblazing environmental plan," *The Guardian.*

11. "Our approach to sustainability," Unilever.

12. Ibid.

13. "Five minutes with Santiago Gowland." (2010, October 11). *The Guardian.* Retrieved September 17, 2012, from http://www.guardian.co.uk/sustainable-business/five-minute-interview -santiago-gowland

14. "Unilever sustainable living plan summary." (n.d.). Unilever. Retrieved September 17, 2012, from http://www.unilever.com/sustainable-living/uslp/

15. "Our approach to sustainability," Unilever.

16. Unilever. (2012, September 14). "Unilever named in top spot on Dow Jones Sustainability Index. Retrieved March 6, 2015, from http://www.unileverusa.com/media-center/pressreleases/2012/ UnileverNamedonDJSI.aspx

17. Ibid.

18. "Unilever wants short, soapy showers and long-term investors," *Bloomberg News.*

PART II

THREE COMPONENTS OF CR: ENVIRONMENTAL, SOCIAL, AND GOVERNANCE

Chapter 3

ENVIRONMENTAL RESPONSIBILITY

When consumers think about corporate social responsibility, many first think about environment responsibility (often referred to as "sustainability." There are many definitions of environmental responsibility as it pertains to the corporation. While the standard definition is "the duty that a company has to operate in a way that protects the environment,"[1] researchers at the University of Michigan's Erb Institute for Global Sustainable Enterprise define corporate environmental responsibility as "friendly actions not required by law, also referred to as going beyond compliance, the private provision of public goods, or voluntarily internalizing externalities."[2] The corporation's responsibility to the environment can also be defined as delivering on stakeholder needs without compromising the ability to meet the needs of future stakeholders.[3]

Whatever definition you choose, however, no one would doubt the importance of the environment today for corporations. Sustainable business practices that protect the environment not only help the planet, but also usually have a positive financial and public relations effect. Thus, this is the one area of responsibility corporations have embraced wholeheartedly.

THE EVOLUTION OF CORPORATE ENVIRONMENTAL RESPONSIBILITY

In the 1960s and 1970s, there was some concern over corporate environmental responsibility, but the conversation that occurred mostly pitted business against the environment. The 1960s did, however, see the beginnings of concern over how business growth was negatively affecting the environment.[4] During this time, many companies focused on controlling pollution and adding additional parts to existing machinery in response to rising awareness of the environmental consequences of their business operations.[5] The prevailing mind-set was that business and the environment were entities whose competing interests could not be reconciled.[6]

The situation looked to be a zero-sum game, with decisions that positively affected business necessarily being bad for the environment and vice versa.[7] During the 1970s, there were trade-offs between environmental and financial performance, and the former were viewed as a mere distraction for managers.[8] As noted by Michael Porter and Classe van der Linde:

> The relationship between environmental goals and industrial competitiveness has normally been thought of as involving a tradeoff between social benefits and private costs. The issue was how to balance society's desire for environmental protection with the economic burden on industry.[9]

Beginning in the 1970s and continuing into the mid-1980s, there was resistance to adaptation of environmentally responsible behavior among corporations. Such compliance was mostly spurred by increased regulation, with corporations doing everything in their power to fight the new laws. This period of corporate resistance to environmental compliance was characterized by "delegation of environmental protection to local facilities, a widespread failure to create environmental performance-measurement systems, and a refusal to view environmental issues as realities that needed to be incorporated into business strategy."[10] During the 1980s, however, both corporations and regulatory bodies started to take a different approach to environmental issues. Instead of addressing the symptoms of environmental abuses such as pollution, both groups began focusing more on eliminating the underlying causes. In other words, the focus of the conversation shifted from assigning punishments to perpetrators of environmental offenses to preventing such offenses in the first place.[11]

During the mid-1980s to late 1990s, the approach shifted again—this time, with the conversation centering on "win-win" solutions and eco-efficiency—as a response to increasing concerns about the environment. In 1998, *The Atlantic* called eco-efficiency "the next industrial revolution" and cited a 1987 report by the United Nations' World Commission on Environment and Development as a major catalyst of the movement. The UN report linked business efficiency with environmental sustainability and outlined dire consequences for failure to address environmental concerns, warning that without more stringent pollution control, "property and ecosystems would be threatened, and existence would become unpleasant and even harmful to human health in some cities."[12] The UN commission also argued for the promotion of industries and operations that would use resources efficiently, generate less pollution and waste, rely on renewable resources, and minimize negative effects on both human health and the environment.[13]

Five years later, the Business Council (now the World Business Council) for Sustainable Development, a group of 48 corporate sponsors of the 1992 Earth Summit, including Dow and Chevron, promoted the term *eco-efficiency* following the event. The Summit was a gathering in Rio de Janeiro to address environmental issues and included 30,000 people from around the world, with 167 countries represented and more than 100 world leaders present.[14] What did eco-efficiency mean in actionable terms? Corporations would work to update their machinery with cleaner, faster, quieter engines, without a negative impact on financial prosperity. In other words, the goals of eco-efficiency ran diametric to the conventional wisdom that environmental and business interests were mutually exclusive. Eco-efficiency was designed to "transform human industry from a system that takes, makes, and wastes into one that integrates economic, environmental, and ethical concerns."[15]

One of the catalysts of the shifting views of environmental responsibility was the realization that approaching environmental issues proactively could lead to strategic cost-savings due to win-win measures. During the second half of the 1980s, regulation grew increasingly focused on environmental results versus compliance, and managers began to shift their approach to environmental issues, looking beyond a merely technical approach to think strategically about these concerns.[16]

During the 1990s, this trend continued, with managers beginning to understand that better performance on environmental issues could positively affect a corporation's financial bottom line.[17] A "greening revolution" began, in which some companies began to see the relationship between business and the environment as a strategic opportunity.[18] Companies realized that there were cost-savings to be attained through the minimization of resource usage and waste—win-win situations that both required less operational spending and put less strain on the environment. Managers focused on maximizing efficiency and creating competitive advantage. Eco-efficiency was "perceived as a 'win–win' solution, enabling the twin goals of economic growth and environmental protection to be maintained."[19]

Even so, some strong voices saw eco-efficiency measures as detracting from shareholder value, much in the same way that Milton Friedman saw all of corporate responsibility, with little potential for true gains to be made. A mid-1990s article in *Harvard Business Review* looked not at the cost-savings associated with environmental responsibility but at the additional costs incurred in establishing environmentally responsible business practices—and questioned whether there were really business advantages to be gained from engaging in them:

> Responding to environmental challenges has always been a costly and complicated proposition for managers. In fact, environmental costs at most companies are skyrocketing, with little economic payback in sight . . . win-win situations

do . . . exist . . . but they are very rare and will likely be overshadowed by the total cost of a company's environmental program. Win-win opportunities become insignificant in the face of the enormous environmental expenditures that will never generate a positive financial return.[20]

The authors argued that while the prevailing conversation around finding win-win solutions to environmental issues was rhetorically effective, approaching such issues with the goal of increasing the efficiency and effectiveness of environmental spending would be far better, estimating that one-quarter to one-half of an industry's market value was susceptible to growth in environmental costs and charging that such costs would destroy shareholder value.[21]

There were other drawbacks to the win-win, eco-efficiency approach of the 1990s, namely, that it disguised the most pressing, most difficult to solve environmental challenges by focusing on those with quick paybacks and no need for significant reengineering of operations.[22] Additionally, this approach left some with the mistaken impression that all business resource efficiencies were environmentally sound.[23]

Another issue with eco-efficiency was that it was unsuitable as a long-term strategy. Instead of disrupting the existing approach to business problems to forge a new, strategic path for corporate environmental responsibility, eco-efficiency worked within the existing system and in many ways was a reactive versus proactive approach to environmental issues, marked by "moral proscriptions and punitive demands."[24] Eco-efficiency, rather than introducing new methods of doing business that would allow companies to unlock shared value—identifying cost-savings while preserving natural resources, for example—allowed corporations to focus on mitigating the negative effects of their destructive behavior instead of enacting widespread changes that would eliminate such effects going forward.[25]

From the late 1990s on, the conversation around corporate environmental responsibility moved increasingly toward eco-effectiveness and the idea of a greening revolution. Eco-effectiveness was introduced as a guiding principle of corporate sustainability, under which business practices were expected to stretch beyond pollution control and eco-efficiency to embrace business methods designed to both restore and enhance the environment.[26] What is the difference between the limited eco-efficiency and eco-effectiveness? In short, while eco-efficiency focuses on doing less damage to the environment, eco-effectiveness takes a more proactive approach, seeking instead to do more good for the environment.[27] In an article in *Business Strategy and the Environment*, eco-effectiveness was described as follows:

The alternative to eco-efficiency is to enable business to operate in a manner that allows nature and business to succeed, to be productive, the objective being for business to seek a balance with the natural world in such a way as to remove negative impacts and to develop systems to restore and enhance the natural environment. The term eco-effectiveness was coined to describe these ideas. Eco-effectiveness ultimately requires industry to reinvent itself so that the new ways of doing business result in regenerative, not depletive, practices.[28]

The 1990s saw a steady increase in public concern for the environment, making it an ideal atmosphere in which environmental responsibility and eco-effectiveness in particular could thrive. Climate change became a major topic of discussion, which continued into the 21st century. People voiced deep concerns about the future of the planet, with human overconsumption and irresponsible resource management leading to an unsustainable strain on resources.[29] Climate change, meanwhile, would put additional pressure on the planet, and there was fear about the earth reaching a global "tipping point" at which the earth and its inhabitants would be negatively and permanently affected by the environmental crisis.[30]

A report by Business for Social Responsibility (BSR), a nonprofit that promotes social responsibility in business, described dire consequences if current resource consumption were to continue along the same trajectory:

> With population growth, increasing per capita consumption, and tremendous technological capacity leading to ever greater levels of production and consumption, we have begun to reach planetary limits, threatening the health and function of ecological systems that support all activity on Earth. . . . By recent estimates, our global footprint now exceeds the world's capacity to regenerate by about 30 percent, and if our current demands continue, by 2030 we will need the equivalent of two planets to maintain our lifestyles.[31]

Outside the sustainability realm, other stakeholders such as government officials also expressed fears about the consequences of the strain on the earth's resources. Lord Nicholas Stern, former UK Government and World Bank Chief Economist, expressed his belief that rising carbon emissions would not only have perilous effects on climate change in the short term, but also negatively affect economic growth over the long-term.[32] Stern charged that if nothing was done to curb such emissions, the equivalent of at least 5% of global gross domestic product (GDP) would be lost per year because of increased costs and risks. Going forward, this number could increase to 20% of global GDP. Meanwhile, the costs of addressing carbon emissions would be relatively small—roughly 1% of global GDP per year.[33]

Stakeholder concerns about corporations' externalities have increased as a result of these trends. As a result, corporations have become more serious about engaging in better environmental policies, with corporations across nearly all industries taking eco-friendliness into account in their decisions about product and service development.[34] *Harvard Business Review* described accounting for environmental externalities as "the key to becoming a contemporary corporate leader," explaining that the rules of doing business have changed in response to the negative social and environmental effects of traditional corporate policies.[35] Not only was it impossible to continue to ignore such externalities, but a positive outcome of the increased focus on them has been the development of cheaper, less-complex means of keeping tabs on them.[36]

A surprising turn of events in the early 21st century was the rise of longtime environmentalist and former U.S. vice president Al Gore as a prominent figure in the public conversation about environmental sustainability. Some notable examples of Gore's involvement in environmental initiatives have included co-founding Generation Investment Management, a socially responsible investing management firm,[37] and starring in the Academy Award–winning 2006 documentary film *An Inconvenient Truth*, which educated viewers on the evidence of global warming.[38] For his efforts, Gore was co-recipient of the 2007 Nobel Peace Prize, alongside the Intergovernmental Panel on Climate Change.

Writing in *Review of Environmental Economics and Policy*, Thomas P. Lyon and John W. Maxwell explained how business needs have driven corporate responses to environmental issues: "The growing attention to corporate environmental initiatives in the business press strongly suggests that market forces—in the markets for products, capital, and labor—are increasingly powerful drivers of corporate environmental improvement."[39] Stakeholder demand for corporations to behave responsibly with regard to the environment is growing, particularly the perception that companies must internalize their externalities through the use of sensors that measure corporate environmental impact so that companies can mitigate it.[40] There are consequences for corporations that are believed to be taking minimal or no responsibility for externalities, in the form of riots, consumer boycotts, or regulation.[41]

Other consequences exist as well for corporations that fail to deliver on stakeholders' environmental expectations. Environmental issues increasingly cause obstacles to companies' ability to create value for stakeholders, because of environmental pressures and business liabilities.[42] Growth in areas of the world such as China and India has also resulted in tougher competition over natural resources, adding a new geopolitical dimension to the conversation around sustainability. Refusing to acknowledge or account for externalities can have dire consequences for corporations operating in this new world, as "investors consider them central to a firm's performance and stakeholders expect companies to share information about them."[43] Meanwhile, increased concern about issues including climate change, pollution, food safety, and natural resource consumption means that, globally, many consumers are opting for products and services that are produced and rendered sustainably—and in some cases, demanding that companies alter existing products and services to make them more sustainable.

There are also examples of how environmental concerns can drive positive effects on market demand in emerging markets with weak regulatory systems, where international markets drive corporations to be more environmentally responsible. Colombia exports cut flowers to the European Union, where customers often choose suppliers partly by their pesticide usage. To respond to this demand, the Colombian flower industry started the Florverde program, which encourages its members to adopt environmentally friendly practices.[44] Each year, 1.3 billion stems and over 2,000 hectares of land are certified by Florverde Sustainable Flowers.[45] In this case, the shift in consumer demand arguably plays a larger role in advancing environmental responsibility than the country's pesticide regulations.[46]

There are also opportunities for business in that weak economies that are transformed by sustainable consumption strategies will serve as better environments in which to do business, creating new market opportunities worldwide by innovating new business models and devising new strategies.[47] Corporations at the forefront of innovation will find their competitors hard-pressed to catch up. By using the principles of sustainability to rethink existing business models, companies "will build resilience against the ups and downs of economic cycles and shifting consumer expectations, and they will deliver positive outcomes in new markets for themselves and for consumers."[48]

Sustainable consumption, beyond being a potential marketing tool in areas of the world where corporate environmental responsibility is valued and prioritized by consumers, is crucial to the future of the planet. The future of economic development must provide all people with the resources to meet their basic needs in a way that preserves healthy ecosystems. This would also help business, as corporations can leverage their dedication to sustainable consumption to become more innovative, especially in emerging markets.[49] Over the next two decades the middle class is expected to expand by 3 billion people, increasing the potential market for products and services presently enjoyed by wealthier economies—but only if sufficient attention is paid to developing these economies.[50]

Therefore, corporate environmental responsibility policies have become an essential part of every company's long-term plan. Today, there is widespread concern about sustainability, and corporate leaders must balance stakeholder expectations, which often conflict, with creating value for shareholders. Thinking seriously about environmental sustainability is a necessary means of addressing both goals.[51] Writing in *Business Strategy and the Environment*, Thomas Dyllick and Kai Hockerts declare, "Sustainability has become a mantra for the twenty-first century. It embodies the promise of societal evolution towards a more equitable and wealthy world in which the natural environment and our cultural achievements are preserved for generations to come."[52] Environmental preservation is not just good for society; it is also beneficial to corporations in the form of reduced consumption of resources and the development of new, innovative products that appeal to consumers.[53]

GREENWASHING AND SUSTAINABILITY RANKINGS

One result of the heightened trend of "going green" is greenwashing, which has become a big problem. What is greenwashing? *Greenwashing*, a term coined by New York environmentalist Jay Westerveld in 1986, refers to corporations' practice of disingenuously spinning their products or policies as environmentally friendly or beneficial. Greenwashing involves the deceptive use of green public relations or green marketing. There is great incentive for corporations to engage in greenwashing, which allows them to benefit from the positive public relations associated with environmental friendliness without having to invest resources to develop eco-friendly products and processes.

The Big Green Opportunity report, which collects data from 1,300 small businesses in the U.S., indicates that growth in green segments has outpaced conventional segments in every surveyed industry. For instance, the organic goods segment grew by 238% over a 10-year period from 2002 to 2011, whereas the overall goods market grew only 33% during the same period.[54] If corporations are not willing to create green products or engage in environmentally responsible practices, they may be leaving money on the table.[55] Accordingly, corporations must not only offer green products but must also communicate their eco-friendly business practices to consumers. Green advertising has increased tenfold in the past two decades, nearly tripling since 2006; meanwhile, more than 75% of S&P 500 companies have website sections focusing on their environmental policies.[56] As of March 2013, Worldwatch Institute issued a report saying that the number of new products that used green advertising grew from 100 in 2004 to 1,500 in 2009.[57] With companies intent on publicizing their green practices as a form of competitive advantage, it makes sense that some companies would engage in greenwashing at either the firm level (i.e., misleading consumers about a company's environmental practices) or the product level (misleading consumers about the environmental benefits of a particular product or service).[58]

Figure 3.1   The seven sins of greenwashing

Sin of the Hidden Trade-Off	• A claim that a product is green based on certain positive attributes without addressing other harmful attributes. • Example: "Energy-efficient" electronics containing hazardous materials.
Sin of No Proof	• A claim that a product is environmentally friendly, without substantiation. • Example: A paper product claiming to be "forest-friendly" but lacking verification by an outside agency such as EcoLogo.
Sin of Vagueness	• A claim that is extremely broad or poorly defined. • Example: Products claiming to be 100% natural, when many natural products are hazardous (such as formaldehyde).
Sin of Irrelevance	• An environmental claim that, while truthful, is not pertinent for consumers in evaluating the eco-friendliness of the product relative to competitors' offerings. • Example: Products claiming to be CFC-free when CFCs have been banned for 20 years
Sin of Fibbing	• A product that leads consumers to believe it has outside certification for which it has in fact not met the criteria. • Example: A household appliance falsely claiming to be EnergyStar certified.
Sin of the Lesser of Two Evils	• A claim that is true within the product category but ignores the other negatives qualities associated with the product or product type. • Example: Organic cigarettes or "environmentally friendly" pesticides.
Sin of Worshipping False Labels	• Misleading words or images on products that suggest certification where none exists. • Example: A sticker designed to look like a USDA Organic certification marker affixed to a nonorganic product.

Source: Adapted from Wasserman, E. (2014, April 23). "7 sins of greenwashing (and 5 ways to keep it out of your life." EcoWatch.com. Retrieved March 2015 from http://ecowatch.com/2014/04/23/7-sins-of-greenwashing.

TerraChoice, a Canadian environmental marketing agency that found that 99% of consumer products companies engage in greenwashing, organizes greenwashing into seven sins, as seen in Figure 3.1.[59]

Unsurprisingly, the practice of greenwashing has grown in popularity as more corporations have realized the marketing potential of eco-friendliness. Unfortunately, the prevalence of greenwashing can negatively affect consumer and investor confidence in green products—but trying to limit the effects of this practice can be very challenging, as there is limited regulation in place.[60] One difficulty is that there is no set definition of what qualifies as a green product, and the understanding of what it means to be environmentally friendly can vary greatly among industries, companies, or product classes.[61] Even with unclear rules, companies that fail to engage in the conversation about green products and services are in danger of being judged for not meeting confusing standards, or left in the dust by a competitor with a better understanding of green business—or a more proactive approach to it.[62]

A Harris poll found that corporations, rather than exhibiting a real commitment to sustainable practices, are generally more interested in disseminating propaganda suggesting such a commitment. Corporate executives surveyed expressed skepticism that attention to environmental issues would attract consumers; meanwhile, consumers are in disbelief that corporations' claims of eco-friendliness are genuine.[63]

Greenwashing detracts from the gains made by environmentally friendly products and services by negatively affecting consumer confidence.[64] And it is not just corporations that participate in greenwashing that suffer. When consumers perceive that greenwashing is occurring, they respond by purchasing less from the corporation suspected of the practice. NGOs, meanwhile, respond to greenwashing by attracting negative publicity to businesses. Finally, regulators may assess the validity of a company's claims and fine it for misleading consumers.[65] In 2011, the California attorney general filed suit against ENSO Plastics over the company's false claims that its products would biodegrade within five years.[66]

Even if a particular business has not been the subject of negative attention related to greenwashing, the existence of greenwashing within its industry will hurt competition and should be cause for concern.[67] Greenwashing shatters consumer confidence in environmentally friendly products and can damage investor confidence in eco-friendly companies, creating difficulties for socially responsible investment firms in attracting capital.[68] The prevalence of greenwashing can also lead to increased regulation[69] and slow the progress of environmental initiatives by increasing public skepticism of them.[70] Meanwhile, greenwashing creates obstacles to consumer understanding of the actual environmental impact of the products and services they purchase and use.[71] And dealing with greenwashing is a drain on resources that could be better spent enhancing environmental initiatives.[72]

What are the causes of greenwashing? Unfortunately, the downside of increased consumer demand for green products is increased incidence of false claims of eco-friendliness, as many corporations have responded not by developing better processes but by presenting the illusion of doing so.[73] BSR identifies five drivers of greenwashing as especially important:

1. Increased consumer demand for more environmentally responsible products

While green products were once a niche area that only dedicated environmentalists would choose over their less eco-friendly counterparts, their popularity has grown substantially. A May 2012 survey conducted by Harris Interactive on 2,451 adults in the U.S. showed that 79% of the respondents purchased green products or services, with one-third believing that such behavior was becoming a norm and what was expected of them. Survey respondents also indicated that they would rather dine at a green restaurant despite the higher cost.[74] This trend is not limited to the U.S.—*National Geographic* and GlobeScan's "2012 Greendex" surveyed 17,000 consumers in 17 countries and found that consumer environmental responsibility is on the rise globally as well.[75]

2. Rising sales of environmentally oriented products

Green products have seen rapid growth in the U.S. CBS News reported that green product launches by major U.S. manufacturers grew to 328 during 2007, compared with only five green products launched in 2002. Meanwhile, the organic industry has nearly tripled since 1997, with sales of organic personal-care items now totaling hundreds of millions of dollars.[76]

3. Continued strong demand for green products despite the economic downturn

Consumer attitudes toward green products were unaffected by the state of the economy, according to the 2009 Cone Consumer Environmental Survey conducted by Opinion Research Corporation. Of those surveyed, 34% responded that they were more likely to buy environmentally responsible products at that time, with another 44% stating that their green shopping habits had not been affected by the economy.

4. Pending regulation and government action

Over the next 10 years, $3 trillion is expected to be paid out in stimulus money in 15 countries around the world, much of which will be put toward environmental goals. For example, the U.S. stimulus package is intended to double clean energy capacity and create 2.5 million green jobs. Consequently, the number of climate change lobbyists in Washington has grown significantly, providing additional incentives for corporations to promote an image of eco-friendliness.

5. Lack of standards for communicating environmental messages

The ability of the U.S. Federal Trade Commission (FTC) to regulate and monitor greenwashing is limited, given the sizable scope of the FTC's responsibilities.

Given the motivations for corporations to commit greenwashing, how can the practice be prevented? BSR recommends a three-pronged approach: (1) impact, (2) alignment, and (3) communication.[77] See Table 3.1 for more information.

MEASURING ENVIRONMENTAL FRIENDLINESS

While lists that rank companies and products or services on their eco-friendliness may seem like a good way to evaluate a corporation's environmental commitment, this is not always the case. Rankings are widely used, but not necessarily reliable. Most companies now report on their environmental impacts, with 93% of the 250 largest firms worldwide providing regular updates on their environmental initiatives and 82% of these companies referring to the Global Reporting Initiative's Sustainability Reporting Guidelines.[78] Rankings are important to both consumers and investors, as they enable shoppers to vote with their wallets, workers to evaluate potential employers, and socially responsible investment funds to make appropriate choices.[79] Most rankings, however, include only operational activities and not lobbying and campaign contributions around environmental policy, which often can have more impact than operations. One reason for this is the lack of transparency around corporate political activity, which translates to a lack of transparency about the real impact of a corporation's dealings in terms of environmental policies and regulations.[80]

Table 3.1 A three-pronged approach to preventing greenwashing

Impact: Make sure it's real	Messages about the environmental issues associated with products must be based on real, significant impact, as opposed to being mere PR ploys.
Alignment: Build support internally and externally	The initiative must be aligned with functions throughout the company.
Communication: Communicate it accurately	Communications must be clear and transparent, and companies should avoid self-aggrandizements in dialogue with stakeholders. It is also essential that partner organizations understand these principles.

Source: Adapted from "Understanding and preventing greenwash: A business guide" (pp. 26–27). (2009, July). Business for Social Responsibility and Futerra Sustainability Communications.

While this is a big problem, it can be fixed fairly easily, according to Schendler and Toffel, who argue that "rating systems should factor in political contributions, CEO advocacy work and engagement with nongovernmental organizations among other actions."[81] Rating agencies can better serve stakeholders looking to evaluate corporations' eco-friendliness by partnering with environmental nonprofits to determine whether certain organizations strengthen or weaken environmental policy. The authors state, "Incorporating corporate advocacy can strengthen the competitiveness of ranking systems and enhance their differentiation in a crowded field of company ratings and rankings."[82]

THE CURRENT STATE/HEADING TOWARD A TRIPLE WIN

Even though corporate environmental responsibility has become a "megatrend,"[83] corporations still cite a number of issues surrounding their environmental initiatives that have kept them from becoming fully integrated into most companies' missions and strategies. A 2010 study identified eight inhibitors (see Figure 3.2).

Figure 3.2   Eight inhibitors of integrating environmental initiatives into missions and strategies

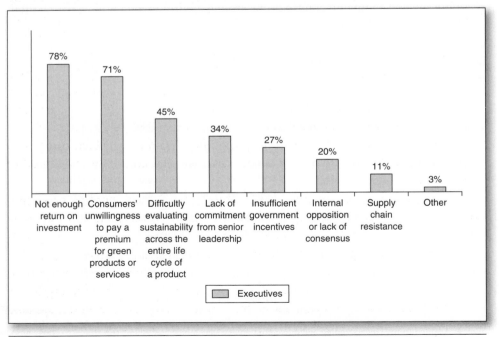

Source: "Perspectives on corporate sustainability." (2010). *Gibbs & Soell Sense and Sustainability™ study* (p. 10).

The number one cited obstacle to full integration of environmental policy into core business strategy and mission was the lack of return on investment (ROI) associated with environmental initiatives, with 78% of the executives surveyed citing insufficient ROI as a roadblock to going green.[84] In particular, such ROI is difficult to measure and prove in the short term, as we will see in Chapter 8's detailed discussion on the difficulties in measuring and reporting CR (viewed through the lens of corporate philanthropy). It can be difficult for companies to reconcile a long-term, visionary approach to sustainability with the need to demonstrate evidence of financial gains in the short term to validate the attention paid to environmental impact.[85] A study based on interviews with 400 CFOs of U.S. corporations found that 78% had sacrificed long-term value to "maintain short-term predictability in earnings and financial disclosures."[86]

A second obstacle to integrating environmental responsibility into core business practices was low willingness to pay—or at least the perception of it. In this case, 71% of the executives surveyed cited consumers' unwillingness to pay a premium for eco-friendly products or services as an obstacle to going green.[87] While it is true that consumers are likely unwilling to pay a premium for environmentally friendly products, 73% of consumers will choose a brand or product that is socially or environmentally responsible over a similar offering.[88]

The third most commonly cited inhibitor was difficulties with measurement, with more than two out of five executives reporting challenges in evaluating the sustainability over the life cycle of a product.[89] For example, some corporations have tried to calculate expenses associated with externalities to include in their analyses of profits and losses.[90] Such externalities could eventually be taxed by governments, forcing businesses to do a better job of managing the negative impact of their policies on the environment.[91] While these concerns are a source of motivation for companies to do a better job of accounting for environmental impact, measurement is a challenging component of all corporate responsibility initiatives, including environmental responsibility. Chapter 8, which deals with corporate philanthropy, provides a deeper discussion of corporate responsibility measurement systems.

And yet, there are companies that are overcoming these hurdles or simply proving them to be misconceptions, and in doing so creating entirely new dimensions of competitive advantage. Some companies have realized the ROI of environmental responsibility by unlocking measurable cost-savings in the form of reduced consumption of inputs. Being environmentally responsible also enables corporations to generate additional revenues by developing better products or introducing new business lines. Fortuitously, such benefits are also the goals of corporate innovation, so that "smart companies now treat sustainability as innovation's new frontier."[92] While attempts to minimize negative externalities such as pollution were in the past believed to incur costs to business and to be motivated only in response to regulatory changes and taxes, Michael Porter and Mark Kramer point out that "today there is a growing consensus that major improvements in environmental performance can often be achieved with better technology at nominal incremental cost and can even yield net cost savings through enhanced resource utilization, process efficiency, and quality."[93]

Another way that corporations can overcome obstacles to engaging in environmentally responsible behavior is by delivering superior financial performance. A study of 180 corporations by *The Guardian* found that, over an 18-year period, high-sustainability companies had market returns of 4.8% more on average than low-sustainability companies, with the former's returns also being less volatile than the latter's.[94] The study differentiated between high-sustainability and low-sustainability corporations based on whether or not the companies had been voluntary early adopters of environmental and social policies.

While opponents of corporate environmental responsibility have argued that sustainability destroys shareholder value, the study found the opposite to be true, with companies that behave socially and environmentally responsibly creating more value for shareholders by increasing the loyalty of their customers and employees.[95] With consumer expectations of corporate responsibility continuing to increase, companies that behave responsibly will see their competitive advantage grow. According to *The Guardian*, "the argument about sustainability is over. It is the key to creating value for shareholders and all other stakeholders over the long term, thus ensuring the sustainability of the company itself."[96]

Additionally, at high-sustainability companies, the boards of directors are more likely to include sustainability initiatives in their purview, plus top-executive incentives are more likely to be a function of sustainability metrics, than at their low-sustainability counterparts. Such corporations also think strategically, having procedures in place to engage stakeholders while keeping close tabs on nonfinancial information through measurement and reporting systems.[97] It is no surprise, then, that high-sustainability companies significantly outperform low-sustainability companies over the long term, in both stock market and accounting performance.[98]

Even under special circumstances such as market duress, the findings held true:

Even in extreme market conditions, performance was not negatively impacted. Not only that, but outperformance was seen across the range of global sectors and geographies . . . the introduction of ESG [environmental, social, and governance] values into corporate strategy can lead to increased efficiency and innovation, and a consequent boost to revenues and profits.[99]

GROWING INVESTOR INTEREST

Beyond consumers and employees, there is another group of stakeholders for whom environmental responsibility is an important component of engagement with a corporation: investors. PricewaterhouseCoopers (PwC) found that investors are growing increasingly concerned with corporations' environmental behavior, meaning that being eco-friendly could have the added benefit of ROI in the form of increased investments.[100] According to PwC, "investors have begun to recognize that the social and environmental conditions in society can have a direct impact on the business operations of a company and its long-term viability." Sustainable practices are not just the right thing to do; they are also good business policies. The longtime perception of environmental responsibility as a minor issue has changed, with many investors now considering sustainability to be a vital component of their overall approach.[101] Both institutional and retail investors take sustainability into account. Some investors even use sustainability as an investment strategy itself, with an increasing number of funds focusing on ESG concerns.

There are concrete financial reasons for investors to take such concerns into account, with climate change risk being intertwined with expected population changes and growth of the middle class in emerging markets, as shown in Figure 3.3.[102]

Figure 3.3 Estimated population and global middle class

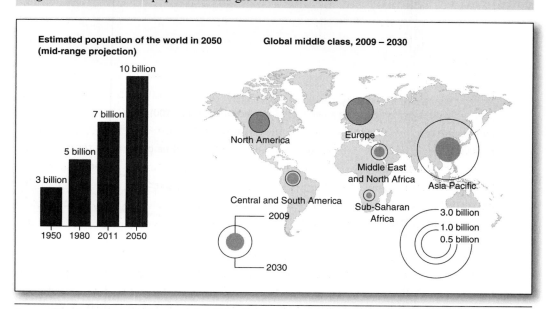

Source: "Do investors care about sustainability? Seven trends provide clues" (p. 2). (2012, March). PricewaterhouseCoopers.

Such changes are projected to result in strains on resources, including water, food, and energy, which will increase the prices of commodities (see Figure 3.4). Corporations that inventory their usage of such natural resources will be better equipped to comprehend social and environmental risks, as well as how such risks stand to affect their businesses, empowering them to create better, adaptive strategies for the future.

Interestingly, sustainable investing has seen faster growth than the broader investment universe in the U.S.—nearly one out of every eight dollars under professional management is involved in sustainable and responsible investing.[103] Echoing *The Guardian*'s findings, a Harvard Business School working paper discovered that sustainability leaders can be expected to have "better stock performance, lower volatility,

Figure 3.4   World demand for energy fuels, 2010–2036

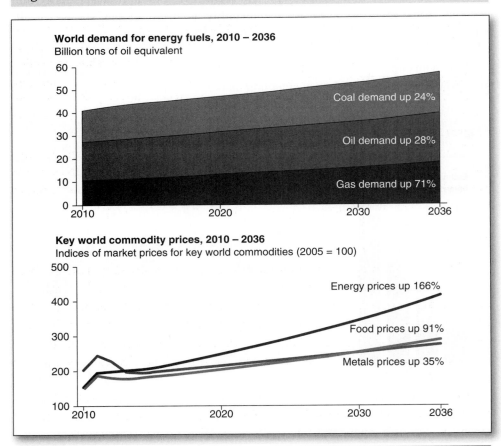

Source: "Do investors care about sustainability? Seven trends provide clues (p. 2)." (2012, March). Pricewater houseCoopers.

and greater return on assets (ROA) and return on equity (ROE)," which the authors attribute to superior governance structures and stakeholder engagement.[104]

There are also benefits of environmental responsibility in terms of research and development. Higher attention to environmental issues, coupled with the greater availability of data, will result in corporations having more room for innovative, environmentally friendly products for which consumers will be willing to pay. According to *Harvard Business Review*:

> The developments we are seeing in scale, sensors, and sensibilities all fuel one another. The average company feels the effects because as measurement improves and access to those measurements becomes ubiquitous, people act on the information, thanks to heightened sensibilities. Formerly unseen and unremarked effects of doing business start getting measured, and affected people, armed with data, seek recourse.[105]

Porter and Kramer echoed this position in their own *Harvard Business Review* piece "Strategy and Society: The Link Between Competitive Advantage and CSR," explaining that corporations that include a social dimension in their value proposition are better placed in the competitive atmosphere. "Government regulation, exposure to criticism and liability, and consumers' attention to social issues are all persistently increasing. As a result, the number of industries and companies whose competitive advantage can involve social value propositions is constantly growing."[106]

Though measurement can be a challenge, it is possible and distinguishes companies that do it well. Corporate environmental responsibility initiatives create value in three key ways that are already measured by the market: growth, return on capital, and risk management.

Growth

While innovation is often a by-product of adopting eco-friendly policies, there is also an opportunity for corporations to deliver new products specifically designed to meet customers' environmental concerns. One such example is IBM's collaboration with the Nature Conservancy, through which the organizations are developing 3D imaging technology that will help them improve water quality, simultaneously addressing an environmental issue and identifying a new business opportunity for IBM.[107]

Another type of growth driven by corporate environmental responsibility initiatives is market share growth. Coca-Cola's eKOfreshment line includes coolers, vending machines, and soda fountains that are environmentally friendly, removing the need for hydrofluorocarbons (greenhouse gases) as a refrigerant and reducing energy consumption. This new technology provides benefits not only to the environment but also to retailers who stock Coke products. It increases the equipment's energy efficiency by as much as 35%, meaning retailers realize financial savings on their energy bills, which Coke delivers in exchange for access to the best locations in retail outlets.[108]

Return on Capital

As we discussed earlier in the chapter, environmental initiatives enable corporations to realize cost-savings by improving energy efficiency, decreasing input usage, and developing better processes. While there are often upfront costs associated with improvements to existing equipment, upgrading technologies, systems, and products to be more environmentally friendly presents an opportunity for substantial cost-savings.[109] One example is Novo Nordisk's improvements to its operational efficiency after setting a 2006 goal of reducing the company's carbon dioxide emissions by 10% over the next 10 years. Novo Nordisk partnered with a local energy supplier to unlock energy savings at its production facilities in Denmark, which produced 85% of the corporation's carbon dioxide emissions worldwide. By using the cost-savings to pay a premium for wind power, the company eliminated a substantial portion of its emissions. The company set a goal that by 2014 all their activities in Denmark would be powered by green electricity. As of the 2013 annual report, the company was on track despite an increase in energy consumption by the firm. Additionally, Novo Nordisk has also optimized water and energy consumption at their production sites, reducing the company's total resource consumption in 2013. The company reduced its emissions, increased its energy efficiency, and cut costs— while helping to develop the country's renewable energy market.[110]

Risk Management

One way in which environmental responsibility assists corporations with risk management is by allowing them to take a proactive approach to their relationships with stakeholders such as policymakers. Verizon is an example of a company that prioritizes relationships with stakeholders and has sponsored research on how information communications technology leads to energy efficiency. One such example is their sponsorship of the research behind the SMART 2020 report, which details how this technology, along with broadband Internet connections, could allow the U.S. to reduce carbon emissions by 22% and reliance on foreign oil by 36% by 2020.[111]

Writing in *Harvard Business Review*, David A. Lubin and Daniel C. Esty identify four stages of value creation (see Table 3.2).[112]

Thus, in the four stages of value creation, some firms are finally entering the fourth, which will be necessary for long-term success due to increased consumerism and its effects on climate change. The fourth stage, new business model creation and differentiation, allows for the most significant opportunities for

Table 3.2 Lubin and Esty's four stages of value creation

Stage 1: Do old things in new ways.	Outperform competitors on regulatory compliance and environment-related cost and risk management.
Stage 2: Do new things in new ways.	Redesign existing products, processes, and systems to optimize natural resource efficiencies and risk management across value chains.
Stage 3: Transform core business.	Create new revenues and growth through sustainability innovations.
Stage 4: New business model creation and differentiation.	Exploit the megatrend as a source of differentiation in business model, brand, employee engagement, and other intangibles, fundamentally repositioning the company and redefining its strategy for competitive advantage.

Source: Lubin, D. A., & Esty, D. C. (2010, May). "The sustainability imperative." *Harvard Business Review.* Retrieved from https://hbr.org/2010/05/the-sustainability-imperative.

competitive advantage. To unlock competitive advantage through sustainability, corporations must come up with a vision for value creation and execute it.[113] The "quest for sustainability" has had a profound effect on the competitive landscape, with companies being forced to rethink their approach to products, technologies, processes, and business models.[114] Taking a proactive approach to sustainability issues will allow companies to develop capabilities ahead of the competition.

The growth of emerging economies will compound with the upward consumption trends, increasingly taxing the environment. Companies need to lead the way in influencing consumer demand for more environmentally friendly products and services to ensure their own long-term sustainability. According to *Harvard Business Review*, "Commercial activity has achieved planetary scale. The rapid growth of emerging economies will only accelerate the trend."[115] As transparency increases around the effects of human activity on the environment, consumer attention and concern about this impact—and how it relates to threats to human health and safety—will increase.[116] Corporations must balance the need to deliver environmentally friendly products and services against satisfying the practical needs of consumers.

HUMAN CAPITAL AND SUSTAINABILITY

Human capital is a crucial component of the creation of a low-carbon economy, with both leadership and talent being necessary resources. While today's economy has placed considerable stress on the planet, rapid changes in emerging markets mean that our global economic system, which presently delivers on the needs of about a quarter of the people on earth, will need to fulfill the needs of twice as many people over the next decade. According to Nidumolu et al. in *Harvard Business Review*, "Traditional approaches to business will collapse, and companies will have to develop innovative solutions. That will happen only when executives recognize a simple truth: Sustainability = Innovation."[117]

In this rapidly changing world, adaptability is key. Corporations that wish to succeed must adjust to "the political, social, economic and fiscal drive towards a global low carbon economy," according to the SMART 2020 report, which notes that companies that turn challenges into opportunities are best positioned for success.[118] They will be better prepared than their competitors to develop necessary business models for adoption of low-carbon solutions, control their carbon emissions, and adapt to the changing world. According to SMART 2020, "A radical approach is required that incorporates different ways of thinking, living, working, playing, doing business and developing solutions. Action is no longer an option; it has become an urgent necessity."[119]

Another aspect of adaptability is conforming to or improving upon regulation's best practices. While many corporations have dragged their feet on complying with environmental standards, doing so only when absolutely required by law, taking a proactive approach is more beneficial over the long run. According to *Harvard Business Review*:

> It's smarter to comply with the most stringent rules, and to do so before they are enforced. This yields substantial first-mover advantages in terms of fostering innovation. . . . Contrary to popular perceptions, conforming to the gold standard globally actually saves companies money.[120]

Why is this the case? When corporations opt to conform only to minimal environmental standards, they run into different rules in each country in which they conduct business or source materials. Meanwhile, companies such as HP and Cisco that comply with the most stringent standards can establish a single norm throughout all facilities worldwide, enabling them to optimize supply chain operations.[121] It makes sense that, to ensure that the company is meeting the standards of the most harshly regulated country, the strictest standards become the universal norm.

As Charles Handy explained in his seminal *Harvard Business Review* piece "What's Business For?":

> Doing no harm goes beyond meeting the legal requirements regarding the environment, conditions of employment, community relations, and ethics. The law always lags behind best practice. Business needs to take the lead in areas such as environmental and social sustainability instead of forever letting itself be pushed onto the defensive.[122]

BSR offers strategic advice for companies looking to move forward to the next frontier of environmental responsibility. The nonprofit sees significant opportunity for sustainability growth "through a heightened focus on product design, consumer engagement, use, and end-of-use elements of the value chain cycle," and stresses the need to think of these elements as components of a common system (see Figure 3.5).[123]

BSR also provides a framework that corporations can use to articulate their sustainability strategies in the new frontier. The organization advises that companies look at redefining core business activities through four pillars: innovation, education, collaboration, and measurement. See Figure 3.6 for a better understanding of how looking at sustainability decisions through each of these lenses works in practice.

The ultimate goal of an effective, adaptive sustainability strategy should be the creation of a triple win through innovation in product development and production processes: (1) creating competitive advantage in the marketplace, (2) delivering new value

Figure 3.5   Opportunities to address sustainable consumption in the value chain

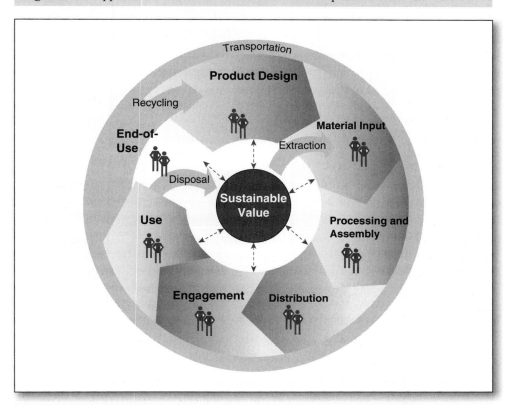

Source: "New frontier in sustainability" (p. 10). (2010, July). Business for Social Responsibility.

Figure 3.6 Framework for redefining core business activities

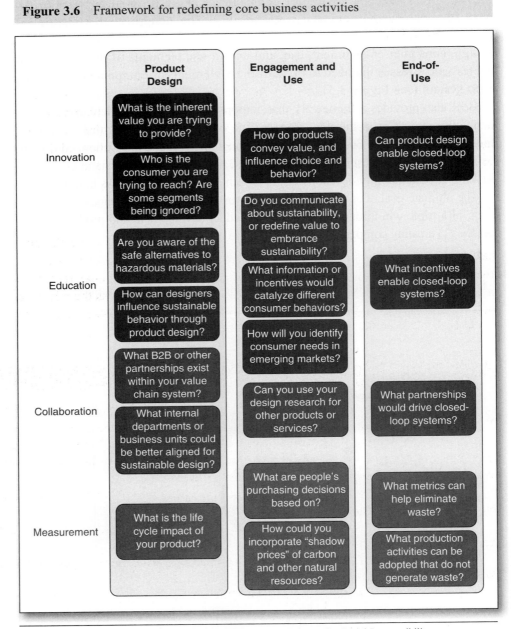

Source: "New frontier in sustainability" (p. 11). (2010, July). Business for Social Responsibility.

to consumers, and (3) transforming economic systems.[124] According to BSR, business today has an unprecedented opportunity "to develop economies that deliver more economic value and better human outcomes while significantly reducing environmental impacts." Remember, however, that it is not enough to simply improve product offerings; instead, corporations must not only approach things differently, but do new and different things.[125]

A report from the Amsterdam Global Conference on Sustainability and Transparency noted that while it is evident that business is capable of innovating new technologies, systems, and services, "the full potential of capital markets to incentivize sustainable behavior has yet to be exploited and will be essential to achieving a sustainable global economy."[126] Not only will committing to sustainability have positive effects on the environment, but it also stands to pay dividends in the form of new technologies and jobs and reduce poverty and pollution.[127]

CONCLUSION

Corporate environmental responsibility has evolved dramatically over the past half century. While environmental responsibility was initially seen as a detraction from core business strategy, forward-thinking corporate leaders of today recognize it as a key component of business operations, one that not only has the power to deliver cost-savings in the form of smarter resource usage but is also a means of developing competitive advantage through innovation.

NOTES

1. "Environmental responsibility." (n.d.). *Cambridge Dictionaries Online.* Retrieved July 22, 2014, from http://dictionary.cambridge.org/dictionary/business-english/environmental-responsibility

2. Lyon, T. P., & Maxwell, J. W. (2006, July 11). "Corporate social responsibility and the environment: A theoretical perspective." Retrieved July 22, 2014, from http://www.erb.umich.edu/Research/Initiatives/colloquiaPapers/LyonMaxwellREEP.pdf

3. Dyllick, T., & Hockerts, K. (2002). "Beyond the business case for corporate sustainability." *Business Strategy and the Environment, 11*(2), 130–141.

4. Blowfield, M., & Murray, A. (2011). *Corporate responsibility* (2nd ed., p. 41). New York, NY: Oxford University Press.

5. Young, W., & Tilley, F. (2006, March.) "Can businesses move beyond efficiency?" *Business Strategy and the Environment.*

6. Walley, N., & Whitehead, B. (1994). "It's not easy being green." *Harvard Business Review, 72*(3), 46–50.

7. Ibid.

8. Blowfield & Murray, *Corporate responsibility*, p. 59.

9. Porter, M. E., & van der Linde, C. (1995). "Toward a new conception of the environment–competitiveness relationship." *Journal of Economic Perspectives, 9,* 97–118.

10. Walley & Whitehead, "It's not easy being green."

11. Blowfield & Murray, *Corporate responsibility*, p. 60.

12. McDonough, W., & Braungart, M. (1998, October). "The next industrial revolution." *Atlantic Monthly.*

13. Ibid.

14. Ibid.

15. McDonough & Braungart, "The next industrial revolution."

16. Walley & Whitehead, "It's not easy being green."

17. Blowfield & Murray, *Corporate responsibility*, pp. 22–23.

18. Ibid., pp. 22–23.

19. Young & Tilley, "Can businesses move beyond efficiency?"

20. Walley & Whitehead, "It's not easy being green."

21. Ibid.

22. Young & Tilley, "Can businesses move beyond efficiency?"

23. Ibid.

24. McDonough & Braungart, "The next industrial revolution."

25. Young & Tilley, "Can businesses move beyond efficiency?"

26. Ibid.

27. Blowfield, M., & Murray, A. (2008). *Corporate responsibility: A critical introduction* (p. 23). New York, NY: Oxford University Press.

28. Young & Tilley, "Can businesses move beyond efficiency?"

29. "The Amsterdam Global Conference on Sustainability and Transparency. Rethink. Rebuild. Report." (2010, May). Global Reporting Initiative.

30. Ibid.

31. "New frontier in sustainability." (2010, July). Business for Social Responsibility.

32. "SMART 2020: Enabling the low carbon economy in the Information Age." (2008). Climate Group & Global eSustainability Initiative.

33. Ibid.

34. Ginsberg & Bloom, "Choosing the right green marketing strategy."

35. Meyer, C., & Kirby, J. (2010, April). "Leadership in the age of transparency." *Harvard Business Review.*

36. Ibid.

37. Generation Investment Management, http://www.generationim.com/ (accessed July 22, 2014).

38. See http://www.takepart.com/an-inconvenient-truth/film (accessed July 22, 2014).

39. Lyon & Maxwell, "Corporate social responsibility and the environment."

40. Meyer & Kirby, "Leadership in the age of transparency."

41. Ibid.

42. Lubin, D. A., & Esty, D. C. (2010, May). "The sustainability imperative." *Harvard Business Review.*

43. Ibid.

44. Lyon & Maxwell, "Corporate social responsibility and the environment."

45. Florverde Sustainable Flowers, http://www.florverde.org/ (accessed July 22, 2014).

46. Lyon & Maxwell, "Corporate social responsibility and the environment."

47. "New frontier in sustainability," Business for Social Responsibility.

48. Ibid.

49. Ibid.

50. Ernst & Young. (2013). "Hitting the sweet spot: The growth of the middle class in emerging economies." Retrieved July 22, 2014, from http://www.ey.com/Publication/vwLUAssets/Hitting_the_sweet_spot/$FILE/Hitting_the_sweet_spot.pdf

51. Eccles, R., Ioannou, J., & Serafeim, G. (2012, January 6). "Is sustainability now the key to corporate success?" Guardian Professional Network.

52. Dyllick, T., & Hockerts, K. (2002). "Beyond the business case for corporate sustainability." Business Strategy and the Environment.

53. Porter, M. E., & Kramer, M. R. (2002). "The competitive advantage of corporate philanthropy." Retrieved July 22, 2014, from http://www.expert2business.com/itson/Porter%20HBR%20Corporate%20philantropy.pdf

54. Big Green Opportunity. (2013). "Small business sustainability report 2013." Retrieved July 20, 2014, from http://biggreenopportunity.org/wp-content/uploads/2013/05/Big-Green-Opportunity-Report-FINAL-WEB.pdf

55. Delmas, M., & Cuerel Burbano, V. (2011, Fall). "The drivers of greenwashing." *California Management Review*.

56. Ibid.

57. Worldwatch Institute. (2013). "Advertising spending continues gradual rebound." Retrieved July 20, 2014, from http://www.worldwatch.org/advertising-spending-continues-gradual-rebound

58. Delmas & Cuerel Burbano, "The drivers of greenwashing."

59. Ibid.

60. Ibid.

61. Unruh, G., & Ettenson, R. (2010, November). "Winning the green frenzy." *Harvard Business Review*.

62. Ibid.

63. Wilson, D. (2010, October 4). "Corporate environmental responsibility." *Harvard Political Review*.

64. Delmas & Cuerel Burbano, "The drivers of greenwashing."

65. "Understanding and preventing greenwash: A business guide." (2009, July). Business for Social Responsibility & Futerra Sustainability Communications.

66. Schwartz, N. (2011, October 26). "Water bottle lawsuit: California attorney general sues companies over false biodegradable claims." *Huffington Post*. Retrieved July 22, 2014, from http://www.huffingtonpost.com/2011/10/26/water-bottle-lawsuit_n_1033795.html

67. "Understanding and preventing greenwash," Business for Social Responsibility & Futerra Sustainability Communications.

68. Delmas & Cuerel Burbano, "The drivers of greenwashing."

69. "Understanding and preventing greenwash," Business for Social Responsibility & Futerra Sustainability Communications.

70. Ibid.

71. Ibid.

72. Ibid.

73. Ibid.

74. "Green still follows green: The environment retains influence on spending." (2012, May 30). *Harris Interactive*. Retrieved July 18, 2014, from http://www.harrisinteractive.com/NewsRoom/HarrisPolls/tabid/447/ctl/ReadCustompercent20Default/mid/1508/ArticleId/1070/Default.aspx

75. "Greendex 2012: Consumer choice and the environment: A worldwide tracking survey." (2012). *National Geographic*. Retrieved from http://images.nationalgeographic.com/wpf/media -content/file/NGS_2012_Final_Global_report_Jul20-cb1343059672.pdf

76. "A closer look at 'green' products." (2008, May 18). *CBS News*. Retrieved March 13, 2015, from http://www.cbsnews.com/news/a-closer-look-at-green-products/

77. Ibid.

78. KPMG International. (2013). "The KPMG survey of corporate responsibility reporting 2013." Retrieved July 22, 2014, from http://www.kpmg.com/global/en/issuesandinsights/articlespub lications/corporate-responsibility/pages/corporate-responsibility-reporting-survey-2013.aspx

79. Schendler, A., & Toffel, M. (2011, September). "The factor environmental ratings miss." *MIT Sloan Management Review*.

80. Chatterji, A., & Toffel, M. (2012, October 24). "The big flaw in corporate sustainability rankings." *Harvard Business Review*. Retrieved March 7, 2015, from https://hbr.org/2012/10/the -big-flaw-in-corporate-sustainability-rankings/

81. Schendler & Toffel, "The factor environmental ratings miss."

82. Ibid.

83. Lubin & Esty, "The sustainability imperative."

84. Cheeseman, G. M. (2010, September). "Majority of executives and consumers think businesses not committed to sustainability." *Triple Pundit*.

85. "New frontier in sustainability," Business for Social Responsibility.

86. Ibid.

87. Cheeseman, "Majority of executives and consumers think businesses not committed to sustainability."

88. Edelman. 2012. "2012 Edelman goodpurpose study." Retrieved July 13, 2014, from http://purpose.edelman.com/

89. Cheeseman, "Majority of executives and consumers think businesses not committed to sustainability."

90. Porter, M. E., Hills, G., Pfitzer, M., Patscheke, S., & Hawkins, E. (2012). "Measuring shared value: How to unlock value by linking social and business results." FSG.

91. Ibid.

92. Nidumolu, R., Prahalad, C. K., & Rangaswami, M. R. (2009, September). "Why sustainability is now the key driver of innovation." *Harvard Business Review*.

93. Porter, M. E., & Kramer, M. R. (2011, January/February). "Creating shared value." *Harvard Business Review*.

94. Eccles et al., "Is sustainability now the key to corporate success?"

95. Ibid.

96. Ibid.

97. Ibid.

98. Eccles, R., Iaonnou, I., & Serafeim, G. (2011, November 25). "The impact of a corporate culture of sustainability on corporate behavior and performance" [Working paper]. Harvard Business School.

99. "Sustainability: Opportunity or opportunity cost?" [White paper]. (2011, July). RCM.

100. "Sustainability goes mainstream: Insights into investor views." (2014, May). PricewaterhouseCoopers.

101. "Sustainability: Opportunity or opportunity cost?," RCM.

102. "Do investors care about sustainability? Seven trends provide clues." (2012, March.) PricewaterhouseCoopers.

103. Ibid.

104. Ibid.

105. Meyer & Kirby, "Leadership in the age of transparency."

106. Porter, M. E., & Kramer, M. R. (2006, December). "Strategy and society: The link between competitive advantage and CSR." *Harvard Business Review.*

107. Bonini, S., Koller, T. M., & Mirvis, P. H. (2009). "Valuing social responsibility programs." *McKinsey Quarterly.*

108. Ibid.

109. Ibid.

110. Novo Nordisk. (2013). "Novo Nordisk annual report 2013." Retrieved from http://www .novonordisk.com/content/dam/Denmark/HQ/Commons/documents/Novo-Nordisk-Annual-Report-2013-UK.pdf

111. Bonini et al., "Valuing social responsibility programs."

112. Lubin & Esty, "The sustainability imperative."

113. Ibid.

114. Nidumolu et al., "Why sustainability is now the key driver of innovation."

115. Meyer & Kirby, "Leadership in the age of transparency."

116. Ginsberg & Bloom, "Choosing the right green marketing strategy."

117. Nidumolu et al., "Why sustainability is now the key driver of innovation."

118. "SMART 2020," Climate Group & Global eSustainability Initiative.

119. Ibid.

120. Nidumolu et al., "Why sustainability is now the key driver of innovation."

121. Ibid.

122. Handy, C. (2002, December). "What's a business for?" *Harvard Business Review.*

123. "New frontier in sustainability," Business for Social Responsibility.

124. Ibid.

125. Ibid.

126. "The Amsterdam Global Conference on Sustainability and Transparency," Global Reporting Initiative.

127. Ibid.

WAL-MART'S SUSTAINABILITY STRATEGY

We've come to believe through experience that you really can create environmental progress by leveraging corporate purchasing power. And who's got more purchasing power than Wal-Mart?

—Gwen Rutta, director of corporate partnerships at Environmental Defense, in a July 2004 article[1]

In October 2005, in an auditorium filled to capacity in Bentonville, Arkansas, Lee Scott, Wal-Mart's president and CEO, made the first speech in the history of Wal-Mart to be broadcast to the company's 1.6 million associates (employees) in all its 6,000-plus stores worldwide and shared with its 60,000-plus suppliers. Scott announced that Wal-Mart was launching a sweeping business sustainability strategy to dramatically reduce the company's impact on the global environment and thus become "the most competitive and innovative company in the world." He argued that "being a good steward of the environment and being profitable are not mutually exclusive. They are one and the same." He also committed Wal-Mart to three aspirational goals: "to be supplied 100 percent by renewable energy; to create zero waste; and to sell products that sustain our resources and the environment."[2]

In the past, Wal-Mart had dealt with environmental issues defensively, rather than proactively and as a profit opportunity. In 1989, in response to letters from customers about environmental concerns, the company launched a campaign to encourage its suppliers to provide environmentally safe products in recyclable or biodegradable packaging at no additional cost. As *Discount Stores News* reported, "What Wal-Mart has chosen to do, apart from reaping a large public relations windfall, is to deploy its clout with vendors to influence them to spend more on R&D to develop safer packaging—without passing those costs on to Wal-Mart."[3] The company's CEO at the time, David Glass, denied that the program was meant to be self-serving.

Regardless of the motive, the company did earn some "goodwill among environmentalists [as] the first major retailer to speak out in favor of the environment in 1989."[4] When vendors claimed they had made environmental improvements to products, Wal-Mart began promoting the products to consumers with "green" shelf tags (without measuring or monitoring the improvements themselves). At one point, the company had as many as 300 products with green tags in its stores.

However, not all the press was positive. In response to Wal-Mart's 1989 campaign, Procter & Gamble labeled a brand of their paper towels as "green" when the inner tube was made of recycled content but the towels themselves were made of unrecycled paper treated with chlorine bleach. When the details behind the product were exposed, both organizations were heavily criticized.[5] By1991, Wal-Mart's green tags had declined to roughly 200 products.[6] Within another couple of years, the program seemed to disappear altogether.

In contrast to the environmental campaign of 1989, the sustainability strategy launched in 2005 would need to be long-lasting and deeply embedded in Wal-Mart's operations to meet Scott's ambitious public goals. Andrew Ruben, vice president of corporate strategy and business sustainability, and Tyler Elm, senior director of the same group, had been named by Scott to lead the sustainability strategy. As they looked to 2007, Ruben and Elm knew they had to keep environmental improvement tightly coupled with business value and profitability for the strategy to succeed, and they challenged themselves to find new ways to drive measurable results.

While Wal-Mart's environmental impact had not been as problematic as these other issues, "the company's environmental record was nothing to boast about either," said one *Fortune* article. "It had paid millions of dollars in fines to state and federal regulators for violating air and water pollution laws."[7] Wal-Mart had huge environmental impacts simply because of the scale of its operations. For example, in its retail operations, Wal-Mart was the biggest private user of electricity in the U.S. and emitted more than 19.1 million metric tons of carbon dioxide annually[8]—an amount equal to the pollution created by roughly 2.8 million households. Taking into account the emissions of Wal-Mart's suppliers, the quantity was estimated to be more than 10 times greater.[9]

For these reasons, Wal-Mart's reputation among consumers and environmentalists was deteriorating. According to a study conducted by McKinsey and leaked to the public by the public watchdog organization Wal-Mart Watch, between 2% and 8% of consumers said they had stopped shopping at Wal-Mart because of the company's practices.[10] Another study, performed by Communications Consulting Worldwide (CCW), claimed that if Wal-Mart had a reputation similar to that of its rival Target, its stock would be worth 8.4% more, adding $16 billion to the company's market capitalization.[11] Compounding Wal-Mart's problems, sales growth was slowing and the company was facing increasing resistance from local communities as it sought to expand geographically.

THE SUSTAINABILITY STRATEGY

Against this backdrop, Scott initiated a review of Wal-Mart's legal and public relations challenges in 2004. One area that the company wanted to evaluate was its environmental impact. "They were looking for help defensively from a strategic standpoint—'Where are we vulnerable?'" explained Jib Ellison, founder of Blu Skye Sustainability Consultants.[12] However, Ellison had bigger ideas for how Wal-Mart could profitably reduce environmental impacts, which he pitched to Scott in June 2004. The basic proposal was that Wal-Mart could differentiate itself from its competition, continue to grow, and remain consistent to its commitment to serving customers through everyday low prices by pursuing an offensive strategy. "Sustainability represents the biggest business opportunity of the 21st century," said Ellison. In addition, he asserted that Wal-Mart and its complex supply chain could become even more efficient by making its operations more environmentally friendly. Intrigued by the idea, Scott hired Blu Skye to perform an environmental impact assessment and to consult with Wal-Mart on how it might launch such an initiative.

Getting Started

The next challenge was to figure out where to focus. Over the next four to six months, Wal-Mart worked with Blu Skye and a coalition of nongovernmental organizations (NGOs) to identify which of its products and processes created the greatest environmental impacts across five primary areas (greenhouse gas emissions, air pollution, water pollution, water use, and land use).[13] For each of the 134 product categories and impact areas under review, the Union of Concerned Scientists (UCS) estimated an environmental impact score per $1 spent by a consumer (e.g., greenhouse gas emissions in tons of CO_2 equivalents per $1 spent on electronics). Wal-Mart multiplied these environmental impact scores by 2003 sales in each product category to estimate its overall environmental impact in each of the five areas.

By June 2005, a team of top Wal-Mart executives, high-potential employees, and the consultants had identified three primary areas around which it would set environmental goals for reducing Wal-Mart's impact on the environment: energy, waste, and products. Increasing energy efficiency, transitioning to renewable energy, and reducing waste in retail operations were direct goals—goals that could be achieved by making changes that were within Wal-Mart's more immediate control. Providing more sustainable products, however, was an indirect goal that would require the involvement of Wal-Mart suppliers, and even its suppliers' suppliers, to accomplish. "We recognized early on that we had to look at the entire value chain," said Elm. "If we had focused on just our own operations, we would have limited ourselves to 10 percent of our effect on the environment and, quite frankly, eliminated 90 percent of the opportunity that's out there."

Wal-Mart's commitment to pursuing its sustainability strategy was galvanized shortly thereafter by Hurricane Katrina. The company played a sizable role in helping provide relief to people in New Orleans and its surrounding areas and, as a result, was "showered with gratitude, kindness, and acknowledgments," said Scott.[14] Joel Swisher of Rocky Mountain Institute (RMI) commented:

The overwhelmingly positive reaction that Wal-Mart received from its efforts to help the victims of the hurricane convinced Lee Scott that doing good things for people was the best way to generate goodwill, and was far more effective than any legal or PR activities the company had tried.

Wal-Mart was ready to take action.

Next Steps

The company defined 14 specific sustainability teams, known as *sustainable value networks*, to drive environmental improvements related to energy, waste, and products. An executive sponsor was identified for each network, as well as a network captain. The network captains were typically senior-level managers from Sam's Club or Wal-Mart who were considered to be among the company's top performers. Each one was responsible for leading a cross-functional team of Wal-Mart associates that would be focused on driving sustainability in different parts of the business.

Importantly, Wal-Mart decided to make sustainability a new responsibility for people in their existing positions rather than creating new jobs or building a separate sustainability-related organization. This way, sustainability was less likely to be considered a fringe initiative led by a disconnected group of individuals in the home office, but rather an integral part of the way work was performed. Aside from a small core team of five dedicated staff members, which included Ruben and Elm, no Wal-Mart associates were assigned to work on sustainability full time (with only a few exceptions in textiles and global logistics). Elm explained the approach: "Business sustainability isn't something you're doing in addition to your job. It is a new way of approaching your job." Ruben concurred: "People are absolutely stretched thin, but there's incredible power that comes from keeping sustainability within the business." To help make the model viable, in most cases each network was staffed with one or more external consultants from Blu Skye or RMI.

Another essential element of the sustainability strategy was to look outside "the Bentonville Bubble" for input. Over the years, Wal-Mart had become notorious for being internally and operationally focused. To open its door and seek strategic level input from outside parties represented a major cultural change for the organization, but Wal-Mart started "pulling ideas from everywhere"[15]—consultants, NGOs, suppliers, eco-friendly competitors, academics, and even critics. "What we found is that, when you're focused on heads-down execution and have an internally focused culture, it often results in a reduction in the diversity of ideas and a growing disconnect with external stakeholders," commented Elm.

Wal-Mart also began to engage in dialogue with government policymakers regarding climate change. In the U.S., either a tax or a cap-and-trade system for curbing greenhouse gases seemed imminent. Wal-Mart opposed a carbon tax as regressive and costly to its customers. If allowed to participate in a cap-and-trade system, the company could unlock a "virtual gold mine"[16] of credits for CO_2 reduction in its supply chain. In testimony before the U.S. senate, Ruben testified in favor of immediate, strong federal regulation, and the company later publicly endorsed proposals for "market-based programs for greenhouse gas reductions."[17]

More About the Sustainable Value Networks

When the sustainable value networks were formed, they were given explicit guidance by Elm: "It's not an environmental initiative, it's a business strategy. Your overall objective is to derive economic benefits from improved environmental and social outcomes. It's not philanthropy." Furthermore, according to Elm, the networks were encouraged "to develop a 'sensing organization' that is aware of the external business environment, and able to incorporate this perspective into business decisions that create long-term value. And, also to transition the company from an organization that derives value primarily from transactions to one that also derives value from relationships." Beyond that, the networks were given the freedom to define their own sustainability objectives and plot their own course. Elm continued:

> Once we've identified all the issues that are out there, we develop a desired future outcome, and we look at developing a pathway to get from where we are today to that desired future state. We call that the sustainable pathway, which is made up of projects of different sizes. We've got *quick wins* that the business and stakeholders can immediately go after. We have *innovation projects*, which may take one to three years. These initiatives involve Wal-Mart, but often change entire industries. Then we also identify *game changers*.

Game changers were intended to result in a radical departure from traditional business practices (see Exhibit 3.1). Each network was asked to define six quick wins, at least two innovation projects, and one game changer. While some of the networks embraced this structure whole-heartedly, others seemed to pursue their sustainability initiatives ad hoc or opportunistically, taking advantage of the high level of autonomy they were given in developing and executing their plans.

In the early phases of the program, some networks, such as Global Logistics, were able to leverage existing programs to hit the ground running. By October 2006, the logistics network was moving so quickly that Tim Yatsko, network captain for that team, said, "I can tell you that we're already there . . . in terms of our short-term goal to achieve a 25-percent improvement in fuel efficiency by 2007. That equates to almost $75 million in annual savings to Wal-Mart and probably 400,000 tons of CO_2 per year out of the atmosphere."

For other networks, like the China Sustainable Value Network, more time and planning was required to define a focus. In 2005, Wal-Mart's Chinese exports climbed to an estimated $23 billion (greater than 1% of China's $2.25 trillion GDP). In total, the company worked with more than 50,000 Chinese suppliers and was the country's seventh largest trading partner.

After researching a broad range of environmental issues, Rob Kusiciel, captain of the network, and his team realized that Wal-Mart needed to consolidate its supply base and develop a more collaborative, long-term, influential relationship with each supplier. They decided to begin working with Wal-Mart's 20 largest Chinese suppliers to improve environmental performance and to build a sustainable and transferable sourcing model.

OPERATIONAL CHANGES

A closer examination of Wal-Mart's sustainable value networks for seafood and electronics demonstrates how the sustainability strategy was being operationalized.

Seafood

According to an international study released in 2006, all species of wild seafood were greatly depleted and predicted to collapse within 50 years.[18] Furthermore, fishing was an inefficient industry in terms of its fuel use; in 2000, fisheries around the world burned roughly 13 billion gallons of fuel to catch 80 million tons of fish, accounting for approximately 1.2% of global oil consumption.[19]

As wild fish stocks declined, an increasing percentage of the seafood supply was farm-raised.[20] Yet some studies had shown that farm-raised fish provided lesser health benefits in terms of nutrients, as well as increased health risks in the form of harmful chemicals and antibiotics used to fight disease in fish-farming environments. In addition, the conversion of coastal ecosystems to aquaculture ponds also destroyed wild ocean fisheries by degrading coastal waters with antibiotics, chemicals, feed, and feces, as well as increasing the risk of disease and genetic contamination when fish escaped from the farms.

Within this complex and ominous business environment, Wal-Mart was sourcing approximately $750 million in seafood annually, and the business was growing at roughly 25% per year. "I was already having a hard time getting supply," said Peter Redmond, vice president for seafood and deli and captain of the Wal-Mart seafood network. When Redmond learned about the Marine Stewardship Council's certification program for wild-caught fish, he saw it as a potential solution to Wal-Mart's near-term and long-term supply-related challenges.

The MSC program, established by Unilever and the World Wildlife Fund (WWF) in 1997, established a broad set of certification standards based on the United Nations' Code of Conduct for Responsible Fishing. Certified fisheries displayed an MSC eco-label on their finished products as a signal that the fish was harvested in a sustainable manner, thus raising consumer awareness, which the MSC hoped would pressure the industry to shift to more sustainable fishing practices.[21]

Redmond recognized the benefits of leveraging a well-defined, established, and objective program that was developed and endorsed by organizations respected in the field. "It is a completely impartial process that is reviewed by a lot of different NGOs, including WWF and Greenpeace—groups that potentially could have been critical of us if we had decided to come out with our own standard and then go police them with our own people," he said. Tapping into the MSC program would also enable the seafood network to make faster progress. Wal-Mart went public with an ambitious seafood goal: the company committed to moving its wild catch to *22% MSC certified seafood within three to five years*.

WAL-MART'S APPROACH TO MSC CERTIFICATION

To accomplish this goal, Wal-Mart would have to work through its suppliers to increase the number of fisheries and processing plants in the MSC certification program. Suppliers would identify fisheries already using primarily sustainable practices to catch wild fish, refer them to the MSC for certification, and have them use MSC eco-labels on their products within six months.

Wild-seafood suppliers were also instructed to begin working with the WWF and a group of other experts to identify those fisheries that were potential candidates for certification, but might first need to adjust processes or practices. The WWF remained closely involved in the MSC program and could help fisheries and processors prepare to enter the certification process.

There was a third group of fisheries—many in countries such as Russia with no effective government regulation of fishing—that would require long-term, severe restrictions in the catch to become sustainable. Given the volume of Wal-Mart's demand, the company remained dependent on fish from these areas, at least in the near term, to adequately supply its customers. Fish from these areas was approximately 20 cents per pound less expensive than MSC-certified fish.

The Role of Suppliers

Because Wal-Mart had delegated the implementation of the MSC certification program to its suppliers (as well as NGO partners), companies willing to take the lead in driving sustainability into the supply base stood to differentiate themselves from the competition and further strengthen their relationships with the company. Manish Kumar,

CEO of The Fishin' Company, felt that his efforts were helping to secure and expand his business with Wal-Mart in the long term. "It's definitely brought us closer. I think there's a lot more trust now in our relationship," he said. "They're willing to let us talk on their behalf, defend their points, and explain to the businesses we work with how important this effort is. And, because we have the muscle of their business behind us, we can go to a plant or a fishery and persuade them to become certified." Additionally, because Wal-Mart was interested in acquiring as much certified fish as possible, suppliers were able to begin taking a longer-term perspective toward their business with Wal-Mart.

The Cost of Certification

The direct cost of MSC certification was paid for by boat operators and processing plants. Getting through the rigorous certification process could cost between $50,000 and $500,000 and take one to two years to complete. According to one estimate, another way of understanding the cost of certification was to add $0.03 to every pound of fish. There were other indirect costs associated with certification; for example, fisheries with the most depleted fish stocks were forced to reduce their catches while repopulation occurred.

Progress as of Late 2006

By the end of 2006, Wal-Mart expected to have 30% to 40% of its total wild-caught fish certified under the MSC. And, in the spirit of everyday low prices, there was no price premium, partly because consumers were unwilling to pay extra for sustainably caught fish. At that time, according to Redmond, the company would consider beginning to promote certified fish to its customers. "Right now, we have not put out anything from a marketing point of view," he said. "We want to have a greater percentage of our product MSC certified before we go out with the message."

ELECTRONICS

The electronics network was formed to address issues across the consumer electronics products and small appliances. Across these product lines, Wal-Mart had approximately 25 domestic electronics buyers, while Sam's had another 15. Within the U.S. electronics industry, the company had the second highest market share, just behind Best Buy.

The electronics network was led by two co-captains: Laura Phillips, vice president and divisional merchandise manager for entertainment/wireless for Wal-Mart, and Seong Ohm, vice president and divisional merchandise manager for electronics for Sam's Club. During its initial start-up phase, the team defined six key areas where it would focus:

- **Materials innovation**: Working on near-term product modifications to reduce environmental impact—for example, energy efficiency and transparency, elimination of hazardous substances (initiatives under way in 2006).
- **E-waste:** Recovery and safe disposal of electronics (piloting programs in 2006).
- **Legislation:** Collaborating with external stakeholders and governmental agencies to affect policy and regulation related to electronics (preliminary efforts under way in 2006).
- **Green engineering:** Working with suppliers and their research and development functions to rethink how products are designed and manufactured to drive fundamental change in the industry on sustainability-related issues—for example, designing for recyclability (started in late 2006).
- **Metrics:** Measuring and monitoring the performance of associates, the network, and suppliers in the area of sustainability (started in late 2006).
- **Training and education:** Informing internal and external stakeholders about changes in the electronics industry and the potential implications and opportunities related to sustainability (under way internally, but just getting started in late 2006 relative to external customers).

Subteams of eight or nine network members were designated to support each initiative. The teams also worked collaboratively, since many projects were interconnected and shared common goals. One such example was related to hazardous substances, such as lead, cadmium, and mercury, contained in many electronics. Computers and other electronics accounted for as much as 40% of the lead in U.S. landfills,[22] even though 80% of the e-waste collected for recycling was being exported to developing countries where the toxic components led to pollution levels that were hundreds of thousands of times higher than those allowed in developed countries,[23] as well as tragic, large-scale human health effects. While the e-waste team was working to dispose safely of lead and other hazardous substances in electronics, the materials innovation group was seeking ways to get them removed from computers in the first place.

Materials Innovation Project: Buying RoHs-Compliant Computers

One of the first quick wins in the electronics network was related to the issue of eliminating hazardous chemicals from production. Alex Cook, an electronics buyer and member of the sustainability network, was making a standard visit to a computer supplier in China in March 2005 when he noticed that the company was running two manufacturing lines for the same product. Inquiring about the reason, he was told that one line made traditional computers for the U.S. while the other made RoHS-compliant computers for customers in Europe. RoHS (Restriction on Hazardous Substances) was a new directive by the European Parliament to restrict the use of certain hazardous substances in electrical and electronic equipment This particular manufacturer planned to ship RoHS-compliant products to Europe in January 2006. On learning more about the program, Cook asked if he could buy these machines on the same timeline.

Ultimately, the supplier agreed to sell the RoHS-compliant product to Wal-Mart as long as Wal-Mart would guarantee the order, essentially eliminating risk to the supplier by making a commitment for 12 weeks of inventory as opposed to the more typical four-week commitment. Wal-Mart's commitment also created an economic benefit for the supplier because it did not have to shift its production line between RoHS-compliant and non-RoHS-compliant machines, which was a costly and time-consuming process.

Shortly after Wal-Mart made its first purchase of RoHS-compliant computers, it started to ask other computer manufacturers for RoHS-compliant products. Before long, many of them informed Wal-Mart that they were switching all their U.S. customers to products meeting RoHS standards. "By July 2006, which was actually when the European mandate took effect, every computer that we bought and every monitor that we acquired from every supplier was RoHS-compliant," said Cook, even though there was still no such mandate in the U.S. The network also had started working on meeting RoHS standards for its TVs.

E-waste

E-waste brought the network greater trial and error. Initially, the team tried to leverage return centers within the stores to run recycling take-back programs for electronics, but the return centers did not have adequate space and labor to deal with even small recycling volumes. The next attempt was focused on Wal-Mart's "Box Program," run in partnership with the U.S. Postal Service, HP, and Noranda Recycling. This program offered store customers postage-paid boxes to package and ship their used electronics for recycling. The boxes (including postage) sold for approximately $15—roughly 35% to 50% of the actual cost. Unfortunately, even in affluent geographic areas, customers appeared unwilling to pay to participate in the program.

Wal-Mart then sponsored a series of electronics-recycling days at stores across the country. "We collected just over 70 tons of electronics at five events in September 2006," said Jenni Dinger, a Wal-Mart music buyer and leader of the e-waste subteam. However, even with the continued participation of HP and Noranda, the events were costly and there was no measurable connection between customer participation and increased in-store sales.

Legislation

As of 2006, the U.S. had no federal electronics regulation, but states were taking action; 19 bills were in play in eight states and at least three states had e-waste laws.

However, each state was implementing a different policy. For example, California required retailers to collect a $6 to $10 fee when selling any laptop, monitor, television, or similar "covered" electronic device, used to certify and compensate other firms for the collection ($0.20 per pound) and recycling ($0.28 per pound) of used electronics. The advance recovery fee would increase as needed to cover all collection, recycling, and administrative costs.[24] California also imposed RoHS for laptops and monitors (effective January 2007).[25] In contrast, Maine and Maryland required producers to take responsibility for collecting and recycling used electronics.

Against this backdrop, Wal-Mart focused primarily on advocating national standards for both hazardous substances and e-waste. "We can't effectively manage a national program with state-by-state solutions. It's burdensome and very costly for us. There's also a need to do something at the national level since some states are doing nothing," said Phillips. U.S. Environmental Protection Agency (EPA) administrators were interested in the take-back programs sponsored by Wal-Mart, HP, and Noranda. By demonstrating successful and cost-effective collection and recycling, the partners could influence the federal government to pursue "producer responsibility" rather than the California model of advanced recycling fees and government administration of collection and recycling.

Progress as of Late 2006

Commenting on the overall progress of the electronics network, Phillips noted, "We've made a lot of progress because most of the changes make business sense to our suppliers." She added, "Where they push back is when they have to take on added costs," citing e-waste as an example of a project where cost-savings had not been realized through increased efficiency.

Another complicating factor in the electronics arena was supplier sensitivity around intellectual property. Scot Case of Blu Skye explained, "For example, if one factory is significantly more energy efficient than others, it's got an advantage. And if it shares that information, the competition might gain a much better understanding of its production costs and, therefore, its profit margins." Some even feared that this type of information could be used by Wal-Mart in its price negotiations with the supplier.

On the other hand, said Case, "anything that can be easily tested, most suppliers are more comfortable providing. Information about how much energy a product consumes is not particularly sensitive." This hesitancy to disclose was challenging to Wal-Mart not only from a performance management perspective. Ohm added, "If someone comes up with a better, more sustainable way to do something, we want to encourage them to share that with other suppliers to increase the impact." One way the network was encouraging its suppliers to accomplish this was by encouraging suppliers to license their environmental innovations. The opportunity to derive additional revenue from an environmental innovation would increase the incentive to suppliers for investment in innovation, while licensing the innovation also would lead to improved environmental performance across the industry and more widespread benefits for Wal-Mart.

MEASURING SUSTAINABILITY

As of late 2006, sustainability metrics and monitoring processes were still under development. At the network level, each team had been asked to define the "sustainability attributes" of its products and services. These sustainability attributes would become the "North Star" toward which each network would direct its improvement efforts. Next, each network would define specific performance metrics that corresponded to its sustainability attributes to support decision-making (e.g., regarding product assortment and pricing) and to enable communication with customers and the public, as well as to motivate suppliers and associates.

Product Assortment, Pricing, and Communication With Customers

Wal-Mart needed new metrics to drive sustainability into its product assortment and pricing decisions. Expanding the product assortment would increase the company's sourcing and inventory costs. While new green products might draw new customers or result in additional purchases, they also cannibalized sales of conventional products. As Wal-Mart considered adding green products, new metrics were needed to help the company decide how many and which of these green products to offer, which conventional products should be retired, and how to price the related green and conventional products.

Wal-Mart had to consider multiple perspectives when devising these new metrics. For example, many NGO partners advocated against the use of PVC due to negative human health effects associated with toxins generated by the production and incineration of PVC. On the other hand, some suppliers argued that the negative health effects of PVC were unproven and that customers demanded the strength and flexibility in certain products (e.g., shower curtains, inflatable swimming pools) that only PVC could provide. Wal-Mart had to manage this tension as it decided on what metrics would drive its product assortment and pricing decisions.

Wal-Mart also needed new metrics for communicating with customers. Wal-Mart faced two primary problems with communicating products' sustainability-related attributes. First, the networks had to be careful about promoting the performance of green products in such a way that conventional alternatives would appear undesirable (e.g., MSC-certified versus noncertified fish). Second, Wal-Mart often did not have enough reliable information to definitively explain or defend a product's environmental and health benefits to customers. If the company was uncertain about the safety, effectiveness, or environmental impact of a product, for example, because it relied on suppliers to self-police (e.g., RoHS-compliant PCs), it could not promote those attributes. These two problems were evident in the compact fluorescent light bulb (CFL) initiative, coordinated by the global greenhouse gas network.

Compact Fluorescent Light Bulbs

In 2006, driven by the sustainability attribute of improved energy efficiency, Wal-Mart announced a goal to sell 100 million energy-saving compact fluorescent light bulbs (CFLs) per year by 2008. If the company accomplished this objective, total sales of the bulbs in the U.S. would increase by 50% and the corresponding savings to Americans in electricity costs would be approximately $3 billion.[26] It would also result in a dramatic reduction in CO_2 emissions, since lighting accounted for approximately 8% of total U.S. CO_2 output[27] and each CFL used 75% less electricity.[28] From August 2005 to August 2006, Wal-Mart sold only 40 million CFLs compared to roughly 350 million incandescent bulbs.[29]

Sales of CFLs would directly cannibalize Wal-Mart's own lighting business, because each CFL lasted 10 times longer than an incandescent bulb. Nevertheless, Wal-Mart lowered its prices on CFLs from roughly $8.10 for a three-pack of bulbs to $7.59 (versus approximately $1.50 for three incandescents), expanded the presence of CFLs in the stores by moving the bulbs to eye level on the shelves, and heavily promoted CFL technology through creative marketing partnerships, media product placements, and other less-traditional communication strategies.

Wal-Mart further invested in in-store displays to help educate consumers on the benefits of CFLs, giving up precious selling space to showcase information about the value of the bulbs (each CFL was expected to save the consumer $30 in energy costs over its lifetime).[30] Concurrent with these promotional efforts, Wal-Mart was closely monitoring the reduction in CO_2 emissions achieved by its CFL initiative and other energy efficiency projects, but had not yet shared the detailed CO_2 emissions data with policymakers and the public.

Communication With the Public

In his October 2005 presentation to Wal-Mart associates and suppliers, Lee Scott admitted that the goals he announced were "ambitious and aspirational and I'm not sure how to achieve them . . . at least not yet."[31] According to Roger Deromedi, the CEO of Kraft at the time of Scott's speech, Wal-Mart exposed itself to risk in publicizing such bold objectives, particularly when it would be dependent on suppliers to achieve them.

Specific and measurable goals (e.g., to carry only MSC-certified wild fish within five years) were more compelling to the public, but also more risky. McDonald's was sued for failing to keep a public promise to eliminate trans fats in its products by early 2003, and settled the suit by donating $7 million to the American Heart Association and spending $1.5 million to notify the public about the trans fats in its cooking oils.[32] By publishing goals that were aspirational but nonspecific, Wal-Mart invited less positive attention, but also reduced the risk of future criticism and liability.

Despite the risks, Ruben favored publicizing goals and results. He commented, "We get a lawsuit every few seconds anyway. One of the really liberating factors is how much criticism already exists." He also seemed relatively unconcerned about missing some of the deadlines made public as part of the company's efforts:

> We're going to miss some things. If we miss 90 percent of what we say, I think there are big costs. If we miss nothing, I think there are also costs. If we miss 10 percent, then I think we're about right. There's a believability about it, a realness about it, and an aggressiveness about it.

Supplier Performance Measurement

More than ever before, Wal-Mart was dependent on the cooperation of its suppliers to meet its public goals. As a result, effective supplier measurement and motivation was essential. The packaging network, under captain Matt Kistler, vice president of package and product innovations, was furthest ahead in this area. This group was in the process of implementing a web-based scorecard that would evaluate each product's packaging against nine metrics, such as the percentage of recycled content and the product-to-package ratio.

On February 1, 2007, Wal-Mart's 60,000-plus suppliers would be asked to begin using the scorecard for a one-year trial period to determine how their packaging innovations, environmental standards, energy efficiencies, and use of materials rated relative to their peers. The scorecard was perceived as an important enabler for helping the company achieve its public goal of reducing the packaging used by all its suppliers by 5% between 2008 and 2013. If achieved, this five-year program was expected to generate $3.4 billion in savings.

Ruben explained how Wal-Mart would seek to exert more influence over supplier behaviors as it sought to consolidate its business with a more select group of high-performing direct suppliers. "Right now we account for 2 percent of a lot of people's business, especially overseas. We know that needs to be a lot larger—maybe in the 50 or 60 percent," he said. This positioning would motivate suppliers to participate to maintain or expand the amount of business they received from Wal-Mart. "We're trying to stimulate a race for the top," said Phillips.

Associate Performance Measurement

Internally, Wal-Mart planned to translate sustainability attributes into an objective measurement system to track the performance of associates in important functions such as merchandising, strategic sourcing, and other roles that were directly linked to its sustainability efforts. However, as of late 2006, decisions regarding how (and if) to measure these contributions had been left to the discretion of the networks captains. In some areas, such as electronics, broad preliminary metrics had been put into place. For example, electronics buyers for Sam's Club were required by Ohm to have at least 25% of the products they bought (by SKU) involved in some form of sustainability initiative (e.g., packaging reduction, RoHS compliance, improved energy efficiency). However, in most areas of the business, a formal system for measuring associate involvement in sustainability did not exist, which meant that individuals were forced to try to distinguish their sustainability-related contributions against largely subjective criteria.

LOOKING FORWARD

At the end of 2006, Ruben and Elm estimated that the profits generated by the sustainability strategy's quick wins in the first year were roughly equivalent to the profits from several Supercenters. They saw an overwhelmingly large array of opportunities that remained untapped, and resolved to continue to identify and pursue the opportunities with greatest environmental benefits and business value.

Case Questions

1. Thinking about Wal-Mart's environmental strategy as described in the case, where does it fit into the different approaches to sustainability discussed in the chapter? For example, is Wal-Mart proactive or reactive in addressing environmental concerns?

2. Do Wal-Mart's environmental stewardship efforts compensate for its shortcomings in other areas of corporate responsibility?

3. Wal-Mart's consumers, in general, are unwilling to pay a premium for environmentally friendly products. In light of this, how is Wal-Mart's environmental strategy an example of shared value creation?

4. What are some ways in which Wal-Mart ensures that it keeps deriving commercial value through sustainability?

5. Wal-Mart's sustainability strategy has generally been very profitable; however, two initiatives described in the case benefit society and the environment but apparently decrease Wal-Mart's profits. How would you justify pursuing those initiatives?

Exhibit 3.1   How Networks Drive Sustainability Goals

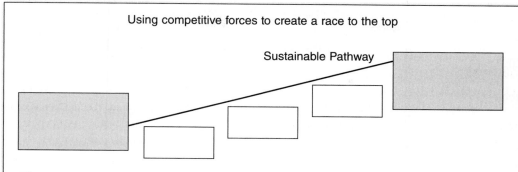

Using competitive forces to create a race to the top

Sustainable Pathway

TO

FROM

Today's Business Practices

- Fossil fuel dependence
- Waste in many forms
- Products that don't account for full costs to society

Unintended negative consequences for our customers and business

Quick Wins

< 1 year

- Actions that make business sense based on available technologies, products, and processes

Innovation

Projects

1 to 3 years

- Opportunities that make sense based on emerging technology, processes, and innovation

Big Game Change

Ongoing

- Changing the "rules of the game" to tilt the playing field to favor sustainable practices, in areas where we can lead, so that the market works for sustainability, not against it

Sustainable Business Practices

- Use 100% renewable energy
- Produce zero waste
- Sell products that sustain our resources and environment
- A win for society and a win for business

NOTES

1. "Environmental group moves in near Wal-Mart." (2004, July 16). *Commercial Appeal*, p. D4.

2. Scott, L. (2005, October 23). "Twentieth century leadership." Retrieved January 29, 2007, from http://news.walmart.com/executive-viewpoints/twenty-first-century-leadership (January 29, 2007).

3. "Tough talk and soothing speech: Managing reputations for being tough and for being good" (1999). *Corporate Reputation Review*, p. 317.

4. Halverson, R. (1991, March 18). "Big three take high road on environmental front." *Discount Store News*. Retrieved January 11, 2007.

5. Ginsberg, J. M., & Bloom, P. N. (2004, Fall). "Choosing the right green marketing strategy." *MIT Sloan Management Review*. Retrieved January 31, 2007, from http://sloanreview.mit.edu/smr/issue/2004/fall/12/

6. Halverson, "Big three take high road on environmental front."

7. Gunther, M. (2006, July 31). "The green machine." *Fortune*. Retrieved November 28, 2006, from http://money.cnn.com/sales/executive_resource_center/articles2/8382593/index.htm

8. "Wal-Mart response, Carbon Disclosure Project." (2006). Retrieved February 6, 2007.

9. Ibid.

10. Hanft, A. "10 steps to turn around Wal-Mart." *Fast Company*. Retrieved November 28, 2006, from http://www.fastcompany.com/resources/innovation/Hanft/120105.html

11. Engardio, P. (2007, January 19). "Beyond the green corporation." *BusinessWeek Online*. Retrieved January 29, 2007, from http://www.msnbc.msn.com/id/16710668/

12. All quotations from interviews conducted by authors unless otherwise cited.

13. Brower, M., & Leon, W. (1999). *A consumer's guide to effective environmental choices: Practical advice from the Union of Concerned Scientists.* New York, NY: Three Rivers Press.

14. Scott, "Twentieth century leadership."

15. Gunther, "The green machine."

16. "Wal-Mart eyes carbon bounty in its supply chain." (2006, November 1). *Planet Ark*. Retrieved February 21, 2007, from http://www.planetark.com/dailynewsstory.cfm/newsid/38765/story.htm

17. Aluminum Association. (2007, January 22). "Alliance gets Wal-Mart's backing in push for caps on carbon emissions." Retrieved February 21, 2007.

18. "*Science* study predicts collapse of all seafood fisheries by 2050." (2006, November 2). *Stanford Report*. Retrieved December 14, 2006, from http://news-service.stanford.edu/news/2006/november8/ocean-110806.html

19. Dean, C. (2005, December 20). "Fishing industry's fuel efficiency gets worse as ocean stocks get thinner." *New York Times*.

20. Delicious Organics.com. (n.d.). "Wild versus farm- or ocean-raised fish?" Retrieved January 4, 2007.

21. Duecy, E. (2006, February 13). "Darden, Wal-Mart ride seafood sustainability wave, buoy advocates." *Nation's Restaurant News*, p. 8.

22. Laptopical.com. (n.d.). "The green laptop RoHS revolution." Retrieved November 22, 2006.

23. Mohamed, S. (2002, April 24). *Dumping electronic waste in developing countries.* Society for Conservation and Protection of the Environment. Retrieved January 9, 2007.

24. U.S. Department of Commerce, Office of Technology Policy. (2006, July). "Recycling technology products: An overview of e-waste policy issues." Author.

25. California Department of Toxic Substances Control. "Restrictions on the use of Certain Hazardous Substances (RoHS) in Eletcronic Devices." Retrieved January 16, 2007, from https://www.dtsc.ca.gov/HazardousWaste/RoHS.cfm

26. Barbaro, M. (2007, January 2). "Wal-Mart puts some muscle behind power-sipping bulbs." *New York Times.* Retrieved January 16, 2007, from http://www.nytimes.com/2007/01/02/business/02bulb.html?ex=1325394000&en=78dfdd6856cb7590&ei=5090&partner=rssuserland&emc=rss&pagewanted=all&pagewanted=all

27. Azevedo, I. (2007). Presentation at the Climate Decision Making Center Meeting, Carnegie Mellon University, Pittsburgh, PA.

28. Barbaro, "Wal-Mart puts some muscle behind power-sipping bulbs."

29. Ibid.

30. Ibid.

31. "Sen. Jeffords introduces legislation to protect Americans from hazardous chemicals in consumer products." (2005, July 13). Retrieved January 25, 2007, from http://www.epw.senate.gov/pressitem.cfm?id=240542&party=dem

32. Ibid.

Chapter 4

THE CORPORATION'S RESPONSIBILITY TO SOCIETY: HUMAN RIGHTS AND LABOR ISSUES

In this chapter, we examine the corporation's responsibility toward its employees and the communities surrounding its operations.

In Chapter 1, we defined corporate responsibility as a corporation's environmental and social obligations to its constituencies and greater society. Fulfilling these obligations includes paying attention to human rights issues as well as the interests of a corporation's workforce and suppliers.[1] Corporations have a responsibility not only to those immediately affected by their business dealings, such as their employees and consumers, but also to remote constituents, such as citizens of the developing nations where they obtain raw materials or employ labor forces.

If they seek to take a comprehensive approach to human rights issues, corporations must consider myriad concerns including discrimination, health and safety, poverty, and environmental issues that affect health.[2] Companies affect human rights in all their relationships with constituents.[3]

Corporations are also beginning to understand the role they play in human rights issues. As the Institute for Corporate Culture (ICCA), a nonprofit organization that helps corporations mainstream their CR activities, explains in its *Handbook on Corporate Social Responsibility*, "firms have discovered that moral problems are economic problems, be they the need to deal honestly with employees, suppliers and customers or the emphasis on environmental protection and responsible behavior towards people in developing countries."[4] Corporations are now expected to behave in socially responsible ways, seeking not only to increase their profits but also to assume responsibility for the effect their activities have on the cultural and political contexts in which they are based.[5] As a result, companies have adopted socially responsible business practices as a means of ensuring that they meet these expectations.

We begin by looking at the definition and history of socially responsible business practices and labor practices in particular, then examine different forms of workplace discrimination and examples of how corporations have engaged in each in recent history. Then, we will look at the complicated nature of human rights violations in multinational corporations, and how international bodies such as the United Nations are working to provide guidelines for corporations to ensure their compliance on such issues.

INTRODUCTION TO SOCIALLY RESPONSIBLE BUSINESS PRACTICES

What distinguishes socially responsible business practices from other practices conducted within a corporation that improve communities and protect the environment? A key difference is that socially responsible practices are done at the company's discretion, rather than because of an outside force such as regulation.[6] Over the past couple of decades, there has been a shift from engaging in socially responsible business practices as a reaction to regulations and complaints by antagonists to taking on CR initiatives as a strategic imperative designed to solve social and environmental problems while benefiting a corporation's financial bottom line.[7]

Why has this shift occurred? As seen in Chapter 2, a strong business case exists for corporate responsibility. Socially responsible practices in many cases involve activities that increase revenues and reduce or eliminate business costs.[8] Thanks to advancements in technology and reduced barriers to entry for firms, consumers now have more options than ever when it comes to purchasing goods or services, and they are likely to make buying decisions based on factors beyond the 4P model (product, price, promotion, and place) marketers have traditionally used to entice buyers.[9] As seen in the Edelman goodpurpose® study, more and more consumers are taking corporate responsibility into account when they buy.[10] The knowledge that consumers have this power incentivizes companies to behave in socially responsible ways. Meanwhile, the increased public scrutiny resulting from consumer expectation causes a corporation's investors and other stakeholders to become invested in ensuring that the corporation is adhering to socially responsible business practices.[11]

Corporations are also interested in higher worker productivity and workforce retention. Because three-quarters of job-seekers in the United States consider a corporation's social and environmental practices when choosing potential employers,[12] socially responsible business practices not only allow corporations to gain favor with the public, but can be a crucial tool for recruiting top talent, as well as increasing morale and well-being.[13]

Advancements in information technology have led to increased visibility of corporate activities, as well as more negative publicity when things go wrong.[14] The social-networking platform Twitter has provided a means for consumers to instantly publicize grievances against corporations. Meanwhile, immediate access to the ideas of both traditional journalists and bloggers allows even a person with minimal CR expertise to stay informed about the basic facts of a corporation's CR blunders.

Another side to the increased availability of information is that consumers' expectations have risen with their access to information. Customers now expect to be fully informed of corporations' practices; corporate transparency is imperative.[15] The food industry in particular has been affected by the increase in consumer awareness. Today, labels often identify not only traditional information such as ingredients and nutrient values, but also the methods used in farming, as well as information about the facilities used to manufacture packaged foods. For example, Stonyfield Farm, a subsidiary of Groupe Danone specializing in organic dairy products, includes the names of its supplier farms on its labels and provides additional information about them, including videos featuring the farmers, on its website.[16]

While there are risks inherent to this atmosphere of increased scrutiny, corporations also have an opportunity to benefit from it. In financial terms, we have already looked at the opportunities to decrease operating costs, as well as to benefit from monetary incentives from regulatory agencies. By increasing employee morale and well-being, CR activities contribute to a work environment with less personnel turnover, meaning the company saves money on training and recruitment costs. Employees who are happy and healthy also tend to be more productive, upping a corporation's work capacity.

There are also marketing opportunities. Socially responsible business practices increase a corporation's goodwill in the communities in which it operates and lead to brand preference in the marketplace, as seen in the Edelman survey. They are also a brand-positioning tool, allowing corporations to distinguish themselves from competitors through their social and environmental efforts and courting segments of the population who are especially attuned to these issues. As seen in Chapter 2, adherence to sustainability requirements also presents an opportunity to improve product quality. Similarly, voluntary reforms designed to benefit society or the environment may also pay dividends in the form of improved product quality. Corporations may also find opportunities for partnerships with outside organizations such as regulatory agencies, suppliers, and nonprofits.[17] Such partnerships legitimize corporations' commitment to CR in the eyes of constituents, including consumers and NGOs.

Given increased consumer awareness of the role of socially responsible corporate behavior as a marketing tool, there are also risks in promoting awareness of a corporation's socially responsible practices. Savvy consumers may question the motives of corporations that brand themselves as socially responsible, wondering whether the company's goals are truly aligned with a cause or if the company is simply trying to generate positive PR.[18] Greenwashing, the practice of using environmental benefits as a marketing technique, has been a successful effort in the past, but as consumers become better informed and increasingly skeptical, corporations can expect their CR initiatives to come under greater scrutiny. Consumers will look for actions to support a corporation's promises, and if statements and actions do not line up, the corporation runs the risk of suffering reputational setbacks.

A key item that constituents will look for in evaluating a corporation's commitment to its social programs is whether the announced program or programs are long-term commitments or short-term campaigns.[19] While we have already discussed how incorporating CR into a company's strategic plan is good for business, here we see that looking at CR in the long term also legitimizes social and environmental commitments in the eyes of stakeholders.

Stakeholders may also question how the corporation's new practices will make a difference. They may ask for greater transparency into how new practices will differ from old, and what the expected results will be. They will also seek to see measurable results.[20] Another issue may be concerns over whether new, more responsible business methods will result in inferior products.

How can a corporation address these challenges? First, being proactive is essential. Corporations can do this by choosing a social or environmental issue whose solution also meets a business need of the firm. It is also essential to make a long-term commitment to demonstrate that the corporation's commitment to CR is not a passing fad but a crucial piece of its strategic plan. A corporation should also cultivate enthusiasm among its employees to ensure support from the bottom up; however, this internal buy-in, while necessary to the success of a CR program, is meaningless unless the corporation puts resources toward building the infrastructure necessary for the initiative to succeed. Finally, as with any other major change in an organization, it is imperative that the change in business practices be accompanied by honest and direct communication with all constituencies—top management, shareholders, consumers, and other stakeholders.

SOCIALLY RESPONSIBLE LABOR PRACTICES

A crucial component of the relationship between the corporation and society is the former's adherence to socially responsible labor practices. Guidelines for business's duty to society in terms of labor practices can be found in the United Nations Global Compact, which includes four standards regarding fair labor practices among its Ten Principles:

- Principle 3: Businesses should uphold the freedom of association and the effective recognition of the right to collective bargaining;
- Principle 4: the elimination of all forms of forced and compulsory labour;
- Principle 5: the effective abolition of child labour; and
- Principle 6: the elimination of discrimination in respect of employment and occupation.[21]

The above principles are also incorporated into the International Labour Organization's (ILO's) Declaration on Fundamental Principles and Rights at Work, "an expression of commitment by governments, employers' and workers' organizations to uphold basic human values."[22] The ILO is a United Nations agency dealing with labor issues, of which nearly all UN members (185 out of 193) take part. Meanwhile, the Global Compact is of limited impact because it relies on voluntary public accountability, rather than legally binding mandates, but it provides a foundation for industry-specific regulation.[23]

While the UN and ILO have limitations in terms of their ability to enforce the practices they advocate, other organizations exist whose goal is to create accountability for corporations in dealing with labor issues. One such organization is the Fair Labor Association (FLA), formed in 1999 as an industry-specific regulatory organization with the goal of promoting respect for labor rights around the world.[24] The FLA seeks to reach this goal by addressing worker exploitation, including forced and child labor; work environment issues such as harassment and abuse, discrimination, and health and safety; and employment criteria, such as freedom of association and collective bargaining, wages and benefits, hours of work, and overtime compensation.[25]

The FLA code allows it to enforce corporate compliance with its principles in several ways. Companies are asked to establish clear, written workforce standards for their suppliers, which serves as a means of managing supplier risk. The FLA then monitors compliance with its labor standards through data collection and audits, soliciting information from parties including corporate employees as well as labor, human rights, and religious organizations. The organization operates as a mediator, using independent, third-party monitors to audit corporations according to its regulations, and the monitors' fees are paid by FLA.[26]

Does self-regulation by the FLA and organizations work? The answer is both yes and no. The FLA does create competitive pressure for suppliers who work with FLA-participating companies.[27] The organization releases periodic reports on its participating companies; consumers can use the information contained in the reports to put pressure on companies that are not currently FLA members.[28]

The FLA uses remediation to correct violations by member companies, as the organization's goal is to have companies fix problems instead of just relinquishing their membership.[29] One example of how the FLA operates is a situation at an athletic apparel factory in Thailand, in which factory workers were being under-paid. An FLA-member company that used the factory as a supplier required the factory to allow its workers to record their hours electronically, thus ensuring that employee pay corresponded to hours worked.[30] In this situation and others, FLA member companies have extended their responsibility to workers beyond their own internal operations, ensuring the welfare not only of their own workers but also of those whom they do not directly employ.[31]

At the same time, there are limitations to what the FLA is able to accomplish, particularly because of issues with implementation and accountability. One example of these difficulties is the absence of unions in China. As a result, the factories that are inspected are not named, which makes it harder for watchdog organizations such as the FLA to verify inspection results.[32] The 2011 explosion at a factory owned by Apple supplier Foxconn, which we will discuss in more detail later in the chapter, brought attention to a series of violations of Apple's labor rules by the company's suppliers. While Apple has a clear code of conduct for its suppliers to follow, the company's ability to ensure compliance is limited, especially abroad. Another issue is that FLA code can be very confusing to suppliers, which tend to undergo different audits by companies that participate in voluntary regulatory organizations. Suppliers are subject to various standards that are imposed via the participation of the companies they supply in organizations such as the FLA. The lack of understanding of specific regulations can lead to factories being rejected by compliance organizations, which puts factory managers in a difficult position.[33]

A major subset of labor issues that has received increased attention over the past few decades is workplace discrimination, which has been used to limit members of underprivileged groups from achieving professional success. Workplace discrimination often operates in hidden, insidious ways and can be difficult to identify and combat. We will now explore three types of discrimination in the workplace.

WORKPLACE DISCRIMINATION

Despite the strides made by women, minorities, and other historically disenfranchised groups during the past few decades, workplace discrimination persists. In 2011, the Equal Employment Opportunity Commission (EEOC) reported that the number of private-sector workplace discrimination charges throughout the U.S. during fiscal 2010 had hit an all-time high of 99,922. In 2013, workplace discrimination charges were still high at 93,727.[34]

Discriminatory practices include those that marginalize and disadvantage workers based on gender, race or ethnicity, sexual orientation, or disability. Engaging in such practices is not only a human rights violation, but can also put corporations in danger of jeopardizing business through damaged corporate reputation or risks to their licenses to operate.

Increasing the Role of Women in the Workplace

An important issue related to the corporation's responsibility to society in general and to workplace discrimination in particular is the goal to increase the role of women in the workplace. While ending discriminatory practices would seem to be an inherent good, there is also a business case for creating more corporate opportunities for women. A report by McKinsey reported that gender diversity in the boardrooms is correlated with better financial performance on several measures. For example, firms whose boards include women have, on average, 47% better return on equity and 55% better earnings before interest and tax than firms without gender diversity among board members.[35] Another study by Catalyst Inc. found that companies with more women board directors outperform companies with the fewest women board directors by 53% in terms of ROE, by 42% in terms of return on sales, and by 66% in terms of return on invested capital (see Figure 4.1).[36]

Despite such findings about the relationship between women board directors and financial performance, the number of women in U.S. boardrooms continues to be disappointing. While the ranks of women on corporate boards are growing around the world, the proportion of women in U.S. boardrooms lags behind that of most in the Western world.[37] As noted in a 2012 article for *The Guardian*, the number of female board directors at U.S. corporations grew only half a percentage point from 2009 to 2011.[38] While, at 12.6%, it's still higher than the global average, the 0.5% increase is significantly smaller than gains made in countries such as France, where the number grew 7.5% during the same period, and Australia, where the number increased by 5.4%, according to a report from watchdog group GovernanceMetrics International.[39]

Figure 4.1   Return on equity, sales, and invested capital by women's representation on the board

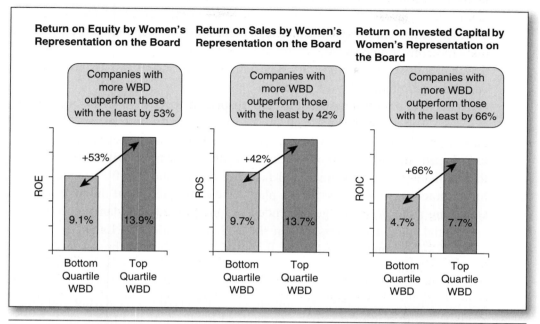

Source: "The bottom line: Corporate performance and women's representation on boards" (p. 1). (2007). Catalyst. Retrieved August 3, 2014, from http://www.catalyst.org/file/139/bottom%20line%202.pdf.

What accounts for the differentials between the U.S. and these other countries? In the case of France, the country passed a national law in 2010 mandating that boards meet certain benchmarks—specifically, they are required to be 20% female by 2013 and 40% female by 2016.[40] Australia, on the other hand, has seen similar success without instituting national laws; the country has instead introduced a transparency requirement for corporations, ensuring that they report on their diversity policies and histories.[41]

Meanwhile, the European Commission has taken steps to create a quota program similar to that of France throughout the European Union, citing failed attempts to rectify the situation through voluntary measures. Previously, there had been calls for large companies throughout the EU to increase their percentage of women board members to 30% by 2015 and 40% by 2020.[42] These recommendations were unsuccessful, however. As explained by Dutch Member of the European Parliament Sophia in't Veld, "quotas are a necessary evil, because voluntary measures have got us nowhere."[43] In March 2012, the European Parliament adopted a resolution drafted by in't Veld that will make it mandatory for EU corporations to fulfill the proposed 2015 and 2020 corporate board quota goals. As it currently stands, only 12% of board members, on average, of the largest public companies in Europe are women.[44] The quotas therefore represent an aggressive, swift approach to the issue of female board representation. Differing views exist on whether quotas are the correct means of remedying the gap between female and male representation on corporate boards.

What consequences exist for corporations that discriminate against employees and potential employees based on gender? Reputational risk is an obvious consequence, as corporations that are suspected to engage in discriminatory practices can expect a great deal of negative publicity both in traditional and new media. There are also other, more tangible consequences. In late 2011, U.S.-based multinational corporation Cargill was charged with systematically discriminating against women and favoring Asians and Pacific Islanders in its hiring practices at a Southern U.S. plant. The consequences of the investigation stemming from these charges extended beyond reputational damage to include substantial loss of business. When the U.S. Department of Labor discovered Cargill's discriminatory practices, the situation resulted in threats to Cargill's existing federal contracts, which included agreements worth over $550 million with the Department of Defense.[45] In addition to canceling the current contracts, federal officials stated their intention to prevent Cargill from entering into future federal contracts until the company showed evidence that it had ended its discriminatory practices.[46]

Another example of how sex discrimination hurts corporations is a Wal-Mart class action suit brought by female employees who claimed that the company's policies and practices had resulted in discriminatory decisions over pay and promotions.[47] The suit was rejected by the Supreme Court in June 2011. The ruling was not a judgment on the question of whether Wal-Mart had in fact engaged in discriminatory practices against the women, but instead represented the determination by the Court that the case could not be tried as a class action suit.[48] Four months later, the women filed a new lawsuit narrowing their prior claims to Wal-Mart stores in the State of California, with the women's lawyers announcing their intention to follow this initial suit with similar allegations in other regions of the U.S.[49] If this new case and those to follow are admitted in court, the company potentially stands to lose billions of dollars, in addition to having to grapple with the reputational issues resulting from the negative publicity around the story.

Retailers such as Wal-Mart may have unique concerns relative to other types of businesses, as they have to contend with concerns about losing customers over their alleged discriminatory practices. According to the 2011 Survey of the American Consumer conducted by GfK Mediamark Research & Intelligence, 74.9% of women identify themselves as the primary shoppers for their households.[50] Having a reputation as a company that actively discriminates against women risks alienating a group with a great deal of purchasing power.

Racial Discrimination

Even in the 21st century, discrimination based on race remains the most common form of workplace discrimination. During 2013, the EEOC received 33,068 complaints related to racial discrimination throughout the U.S.[51] Workplace discrimination based on race is illegal under Title VII of the Civil Rights Act of 1964, which prohibits employers with 15 or more employees from discriminating against individuals based on race, national origin, religion, or sex. Yet despite attempts by both state and federal lawmakers to eliminate racial discrimination, it persists even in the most renowned major corporations.

Coca-Cola is one major multinational corporation that has had a disturbing history of accusations of racial discrimination. In late 2000, the company settled a federal lawsuit brought by black employees for $156 million—one of the largest settlements ever reached in a racial discrimination case.[52] The lawsuit alleged that Coke's corporate hierarchy kept black employees at the bottom of the pay scale, earning on average $26,000 less per year than their white colleagues.

The settlement included a provision mandating that Coca-Cola put $36 million toward internal changes designed to prevent similar situations going forward.[53] Even so, in early 2012 the company once again found itself the target of another suit, with 16 black and Hispanic employees calling the company a "cesspool of racial discrimination."[54] These allegations came from employees in two New York State plants, where they were subject to injustices including "biased work assignments and allotment of hours, unfair discipline and retaliation, and a caustic work environment."[55]

LGBT Discrimination

In recent years, discrimination against people who identify as lesbian, gay, bisexual, or transgender has been receiving a great deal of press as these groups make gains in their efforts to achieve many rights already afforded straight people. One organization that came under fire in the media during 2012 for poor handling of LGBT issues is the Boy Scouts of America.

In the summer of 2012, technology and culture blog *Boing Boing* reported that Eagle Scouts around the U.S. were returning their medals to the Boy Scouts of America in response to the BSA's July 12 decision to reaffirm its long-term ban on openly gay scouts and leaders.[56] Citing the tremendous work and commitment required to earn the Eagle Scout medal and the value it holds for the young men who have reached this achievement, the *Boing Boing* post printed a collection of letters enclosed with the returned medals (see Figure 4.2 for an example).

Figure 4.2 Christopher Banker letter

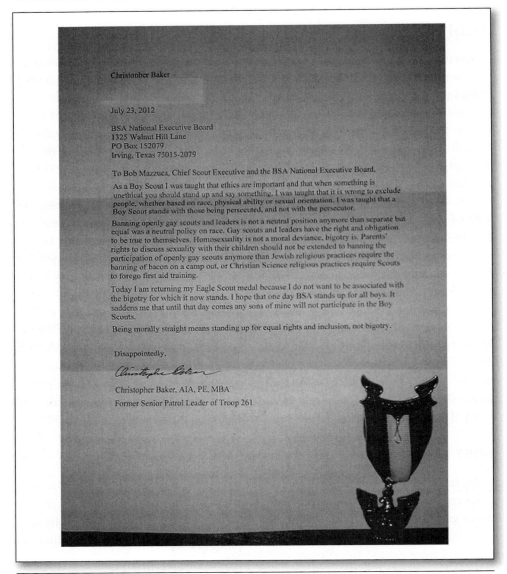

Christopher Baker

July 23, 2012

BSA National Executive Board
1325 Walnut Hill Lane
PO Box 152079
Irving, Texas 75015-2079

To Bob Mazzuca, Chief Scout Executive and the BSA National Executive Board,

As a Boy Scout I was taught that ethics are important and that when something is unethical you should stand up and say something. I was taught that it is wrong to exclude people, whether based on race, physical ability or sexual orientation. I was taught that a Boy Scout stands with those being persecuted, and not with the persecutor.

Banning openly gay scouts and leaders is not a neutral position anymore than separate but equal was a neutral policy on race. Gay scouts and leaders have the right and obligation to be true to themselves. Homosexuality is not a moral deviance, bigotry is. Parents' rights to discuss sexuality with their children should not be extended to banning the participation of openly gay scouts anymore than Jewish religious practices require the banning of bacon on a camp out, or Christian Science religious practices require Scouts to forego first aid training.

Today I am returning my Eagle Scout medal because I do not want to be associated with the bigotry for which it now stands. I hope that one day BSA stands up for all boys. It saddens me that until that day comes any sons of mine will not participate in the Boy Scouts.

Being morally straight means standing up for equal rights and inclusion, not bigotry.

Disappointedly,

Christopher Baker, AIA, PE, MBA
Former Senior Patrol Leader of Troop 261

Source: Koerth-Baker, M. (2012, July 23). "Eagle Scouts stand up to the Boy Scouts of America." *Boing Boing.* Retrieved from http://boingboing.net/2012/07/23/eagle-scouts-stand-up-to-the-b.html.

In a statement, BSA Chief Scout Executive Bob Mazzuca claimed that a majority of BSA's membership agreed with the policy.[57] But the language used in the letters shared online suggests not only that multiple BSA members disagree, but also that they returned their medals *because* of the values they had been taught as members of the organization. As the Eagle Scout stated in the letter featured in Figure 4.2:

> As a Boy Scout I was taught that ethics are important and that when something is unethical you should stand up and say something. I was taught that it is wrong to exclude people, whether based on race, physical ability or sexual orientation. I was taught that a Boy Scout stands with those being persecuted, and not with the persecutor.[58]

Another Eagle Scout expressed his belief that the decision was "a stain on the otherwise exceptional reputation of the Boy Scouts of America." He went on to say, "As well you know, a Scout is courteous and kind, and this discriminatory policy is in violation of at least those two tenants of the Scout Law. It is certainly not a 'brave' decision."[59] A third Eagle Scout expressed his dismay that "the organization which I believe guided me into becoming the man I am today, has practices that go against the very principles I took from it."[60]

The Eagle Scouts quoted above demonstrate a perceived disconnection between the values BSA claims to espouse and its discriminatory practices against LGBT individuals. Engaging in practices that conflict with an organization's core values can negatively affect corporate reputation. While the BSA has long been known for its service to communities throughout the U.S., the increased expectations of its stakeholders around human rights issues could eventually put sufficient pressure on the organization to change its systematic discriminatory policies.

Sometimes discrimination doesn't involve overt denial of privileges to employees or volunteers. Take, for example, the case of Atlanta-based fast-food chain Chick-fil-A, which in 2012 came under fire for contributing corporate dollars to anti-gay groups. The LGBT advocacy organization Equality Matters found that Chick-fil-A gave nearly $2 million to anti-gay organizations during 2010 through its charitable arm, WinShape.[61] Between 2003 and 2009, Chick-fil-A had given $3 million to such organizations.[62] In 2012, public sentiment against such practices was strong enough to convince Chick-fil-A's president, Dan Cathy, to cease donations—even though Cathy had previously stated that the company was supportive of "the biblical definition of the family unit.[63] After meeting with another LGBT advocacy group, the Civil Rights Agenda, Chick-fil-A stated that the company "is now taking a much closer look at the organizations it considers helping, and in that process will remain true to its stated philosophy of not supporting organizations with political agendas."[64] Although the corporation did not come under fire for its mistreatment of employees based on its values, Chick-fil-A also agreed to amend an official company document called "Chick-fil-A: Who We Are" to state that the company will "treat every person with honor, dignity and respect—regardless of their beliefs, race, creed, sexual orientation and gender."[65]

Subtle Forms of Discrimination

An article published in *Forbes* in late 2009 states that despite significant advancements in discrimination labor laws, discrimination still persists.[66] The researchers claim that people categorize others based on warmth and competence. They describe how such categorization works as follows: "Warmth is a matter of positive or negative intentions. Another person is either friend or foe, with you or against you. Competence involves that person's effectiveness: He or she is either capable or not of realizing those intentions."[67]

The model in Figure 4.3 has four quadrants representing high or low on each dimension. While these factors may seem unrelated to workplace discrimination, the researchers found that a person's class, race, ethnic origin, and other traits tend to determine to a large extent what others think of him or her, including perceptions of where the individual falls on the warmth and competence scales. This is a more subtle form of discrimination than overtly denying workplace recognition or advancement based on race, class, or gender. It is particularly insidious due to its largely invisible nature—the article notes that many people who discriminate against colleagues are unaware they are doing so.

Figure 4.3   The Warmth and Competence Scale

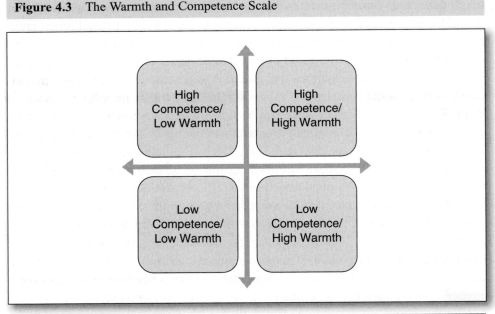

Source: Adapted from Morris, M., & Fiske, S. (2009, November 12). "The new face of workplace discrimination." *Forbes.* Retrieved March 5, 2015, from http://www.forbes.com/2009/11/12/discrimination-workplace-prejudice-leadership-managing-bias.html.

Additionally, such discrimination occurs not only in major events such as promotions or salary increases. Instead, the authors argue, it "occurs in everyday activities such as task assignments, informal mentoring and performance appraisals."[68] As noted in *Forbes*, Laura Liswood, a senior adviser to Goldman Sachs, conducted focus groups of finance-industry professionals, with each group including a mix of white men, white women, nonwhite men, and nonwhite women. The white men included in the study tended to believe their firms were meritocracies, while members of all the other participating groups cited various kinds of discrimination they had experienced firsthand or observed occurring toward others.[69]

As for the question of why the white men had failed to notice the discriminatory practices cited by the other participants, Liswood says the results show that those who thrive in a workplace where subtle inequities exist tend not to notice that they are advantaged.[70] What are the implications of this? As stated in the article, "when diversity efforts focus exclusively on recruiting, the result is too often that the firm hires people because they are different but then fails to promote them—precisely because they are the not the same."[71]

LABOR ISSUES IN THE SUPPLY CHAIN

Whereas internal labor issues such as discrimination are complex on their own, labor issues that exist along a company's supply chain are in many ways more difficult to control given corporations' limited purview over external organizations. Transparency is an important tool in managing such issues, as it "can provoke learning and also positive institutional change by empowering private watchdogs to monitor and pressure business leaders to alter harmful behavior."[72] Both Nike and Levi's started out being resistant to enhancing supply chain transparency but eventually grew to become industry leaders in factory disclosure, first publishing their global supplier lists in 2005.[73] The disclosure of supply chain information such as the identity of corporations' suppliers is a powerful piece of the CR puzzle, as factory disclosure enables stakeholders such as NGOs, unions, journalists, and academics to access information about a corporation's supply chain practices and use the information to target the brands in negative campaigns.[74] As a result, corporations who hope to limit the ability of such antagonists to damage their brands should have deep incentives to keep close tabs on the activities along their supply chains and take a proactive approach to addressing concerns before external forces get hold of negative information.

In the case of Nike, the company's shift toward greater supply chain transparency came after journalists, including filmmaker Michael Moore and author Naomi Klein, brought greater attention to Nike's labor practices during the 1990s.

In particular, Nike came under fire over the discovery that its overseas factories were using child labor, violating minimum wage and overtime laws, and fostering poor working conditions for employees.

To date, only a handful of corporations have adopted factory disclosure, but those who have understand it to be a CR strategy that enables them to deflect criticism about supply chain labor practices. In a world where consumers have increased transparency into corporate activity and heightened expectations of corporate behavior, consumers see a company's willingness to disclose its factory information as a signal that it has nothing to hide.[75]

In recent years, there has been an increased focus on eliminating coerced labor and child labor. Supply chain transparency is necessary to ensure that corporations are meeting such goals globally. While factory disclosure has had limited success in terms of broad adoption by corporations, many global corporations report to some extent on their supply chain labor practices. Three examples of companies that disclose aspects of these practices include HP, Nokia, and Cargill. Since launching its supply chain audit program in 2011, HP has performed over 760 supplier audits to ensure that suppliers meet company standards.[76] Nokia, meanwhile, states its labor-practice goals on its Nokia website, along with the steps the company takes to meet them throughout its supply chain:

> It is extremely important to Nokia that labor conditions at all our production sites meet recognized international standards. Each of our sites must comply with our global employment guidelines. We assess their performance regularly and those of our suppliers. . . . to improve management of working conditions at factories, we developed the Nokia Labor Conditions Standard in 2006. It is based on International Labor Organization and UN Human Rights conventions, and has been benchmarked against international labor laws and standards.[77]

In addition, Cargill, despite its previously discussed discrimination allegations, has exhibited responsible behavior in terms of its supply-chain transparency.[78] The corporation has taken a hard stance on coerced and other illegal labor, and includes information about how it has sought to crack down on these issues in different markets around the world.

Beyond its commitment to factory disclosure, Nike, a corporation with a checkered past regarding labor issue allegations, started a supply chain audit program internally, and has also collaborated with human rights groups to found an external inspection agency. By working with external partners, Nike has gained credibility as an organization that seeks to be socially responsible.[79] Additionally, when issues do arise along Nike's supply chain, the complaints are directed to the company, allowing Nike to investigate and address concerns. Contrast this with the early CR cases discussed in Chapter 1, in which NGOs and other external bodies would draw attention to issues and companies had no choice but to react. In Nike's case, the corporation is able to take a proactive approach to dealing with CR crises.

Nike's program involves a staff of 97 who inspect several hundred factories each year. In these inspections, the inspectors grade the factories on labor standards and work with managers to address problems. Nike also allows the FLA to conduct factory inspections at random.[80]

Another recent example of a supply chain issue that has negatively affected the public perception of a popular corporation is the 2011 explosion at the Foxconn factory in Chengdu, China—a major manufacturer of iPads for Apple.[81] Between this incident and an explosion at another factory, four workers were killed and 77 wounded within a seven-month period. In the case of the Chengdu explosion, a Chinese organization had inspected the plant and alerted Apple to concerns about hazardous conditions.[82] Nicholas Ashford, former chairman of the National Advisory Committee on Occupational Safety and Health, highlights one of the most troubling implications of this situation: "If Apple was warned, and didn't act, that's reprehensible. But what's morally repugnant in one country is accepted business practices in another, and companies take advantage of that."[83]

Apple publishes an annual report on its suppliers' compliance with Apple's Supplier Code of Conduct. The code includes labor rights, health and safety precautions, and ethics, and while details are provided on suppliers' results in each area, many of the rules are not adhered to by factories.[84] More than half of Apple's manufacturing facilities have had at least one violation each year since 2007.[85] Past violations include the following:

- **Discrimination:** In 2011, 18 of Apple's factories screened potential employees for hepatitis B, while 24 gave their employees pregnancy tests
- **Labor rules:** The Code of Conduct stipulates that employees should not work more than 60 hours a week; however, in 2011, there were 93 facilities where more than half of all employees exceeded the limit.
- **Health and safety:** In 2009, 137 workers were injured while using the toxic chemical n-hexane to clean iPhone screens.
- **Management:** Apple requires its suppliers to establish management systems that ensure compliance with the Code of Conduct; however, fewer than 70% of suppliers were found to have such systems in place.

In the aftermath of the situation, Apple and Foxconn agreed to address the working condition violations affecting 1.2 million workers assembling iPhones and iPads.[86] Beyond the immediate impact on Apple and its suppliers, the decision has the potential to affect how Western companies do business in China.[87]

THE SCOPE OF HUMAN RIGHTS RESPONSIBILITY

A key issue for corporations grappling with their role in human rights issues is determining where the corporation's responsibility begins and ends. The first two principles of the United Nations Global Compact address human rights issues:

- Principle 1: Businesses should support and respect the protection of internationally proclaimed human rights; and
- Principle 2: make sure that they are not complicit in human rights abuses.[88]

There are increasing expectations around human rights, from many different stakeholders. NGOs are paying attention to the impact of company actions and forming influential coalitions to campaign for accountability. Consumers are considering corporations' involvement in human rights issues when making purchasing decisions. Meanwhile, employees and prospective employees place value on working for corporations with favorable records on human rights issues. Investors seek to invest in companies that are less likely to become entangled in a crisis, while more and more financial institutions are beginning to apply social and environmental criteria to their investments. The Forum for Sustainable and Responsible Investment, a U.S. organization, provides resources for member individuals and organizations who are committed to advancing investment practices that consider ESG factors rather than simply financial returns. The organization describes its vision as "a world in which investment capital helps build a sustainable and equitable economy."[89]

Governments are also invested in the conversation around human rights violations at companies, and more are embarking on ways to encourage companies to address human rights.[90] This is especially important given that transnational corporations often violate human rights (as seen in the case of Nike) by providing below-subsistence wages, unsafe working conditions, and harmful environmental pollution; engaging in bribery; harming indigenous populations; and ignoring host nations' laws.[91]

The *ICCA Handbook of Corporate Responsibility* states:

The focus on business and human rights is here to stay. Never before have development, environmental and civil/political rights organizations joined together with such determination on a single issue—not just international organizations, but also national and local grassroots groups.[92]

While some may argue that responsibility for human rights issues should lie solely with governments, corporations have a responsibility to ensure that the rights assured by governmental bodies are granted to their constituents.[93] According to the *ICCA Handbook*:

> Human rights are rooted in law. Respecting and protecting them was never meant to be an optional extra, a matter of choice. It is expected and required. It should be part of the mainstream of any company's strategy, not only seen as part of its corporate social responsibility strategy.[94]

Sir Geoffrey Chandler, the founding chair of Amnesty International UK Business Group and former director of Shell International, stated that failure to speak out on issues can often equal tacit complicity: "Silence or inaction will be seen to provide comfort to oppression. . . . Silence is not neutrality. To do nothing is not an option."[95]

There is pressure on corporations not merely to take action, but to take substantive action; companies that address human rights as a PR issue meet with skepticism from constituents.[96] Beyond reputational risk, there are other consequences for corporations that choose to ignore human rights issues, including legal action, protests, shareholder action, and consumer boycotts.[97] Meanwhile, companies stand to benefit from taking a proactive stance on human rights.[98] An environment in which human rights are protected is clearly better for business than one in which widespread abuses take place; the rule of law is important for business investments and operations around the world.

What are some of the benefits of taking a proactive corporate approach to human rights issues? Enhanced corporate reputation is one, along with the opportunity to make the corporation's license to operate more secure. Corporations that care about human rights can also expect to see improvements in employee recruitment and retention as well as morale. Improved stakeholder relations overall is a compelling reason for corporations to protect human rights. It is obvious that there is a business case for attention to human rights concerns; however, this does not mean that business benefits should be necessary for corporations to want to respect human rights.[99] The *ICCA Handbook* argues that the case for companies taking a proactive stance on human rights demonstrates the clear need for the adoption of a set of principles that would act as a minimum human rights floor.[100]

Creating and adopting a set of minimum human rights standards is easier said than done, however. Currently, the United Nations Global Compact is the predominant set of standards applied to corporate behavior regarding human rights. While the Global Compact is helpful in terms of setting guidelines, there are several factors that limit its effectiveness and make it difficult for companies to uphold:

- Lack of definitional clarity on key concepts such as "sphere of influence" and "complicity" in human rights abuses
- Lack of clarity on the distinct duties of corporations and other business enterprises as opposed to nation states
- Limited guidance regarding how to measure and report on compliance with the principles
- Lack of penalties for failing to adhere to the principles beyond being delisted for failing to file annual reports

The UN, aware of the Global Compact's limitations, created a Sub-Commission on the Promotion and Protection of Human Rights to explore the role of corporations in human rights.[101] In 2003, the Sub-Commission presented a report on "Norms on the Responsibilities of Transnational Corporations and Other Business Enterprises With Regard to Human Rights," which was endorsed by NGOs such as Amnesty International, Human Rights Watch, and the Prince of Wales International Business Leaders Forum. At the same time, the report was harshly criticized by business organizations including the International Chamber of Commerce, International Organization of Employers, and U.S. Council for International Business.[102]

The Norms established by the Sub-Commission on the Promotion and Protection of Human Rights have three characteristics that distinguish them from previous codes of conduct, and specific challenges and issues come with each, as seen in Table 4.1.[103]

The confusing nature of the third issue blurs the line between voluntary and legal actions and makes compliance virtually impossible for corporations.[104] Because of these challenges, the UN Commission on Human Rights chose not to endorse the Norms. Instead, the UN in 2005 appointed a Special Representative to the Secretary General (SRSG) on the Issue of Human Rights and Transnational Corporations and Other Business Enterprises.[105] The Representative, John Ruggie, published the tripartite framework of the duties of transnational corporations (TNCs) and national governments regarding human rights in 2008. The three elements of this framework are as follows: (1) states have a primary duty to protect against human rights abuses by third parties (including TNCs), (2) TNCs and other businesses have a duty to respect human rights, and (3) access to remedy must be made available to victims of human rights abuses. This framework was endorsed by the Human Rights Council.[106]

The framework, while a step in the right direction, is not sustainable. There is no clear distinction between duty and responsibility.[107] Meanwhile, states have a moral and legal duty to protect human rights, but TNCs and businesses may only be blamed or criticized for failing to respect human rights.[108] Many TNCs operate

Table 4.1   Three distinguishing characteristics of the Norms established by the Sub-Commission on the Promotion and Protection of Human Rights and their accompanying challenges

Differentiating Factor	*Challenges*
The Norms unify and integrate principles and codes of conduct previously adopted by organizations, including the Organisation for Economic Co-operation and Development (OECD), International Labour Organization (ILO), and World Health Organization (WHO), as well as general human rights agreements such as the UN Universal Declaration of Human Rights (1948), UN Rio Declaration on the Environment and Development, WHO Health for All Policy, and UN World Summit on Sustainable Development.	The Norms fail to differentiate between nations and corporations, which results in confusion regarding human rights duties, which undermines the integrity of the Norms and the effort to enhance human rights.
The Norms are aspirational—they identify ideals of transnational corporation (TNC) behavior rather than minimum standards.	The Norms extend far beyond issues of human rights and cover a wide range of political, social, and economic rights that should be decided by national governments (e.g., the requirement in Article 12 that TNCs contribute to "the highest attainable standard" of physical and mental health, adequate housing, and education; many developed and wealthy nations have problems providing these things).
The drafters of the Norms claim that they are nonvoluntary and are legally binding, with their evidence of this being that their implementation provisions require reporting and oversight.	Despite the claim that the Norms are "soft law" but will transition to "hard law," there is in fact no legal obligation for corporations to comply.

Source: Adapted from Arnold, D. (2010, July). "Transnational corporations and the duty to respect basic human rights" (pp. 373–375). *Business Ethics Quarterly, 3*(20).

in states that do not adequately protect human rights, and TNCs may be more readily able to do something about it, but it is not clear what TNC responsibility is in these circumstances.[109]

So is the UN Global Compact successful, along with the Norms and SRSG framework? The UN follows up with corporations that have signed onto the Global Compact to ensure compliance. The minimum participation requirement for continued membership is a "Communication on Progress" (COP), which is a report on a corporation's progress in implementing all 10 principles. The first Communication occurs 27 months after a company agrees to the compact and annually after the initial report.[110]

Based on the status of the Communications, a company could be in danger of jeopardizing its status. Missing one reporting deadline moves a corporation to "noncommunicating" status; missing two deadlines places the company in "inactive" status. A study looking at actual and predicted compliance with the reporting requirements found that roughly two-thirds of all existing Compact members have failed to meet them.[111] The report noted that, as of October 2008, only 31% (1,754) of the 5,654 Global Compact member companies were expected to be in compliance with the reporting requirements.[112] As of the 2013 Activity Report from the UN, 72% of business participants had submitted a COP demonstrating significant improvement in terms of participation.[113] However, this does not mean that all business participants were in compliance.

Human rights violations can also occur in the context of the extraction of natural resources from countries where environmental laws are lax and there is limited supervision over operations. These are mainly developing countries, as we will see from the example of Shell in Nigeria in the case at the end of this chapter. In situations where multinational corporations collaborate with unstable or corrupt governments, there are often issues with local communities not receiving their fair share of the wealth created by corporate operations. Examples of this are the mining industry in South and Central America and oil drilling in the Gulf of Mexico.

Another major concern is human rights violations by local governments and military personnel in the name of conserving business interests. ExxonMobil was sued by Indonesian villagers who claimed that the company enabled the commission of murder, torture, and sexual assault by its security forces in Indonesia's Aceh province.[114] ExxonMobil was initially able to have the case thrown out by a trial judge on the grounds that the villagers were not allowed to use U.S. courts to sue over alleged actions that took place in Indonesia and involved the Indonesian military during a period of martial law. Later, however, the U.S. Court of Appeals in Washington reinstated the suit, stating that the corporation did not have corporate immunity from claims filed by the Indonesian villagers under the Alien Tort Statute.[115] The abuse was committed by an Indonesian military unit dedicated only to Exxon's Aceh facility and under the company's direction and control.

The ruling in the Exxon case was "at odds with a landmark ruling last September by the federal appeals court in New York, raising the prospect that the U.S. Supreme Court could try to resolve the dispute."[116] This case could have had huge implications for multinationals if the Supreme Court determined that they can be sued for human rights violations in U.S. courts.

However, in April 2012, the court ruled that corporations cannot be held liable under the Torture Victim Protection Act.[117] Then in April 2013, the U.S. Supreme Court ruled in favor of ExxonMobil, "stating that a US federal law, the Alien Tort Statute, could not be used to hold corporations liable for abuses committed on foreign soil."[118] This was a major win for multinationals, but at the moment it's unclear how this will affect the ExxonMobil case. Another example of governmental human rights violations in the name of preserving business interests is Shell in Nigeria, which will be discussed in more detail at the end of this chapter.

The violation of free-speech "rights"—which are not considered rights in many countries around the world—is also an issue that arises when discussing basic human rights. With the advent of new technology and social media in particular, it has grown increasingly difficult for governments that monitor or forbid free speech to prevent their constituents from speaking out on human rights violations, as people around the world have been successful in using technology to advance democracy. Two examples of how technology is changing the face of human rights protests are the role of social networks in the Arab Spring, and the tool created by a pro-democracy group for analyzing election results and detecting fraud in an Afghani presidential election.[119] These are cases of organizations and individuals making use of available technology. A key question is whether corporations have a responsibility to provide access. Do technology companies have a "duty" to their users, particularly those in countries that restrict communication about controversial issues?

Both Yahoo and Google, as well as other technology companies, have come under fire over censorship in China. In 2004, Yahoo provided the Chinese government access to email accounts belonging to opposition leaders and others.[120] As a result, journalist Shi Tao was sentenced to 10 years in jail. Yahoo's Hong Kong subsidiary was sued for this, but the court did not find it responsible.

> Hong Kong's privacy commission said there was "insufficient evidence" to hold Yahoo Hong Kong liable under the local privacy regulations. The ruling can be appealed. Yahoo and Google have been criticized for cooperating with officials in China on Internet censorship efforts but Yahoo has been singled out for providing information that helped officials convict Chinese journalist Shi Tao.[121]

CONCLUSION

Corporate responsibility in the realm of human rights and labor issues has grown increasingly complex with increased globalization. Corporations must not only address easily identifiable and quantifiable wrongs such as pay discrepancies, but also pay attention to hidden, insidious forms of workplace discrimination. Despite lax human rights laws in certain countries, corporations have a responsibility to ensure that their labor practices abroad reflect corporate ethics as practiced in their home countries. Advancements in technology continue to make it easier for corporations to be held accountable for their human rights practices worldwide.

NOTES

1. Holzinger, M., Richter, K., & Thomsen, D. (2006). "A company's social side" (p. 310). In J. Hennigfeld, M. Pohl, & N. Tohurst (Eds.), *ICCA handbook on corporate social responsibility.* Hoboken, NJ: John Wiley.

2. Ibid., p. 69.

3. Ibid.

4. Ibid., p. 309.

5. Ibid., p. 329.

6. Kotler, P., & Lee, N. (2005). *Corporate social responsibility: Doing the most good for your company and your cause* (p. 208). Hoboken, NJ: John Wiley.

7. Ibid., p. 208.

8. Ibid.

9. Ibid.

10. Edelman. (2012). "2012 Edelman goodpurpose study." Retrieved July 13, 2014, from http://purpose.edelman.com/

11. Ibid.

12. Nidumolu, R., Prahalad, C. K., & Rangaswami, M. R. (2009, September). "Why sustainability is now the key driver of innovation" (p. 64). *Harvard Business Review.*

13. Kotler & Lee, *Corporate social responsibility*, p. 209.

14. Ibid.

15. Ibid., p. 209.

16. Stonyfield Organic, http://www.stonyfield.com (accessed July 24, 2014).

17. Ibid., p. 211.

18. Ibid., p. 221.

19. Ibid., p. 222.

20. Ibid., p. 222.

21. United Nations Global Compact. (n.d.). "The ten principles." Retrieved March 1, 2015, from https://www.unglobalcompact.org/AboutTheGC/TheTenPrinciples/index.html

22. International Labour Organization. (n.d.). "ILO Declaration on Fundamental Principles and Rights at Work." Retrieved July 24, 2014, from http://www.ilo.org/declaration/lang--en/index.htm

23. Hemphill, T. (2004, Summer). "Monitoring global corporate citizenship: Industry self-regulation at a crossroads." *Journal of Corporate Citizenship, 14,* 89.

24. Jonker, J., & de Witte, M. (2006). *Management models for corporate social responsibility* (p. 180). Springer.

25. Ibid.

26. Hemphill, "Monitoring global corporate citizenship," pp. 85–86.

27. Jonker & de Witte, "Management models for corporate social responsibility," p. 185.

28. Ibid., p. 86.

29. Ibid., p. 90.

30. Ibid.

31. Ibid., p. 91.

32. Ibid., p. 90.

33. Ibid., p. 185.

34. U.S. Equal Employment Opportunity Commission. (n.d.). "Charge statistics: FY 1997 through FY 2014." Retrieved July 24, 2014, from http://www.eeoc.gov/eeoc/statistics/enforce ment/charges.cfm

35. "Women matter: Gender diversity, a corporate performance driver." (2013). McKinsey & Company. Retrieved July 24, 2014, from http://www.mckinsey.com/Features/Women_Matter

36. "The bottom line: Corporate performance and women's representation on boards." Catalyst. Retrieved August 3, 2014, from http://www.catalyst.org/file/139/bottom%20 line%202.pdf

37. McCarthy, T. (2012, March 8). "Women make gains in boardrooms worldwide, but US still lags behind." Retrieved July 24, 2014, from http://www.guardian.co.uk/society/2012/mar/08/ equality-usa

38. Ibid.

39. Ibid.

40. Ibid.

41. Ibid.

42. "MEPs back quotas to get more women in boardrooms." (2012, March 14). *EurActive. com.* Retrieved July 24, 2014, from http://www.euractiv.com/socialeurope/meps-back-quotas-get-women-board-news-511501

43. Ibid.

44. Ibid.

45. Nuss, J. (2011, November 29). "US Labor Dept. alleges discrimination by Cargill." *Associated Press.* Retrieved July 24, 2014, from http://www.businessweek.com/ap/financialnews/ D9RAK7483.htm

46. Ibid.

47. Liptak, A. (2011, June 20). "Justices rule for Wal-Mart in class-action bias case." *New York Times.* Retrieved July 24, 2014, from http://www.nytimes.com/2011/06/21/business/21bizcourt .html?pagewanted=all

48. Ibid.

49. Martin, A. (2011, October 27). "Female Wal-Mart employees file new bias case." *New York Times.* Retrieved July 24, 2014, from http://www.nytimes.com/2011/10/28/business/women-file-new-class-action-bias-case-against-wal-mart.html

50. GfK Mediamark Research & Intelligence. (2011). "The survey of the American consumer." Author.

51. U.S. Equal Opportunity Commission. (n.d.). "Race-based charges: FY 1997–FY 2014." Retrieved July 24, 2014, from http://www.eeoc.gov/eeoc/statistics/enforcement/race.cfm

52. Winter, G. (2000, November 17). "Coca-Cola settles racial bias case." *New York Times*.

53. Ibid.

54. Marzulli, J. (2012, March 16). "Coke's not it: 16 workers sue, call giant 'cesspool' of racial discrimination." *New York Daily News*.

55. Greenwald, J. (2012, March 20). "Coca-Cola unit sued for alleged racial discrimination." *Workforce*. Retrieved July 24, 2014, from http://www.workforce.com/articles/coca-cola-unit -sued-for-alleged-racial-discrimination

56. Koerth-Baker, M. (2012, July 23). "Eagle Scouts stand up to the Boy Scouts of America." *Boing Boing* (blog). Retrieved July 24, 2014, from http://boingboing.net/2012/07/23/eagle-scouts -stand-up-to-the-b.html

57. Eckholm, E. (2012, July 17). "Boy Scouts to continue excluding gay people." *New York Times*.

58. Koerth-Baker, "Eagle Scouts stand up to the Boy Scouts of America."

59. Ibid.

60. Ibid.

61. Equality Matters, http://equalitymatters.org/factcheck/201207020001 (accessed July 24, 2014).

62. Hsu, T. (2012, September 19). "Chick-fil-A promises to stop giving money to anti-gay groups." *Los Angeles Times*. Retrieved July 24, 2014, from http://articles.latimes.com/2012/ sep/19/business/la-fi-mo-chickfila-gay-moreno-20120919

63. Hsu, T. (2012, July 18). "Is Chick-fil-A anti-gay marriage? 'Guilty as charged,' leader says. *Los Angeles Times*. Retrieved July 24, 2014, from http://articles.latimes.com/2012/jul/18/ business/la-fi-mo-chick-fil-a-gay-20120718

64. Hsu, "Chick-fil-A promises to stop giving money to anti-gay groups."

65. "Chick-fil-A: Who we are." (2012, August 15). Retrieved March 2015 from http://media .chick-fil-a.com/Media/pdf/who-we-are.pdf

66. Morris, M., & Fiske, S. (2009, November 12). "The new face of workplace discrimination." *Forbes*. Retrieved July 24, 2014, from http://www.forbes.com/2009/11/12/discrimination -workplace-prejudice-leadership-managing-bias.html

67. Ibid.

68. Ibid.

69. Ibid.

70. Ibid.

71. Ibid.

72. Doorey, D. J. (2011, May 19). "The transparent supply chain: From resistance to implementation at Nike and Levi-Strauss." *Journal of Business Ethics*.

73. Ibid., p. 1.

74. Ibid., p. 3.

75. Ibid.

76. HP. (n.d.) "About supply chain responsibility." Retrieved July 24, 2014, from http://www.hp.com/hpinfo/globalcitizenship/society/supplychain.html

77. https://networks.nokia.com/

78. Cargill. (n.d.). "Responsible supply chains in action: Ensuring responsible labor practices." Retrieved July 24, 2014, from http://www.cargill.com/corporate-responsibility/responsible-supply-chains/responsible-labor/index.jsp

79. Bernstein, A. (2004, September). "Nike's new game plan for sweatshops." *BusinessWeek.* Retrieved July 24, 2014, from http://www.businessweek.com/stories/2004-09-19/online-extra-nikes-new-game-plan-for-sweatshops

80. Ibid.

81. Duhigg, C., & Barboza, D. (2012, January 25). "NYT: In China, human costs are built into an iPad." Retrieved July 24, 2014, from http://www.nytimes.com/2012/01/26/business/ieconomy-apples-ipad-and-the-human-costs-for-workers-in-china.html?_r=1&pagewanted=all

82. Ibid.

83. Ibid.

84. "Compliance by the numbers." (n.d.). *New York Times.* Retrieved July 24, 2014, from http://www.nytimes.com/interactive/2012/01/26/business/apple-suppliers-compliance-by-the-numbers.html?ref=business

85. Duhigg, "NYT: In China, human costs are built into an iPad."

86. Gupta, P., & Chan, E. (2012, March 30). "Reuters: Apple, Foxconn set new standard for Chinese workers." Retrieved July 24, 2014, from http://www.reuters.com/article/2012/03/30/us-apple-foxconn-idUSBRE82S19720120330

87. Ibid.

88. United Nations Global Compact, "The ten principles."

89. USSIF, http://ussif.org/ (accessed July 24, 2014).

90. Holzinger et al., "A company's social side."

91. Arnold, D. (2010, July). "Transnational corporations and the duty to respect basic human rights" (pp. 371). *Business Ethics Quarterly, 3*(20).

92. Hennigfeld et al., *ICCA handbook on corporate social responsibility.*

93. Ibid., p. 71.

94. Ibid., p. 71.

95. Ibid., p. 74.

96. Ibid., p. 75.

97. Ibid.

98. Ibid., p. 77.

99. Ibid., p. 77.

100. Ibid., p. 79.

101. Arnold, D. (2010, July). "Transnational corporations and the duty to respect basic human rights" (p. 373). *Business Ethics Quarterly, 3*(20).

102. Ibid.

103. Ibid.

104. Ibid., p. 375.

105. Ibid., p. 376.

106. Ibid., p. 377.

107. Ibid., p. 378.

108. Ibid., p. 378.

109. Ibid., pp. 380–381.

110. Barkemeyer, R., & Napolitano, G. (2009). "The UN global compact: Moving towards a critical mass or a critical state?" *Academy of Management Proceedings.*

111. Ibid., p. 3.

112. Ibid., p. 4.

113. United Nations Global Compact. (2014, May). "Activity report." Retrieved July 24, 2014, from http://www.unglobalcompact.org/docs/about_the_gc/ActivityReport-2013-web.pdf

114. Exxon Mobil to face Indonesia human rights suit, court says. (2011, July 8). *Bloomberg News.* Retrieved July 24, 2014, from http://www.bloomberg.com/news/2011-07-08/exxon-mobil-to-face-indonesia-human-rights-claims-court-rules.html

115. Ibid.

116. Mears, B. (2011, July 8). "Exxon Mobil to face lawsuit over alleged human rights violations." *CNN.* Retrieved July 24, 2014, from http://articles.cnn.com/2011-07-08/justice/exxon.mobil.lawsuit_1_claim-immunity-face-lawsuit-aceh?_s=PM:CRIME

117. "Supreme Court: No liability for organizations under Torture Victims Protection Act." (2012, April 18). *DC Circuit Review.* Retrieved July 24, 2014, from http://dccircuitreview.com/2012/04/18/supreme-court-no-liability-for-organizations-under-torture-victims-protection-act/#more-1193

118. Schonhardt, S. (2013, April 26). "Indonesians sue ExxonMobil in US court." Retrieved July 24, 2014, from http://www.globalpost.com/dispatch/news/regions/asia-pacific/indonesia/130424/aceh-exxonmobil-us-court-human-rights-abuses?page=0,2

119. "ICT at work: Afghanistan election mapping and Uganda Citizen Hotline." Retrieved July 24, 2014.

120. Mills, E. (2007, March 14). "Yahoo wins ruling in China censorship case." Retrieved July 24, 2014, from http://www.cnet.com/news/yahoo-wins-ruling-in-china-censorship-case/

121. Ibid.

ROYAL DUTCH/SHELL GROUP: BRENT SPAR AND NIGERIA

Shell companies should endeavor always to act commercially, operating within existing national laws in a socially responsible manner and avoid involvement in politics.

—Shell's Business Principles, est. 1976

In 1995, the Royal Dutch/Shell Group found itself in the midst of two crises in which the petroleum-products company was targeted by international protest and the threat of boycotts. The first crisis had sprung from Shell UK's proposed action to dispose of the Brent Spar, an enormous superannuated oil storage and loading platform, in the deep waters of the North Atlantic. The second resulted from Shell's failure to take a public stance against the Nigerian government, Shell's local business partner, when the government executed nine environmentalists in the Ogoni region, including internationally renowned journalist Ken Saro-Wiwa.

Both crises forced the company to rethink its approach to its social and environmental responsibilities.[1] Instead of continuing along a path of economic development with minimal regard for social and environmental impact, Shell began working toward sustainable development, taking into account environmental well-being. The company used the crises as an opportunity to engage stakeholders and increase transparency into its social and environmental practices.

THE BRENT SPAR—"BEST PRACTICE ENVIRONMENTAL OPTION" OR "TOXIC TIME BOMB"?

In 1992, Shell UK made the decision to dispose of the Brent Spar, an oil storage buoy that had been used to hold oil for tankers, since it was no longer needed following the construction of an oil pipeline that had become operational in 1989.[2] By 1995, Shell had identified four possible options for the disposal of the Brent Spar and commissioned 30 studies to determine the technical, safety, and environmental implications of each. The options were (1) on-land disposal, (2) sinking the buoy at its current location in British territorial waters, (3) decomposition of the buoy on the spot, and (4) deep-sea dumping within UK territorial waters.[3]

Shell selected the fourth option based on the relatively low cost and environmental impact. The company decided to dispose of the Brent Spar in the Atlantic Ocean at North

---

Source: This case was written by Dafna Eshet, T'12, under the supervision of Professor Paul A. Argenti at the Tuck School of Business at Dartmouth. This case was prepared with publicly available information. © 2014 Trustees of Dartmouth College. All rights reserved.

Feni Ridge, near the west coast of Scotland, in waters approximately 2.5 kilometers deep. The UK government approved the disposal plan, but before the disposal could occur, a group of activists from environmentalist NGO Greenpeace, along with journalists, occupied the Brent Spar on April 30, 1995. The protestors chained themselves to the buoy, and a Shell team removed them. The media latched onto the story, with Greenpeace activists being portrayed positively as defenders of the environment.

In June 1995, the countries bordering the North Sea participated in the North Sea Protection Conference, at which all but the UK and Norway condemned Shell's proposed plan for the Brent Spar. Later that month, Greenpeace activists once again occupied the Brent Spar. This time, Shell dispatched a tugboat to spray the activists with water to prevent them from boarding the buoy. Photographs of the protestors being blasted with water were printed on newspaper covers around the world. Greenpeace also began to question the accuracy of Shell's findings that the disposal plan would have limited environmental impact.

The negative publicity and public protests eventually led several European heads of state to criticize not only Shell, but also the British government, which had approved Shell's proposal. While the company was initially resistant to criticism, by the end of June 1995 Shell had agreed to rethink its plans for the Brent Spar.[4]

Greenpeace alleged that the Brent Spar was nothing less than a "toxic time bomb" with dangerous chemical residues and radioactive wastes in its storage tanks and a platform "laden with toxic cocktails."[5] The NGO accused Shell of "contempt for public concern about its operations, fishermen's livelihoods and for the health of the North Sea" and of hiding behind a "veil of secrecy."[6]

Greenpeace also alleged that Shell's decision to dispose of the Spar was purely motivated by profit, with little concern for the environmental impact.[7] Similarly, Greenpeace attacked the British government for what the NGO saw as the latest in a string of incidents in which governments had allowed corporations to "treat the seas as a toxic dump."[8] The media quickly latched onto Greenpeace's charges against both institutions, leading to ugly headlines such as "Murder at Sea."[9]

Meanwhile, at Shell UK, director of public affairs and planning John Wybrew defended the Spar plan, arguing that the case for deepwater disposal had been sound and that ocean dumping represented the "Best Practice Environmental Option" (BPEO).[10] Shell had concluded that sinking the Spar would have a negligible impact on the marine environment, whereas the safety risks of onshore disposal would be six times higher.[11] Wybrew pointed out that Shell's assessment of the disposal options had been supported by a variety of stakeholders, including independent experts and oceanographers, environmentalists, conservationists, and fishermen, and criticized both Greenpeace for spreading misinformation and the media for accepting Greenpeace's biased accounts as fact.[12] Because Shell had done its homework, Wybrew believed that Greenpeace's exaggerated account of the situation would eventually be discredited, with the misinformation spread by the NGO being publicly revealed as such and Shell's good name restored.

Although Shell was confident that it had both accurately represented and appropriately handled the Spar situation, Wybrew still saw a valuable lesson in the negative publicity—namely, that, in approaching CR issues, corporations would need to contend with "deep-seated emotions, subconscious instincts, and symbolic gestures" in addition to rational arguments.[13] The company felt that it had acted appropriately in terms of the science behind its decision but had failed to adequately deliver on the emotional expectations of stakeholders. Yet Shell believed that Greenpeace's messages would ultimately be discredited and the media chastened.[14] Accordingly, the company's goal was to assert greater control over the conversation around the crisis to advance its own version of the truth.

Meanwhile, Greenpeace sought for Shell not only to pay for the cleanup but also to begin accounting for its full cost of doing business, including the impact of its practices on the environment, instead of leaving the public to "pay . . . for the aftermath."[15] According to Greenpeace, it "took action against Shell based on a simple principle: the ocean is not a dumping ground."[16] Greenpeace's actions were part of a larger campaign designed to protect the ocean environment, which the NGO had been running since the 1970s. Brent Spar was but one example of how Greenpeace spent many years confronting corporations and governments with the goal of convincing them to take a more responsible approach in their dealings with the marine environment.[17]

In line with Wybrew's realization that the conversation around CR issues often involves murky emotional issues in addition to hard facts, Greenpeace eventually admitted that some of its "facts" had been inaccurate—but the picture it had painted of fishermen and marine life struggling against a major petroleum company had lasting effects. The crisis at Shell came to represent the environmental and political issues associated with the oil industry, which was perceived as risky and unsustainable.[18]

SHELL IN NIGERIA

As Shell UK continued trying to resolve the Brent Spar crisis, Shell Nigeria was grappling with its own catastrophe, one that highlighted issues of environmentalism in the nonindustrialized world and sociopolitical tensions between developed and developing nations.[19] Because oil and gas corporations operate heavily in developing countries, the crisis in Nigeria arguably represented even more of a fundamental threat to Shell's identity and social license to operate than the Brent Spar situation.[20]

Shell was the biggest oil producer in Nigeria and operated as a joint venture with the Nigerian government through its local subsidiary, Shell Petroleum Development Company of Nigeria (SPDC). In 1995, SPDC represented roughly 14% of Shell's total oil production worldwide, and the Nigerian government derived 80% of its federal revenues and 90% of its foreign exchange from royalties and taxes provided by multinational oil companies.[21] Meanwhile, ethnic minority communities living in the Niger Delta, where much of the oil was produced, received almost no share of revenues.

Because of weak environmental regulation, such communities, who relied heavily on fishing and farming, suffered severe ecological and health consequences from oil production. Between 1982 and 1992, 40% of Shell's total spills worldwide occurred in Nigeria.[22] Meanwhile, a dangerous practice called flaring, in which gas by-products from oil drilling are burned off in the open air, caused catastrophic environmental pollution in Nigeria and also contributed to global warming.[23] Finally, oil spills and exploration in Nigeria threatened one of the largest and most ecologically sensitive wetlands in the world.[24]

The Ogoni and Ogoniland

The Ogoni were one of the ethnic minority groups living in the Niger Delta. Journalist and poet Ken Saro-Wiwa considered the land to be the Ogoni's "ultimate heritage," from which the people derived both their sustenance and their identity. In the local languages, the words for the land and the people are indistinct from one another.[25] Beginning in the early 1990s, Ogoni activists and Delta tribal chiefs had documented the ill effects of oil company activity in the region, which were reported in the African media.

The Movement for the Survival of the Ogoni People (MOSOP), an Ogoni-based NGO, attacked Shell, accusing the corporation of offenses including "heartless exploitation" of the region,[26] "ecological war,"[27] and complicity in the "extinction" of the Ogoni people.[28] Saro-Wiwa believed that the Ogoni problem represented "the root of the Nigerian malaise and must be rooted out if coming generations are to find peace and progress. The union between international capitalist and local oppressors which denigrates our people must now be broken."[29] The relationship between Shell and Nigerians was especially dangerous in his mind because it made some Nigerians their brothers' oppressors.

MOSOP estimated that $30 billion of oil had been pumped from Ogoni territories by 1990, while the Ogoni people were seeing none of this wealth themselves.[30] "Black gold" had destroyed their environment and become "a curse for them while feeding others fat."[31] MOSOP believed that "Ogoni deserved to control its own resources, environment, and the right to rule itself."[32] Meanwhile, because legal ownership determined the flow of the region's benefits, the Ogoni saw little of the gains from the exploitation of their resources.

Greenpeace also equated Ogoni suffering with international capital, characterizing the situation in Nigeria as exposing the need for "proper policing" of Big Oil in the developing world.[33] The NGO also identified "the brutality waged upon the Ogoni . . . [as] a byproduct of society's increasing consumption of natural resources" and argued that Ogoniland demonstrated in "microcosm . . . what we are doing to the entire earth—just less visibly."[34]

The Execution of Saro-Wiwa and Shell's Response

They are going to arrest us all and execute us. All for Shell.

—Ken Saro-Wiwa to Greenpeace[35]

In 1993, MOSOP organized a large-scale nonviolent protest against Shell and other oil companies, leading Shell to close its operations in Ogoni.[36] The Nigerian government, as Shell's partner, blamed the MOSOP leadership for local resistance.[37] In May 1994, four Ogoni leaders were killed and Saro-Wiwa arrested, accused of inciting the murders. Ultimately, Saro-Wiwa and others were tried, and he and eight other Ogonis were executed on November 10, 1995.[38]

As in the Brent Spar situation, Shell clung to the story that it had acted appropriately, claiming that it had pursued quiet diplomacy with General Sani Abacha, the Nigerian dictator. MOSOP and other NGOs, however, accused Shell of doing too little. Other institutions and individuals protesting at Shell's UK headquarters and elsewhere—including human rights and environmental organizations, church and writers' groups, and progressive corporations—held Shell accountable for the nine murders and called for boycotts of the company.

There were two major results of the negative publicity Shell received for the situation in Ogoni: (1) the increased attention to oil company operations in Nigeria led to more investigative studies, and (2) the killing of Saro-Wiwa forced Shell to pull together a high-profile public relations response. The company had no choice but to deal with both the executions and the corporation's track record of environmental transgressions in Ogoni and elsewhere. Backed into a corner, both the Royal Dutch/Shell Group and Shell Nigeria released statements about their "shock" and "sadness" over Saro-Wiwa's death.[39] At the same time, however, both institutions failed to accept full responsibility for Shell's role in the events leading up to the executions.

Instead, in 1997, Shell Nigeria released a "Brief" on the Ogoni crisis that echoed the piece written by John Wybrew following the Brent Spar crisis.[40] Similar to Wybrew's article, the Brief was defensive in tone and failed to represent a true mea culpa on behalf of the corporation. Instead of fully acknowledging the extent to which the company's dealings in the region had led to the Ogoni tragedy, Shell opted to portray itself as a victim whose misfortunes had been "unfairly used to raise the international profile" of the MOSOP campaign against the Nigerian government.[41]

Even when Shell did acknowledge environmental problems in the Brief, it downplayed the impact of corporate activities on environmental degradation. With regard to the frequency of oil spills in Nigeria, for example, the company admitted the need to upgrade its facilities; however, it blamed sabotage for most of the spills, instead of the corrosion of aging flowlines.[42] The Brief also alleged that Ogoni claims of environmental "devastation" were exaggerated.[43]

Meanwhile, Shell cited a 1995 World Bank study that considered the issue of oil pollution to be "only of moderate priority" in comparison with other poverty-related factors—including population growth, deforestation, erosion, and over-farming—that contribute to environmental deterioration.[44] It used this study to imply that oil pollution was therefore not a major cause of environmental issues in Nigeria. Furthermore, the Brief used the World Bank study, as well as a report by the World Health Organization, as evidence to dispute the connection between Shell's dangerous gas flaring practices and health issues among Nigerians.[45]

Shell also used other factors to justify its practices in Nigeria. The corporation provided as evidence of its responsible corporate citizenship reparation agreements "signed by all parties" in the aftermath of the Ogoni crisis.[46] The company cited its own willingness to discuss conflicts and revisit past agreements "where new leaders of communities emerge and want to change."[47] But, as Professor Sharon Livesey's research points out, "this argument . . . ignored the power relations implicit in institutional procedures and structures."[48] According to Human Rights Watch, the Nigerian government's lenient attitude toward oil companies allowed the companies to control the process of valuation, negotiation, and compensation.[49]

Meanwhile, Shell's own perspective was that the corporation had limited influence over the Nigerian government. Regarding human rights issues within Nigeria, Shell Nigeria's position was that it lacked the power to force the hand of the Nigerian government. Accordingly, Shell Nigeria absolved itself, to some degree, of having to answer the question of its moral obligations within the country: "What force could we apply—leaving aside the question of whether it would be right for us to do so?"[50] The chairman of the larger Shell Group, Cor Herkstroter, stated his belief that Shell's role in the country was strictly economic and commercial. Herkstroter argued that Shell lacked "license" to interfere in local politics or the sovereign mandate of government.[51]

As a result of Shell's position that its hands were tied with regard to human rights violations in Nigeria, the Ogoni people found that their demands that the company intervene on both these and environmental issues were unmet by real action on the part of Shell. While the corporation claimed to be sympathetic to the Ogoni for the injustices suffered in the region, Shell attempted to deflect blame for its role in creating these injustices, and responsibility for alleviating them, by stating that such actions were outside the company's authority. But in making such statements, Shell failed to account for the fact that the corporation was the primary source of revenues to the Nigerian government—and that the company benefited heavily from the government's decision to continue exploiting the Ogoni land and people.

Shifts in CR at Shell

While Shell initially approached both the Brent Spar and Nigeria crises with the attitude that the corporation's responsibility for the events leading up to them was limited, both incidents that occurred in 1995 eventually spurred changes in Shell Group's approach to CR—referred to internally as Shell's "Transformation."[52] Unsurprisingly, change at Shell was neither instantaneous nor embraced evenly across the organization.

John Elkington, founder of SustainAbility and possibly best known as the originator of the term "triple bottom line," who later became Shell's sustainability consultant, initially resisted the corporation's request for help. Elkington did so because he believed that many Shell executives continued to be "in denial" about the company's CR failures.[53] Interestingly, Shell believed that its reputational problems stemming from crises such as Brent Spar and Ogoni were the result of the corporation being forced to operate in a "global fishbowl."[54] In a speech at Shell's 1997 annual meeting, chairman Cor Herkstroter stated that "modern communications can quickly run local shortcomings into international issues, affecting reputation everywhere."[55] While Herkstroter seemed to view advancements in communication technology as support for his view that Shell's international reputation had been unfairly tarnished, the truth was that Shell was experiencing an important component of the way in which society's view of corporate responsibility and accountability was beginning to change.

Despite Herkstroter's attempts to minimize Shell's responsibility for social and environmental blunders, in 1996 the corporation decided to put resources into market research and stakeholder consultation designed to get a better sense of how the Shell Group was perceived by outsiders, as well as what expectations society held of Shell regarding environmental and social issues. Shell's findings seemed to finally stir the type of internal reaction necessary to advance the case for a sea change within the organization: "We looked in the mirror and we neither recognized nor liked some of what we saw. We have set about putting it right."[56]

Herkstroter, for his part, also showed signs of greater awareness on occasion. In a 1996 speech, discussing why Shell had "stumbled" in the cases of Brent Spar and Nigeria, Herkstroter described both incidents as challenges stemming from shifts in societal demands on corporations in the modern world and explained that "the institutions of global society are being reinvented" by social and technological change.[57] As a result, Shell Group had to shift its institutional approach to incidents such as Spar and Ogoni, learning how to navigate "a very fluid world . . . in which the technological and communications revolution is redefining our perceptions of reality; of authority, and of what is appropriate and what is not."[58] This was a far more nuanced view than the one Herkstroter expressed the following year at the annual meeting. Herkstroter also recognized that Shell and other companies had missed a crucial opportunity by failing to anticipate how changes in the world might affect corporate accountability, noting that where "the more traditional structures [of business and government had] failed to adapt," more-proactive groups such as NGOs had "gained an authoritative voice."[59]

Moreover, in the same speech, Herkstroter attributed this failure to Shell's "techno-logical arrogance," elaborating on this view as follows:

> Most of us at Royal Dutch/Shell come from a scientific, technological back-ground. That type of education, along with our corporate culture, teaches us that we must identify a problem, isolate it and then fix it. That sort of approach works well with a physical problem—but it is not so useful when we are faced with, say, a human rights issue. For most engineering problems there is a correct answer. For most social and political dilemmas there is a range of possible answers, almost all compromises.[60]

While Shell had attempted to respond to crises by pointing out the technical legiti-macy of its actions—insisting, as it had in both Spar and Ogoni, that the support of certain stakeholders was sufficient to justify its actions—Herkstroter now realized the importance of the less black-and-white viewpoints espoused by Greenpeace, MOSOP, and others. Herkstroter acknowledged that Shell should have engaged such outsiders: "alone we could never have reached the right approach; . . . we should have discussed [the incidents] in a more open and frank way with others in order to reach acceptable solutions."[61]

Out of both crises grew a shift in the rhetoric used by Shell to discuss social and envi-ronmental issues.[62] The incidents also affected Shell's material practices, most strikingly evident in two examples from the regions where the crises occurred. First, the Brent Spar was recycled as the base for a quay in Norway in 1999—a process that incurred twice the costs of sea disposal.[63] Meanwhile, in an abrupt departure from its earlier approach to issues in Nigeria, Shell created and publicized plans to track and report environmental problems, upgrade Nigerian facilities, reduce flaring, and minimize the impact of future exploration activities.[64] Shell Group also made changes to its organizational structure and corporate programs and policies related to CR initiatives including the environment and human rights. Perhaps most crucially, the Spar and Nigeria incidents led to greater trans-parency at Shell.

Both the Brent Spar and Ogoni crises are examples of the shift in societal expectations of corporations that has spurred increased attention to corporate responsibility. Unlike the BP Deepwater Horizon Spill in 2010, neither represented a crisis resulting from a single accident. Instead, both Brent Spar and Nigeria are examples of how, in a world that holds corporations increasingly accountable for failing to deliver on their social and environ-mental obligations, what was once considered business as usual now has the potential to turn into a CR crisis with the right media attention. The significant role of NGOs in bringing such situations to light cannot be ignored, as seen in the cases of Greenpeace with the Brent Spar incident and MOSOP in Ogoni.

Case Questions

1. Why has Shell become the subject of criticism and controversy in the UK and Nigeria? How do the CR issues in the Brent Spar case differ from those in Ogoniland?

2. How could Shell have avoided the negative publicity around the Brent Spar disposal? What lessons has Shell learned from Brent Spar?

3. During its time in Nigeria, what, if anything, should Shell have done differently?

4. How does the quotation from Shell's Business Principles at the beginning of the case relate to the company's actions in the UK and Nigeria? Can a corporation detach itself from local political and social issues related to its negative externalities?

5. As an executive at Shell in Nigeria, what would you recommend to Shell's Committee of Managing Directors regarding the death sentence for Saro-Wiwa and his codefendants? What, if anything, would you do personally about this matter?

NOTES

1. Lawrence, A. (1999). "The transformation of Shell, 1994–1999" [Online case study]. Council for Ethics in Economics. Mirvis, P. H. (2000). "Transformation at Shell: Commerce and citizenship." *Business and Society Review, 105*(1), 63–84.

2. "The Brent Spar" (Handout 22-1). Retrieved from https://training.fema.gov/EMIWeb/edu/docs/hram/Session%2022%20-%20Handout%20-%20The%20Brent%20Spar.doc

3. Ibid.

4. Anderson, A. (1997). "Media, culture and the environment." New Brunswick, NJ: Rutgers University Press; Tsoukas, H. (1999). "David and Goliath in the risk society: Making sense of the conflict between Shell and Greenpeace in the North Sea." *Organization, 6,* 499–528.

5. Knight, P. (1998). "Profits and principles: Does there have to be a choice?" [Report] (p. 41). London, UK: Royal Dutch/Shell Group; Greenpeace International. (1995, April 30). "Greenpeace occupies scrapped North Sea oil platform before it's dumped at sea" [Press release] (paragraph 12). Retrieved from https://www.greenpeace.org/[sim]comms/brent/apr30.html

6. Greenpeace International. (1995, May 13). "Shell attempts to evict Greenpeace from oil platform" [Press release] (paragraph 4). Retrieved from https://www.greenpeace.org/[sim]comms/brent/may13.html; Greenpeace International. (1995, May 14). "Shell attempts to gag the press and Greenpeace: Scottish court upholds press freedom [Press release]" (paragraph 5). Retrieved from https://www.greenpeace.org/[sim]comms/brent/may13.html

7. Greenpeace, "Shell attempts to gag the press and Greenpeace," paragraph 5.

8. Greenpeace, "Greenpeace occupies scrapped North Sea oil platform before it's dumped at sea," paragraph 7.

9. Fay, C. (1996, May 20). "Not black & white but shades of green: A business perspective on reporting the environment" [Speech] (paragraph 1).

10. Wybrew, J. (1996, January). "Brent Spar: The implications for environmental decision-making and public support" [Speech].

11. Wybrew, J. (1995, July). "Brent Spar: A 'public relations disaster'?" (paragraph 2). *Journal of the UK Institute of Public Relations*.

12. Ibid.

13. Wybrew, "Brent Spar," paragraph 5.

14. Fay, "Not black & white but shades of green"; Anderson, "Media, culture and the environment."

15. Greenpeace International. (1995, May 7). "Diary" (paragraph 5).

16. Greenpeace International. (1995). "Shell reverses decision to dump the Brent Spar." Retrieved from http://www.greenpeace.org/international/en/about/history/Victories-timeline/Brent-Spar/

17. Ibid.

18. Anderson, "Media, culture and the environment"; Tsoukas, "David and Goliath in the risk society."

19. Livesey, S. (2002). "The discourse of the middle ground: Citizen Shell commits to sustainable development." *Management Communication Quarterly, 15,* 313. doi: 10.1177/0893318902153001

20. Ibid.

21. Lawrence, A. (1999). "Shell Oil in Nigeria" [Online case study] (section 4). Council for Ethics in Economics.

22. "Oil spill intelligence report," as cited in Rowell, A. (with Andrea Goodall). (1994). "Shell-shocked: The environmental and social cost of living with Shell in Nigeria" (fn. 88). Amsterdam, Netherlands: Greenpeace International.

23. Essential Action. (2000). "Shell in Nigeria: What are the issues?" In *Boycott Shell/Free Nigeria: The main issues* [website] (fn. 7). Retrieved from http://www.essentialaction.org/shell/issues.html

24. Shell Petroleum Development Company of Nigeria Limited (SPDC). (1997). "People and the environment: Annual report 1997" [Report] (p. 15). Available from SPDC, Lagos, Nigeria.

25. Saro-Wiwa, K. (1995b). "Closing statement to the Nigerian military appointed tribunal" (paragraph 1).

26. Ake, C. (1994, July 25). "Nightmare of state violence" (paragraph 4).

27. Movement for the Survival of the Ogoni People (MOSOP). (2000). "The role of Shell in Ogoni." Niboro, I. (1993, October 4). "Death on a sea of oil" (paragraph 2). *African Guardian.*

28. Movement for the Survival of the Ogoni People (MOSOP). (2000). "The story of the Movement for Survival of the Ogoni People (MOSOP)" (paragraph 5). Retrieved from http://www.mosopcanada.org/story.php

29. Saro-Wiwa, K. (1994, August 8). "Message from prison" (paragraph 14). *The News.* Retrieved from

30. MOSOP, "The role of Shell in Ogoni."

31. Ekeocha, O. (1993, May 17). "A cry for justice: Or drum beats of treason?" (paragraph 2). *The African Guardian.*

32. MOSOP, "The story of the Movement for Survival of the Ogoni People," paragraph 11.

33. Rowell, "Shell-shocked," paragraphs 6–7.

34. Ibid.

35. Saro-Wiwa, "Message from prison."

36. Shell Petroleum Development Company of Nigeria Limited (SPDC). (1997, August). "Nigeria Brief: Ogoni and the Niger Delta [Booklet]" (p. 2). Available from SPDC, Lagos, Nigeria.

37. MOSOP, "The story of the Movement for Survival of the Ogoni People."

38. Lawrence, "Shell Oil in Nigeria"; MOSOP, "The story of the Movement for Survival of the Ogoni People."

39. Knight, "Profits and principles," p. 2; Lawrence, "Shell Oil in Nigeria"; SPDC, "Nigeria Brief," p. 7.

40. SPDC, "Nigeria Brief."

41. Ibid.

42. Ibid., p. 9.

43. SPDC, "Nigeria Brief," p. 8; *The Independent*, November 8, 1996, as cited in SPDC, "Nigeria Brief," p. 6.

44. Cited in SPDC, "Nigeria Brief," p. 8.

45. Ibid., p. 10.

46. SPDC, "Nigeria Brief," p. 11.

47. Ibid.

48. Livesey, "The discourse of the middle ground."

49. Human Rights Watch. (1998, February). "The price of oil" (p. 3). Human Rights Watch/Africa. Retrieved from http://www.hrw.org/reports/1999/nigeria/

50. Shell Petroleum Development Company of Nigeria Limited (SPDC). (2000). "Influence" (paragraph 3). *Information Resource* [website]. Retrieved from http://www.Shellnigeria.com/

51. Herkstroter, C. (1996, October 11). "Dealing with contradictory expectations: The dilemmas facing multinationals" [Speech]. Herkstroter, C. (1996, November 25). "Challenge and change: Making a contribution in historic times" [Speech].

52. Knight, "Profits and principles," p. 2.

53. Ibid., p. 46.

54. Herkstroter, "Challenge and change," paragraph 39.

55. Herkstroter, C. (1997, May 14). "Speech at the annual general meeting" [Speech] (paragraph 24). Retrieved from Shell.com/library

56. Knight, "Profits and principles," p. 2.

57. Herkstroter, "Dealing with contradictory expectations."

58. Ibid.

59. Ibid.

60. Ibid.

61. Ibid.

62. Livesey, "The discourse of the middle ground."

63. Shell Expro. (1999, September 1). "Brent Spar decommissioning details given at close out seminar."

64. SPDC, "People and the environment"; Shell Petroleum Development Company of Nigeria Limited (SPDC). (1998). "People and the environment: Annual report 1998" [Report]. Available from SPDC, Lagos, Nigeria.

Chapter 5

THE CORPORATION'S RESPONSIBILITY TO CONSUMERS

As society's expectations of corporations have shifted to include socially and environmentally responsible behavior, a growing body of literature has emerged regarding corporate accountability to the environment, society, and governance issues. Despite the increased conversation around broader issues of corporate responsibility, only limited attention has been dedicated to the corporation's responsibility to its consumers.

Why is that? One reason may be the prevalent neoliberal discourse around consumer choice and personal responsibility. Neoliberalism advocates a limited, laissez-faire approach to issues of government involvement, and the neoliberal view of consumer responsibility involves the notion that a rational consumer will decide whether to pay for a product depending on the value he or she derives from it, and, that by choosing to purchase the product, the consumer liberates the corporation that has produced the product from any responsibility regarding the ill effects of the product.

In recent years, however, consumers have started to hold corporations across a variety of industries accountable for the long-term effects of product use and consumption. While this shift in how consumers view corporations' responsibility to them has occurred concurrently with changes in society's view of corporate responsibility overall, this trend is not usually attributed to the CR discussion.

A joint study by Fleishman-Hillard and the National Consumers League, for example, found that 80% of Americans expect companies to be actively engaged in the communities in which they operate.[1] When asked to define corporate social responsibility, the greatest number of respondents identified it as commitment to communities. When participants were asked to identify their expectations of a corporation's commitment to its community, their responses were as shown in Figure 5.1.

Figure 5.1 Expectations of a corporation's commitment to its community

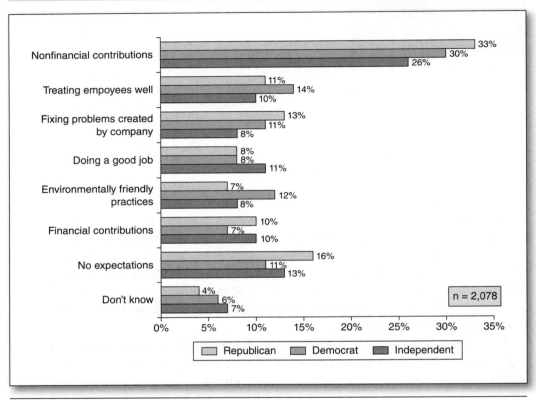

Source: Adapted from Fleishman-Hillard. (2007). "Rethinking corporate social responsibility: A Fleishman-Hillard/ National Consumers League study." Retrieved August 3, 2014, from http://www.csrresults.com/CSR_Executive Summary07.pdf.

That nonfinancial contributions were the number one way for corporations to illustrate their commitment to communities shows that, across political ideologies, American expectations of corporate behavior have shifted to embrace responsibilities beyond philanthropic efforts.

It is important to understand that in introducing the conversation about the corporation's responsibility to consumers, we are not referring to the types of liabilities that arise when products are found to be defective or contaminated—such as the defects in various Toyota vehicles causing dangerous and unintended acceleration that led to numerous recalls in 2009–2010,[2] or the Tylenol poisoning (and subsequent recall by Johnson & Johnson) in the 1980s. Instead, we will focus on situations in which corporations have responsibilities to their consumers regarding the use of fully functional, uncontaminated products or services.

While such responsibilities span a broad spectrum of industries, in this chapter, we will take a look at the food, pharmaceutical, and healthcare industries to understand the different issues related to consumer responsibility. Why these particular industries? Adequate access to food and healthcare are frequently depicted as human rights issues, which may lead to extra scrutiny for companies in these industries. The pharmaceutical industry, meanwhile, raises many questions about the responsibility of corporations in marketing health-related products to consumers. For each industry, we will look at where the personal responsibility of an individual consumer ends and where corporate responsibility begins.

THE FOOD INDUSTRY

In the 2008 documentary film *Food, Inc.*, journalist and food activist Michael Pollan argued, "The way we eat has changed more in the last 50 years than in the previous 10,000."[3] There are various reasons why food consumption and production has changed rapidly since the middle of the 20th century. Between 1930 and 2000, U.S. agricultural output quadrupled.[4] Technological advances in farming and nonfarm economic development were two of the driving forces behind this increase in production, with the former resulting in greater efficiency, consolidation of farmland into fewer and larger farms, and lower production costs.[5]

Beyond farm productivity, social changes also led to shifts in the production and consumption of food in the U.S. With more women entering the workforce, less time for mothers to spend on meal preparation led to the rise of frozen, pre-packaged meals.

A major failure of global food systems can be seen in the fact that there are about 1 billion people in the world who are going hungry, while 2 billion people are overweight.[6] What are the causes of such worldwide nutritional failures?

David Stuckler and Marion Nestle argue that to answer this question, it is first essential to ask, "Who rules global food systems?"[7] Their answer is what is often referred to disparagingly as "Big Food," or a group of multinational food and beverage corporations with enormous market power worldwide. Stucker and Nestle point out that in the U.S., the 10 largest food companies control more than half of all food sales; worldwide, this proportion is 15% and rising.[8] Even more disturbing are the number for processed food items. Worldwide, more than 50% of soft drinks are produced by large multinationals, while 75% of food sales involved processed foods. What are the consequences of Big Food's increasing control over the global food supply? "The world's food system is not a competitive marketplace of small producers but an oligopoly. What people eat is increasingly driven by a few multinational food companies."[9]

Why is food production important? According to the Food Industry Center at the University of Minnesota, the complex, multifaceted food system

> affects human health, the environment, and the economy. It is also closely linked to culture and our sense of community. Knowledge of the current status of the food system and of changes in that status over time is important for food businesses, policy makers, and the stakeholders they serve.[10]

In a 2008 TED Talk, food journalist and author Mark Bittman looked at changes in the production, purchasing, and preparation of food since the middle of the 20th century:

> Every family had a cook, usually a mom. And those moms bought and prepared food. It was like your romantic vision of Europe. Margarine didn't exist. In fact, when margarine was invented, several states passed laws declaring that it had to be dyed pink, so we'd all know that it was a fake. There was no snack food, and until the '20s, until Clarence Birdseye came along, there was no frozen food. There were no restaurant chains. There were neighborhood restaurants run by local people, but none of them would think to open another one.[11]

Occurring concomitantly with these and other changes have been changes in the Western diet, which Bittman identifies as a cause of major human health issues resulting from Americans' overreliance on meat and dairy products at the expense of eating fruits and vegetables. Bittman argues:

> There's no question, none, that so-called lifestyle diseases—diabetes, heart disease, stroke, some cancers—are diseases that are far more prevalent here than in any-where in the rest of the world, and that's the direct result of eating a Western diet.[12]

Americans eat seven times more meat than is recommended by the U.S. Department of Agriculture (USDA).[13] Why do Americans eat a diet that is heavy in foods other than plants? One reason is that government subsidies are given to certain categories of food, including grains, cotton, peanuts, tobacco, and milk.[14] Meanwhile, most fruit and vegetable crops receive minimal government support. Adjusted for inflation, subsidies to farmers have increased greatly since the 1930s. From the 1930s through the 1950s, such subsidies totaled $3 billion annually; in the 1980s they averaged about $11 billion per year, and between 1998 and 2001, this number grew to $20 billion per year (all in 1996 dollars).[15]

How are crops chosen to receive subsidies? Every five years the Food, Conservation, and Energy Act is subject to a vote. Also known as the "U.S. Farm

Bill," the five-year agriculture policy bill includes provisions for government subsidies on various crops.[16] By heavily subsidizing certain crops, the U.S. government is effectively voting on which food products will be pushed onto consumers. Feed grains received a $1.78 billion subsidy in 2012 and a budgeted $2.29 billion subsidy for 2014 according to the fiscal year 2014 Budget Summary and Annual Performance Plan, reducing the price of meat production. That same year, wheat, rice, tobacco, dairy, soybeans, sugar, and others were also heavily subsidized, at a total of $3.6 billion, and $4.25 billion was budgeted for 2014.[17]

Meanwhile, the U.S. meat, fish, and poultry industry continues to grow, with a market value of $155.4 billion in 2013 and a compound annual growth rate (CAGR) of 1.3% from 2007 to 2011.[18] The forecasted market value of the industry in 2016 is $167.2 billion, with a projected CAGR of 1.5% from 2011 to 2016.[19]

Eating more grains and animal products means Americans are eating fewer plants. And as Bittman says, "The evidence is very clear that plants promote health. . . . You eat more plants, you eat less other stuff, you live longer."[20] He argues that heavy marketing of nonessential food products, including meats and packaged foods, has led to inflated demand for foods we do not need to survive. "Their production has been supported by government agencies at the expense of a more health- and earth-friendly diet."[21]

Turning to the food guide pyramid (seen in Figure 5.2) recommended by the USDA, Bittman noted that half the people involved in the development of the pyramid had ties to agribusiness—and thus incentives to make recommendations that served the interests of industrial farming more than the health of individual consumers.[22]

In another TED Talk in 2011, architect and food thinker Carolyn Steel discussed how human beings' relationship to food has changed over time. Echoing thoughts expressed by Bittman, Steel notes that the purchase, preparation, and consumption of food used to be the center of human life and a very social experience. For example, consider the large food markets in urban centers before the 20th century.[23]

Like Bittman, Steel points out that prior to the advent of reliable long-distance transportation in the form of trains, food was locally sourced by necessity. Beyond keeping food consumption limited to what could be produced locally, a larger impact of the absence of such transportation was that urban areas were limited in size because there was no effective means of transporting food, including grains and livestock, into and across large metro areas.[24]

Once a reliable transportation system was in place, there was no need to set aside land for farming within urban areas. The result was the growth of massive urban areas where inhabitants had only a limited relationship with nature. Steel

Figure 5.2 USDA food guide pyramid

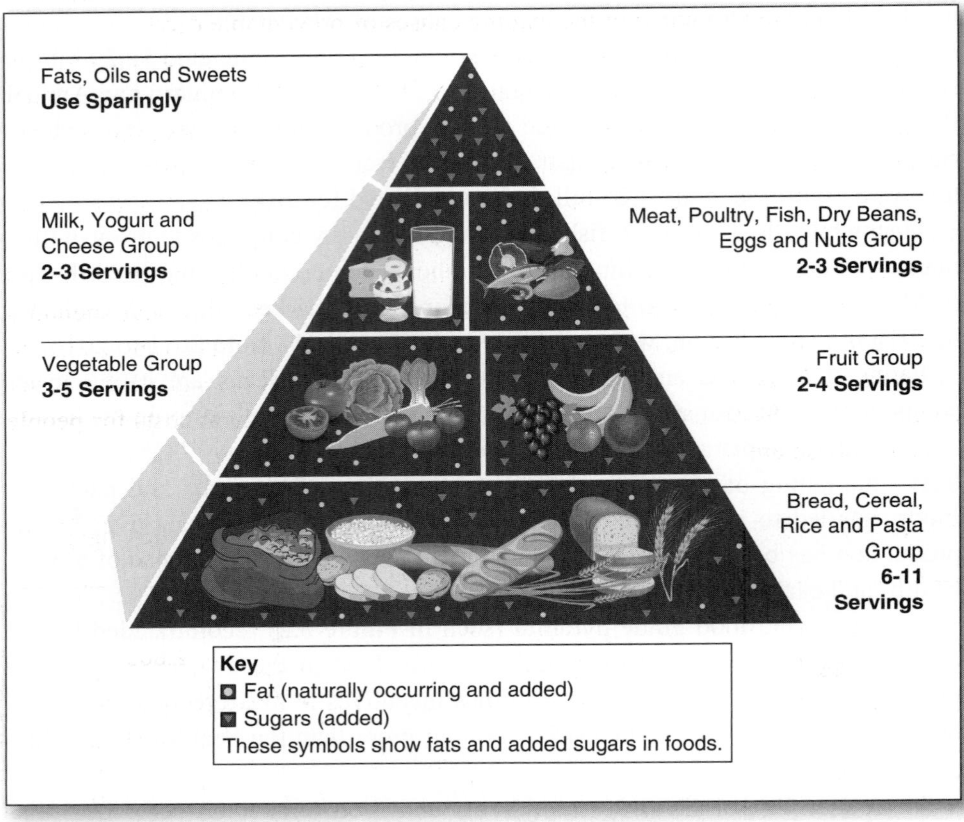

Fats, Oils and Sweets
Use Sparingly

Milk, Yogurt and
Cheese Group
2-3 Servings

Meat, Poultry, Fish, Dry Beans,
Eggs and Nuts Group
2-3 Servings

Vegetable Group
3-5 Servings

Fruit Group
2-4 Servings

Bread, Cereal,
Rice and Pasta
Group
**6-11
Servings**

Key
◻ Fat (naturally occurring and added)
◼ Sugars (added)
These symbols show fats and added sugars in foods.

Source: Food Guide Pyramid. United States Department of Agriculture. http://www.cnpp.usda.gov/FGP.

points out that people in modern societies do not acquire the skills to evaluate food, the way our forefathers needed to do to survive. Today, we determine the edibility of many food items by looking at the date on the box.[25]

Why is food production and consumption an important CR issue? As noted by Bittman, there are social and environmental costs inherent in the way food is produced.[26] Some of these carry externalities, including rising insurance costs and sustainability issues. Today, 75% to 90% of the global food industry is controlled by four multinational corporations who control the raw materials market.[27]

The makeup of the Western diet, which is largely determined by the government subsidies discussed above, has been linked to the rise in obesity among Americans. According to the Centers for Disease Control and Prevention, more than one-third of U.S. adults (34.9%) are obese, and 16.9% of U.S. children and adolescents are already obese.[28] Obesity is associated with many of the lifestyle diseases discussed by Bittman, including heart disease, stroke, type 2 diabetes, and certain types of cancer. These are also some of the leading causes of preventable death.

Figure 5.3 tracks Americans' increase in calorie consumption against the prevalence of obesity in the U.S. between 1970 and 2008. What is driving Americans' increase in caloric intake? Part of the answer is the increase in consumption of energy-dense foods.[29] Americans' demand for meat, dairy, and refined carbohydrates has led them to consume far more calories than are necessary or healthy.[30]

Obesity and associated health conditions have myriad implications with regard to health insurance. Researchers have discovered that annual medical spending associated with obesity is exorbitant.[31] In 2008, such medical costs were estimated to be as high as $147 billion. A Cornell study from 2012 found that obesity accounts for 21% of U.S. healthcare costs.[32] The annual medical costs for people who are obese are $1,429 higher than for those of normal weight.[33]

Figure 5.3   Obesity and calorie consumption in the U.S. between 1970 and 2008

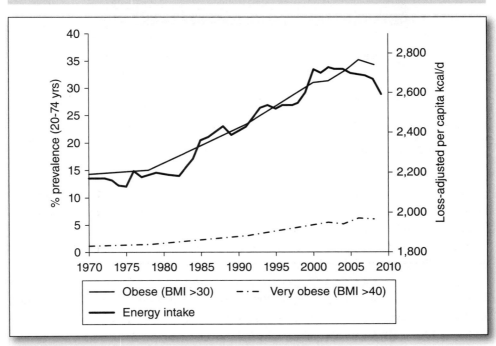

Source: Guyenet, S. (2012, June 5). "Calories still matter." Whole Health Source. Retrieved from http://whole healthsource.blogspot.ca/2012/06/calories-still-matter.html. Image courtesy of Stephan Guyenet. Raw data were obtained from CDC NHANES surveys and USDA Economic Research Service food disappearance records. Image courtesy of Stephan Guyenet.

These numbers represent excessive gains from 10 years earlier. In 1998, medical costs associated with obesity were estimated to be as high as $78.5 billion, and roughly half this number was financed by Medicare and Medicaid.[34] With the introduction of the Affordable Care Act, this information becomes all the more crucial.

Sugar and Obesity

Beyond the impact of overreliance on meat, dairy, and grains, increased sugar consumption in the U.S. is a driving force behind increased calorie consumption. Figure 5.4 shows the increase in per capita sweetener consumption in the U.S. between 1970 and 2010.[35]

Dr. Robert Lustig at the University of California at San Francisco compares overexposure to sugar to overexposure to alcohol, noting that chronic fructose exposure leads to many of the same symptoms as chronic alcohol exposure in human beings (see Figure 5.5).[36]

Figure 5.4   Per capita consumption of caloric sweeteners, 1970–2010

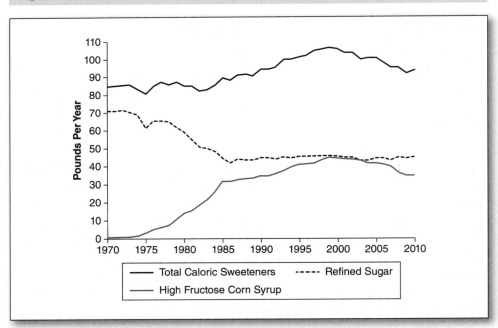

Source: United States Department of Agriculture, Economic Research Service. (n.d.). "Per capita consumption of caloric sweeteners, 1970–2010" [Graph]. Retrieved August 3, 2014, from http://sweetsurprise.com/sites/default/files/pdf/CaloricSweetness.pdf.

Figure 5.5 The deadly effect of chronic fructose exposure

DEADLY EFFECT	
Excessive consumption of fructose can cause many of the same health problems as alcohol.	
Chronic ethanol exposure	*Chronic fructose exposure*
Haematological disorders	
Electrolyte abnormalities	
Hypertension	Hypertension (uric acid)
Cardiac dilatation	
Cardiomyopathy	Myocardial infarction (dyslipidaemia, insulin resistance)
Dyslipidaemia	Dyslipidaemia (*de novo* lipogenesis)
Pancreatitis	Pancreatitis (hypertriglyceridaemia)
Obesity (insulin resistance)	Obesity (insulin resistance)
Malnutrition	Malnutrition (obesity)
Hepatic dysfunction (alcoholic Steatohepatitis)	Hepatic dysfunction (non-alcoholic Steatohepatitis)
Fetal alcohol syndrome	
Addiction	Habituation, if not addiction

Source: Lustig, R. H., Schmidt, L. A., & Brindis, C. D. (2012, February 2). "Public health: The toxic truth about sugar." *Nature, 482,* pp. 27–29. doi: 10.1038/482027a.

Lustig also likens sugar consumption to addiction to cocaine and other drugs.[37] Meanwhile, he is not the only one who believes that sugar consumption has played an instrumental role in the rise of obesity among Americans. Researchers George A. Bray, Samara Joy Nielsen, and Barry M. Popkin looked at the relationship between the intake of high-fructose corn syrup (HFCS), found in soft drinks and other packaged foods, and obesity. They found that consumption of HFCS increased approximately 1,000% between 1970 and 1990, a far greater increase than was seen in the intake of any other food or food group—and the increased use of HFCS in the United States mirrors the rise in obesity.[38]

Aside from the HFCS content in beverages such as Coca-Cola, these sweetened beverages may lead to caloric overconsumption by accelerating the appetite of those who consume them.[39] Therefore, Bray et al. concluded that increased consumption of HFCS is related to the American obesity epidemic, and the overconsumption of HFCS in calorically sweetened beverages may play a role in the epidemic.[40]

Given high social costs and environmental externalities, growing criticism of fast-food chains, soda companies, and big agriculture has ensued. In recent years, the food industry has seen growing comparisons to tobacco. With more and more researchers referring to sugar as an addictive substance, it is hard not to compare its use as an additive in food products to the use of nicotine in cigarettes. In *Food, Inc.*, Michael Pollan notes:

> The industry blames obesity on a crisis of personal responsibility. But when you're engineering foods you are pressing our evolutionary buttons. The fact is we're hardwired to go for three tastes—salt, fat and sugar. These things are very rare in nature. Now sugar is available 24/7 in tremendous quantities. We're eating hundreds of pounds of the stuff a year. This diet of high-fructose corn syrup and refined carbohydrates leads to these spikes of insulin and, gradually, a wearing down of the system by which our body metabolizes sugar.[41]

Former Food and Drug Administration commissioner David Kessler also sees parallels between the food and tobacco industries, with both manipulating consumer behavior to sell products that detrimentally affect health.[42] Kessler's view is that foods with high fat, salt, and sugar content affect the brain's chemistry in a way that causes people to overeat, and the food industry uses this to manipulate people into eating more than they should. How do food companies do this? Such foods stimulate the brain to release dopamine, the neurotransmitter associated with the pleasure center, and over time, the brain "gets wired so that dopamine pathways light up at the mere suggestion of the food, such as driving past a fast-food restaurant, and the urge to eat the food grows insistent."[43] Once the food is eaten, the brain releases opioids, which bring emotional relief. Together, dopamine and opioids create a pathway that can activate every time a person is reminded about the particular food. This happens regardless of whether the person is hungry.[44]

Fast-Food Marketing

One area in which food manufacturers have come under scrutiny is their marketing methods. During 2009, the fast-food industry spent $4.2 billion on marketing.[45] Of this total, $3.2 billion was spent by a group of 12 fast-food restaurant chains analyzed in a report on marketing to children by researchers at Yale's Rudd Center for Food Policy and Obesity.[46] These numbers relate solely to fast-food marketing spending and therefore exclude spending on marketing for other unhealthy products by soft-drink manufacturers such as Coca-Cola and PepsiCo, food manufacturers such as Kraft, and candy and snack manufacturers.

Marketing unhealthy foods and beverages to children is a particular area of concern. Writing for Grist, Tom Philpott noted the effectiveness of marketing to an impressionable young audience:

> How is all of this marketing working? The proof is in the whining. In a survey commissioned by the Rudd Center, 40 percent of parents report that their children ask to go to McDonald's at least once a week, and 15 percent of parents of 2- to 5-year-olds report that their children harangue them for a Mickey D's trip every day. As a result: 84 percent of parents reported taking their child to a fast food restaurant at least once in the past week; 66 percent reported going to McDonald's.[47]

During the early 21st century, U.S. journalists and filmmakers produced a spate of books and documentaries designed to educate consumers on issues around "what we eat." These included films such as Morgan Spurlock's Oscar-nominated *Super Size Me* as well as *Food, Inc.* and *Food Matters*, along with popular books such as Michael Pollan's *The Omnivore's Dilemma*, among many others. As discussed in the case at the end of this chapter, another reaction to concerns about the nutritional value of popular foods has been a series of lawsuits against fast-food companies; McDonald's has been a frequent target.

Some food manufacturers have taken steps to deal with criticism related to the nutritional content of their products, such as reducing portion sizes. For example, Kraft, a $30 billion company, agreed to reduce fats, sugars, and calories across its product line.[48] Kraft's most popular food products include cream cheese, peanut butter, Velveeta Cheese, Oreos, and Oscar Mayer hot dogs—making this decision especially important for children's health, as kids are major consumers of many of these products.

Additionally, not all food companies are part of the problem. Companies such as Stonyfield Farm (a subsidiary of Groupe Danone), a producer of organic dairy products, manufacture healthy packaged foods, some of which are designed to start kids on the path to healthy eating. The rise of largely organic supermarkets such as Whole Foods Market during the late 20th and early 21st centuries is another positive trend.

Corporate Responsibility vs. Government Intervention

In the United States, the responsibility for ensuring that consumers are offered healthy food options is often divided between corporations and governmental bodies.

A notable example of government intervention in portion sizing is the contentious 2012 proposal by New York City mayor Mike Bloomberg to restrict the size of sugary beverages sold by the city's restaurants, food carts, and sports arenas.[49]

At other times, the government has intervened with industry-friendly laws. For example, in 2004, the U.S. House of Representatives passed the Personal Responsibility in Food Consumption Act, known colloquially as the "Cheeseburger Bill," on a 276–139 vote. The bill provided protection from obesity- and weight-based lawsuits unless the weight gain had been due to the violation of a state or federal law. Ric Keller (R-FL), who authored the bill, stated his view that "we need to get back to the old-fashioned principles of common sense and personal responsibility and get away from this new culture where everybody plays the victim and blames other people for their problems." During floor debate, representatives cited a Gallup poll finding that 89% of those surveyed "oppose the idea of holding fast food companies legally responsible for the diet-related health problems of fast food junkies."[50]

Conclusion

Increased discourse around consumer versus corporate responsibility for food-related health concerns has made it difficult to hold corporations accountable for what many see as issues of individual choice and accountability. At the same time, increased attention to food production and consumption issues, spurred by early-21st-century books and documentaries, has led to greater consumer scrutiny of food manufacturers. With increased access to information about food, consumers are more informed than ever, but concerns over obesity-related health issues will likely continue to drive consumers to hold corporations accountable for the damage wrought by their products.

THE HEALTHCARE AND PHARMACEUTICAL INDUSTRIES

The healthcare and pharmaceutical industries are also a compelling example of the shift in the perception of corporate responsibility to consumers over the past few decades. Both types of organizations have long been active in various philanthropic activities; nonetheless, they have also frequently come under fire for being questionable corporate citizens. Healthcare and pharmaceutical corporations exemplify that CR is not only about where and how a company *spends* its money, but also about how a company *makes* its money.

Healthcare differs from other industries in several ways.[51] First, it is an industry in which the supplier (in this case, the physician) has the power to determine demand. There is also asymmetric information and uncertainty regarding the quality and outcomes of products and services. As healthcare journalist Maggie Mayar notes in her book *Money-Driven Medicine*, "Health care providers enjoy nearly unparalleled influence over demand for the services that they sell," making healthcare purchases fundamentally different from other purchases, as they are based on trust.[52]

According to the World Bank, the U.S. has the highest health expenditure as a percentage of total GDP globally (see Table 5.1).[53]

But does greater expenditure necessarily translate to better care? In his 2009 book *The Healing of America: A Global Quest for Better, Cheaper, and Fairer Health Care*, T. R. Reid states that "when it comes to medical care, Americans are shelling out the big bucks without getting what we pay for."[54]

The World Health Organization's (WHO) ranking of the world's health systems concurs with this assessment of the U.S.'s return on investment in healthcare.[55] The WHO ranking of the world's health systems was last produced in 2000; the organization no longer produces such a ranking table because of the complexity of the task. In 2000, the U.S. ranked #37, at a time when the nation was spending 13.4% of GDP on healthcare (see Table 5.2). In contrast, the Netherlands ranked #17 while spending only 8% of its GDP on healthcare. Americans are consuming more healthcare than others and paying more for it while suffering inferior outcomes.

Table 5.1 Countries' health expenditures as a percentage of GDP, per the World Bank

Rank	Country name	2009	2010	2011	2012
1	**United States**	**17.7**	**17.7**	**17.7**	**17.9**
2	Marshall Islands	17.5	16.0	16.0	15.6
7	Netherlands	11.9	12.1	11.9	12.4
8	France	11.7	11.7	11.6	11.7
11	Germany	11.8	11.5	11.3	11.5
12	Canada	11.4	11.4	10.9	10.9
14	Denmark	11.5	11.1	10.9	11.2
15	Switzerland	11.0	10.9	11.0	11.3

Source: "Health expenditure, total (% of GDP)." World Bank. (n.d.). Data | Table. Retrieved from http://data.world bank.org/indicator/SH.XPD.TOTL.ZS/countries?order=wbapi_data_value_2010%20wbapi_data_value%20wbapi_data_value-last&sort=desc&display=default Accessed 7/24/14.

Table 5.2   The World Health Organization's ranking of the world's health systems

Rank	Country	Rank	Country	Rank	Country	Rank	Country
1	France	11	Norway	21	Belgium	31	Finland
2	Italy	12	Portugal	22	Colombia	32	Australia
3	San Marino	13	Monaco	23	Sweden	33	Chile
4	Andorra	14	Greece	24	Cyprus	34	Denmark
5	Malta	15	Iceland	25	Germany	35	Dominica
6	Singapore	16	Luxembourg	26	Saudi Arabia	36	Costa Rica
7	Spain	17	Netherlands	27	UAE	**37**	**USA**
8	Oman	18	United Kingdom	28	Israel	38	Slovenia
9	Austria	19	Ireland	29	Morocco	39	Cuba
10	Japan	20	Switzerland	30	Canada	40	Brunei

Source: Adapted from Coutsoukis, P. (n.d.). "The World Health Organization's ranking of the world's health systems." Retrieved July 24, 2014, from http://www.photius.com/rankings/healthranks.html.

On which metrics did the WHO base its rankings? First, the WHO looked at the overall level of population health. Second, it looked at health inequalities (or disparities) within the population. Third, the organization considered the overall level of health system responsiveness, which was determined by a combination of patient satisfaction and how well the system functioned. The fourth factor was the distribution of responsiveness within the population—in other words, how well people were served by the health system across different levels of socioeconomic status. Finally, the WHO looked at the distribution of the health system's financial burden within the population, or who pays the costs.

Criticism of the healthcare industry includes charges that the industry markets drugs for off-label use, pushes insured patients toward unnecessary and expensive procedures, and prices healthcare services and medication so that they are expensive and unaffordable for many people. Pharmaceutical companies in particular are scrutinized for being aggressive in their attempts to extend patents and, therefore, postpone the market entry of lower-priced generics, which they accomplish by filing for off-label use or use for children, and by making slight modifications to the existing product. One question that has been raised is whether it is ethical for pharmaceutical companies to make record profits on products that are designed to improve consumers' health, a question that is not often relevant to other industries.

Regardless of one's perspective on the ethicality of high profits in Big Pharma, there are some consequences in play for pharmaceutical companies that engage in questionable practices. In 2009, pharmaceutical giant Pfizer was hit with a $2.3 billion fine for promoting the drug Bextra for unapproved uses.[56] Meanwhile, *The New England Journal of Medicine* has frequently spoken out on how Big Pharma has in some cases undermined the integrity of drug research. As an example of pharmaceutical companies' overzealous protection of patents, GlaxoSmithKline (GSK) in 1998 learned that a Canadian drug maker had applied to manufacture a generic form of GSK's popular antidepressant Paxil. With GSK's original patent about to expire, the company filed four patent infringement lawsuits to prevent the Canadian company's version from entering the U.S. market.[57] By preventing generic drugs from entering the marketplace, pharmaceutical companies effectively limit patients' access to affordable medicine. Patented drugs are extremely expensive in the U.S.; meanwhile, pharmaceutical companies have been known to price-discriminate between their consumers in the least-developed countries versus the developed world, as well as between consumers in the U.S. versus those in Western European countries where government exercises bargaining power for the benefit of citizens.[58] Such price discrimination occurs even among citizens within the U.S.

In the past fiscal year, the U.S. federal government recovered $4.3 billion due to healthcare fraud; over the last five years, the number has been $19.2 billion.[59] Settlements in legal cases have included one situation in which GSK agreed to pay $750 million for knowingly selling contaminated baby ointment and ineffective antidepressants. Journalist Andrew Tolve notes that the public perception is that pharmaceutical companies "profit grossly and often unethically from matters of life and death [, leading] to vitriol and mistrust."[60]

The pharmaceutical industry bears the risk of research and development (R&D); however, it has been the most profitable industry since 1982. Is 20% profit a "fair" profit for the risk? Or are critics right?

CNNMoney ranked industries by 2008 profits as percentage of revenues, with pharmaceuticals coming in third (see Table 5.3).

Pharma is not the only health-related industry that is earning high profits. In early 2011, *Businessweek* ranked 97 industries in terms of profitability for small businesses, based on their 2010 net profit margin; four of the top-10 spots were taken by health practitioners (see Table 5.4).

Another 2011 report from Sageworks indicates that four out of the 10 most profitable industries are healthcare-related industries.[61] Johnson & Johnson,

Table 5.3 *CNNMoney*'s ranking of industries by 2008 profits

Industry Rank	Industry	2008 Profits as % of Revenues
1	Network and other communications equipment	20.4%
2	Internet services and retailing	19.4%
3	Pharmaceuticals	19.3%
4	Medical products and equipment	16.3%
6	Financial data services	11.7%
7	Mining, crude-oil production	11.5%
30	Healthcare: Pharmacy and other services	3.0%
34	Healthcare: Medical facilities	2.4%
35	Healthcare: Insurance and managed care	2.2%

Source: Fortune 500 2009, http://money.cnn.com/magazines/fortune/fortune500/2009/performers/industries/profits/ (accessed July 24, 2014).

Table 5.4 *Businessweek*'s ranking of industries by profitability for small businesses

	Offices of Physicians	Offices of Other Health Practitioners	Offices of Dentists	Outpatient Care Centers
Net profit margin rank	6	4	2	7
Net profit margin	13.24%	16.14%	17.04%	12.10%
Change in 2009–2010 sales	3.05%	7.25%	7.18%	8.76%
Number of firms	191,961	113,010	120,676	14,444
Employment	2,169,682	614,171	824,770	695,863

Source: Stonington, J. (2011, January 18). "Most and least profitable business types." Retrieved July 24, 2014, from http://images.businessweek.com/slideshows/20110118/most-and-least-profitable-business-types.html#slide1.

Novartis, Pfizer, and Roche Group also made it to the 2014 Fortune's Global 500 list, which ranks the world's largest corporations based on revenue.[62]

That health practitioners generate such high profits could be cause for concern that their priorities are not in line with patients' needs. In an October 2011 piece for FastCoExist.com, Brian Jackson criticized healthcare companies for valuing short-term profits over the long-term sustainability of the industry and well-being of its patients.[63] He notes that the pharmaceutical industry "has made a business of marketing the use of drugs for off-label purposes, misleading doctors and the public about safety concerns, and falsifying evidence regarding the efficacy of drugs."[64] Beyond pharma, Jackson identifies ways in which hospitals and physicians contribute to an overall lack of ethicality within the healthcare field, citing the overutilization of profitable procedures and tests on well-insured patients. Meanwhile, "underinsured and uninsured patients often struggle to get basic tests and procedures performed. Many of these problems stem from a short-term focus on quarterly profits and shareholder pressure."[65] Jackson also criticizes pharmaceutical companies for increasing their marketing budgets, riding patent coattails for as long as possible to exploit profits, and laying off R&D personnel as a means of manipulating quarterly reports. Hospitals, meanwhile, tend to run on small margins and are not incentivized to improve proper utilization.[66]

In the U.S., the healthcare industry's primary response to such criticism has involved lobbying the government for more favorable regulation, a practice that often leads to additional criticism. In 2013, the healthcare sector spent $226 million on lobbying U.S. politicians about healthcare reform.[67] Data from the Center for Responsive Politics, a research group that tracks money in U.S. politics and its effect on elections and public policy, shows that the pharmaceutical industry is the largest spender on lobbying. From 1998 to 2014, the pharmaceutical industry spent close to $2.86 billion on lobbying, 1.4 times more than the second largest spender—the insurance industry.[68]

Writing for the website of Business for Social Responsibility (BSR), a nonprofit that promotes social responsibility in business, Mark Little says:

> Ethical sales and marketing is no red herring—it is serious and a salient issue for pharmaceutical and medical device industries. But let's ring the death knell for health care companies after they fail to address the health and wellness needs of the bottom 3 billion—this is single handedly the biggest CSR challenge they have to face.[69]

Little responds to Jackson's article by arguing that the biggest challenge for the healthcare industry is and should be "the bottom 3 billion."[70] While Jackson is looking at issues that affect mostly American patients and consumers, Little expands his focus outside the U.S., where other factors come into play.[71]

Certain healthcare-related CR issues are even more complicated outside the United States, including access to medication in areas of the world where infectious diseases are more common than they are in the U.S. HIV is one of the world's leading infectious killers, having claimed more than 25 million lives over the past three decades. In 2013, approximately 35.3 million people were living with HIV.[72] Of those, more than 9.7 million were receiving antiretroviral therapy in low- and middle-income countries—but to meet the WHO goal of providing such therapy to 15 million people by 2015, another 5.3 million people need to be enrolled in treatment.[73]

According to the World Malaria Report 2013, there were approximately 207 million cases of malaria (with an uncertainty range of 135 million to 287 million) and an estimated 627,000 deaths in 2012 (with an uncertainty range of 473,000 to 789,000).[74] Malaria mortality rates have fallen by 42% in all age groups globally since 2000, with particular improvement in the 10 countries that possessed the highest malaria burden in 2000. Approximately 90% of the deaths averted from 2001 to 2012 were estimated to be children aged five and below who were living in Sub-Saharan Africa. Most deaths from malaria occur among children living in Africa, where a child dies each minute from malaria.[75]

After HIV/AIDS, tuberculosis (TB) is the second greatest killer worldwide due to a single infectious agent.[76] In 2012, 8.6 million people became infected with TB, and 1.3 million died from the disease.[77] Deaths from TB disproportionately affect individuals in poorer nations, with over 95% of TB deaths occurring in low- and middle-income countries, and TB is among the top three causes of death for women aged 15 to 44.[78]

How do these statistics relate to the healthcare and pharmaceutical industries? Former UN Special Rapporteur Paul Hunt argues that pharmaceutical companies have right-to-health responsibilities to their consumers, and though improvements have been made, further progress is necessary.[79] Hunt advocates the use of civil "watchdogs" to keep pharma accountable:

> In short, if others fail to act, a consortium of civil society organisations should appoint a panel of well-respected global leaders, supported by a small but properly resourced secretariat, to monitor the policies and practices of pharmaceutical companies and hold them publicly accountable for the discharge of their right-to-health responsibilities.[80]

One issue pharmaceutical companies must contend with in developing countries is that patent laws are often laxer in the developing world than in the U.S. For example, take the case of Cipla, a generic drug manufacturer. Cipla spends 0.2% of its revenue on R&D, which involves reverse-engineering patented drugs, compared with the much higher 12% to 15% of revenue for the pharmaceutical industry.[81] Meanwhile, Cipla's sales constitute less than 0.3% of the combined sales of GSK, Boehringer Ingelheim, Bristol-Myers Squibb, and Merck.[82]

Big Pharma's perspective on companies such as Cipla has been unfavorable, to say the least. According to J. P. Garnier, former CEO of GSK, "this is economic war. There are a couple of pirate companies who want to undermine the patent system."[83] Another British pharma executive fears that "if the patents go away in [countries like China and India,] it's the end of the pharmaceutical industry as we know it," noting that such a scenario would result in Big Pharma being "shut out of 80% of the world population."[84]

An important question to ask is whether the threat to Big Pharma by Cipla and its peers is the result of the industry's failure to meet its responsibilities to society. Comments from Cipla chairman Dr. Yusuf Hamied suggest that he believes so: "My idea of a better-ordered world is one in which medical discoveries would be free of patents and there would be no profiteering from life or death."[85] He notes that most AIDS drugs were not originally invented by big pharmaceutical companies and are instead mostly in-license products. He adds, "The fact that the MNCs have reduced prices [of their AIDS drugs] from $12,000 to three to four times the present prices of generic companies proves that their conscience has been pricked."[86]

In 1998, a consortium of drug companies filed a lawsuit against the South African government related to the companies' attempt to block the distribution of generic HIV/AIDS drugs. While 39 major pharma companies had patented these drugs, their generic versions were 98% less expensive, and the industry claimed to be protecting its intellectual property. The companies came under siege, however, for price-fixing and for denying the poor access to medicine.

Since then, pharma has faced significant pressure with regards to its practices in the developing world, and many companies have responded by changing tactics. In March 2007, Christopher Murray, head of Pharma International at Roche, noted that "the responsibility of pharmaceutical companies to increase access to their medicines—and indeed, to healthcare as a whole—is frequently raised as an ethical issue."[87] While he acknowledged the view of many HIV/AIDS activists that free drugs and donated funds from pharma companies are the right approach, Murray explained that Roche's strategy is driven by "the need for long-term sustainable solutions," which it identifies according to the Brundtland Report's definition of sustainable development as "meet[ing] the needs of the present without compromising the ability of future generations to meet their own needs."[88] He adds:

At Roche, our scientific commitment to the research and development of new health solutions carries considerable economic risk and is our most important contribution to society. As the International Federation of Pharmaceutical Manufacturers & Associations states, "It should be underlined that the pharmaceutical industry's primal role and social responsibility is to deliver new, innovative medicines."[89]

Andrew Tolve, meanwhile, explains:

CSR can develop good will and access in developing markets. Access to medicines initiatives have long been the focal point of pharma CSR. As sources of revenue tilt toward emerging markets, access to medicine initiatives can create valuable business opportunities.[90]

Corporate Responsibility Initiatives in the Pharmaceutical Industry

At GSK our mission is to improve the quality of human life by enabling people to do more, feel better and live longer. This mission has led us to a world-leading position in developing new medicines, vaccines and consumer healthcare products that are used by millions of people around the world.

The challenge of improving healthcare and expanding access to more people is great, and no single organisation can provide all the solutions. Healthcare companies have a role to play, and we want to be a company that makes a difference.

—GSK's mission statement[91]

In an article on corporate responsibility in the pharmaceutical industry, Dr. Harvey Bale states that the greatest responsibility pharma companies have to society is to develop new medications and treatments, echoing the views of Murray from Roche.[92] CR initiatives in pharma include efforts to improve access to medicines in developing countries, donation programs, putting R&D funds toward diseases prevalent in developing countries, and investments in health-related education and prevention programs, among other programs.[93]

According to Murray from Roche:

For the research-based pharmaceutical industry, CSR is a fully integrated element of strategy and operations. Such companies undertake many activities related to healthcare, in developing as well as developed countries. These cover the many facets of the drug development and supply chain, from conducting R&D, implementing health-related education and prevention programmes, to establishing global safety and ethical standards.[94]

Murray also explains how Roche's clinical trial process is informed by the corporation's ethical standards. While clinical trials are essential to the development of new drugs, there are special circumstances for HIV/AIDS drugs, as HIV/AIDS requires lifelong treatment. Roche does not sponsor HIV/AIDS drug trials in low- and middle-income countries because the company believes it would be irresponsible to sponsor such trials and initiate patients to therapy when the company will be unable to ensure the availability of the drugs after the study ends.

For this reason, Roche will only consider sponsoring or providing support for third party HIV/AIDS clinical trials in developing countries if there is a written agreement outlining how post trial treatment will be assured for as long as the participants benefit from that treatment.[95]

How is Roche providing alternatives to such clinical trials?

Roche's Technology Transfer Initiative, for example, an initiative we established in January 2006 and the first of its kind, has enabled Roche to share its technical expertise with local generic manufacturers in the Least Developed Countries and sub-Saharan Africa. Roche provides eligible manufacturers with on-the-ground technical guidance to support the production of saquinavir, a Roche HIV medicine. Through this initiative, we are helping to strengthen and expand manufacturing capabilities and capacities across Africa to begin to produce their own medicines in the future.[96]

Some organizations have created metrics to hold health-related corporations accountable to society. For example, the Access to Medicine Foundation, an international nonprofit organization tackling the challenges of access to medicine, has created the Access to Medicine Index, which ranks pharmaceutical companies with respect to their efforts to enhance global access to medicine.[97] Microsoft founder and noted philanthropist Bill Gates was quoted on the index's website as to the value of the ranking: "When I talk to executives from pharmaceutical companies, they tell me that they want to do more for neglected diseases, but they at least need to get credit for it. The Access to Medicine Index does exactly that."[98] But until quantifiable consequences exist for pharma companies that fail to increase access to medicine worldwide, the Index will be of limited value beyond serving as a source of information for the savviest consumers.

CONCLUSION

As the public's expectations of corporations have shifted to include social and environmental responsibility, there has been much discussion about where consumer responsibility ends and corporate responsibility begins. As seen from the examples above, this is an especially difficult question to answer with regard to industries where correctly manufactured products nonetheless have a negative effect on human health stemming from long-term usage. As consumer expectations of corporations continue to change in the coming years, the issue of personal versus corporate responsibility will continue to be debated.

NOTES

1. Fleishman-Hillard. (2007). "Rethinking corporate social responsibility: A Fleishman-Hillard/National Consumers League study." Retrieved August 3, 2014, from http://www.csrresults.com/CSR_ExecutiveSummary07.pdf

2. Toyota. (n.d.). "Safety/recall." *Toyota USA Newsroom*. Retrieved August 3, 2014, from http://toyota.tekgroupweb.com/safety-recall

3. Kenner, R. (Director), Pollan, M., & Schlosser, E. (2008). *Food, Inc.* [Film]. Magnolia Pictures.

4. Gardner, B. (2003, June). "U.S. agriculture in the twentieth century." Retrieved August 3, 2014, from http://eh.net/encyclopedia/u-s-agriculture-in-the-twentieth-century/

5. Ibid.

6. Stuckler, D., & Nestle, M. (2012). "Big food, food systems, and global health." *PLoS Med*, 9(6), e1001242. Retrieved August 3, 2014, from http://www.plosmedicine.org/article/info%3Adoi%2F10.1371%2Fjournal.pmed.1001242

7. Ibid.

8. Ibid.

9. Ibid.

10. Food Industry Center. (2012). "2011–2012 annual report." Retrieved August 3, 2014, from http://conservancy.umn.edu/bitstream/handle/11299/168235/2012.pdf?sequence=1&isAllowed=y

11. TED Talks. (2008, May 21). "Mark Bittman: What's Wrong with what we eat" [Video file]. Retrieved July 24, 2014, from https://www.ted.com/playlists/75/what_s_wrong_with_what_we_eat

12. Ibid.

13. Ibid.

14. Gardner, B. (2003, June). "U.S. agriculture in the twentieth century." Retrieved July 24, 2014, from http://eh.net/encyclopedia/u-s-agriculture-in-the-twentieth-century/

15. Ibid.

16. U.S. Department of Agriculture. (2009). "FY 2009 budget summary and annual performance plan." Retrieved July 24, 2014, from http://www.fsa.usda.gov/Internet/FSA_File/fy09budsum.pdf

17. U.S. Department of Agriculture. (2014). "FY 2014 budget summary and annual performance plan." Retrieved August 3, 2014, from http://www.obpa.usda.gov/budsum/FY14budsum.pdf

18. MartketLine. (2013, February). "MarketLine industry profile: Meat, fish and poultry in the United States." Retrieved March 19, 2015, from http://store.marketline.com/Browse/?N=357+368+4294803451&Ns=publicationDate&Nso=0

19. Ibid.

20. TED Talks, "Mark Bittman."

21. Ibid.

22. Ibid.

23. TED Talks. (2009, July). "Carolyn Steel: How food shapes our cities" [Video file]. Retrieved July 24, 2014, from http://www.ted.com/talks/carolyn_steel_how_food_shapes_our_cities.html

24. Ibid.

25. Ibid.

26. TED Talks, "Mark Bittman."

27. Lawrence, F. (2011, June 2). "The global food crisis: ABCD of food—how the multinationals dominate trade." Retrieved July 21, 2014, from http://www.theguardian.com/global-development/poverty-matters/2011/jun/02/abcd-food-giants-dominate-trade

28. Centers for Disease Control and Prevention. (n.d.). "Obesity and overweight for professionals: Data and statistics: Adult obesity." Retrieved July 24, 2014, from http://www.cdc.gov/obesity/data/adult.html

29. Ibid.

30. TED Talks, "Mark Bittman."

31. Finkelstein, E. A., Trogdon, J. G., Cohen, J. W., & Dietz, W. (2009, July). "Annual medical spending attributable to obesity: Payer-and service-specific estimates." Retrieved July 24, 2014, from http://content.healthaffairs.org/content/28/5/w822.full.pdf+html

32. Cornell University. (2012, April 9). "Obesity accounts for 21 percent of U.S. health care costs, study finds." Retrieved July 24, 2014, from http://www.sciencedaily.com/releases/2012/04/120409103247.htm

33. Centers for Disease Control and Prevention, "Obesity and overweight for professionals."

34. Hobbs, L. (2011, December 18). "Medical costs associated with obesity were as high as $147 billion per year in the US as of 2008." *FatNews.com*. Retrieved March 19, 2015, from http://www.fatnews.com/index.php/weblog/tell_a_friend/medical-costs-associated-with-obesity-were-as-high-as-147-billion-per-year

35. U.S. Department of Agriculture, Economic Research Service. (n.d.). "Per capita consumption of caloric sweeteners 1970–2010" [Graph]. Retrieved August 3, 2014, from http://sweetsurprise.com/sites/default/files/pdf/CaloricSweetness.pdf

36. Lustig, R. H., Schmidt, L. A., & Brindis, C. D. (2012, February 2). "The toxic truth about sugar." *Nature, 482,* 27–29.

37. Goldwert, L. (2012, April 2). "Sugar is as addictive as cocaine, and causes obesity, diabetes, cancer and heart disease: Researcher." Retrieved July 24, 2014, from http://articles.nydailynews.com/2012-04-02/news/31276928_1_high-fructose-corn-syrup-sugar-consumption-table-sugar

38. Bray, G. A., Nielsen, S. J., & Popkin, B. M. (2004). "Consumption of high-fructose corn syrup in beverages may play a role in the epidemic of obesity." *American Journal of Clinical Nutrition, 79,* 537–543.

39. Lustig, R. (2012, July 2). "Is sugar toxic?" [Audio podcast]. Retrieved July 24, 2014, from http://www.wnyc.org/shows/heresthething/2012/jul/02/transcript

40. Kenner et al., *Food, Inc.*

41. Bray et al., "Consumption of high-fructose corn syrup in beverages may play a role in the epidemic of obesity."

42. Layton, L. (2009, April 27). "David Kessler: Fat, salt and sugar alter brain chemistry, make us eat junk food." Retrieved July 24, 2014, from http://www.washingtonpost.com/wp-dyn/content/article/2009/04/26/AR2009042602711.html

43. Ibid.

44. Ibid.

45. Philpott, T. (2010, November 10). "The fast-food industry's $4.2 billion marketing blitz." Retrieved July 24, 2014, from http://grist.org/article/food-2010-11-09-the-fast-food-industrys-4-2-billion-marketing-blitz

46. Harris, J. L., Schwartz, M. B., & Brownell, K. D. (2010, November). "Fast food F.A.C.T.S: Evaluating advertising and marketing to children and teens." Yale Rudd Center for Food Policy and Obesity.

47. Philpott, "Fast-food industry's $4.2 billion marketing blitz."

48. Shaw, D. (2003, July 30). "I'll have three Big Macs, two large fries and a lawyer." *Los Angeles Times*. Retrieved July 24, 2014, from http://articles.latimes.com/2003/jul/30/food/fo-matters30

49. Grynbaum, M. M. (2012, October 12). "Soda industry sues to stop Bloomberg's sales limits." Retrieved July 24, 2014, from http://www.nytimes.com/2012/10/13/nyregion/soda-industry-sues-to-stop-bloombergs-sales-limits.html

50. "The Cheeseburger Bill: How deep the tentacles, how big the web" [Forum thread]. (2003, April). Just Pure Fitness. Retrieved March 19, 2015, from http://jpfitness.com/showthread.php?60520-The-Cheeseburger-Bill-How-Deep-the-Tentacles-How-Big-the-Web

51. Mahar, M. (2006). *Money-driven medicine: The real reason health care costs so much* (pp. 1–3). HarperCollins.

52. Ibid.

53. World Bank. (n.d.). "Health expenditure, total (% of GDP)" [Data | Table]. Retrieved July 24, 2014, from http://data.worldbank.org/indicator/SH.XPD.TOTL.ZS/countries?order=wbapi_data_value_2010%20wbapi_data_value%20wbapi_data_value-last&sort=desc&display=default

54. Reid, T. R. (2009). *The healing of America: A global quest for better, cheaper, and fairer health care* (pp. 5–27). Penguin Press.

55. Coutsoukis, P. (n.d.). "The World Health Organization's ranking of the world's health systems." Retrieved July 24, 2014, from http://www.photius.com/rankings/healthranks.html

56. Blowfield, M., & Murray, A. (2011). "What are the limits to responsibility? The case of pharmaceuticals." In *Corporate responsibility* (2nd ed., pp. 28–29). New York, NY: Oxford University Press.

57. Ibid.

58. "What's behind U.S. drug companies' response to the AIDS crisis abroad?" (2001, April 11). Retrieved July 24, 2014, from http://knowledge.wharton.upenn.edu/article.cfm?articleid=344

59. U.S. Department of Health and Human Services. (2014, February 26). "Departments of Justice and Health and Human Services announce record-breaking recoveries resulting from joint

efforts to combat health care fraud." Retrieved July 22, 2014, from http://www.hhs.gov/news/press/2014pres/02/20140226a.html

60. Tolve, A. (2011, March 14). "Pharma and CSR: Why good deeds are good business." Retrieved July 24, 2014, from http://social.eyeforpharma.com/commercial/pharma-and-csr-why-good-deeds-are-good-business

61. Bierman, L. (2011, November 7). "10 most profitable industries." *Forbes*. Retrieved July 24, 2014, from http://www.forbes.com/sites/sageworks/2011/07/11/10-most-profitable-industries

62. "Global 500 2014." (n.d.). *Fortune*. Retrieved July 22, 2014, from http://fortune.com/global500/johnson-johnson-121/?iid=G500_lp_toprr#

63. Jackson, B. (2011, October 21). "Bad medicine: There's no CSR in health care." Fast Company. Retrieved July 24, 2014, from http://www.fastcoexist.com/1678660/bad-medicine-theres-no-csr-in-health-care

64. Ibid.

65. Ibid.

66. Ibid.

67. Center for Responsive Politics. (n.d.). "Lobbying spending database." OpenSecrets. Retrieved July 21, 2014, from https://www.opensecrets.org/lobby/top.php?showYear=2013&indexType=i

68. Ibid.

69. Little, M. (2011, October 26). "Is the healthcare industry really failing at CSR?" Retrieved July 24, 2014, from http://www.bsr.org/en/our-insights/blog-view/is-the-health-care-industry-really-failing-at-csr

70. Ibid.

71. Ibid.

72. United Nations. (2013). "UNAIDS 2013: AIDS by the numbers." Retrieved July 24, 2014, from http://www.unaids.org/en/media/unaids/contentassets/documents/unaidspublication/2013/JC2571_AIDS_by_the_numbers_en.pdf

73. Ibid.

74. World Health Organization. (2013). "World malaria report 2013." Retrieved July 24, 2014, from http://www.who.int/malaria/publications/world_malaria_report_2013/report/en/

75. Ibid.

76. World Health Organization. (2014, March). "Tuberculosis fact sheet." Retrieved July 21, 2014, from http://www.who.int/mediacentre/factsheets/fs104/en/

77. World Health Organization. (2013). "Global tuberculosis report 2013." Retrieved July 24, 2014, from http://apps.who.int/iris/bitstream/10665/91355/1/9789241564656_eng.pdf

78. World Health Organization, "Tuberculosis fact sheet."

79. "Are drug companies living up to human rights responsibilities? The perspective of Paul Hunt, former UN Special Rapporteur (2002–2008), and Rajat Khosla." (2010, September). *PLoS Medicine, 7*(9), e1000330. Retrieved August 3, 2014, from http://journals.plos.org/plosmedicine/article?id=10.1371/journal.pmed.1000330

80. Ibid.

81. Argenti, P. A. (2012). *Corporate communication* (6th ed.). McGraw-Hill Higher Education.

82. Ibid.

83. Ibid.

84. Ibid.

85. Ibid.

86. Ibid.

87. Roche. (2007, March). "CSR innovation across the pharmaceutical industry." *Article 13 and Roche: View from the Field.*

88. Ibid.

89. Ibid.

90. Tolve, "Pharma and CSR."

91. GSK, http://www.gsk.com/en-gb/about-us/our-mission-and-strategy/ (accessed July 24, 2014).

92. Bale, H. "The pharmaceutical industry and corporate social responsibility." Retrieved August 3, 2014.

93. Ibid.

94. Roche, "CSR innovation across the pharmaceutical industry."

95. Ibid.

96. Ibid.

97. Access to Medicine Index. (n.d.). "What is the Index?" Retrieved July 24, 2014, from http://www.accesstomedicineindex.org/what-index

98. Ibid.

CREATING SHARED VALUE AT MCDONALD'S

In mid-2012, McDonald's Corporation's soon-to-be CEO Don Thompson announced a shift in the direction of the McDonald's menu, with the focus of the fast-food behemoth's offerings moving from beef to chicken.[1] This was especially surprising news coming from a company that had for most of its history displayed signs outside its restaurants proudly announcing the billions of hamburgers sold since McDonald's mid-20th-century founding.

What drove McDonald's decision to move away from beef? In January 2012, the company rolled out new commercials featuring conversations with some of the farmers and ranchers who were suppliers of McDonald's. One such spot included a sound bite in which a supplier proclaimed, "Beef's what we do"—a seeming microcosm for the whole of the seven-decade-old company's strategy.[2] Yet during a May 2012 consumer conference, Don Thompson cited chicken as a "tremendous opportunity," and there was plenty of evidence to support his claim.[3] Not only did chicken represent an opportunity to improve the nutritional value of McDonald's menu offerings, but it was also less expensive than other protein sources such as beef, providing supply chain cost-savings to McDonald's that it could pass along to its consumers.

Writing in *Harvard Business Review*, Michael Porter and Mark Kramer defined shared value as "policies and operating practices that enhance the competitiveness of a company while simultaneously advancing the economic and social conditions in the communities in which it operates."[4] Shared value creation is the means by which these practices identify the connections between societal and economic progress and turn them into opportunities for global growth.[5] McDonald's is a company that has wisely used its CR initiatives to further its business objectives while being a good corporate citizen.

Because chicken was less expensive than beef, expanding its chicken-based offerings was another way in which McDonald's increased focus on chicken created shared value for the corporation and its consumers. McDonald's identified an opportunity to entice budget-minded consumers, which is especially valuable during periods of economic distress, when consumers are looking for additional cost-savings.[6] A menu with additional chicken-based options gave McDonald's consumers more budget-friendly choices while allowing McDonald's to find new ways to fulfill its customers' increased demand for chicken-based snacks and meals.

During 2011, for the first time, McDonald's sold more pounds of chicken than beef, a feat *The New York Times* likened to Starbucks selling more tea than coffee.[7] Thompson's

Source: This case was written by Kathleen O'Leary, T'12, under the supervision of Professor Paul A. Argenti at the Tuck School of Business at Dartmouth. This case was prepared with publicly available information. © 2014 Trustees of Dartmouth College. All rights reserved.

May 2012 announcement therefore reflected a shift that was already taking place within McDonald's restaurants and driven by its consumers.

MCDONALD'S BEGINNINGS

In 1954, 52-year-old Multimixer milkshake machine salesman Ray Kroc was surprised by an order for eight mixers from a restaurant in San Bernardino, California.[8] Visiting the restaurant from his home outside Chicago, Kroc was deeply impressed by its operational effectiveness and returned home having secured from its owners, Dick and Mac McDonald, the right to set up McDonald's restaurants throughout the U.S. (save for several California and Arizona territories in which the McDonald brothers had already licensed the name). The following year, Kroc founded the McDonald's Corporation and opened his first McDonald's location in Des Plaines, Illinois. Five years later, he had purchased the exclusive rights to the McDonald's name and brought the total number of restaurants in the chain to over 100 locations.[9]

From the beginning, the McDonald's Corporation was a reflection of Kroc's background and values. Kroc, a high school dropout, deliberately created a corporate culture in which professional success both inside and beyond McDonald's restaurants was driven by merit, rather than by an employee's educational background, pedigree, or connections.[10] The advancement process within the company continued to epitomize this philosophy: even in the 21st century, 70% of U.S. store managers began their careers with McDonald's as restaurant crew, while 50% of corporate employees can make the same claim.[11]

Years after Kroc's death, his emphasis on the importance of hard work and integrity continued to echo throughout the corporation.[12] He was known for his iconic sayings, called Krocisms, which included such perspectives as "If you work just for money, you'll never make it. But if you love what you're doing and you always put the customer first, success will be yours."[13]

While Kroc passed away long before Michael Porter and Mark Kramer advocated a shared-value approach in *Harvard Business Review*, the blueprint he created for his company positioned it well to deliver on such a philosophy in its CR programs.[14]

THE EVOLUTION OF CSR AT MCDONALD'S

The 21st century saw an overall shift in societal expectations of corporate behavior and a corresponding shift in corporations' approach to CR issues. The evolution of McDonald's CR program was no exception, as VP of sustainability Bob Langert explained in a January 2012 interview with AccountAbility, a global organization providing innovative CR and sustainability solutions: "In the beginning, CSR was much more focused on our company values, our heritage of doing the right thing."[15]

This view echoed that espoused in McDonald's first formal CSR report, released in 2002:

> The principles behind our commitment to social responsibility were ingrained in our culture by McDonald's Corporation founder, Ray Kroc, who spoke nearly half a century ago of the importance of giving back to the local communities our restaurants served. Ray Kroc did not articulate this as a corporate strategy nor would he have listed social responsibility on a corporate balance sheet. He simply knew its worth because being a good neighbor and corporate citizen are intrinsic to McDonald's approach to business.[16]

While McDonald's early efforts to deliver on its responsibilities to CR stakeholders were informal, the company grew more and more transparent about its social and environmental efforts in the 21st century. McDonald's initially released its CSR and sustainability reports once every two years, but the corporation switched to annual reports beginning in 2008.[17] In its 2011 Global Sustainability Scorecard, McDonald's divided its CR efforts into five categories reflecting the company's comprehensive stakeholder approach: Nutrition & Well-Being, Sustainable Supply Chain, Environmental Responsibility, Employee Experience, and Community.[18]

By 2012, McDonald's was an example of a corporation where CR initiatives were integrated throughout different departments, rather than being siloed in a dedicated CSR department. As Langert explained, "Sometimes people are working on sustainability, and they don't even know it, because they're not looking through that particular lens in their work."[19] The company moved away from talking about CR as a niche area dealing with social issues and philanthropic efforts and toward a more comprehensive conversation about sustainability as a means of not only delivering on the company's responsibility to society but also a means of ensuring that McDonald's could continue to operate profitably going forward.[20]

According to Kathleen Bannan, senior manager for corporate social responsibility, "CSR is everybody's business."[21] Bannan described how McDonald's sets its CR priorities based on what is internally known as the "Smart Zone"—opportunities that result in win-win solutions, such as "investing in energy efficiency solutions and analyzing an environmental scorecard across departments to chart progress as well as identify struggle points."[22]

In a 2010 interview with *Forbes*, Bannan divided the evolution of CR at McDonald's into three eras, beginning in 1955 (see Exhibit 5.1).[23]

What Bannan described as the Golden Age, 1955 to 1989, fits with McDonald's early commitment to delivering on the principles espoused by Ray Kroc without having a formal means of measuring and reporting the company's efforts to serve as a responsible corporate citizen. During the 1990s, with technological advancements making communication easier

Exhibit 5.1 CSR focus at McDonald's, 1955–present

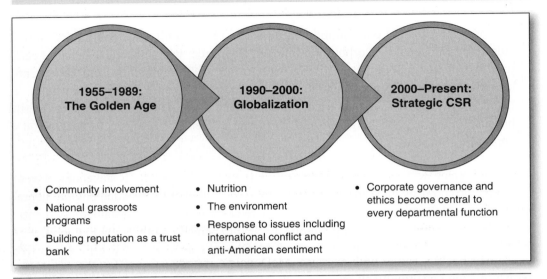

- Community involvement
- National grassroots programs
- Building reputation as a trust bank

- Nutrition
- The environment
- Response to issues including international conflict and anti-American sentiment

- Corporate governance and ethics become central to every departmental function

Source: Adapted from Singh, A. (2010, September 10). "At McDonald's, CSR is everybody's business." *Forbes.* Retrieved August 23, 2012, from http://www.forbes.com/sites/csr/2010/09/10/at-mcdonalds-csr-is-everybodys-business.

and spurring rapid globalization, other issues such as nutrition and the environment became part of the company's CR approach. Anti-American sentiment abroad manifested itself in the form of attacks on major American corporations including McDonald's. As a result, McDonald's approach to CR was reactive rather than strategic. However, the corporation's priorities began to shift in 2000.

Even skeptics such as *Fortune* and GreenBiz.com writer Marc Gunther lauded McDonald's CR efforts under Bob Langert. In a December 2011 GreenBiz article, Gunther described the company's "meaningful progress" in reforming its supply chain to ensure that sources were legal and sustainably managed and cited his trust in Langert as a major reason why he took the company's CR and sustainability efforts seriously.[24] Langert himself described his work for the first 20 years after he was put in charge of McDonald's CSR program as being reactive and defensive. Looking at the spate of films and books targeting McDonald's during the early 2000s (such as *Super Size Me* and *Fast Food Nation*), it is easy to see how CSR personnel were kept busy responding to crises.[25]

In the 21st century, however, McDonald's shifted its perspective on CR and viewed sustainability (which is how the company had chosen to rebrand its CSR efforts) as an opportunity. In delivering on its responsibility to consumers, McDonald's leveraged a key component of Porter and Kramer's road map for creating shared value by using the need to adapt to changing consumer expectations as a launching pad for product and market innovation.

Obesity

Beyond the need to deliver on changing consumer expectations, McDonald's saw other incentives to reorient its menu toward lower-calorie offerings. The events of the first decade of the 21st century provided a challenging backdrop for McDonald's and other fast-food corporations as concerns about the U.S. obesity epidemic—and childhood obesity in particular—brought such companies under increased scrutiny.

In February 2004, the U.S. Centers for Disease Control and Prevention released a study reporting that obesity had become a serious health problem among Americans, whose average weight had grown significantly since the early 1960s—from 168 to 180 pounds for adult males and from 143 to 155 pounds for adult females.[26] That same year, McDonald's discontinued its Supersize option, which had previously allowed customers to upgrade the size of both the soft drink and fries included in their value meals for a nominal uptick in price.[27]

Aside from cutting out the calorie-maximizing Supersize option, the company also took steps to add healthy foods and other resources to its offerings. Encouraging consumers to pair healthy eating with exercise, McDonald's introduced the "Go Active" meal, which included healthy menu options as well as tools designed to help consumers track their physical activity.[28] McDonald's also added nutritional information to its website, breaking with its previous policy of not providing such information for individual menu items. With caloric information provided, certain benefits of choosing chicken over beef became clear—for example, consider the 550 calories in a Big Mac versus the 280 calories in a six-piece order of Chicken McNuggets.[29] In September 2012, McDonald's opted to begin sharing calorie counts for menu items in its U.S. restaurants in advance of requirements to do so under a new healthcare law.[30] During the same month, McDonald's also released its first nutrition progress report, titled "McDonald's USA Nutrition Journey."[31] The report outlined commitments the company had made to its consumers and how it had delivered on them.

While consumers' increased emphasis on healthy eating led McDonald's to take serious, tangible steps to alter its menus and create greater transparency regarding its practices around nutrition, concern about the healthfulness of fast food was nothing new. McDonald's in particular had been the subject of multiple liability lawsuits stemming from the perceived unhealthiness of its menu options, with varying degrees of success.

In 2001, New York lawyer Samuel Hirsch brought a lawsuit against the company on behalf of an obese client alleging that the client's weight problems stemmed from eating at McDonald's and other fast-food restaurants.[32] After this suit was dropped, Hirsch brought a similar suit on behalf of two obese teenagers.[33] In 2002, students at George Washington University Law School filed suit against McDonald's for claiming its French fries were fried in vegetable oil when they were also fried in beef oil; they settled for $12.5 million.

Between 2007 and 2012, McDonald's made additional strides in offering healthy options to a consumer base that increasingly demanded them. Some were simple additions to the menu, including low-calorie wrap sandwiches, 290-calorie servings of oatmeal, and fruit smoothies.[34] Part of the reasoning behind these minor adjustments was a desire to deliver on greater consumer demand for healthy foods. McDonald's had plenty of competition to contend with, between the rise of healthier fast-food options such as Panera Bread and the success of Subway's "Subway Diet" marketing campaign, featuring a customer, Jared Fogle, who had lost 245 pounds through a diet heavily reliant on Subway sandwiches.[35] But beyond heightened competition, because of increased litigation around obesity concerns, McDonald's attention to improving the nutritional content of its menu was a means of protecting its license to operate. In all cases, McDonald's was incentivized to change, but instead of approaching the situation as a necessary evil, the company used it as an opportunity for value creation.

VIEWING THE NEED FOR CHANGE AS OPPORTUNITY

Around the time of Don Thompson's announcement, another top executive, Neil Golden, McDonald's chief marketing officer for its American restaurants, acknowledged a shortfall in public perceptions of the company. While McDonald's served 28 million people every day at the time, Golden believed it could reach more consumers:

> The consumer perception of the quality of our food is not where we want it to be; . . . there are a lot of consumers that love what we're serving. But we believe that they would come more frequently. We also believe that there are more people that would come—if they could feel better about the product.[36]

Langert's view converged with Golden's that the company was potentially leaving money on the table: "Our research shows that the global consumer wants more food choices, wants more incorporation of nutritional aspects into food. We care about that. We want to provide food that people feel good about."[37] It is this perspective that drove McDonald's to upgrade its menu and rebrand its restaurants' offerings as both healthier and more sustainable.[38]

In some cases, U.S. McDonald's menus borrowed from their European counterparts to increase the number of healthier options.[39] Spicy Chicken McBites were one such example; the 410-calorie item was introduced to the U.S. market in June 2012.[40]

McDonald's was acutely aware of how its CR initiatives benefited both the corporation and its constituents. As Bob Langert stated:

Sustainability isn't just about doing the right thing. It's about doing something that's going to benefit our company. There's no need to be bashful about creating value because that's what's going to make our work sustainable and bring value to society at the same time.[41]

One crucial constituency McDonald's tapped for assistance in reformulating its menu was moms—and in particular, mom bloggers. Happy Meals were arguably the section of the McDonald's menu that parents felt most strongly about, and the company was wise to allow leading mom bloggers to influence the direction of its Happy Meal nutrition strategy. In late 2011, McDonald's announced that by March 2012, the company would reformulate its Happy Meals in the United States and Latin America so that every Happy Meal served in McDonald's restaurants in these markets would automatically include fruit.[42]

McDonald's also announced that Happy Meals would include a smaller portion of fries going forward, resulting in a reduction in calories and fat per meal.[43] When the company made these announcements via webcast, it extended invitations not only to traditional journalists but also to a select number of mom bloggers.[44] Rick Wion, McDonald's director of social media at the time, described mom bloggers as "very networked and very linked-in" and said, "They spread information very, very quickly."[45]

In a potentially controversial move, the company also provided perks to influential mom bloggers. In 2010, the company flew 15 mom bloggers to its suburban Chicago headquarters and put them up in hotel rooms. During the visit, the bloggers and their families received a tour of McDonald's headquarters, including the test kitchen and the Ronald McDonald House.[46] Another perk was access to Jan Fields, president of McDonald's USA at the time, herself a mother who had worked her way up through the company after starting as restaurant crew in the 1970s.[47] While travel expenses were paid for, McDonald's did not compensate the bloggers for content posted online or require them to post on specific topics, beyond requesting that they each write one blog post about the trip.[48]

Similarly, McDonald's used the 4,100-attendee BlogHer conference in San Diego during the summer of 2011 as another opportunity to connect with mom bloggers. Once again, the company provided access to Fields, this time in a private luncheon held for 25 bloggers with Fields and other McDonald's executives in attendance.[49] It was mom bloggers who, during the BlogHer luncheon, provided the McDonald's team with ideas for how to improve the nutritional quality of Happy Meals.[50]

The decision by McDonald's to tap into the mom blogger network was a classic example of shared value creation. The relationship between McDonald's and influential mom bloggers provided a series of benefits to both parties, as well as to greater society:

1. **Tapping into consumer knowledge**. Even though McDonald's employees had long included a large number of parents, insights from parents outside the company proved invaluable, offering a different perspective on what worked and what didn't work for busy parents who were committed to feeding their children nutritious meals.

2. **Access to mom bloggers' networks**. Widely read bloggers often have significant influence over the purchasing decisions of their loyal readership, and mom bloggers are no different. Mom bloggers who visited McDonald's headquarters and subsequently wrote about their experiences were likely to include details about the ways in which McDonald's was transforming its menu to provide healthier options for kids.

3. **Reputational rewards**. By building bridges with a group that was likely to be perceived as skeptical about the health benefits of McDonald's food, the corporation enhanced its reputation as a trusted partner in the fight to improve children's nutrition. With the amount of publicity around childhood obesity, McDonald's demonstrated commitment to improving the healthfulness of its menu could be a key differentiator between it and other, similar fast-food restaurants.

4. **Healthier options for kids and families**. The end result of the collaboration between McDonald's and mom bloggers was that McDonald's restaurants offered a menu filled with a greater number of healthy options for kids. By continuing to adapt to changing consumer expectations, McDonald's also identified an opportunity to court future consumers, as today's children grow into tomorrow's parents with a sense of loyalty to the company.

By creating real relationships with mom bloggers through in-person events and demonstrating that McDonald's was serious about their input by using their ideas, the company had the foresight to take steps to win over the group likely to be the most concerned with the nutritional content of Happy Meals. Simultaneously, by tapping into the specialized knowledge of mom bloggers, McDonald's gained access to vital information with the potential to increase revenues and market share.

FOOD SAFETY

McDonald's also had a valuable reputation to protect when it came to food safety, as the company was widely acknowledged to be one of the best companies in the U.S. with regard to this issue.[51] By following extremely stringent procedures throughout the entire process of procuring, shipping, storing, and preparing its meats, McDonald's ensured that it not only protected its consumers from threat of illness or disease but also protected the corporation from potential lawsuits around food safety.

McDonald's was quick to take action whenever it discovered a violation along its supply chain. In August 2012, ABC News reported that McDonald's had terminated its dealings with a California meat supplier, Central Valley Meat (CVM), after an investigation by the same network had uncovered evidence that the plant was treating its animals inhumanely.[52] While there were no food safety issues present in the CVM plant, McDonald's swift actions in terminating its CVM contracts was another example of how the corporation delivered on its responsibility to consumers, who had expectations of McDonald's supply chain behavior that went beyond the nutritional value and safety of the food they purchased. In this case, McDonald's acted in a way that protected the company from coming under attack from an NGO with powerful media connections while communicating to consumers that the company would not stand for animal cruelty along its supply chain.

McDonald's continued to listen to its consumers and adapt to changing societal expectations while retaining the core principles under which it was founded. The company used the evolution of consumer demand as an opportunity to innovate new products and use new media to partner with consumers toward delivering on changing consumer needs.

Case Questions

1. How does McDonald's CR/sustainability strategy fit into the company's overall corporate strategy and culture?

2. What is the relationship between the personal and corporate values espoused by Ray Kroc and McDonald's views of its role as a corporate citizen?

3. How has McDonald's used potential crises as opportunities to better deliver on consumer expectations?

4. What portion of McDonald's decisions to alter its menus do you believe are driven by a desire to increase profits and avoid lawsuits, versus legitimate concern for consumer health? How do McDonald's practices compare with other examples of shared value creation discussed in the book so far?

5. Is McDonald's missing an opportunity by focusing on the health benefits of chicken versus beef, potentially ignoring the additional environmental concerns posed by chicken farming? Should McDonald's increase the percentage of its meals made up of fruit and vegetables to deliver additional environmental benefits, or is this moving too far away from its core business to adequately represent strategic CR?

NOTES

1. Patton, L. (2012, July 2). "McDonald's new CEO focuses on chicken amid shaky economy." *Bloomberg.com.* Retrieved August 21, 2012, from http://www.bloomberg.com/news/print/2012-07-02/mcdonald-s-new-ceo-focuses-on-chicken-amid-shaky-economy.html

2. O'Brien, K. (2012, May 4). "How McDonald's came back bigger than ever." *New York Times Magazine.* Retrieved August 21, 2012, from http://www.nytimes.com/2012/05/06/magazine/how-mcdonalds-came-back-bigger-than-ever.html

3. Ibid.

4. Porter, M. E., & Kramer, M. R. (2011, January/February). "Creating shared value" (p. 6). *Harvard Business Review.*

5. Ibid.

6. Patton, "McDonald's new CEO focuses on chicken amid shaky economy."

7. O'Brien, "How McDonald's came back bigger than ever."

8. McDonald's. (n.d.). "The Ray Kroc Story: McDonalds.com." Retrieved from http://www.mcdonalds.com/us/en/our_story/our_history/the_ray_kroc_story.html

9. Ibid.

10. Wolfe, R., Hartman, L., & Mead, J. (2008). "Started as crew: McDonald's strategy for corporate success and poverty reduction" (Case Study No. UVA-E-0310). Charlottesville, VA: Darden Business Publishing.

11. Ibid.

12. Ibid.

13. Ibid.

14. Porter & Kramer, "Creating shared value."

15. "10 questions: CR leaders corner: Bob Langert." (2012, January 5). Retrieved August 23, 2012, from http://www.accountability.org/about-us/news/cr-leaders-corner/bob-langert.html

16. McDonald's. (2003). "McDonald's social responsibility report." Retrieved March 10, 2015, from http://www.aboutmcdonalds.com/content/dam/AboutMcDonalds/Sustainability/Sustainability%20Library/2002%20Report%20%28English%29.pdf

17. McDonald's. (n.d.). "Sustainability: AboutMcDonalds.com." Retrieved from http://www.aboutmcdonalds.com/mcd/sustainability/library/past_sustainability_CR_reports.html

18. McDonald's. (2011). "McDonald's 2011 global sustainability scorecard." Retrieved from http://www.aboutmcdonalds.com/content/dam/AboutMcDonalds/Sustainability/Sustainability%20Library/2011-Sustainability-Scorecard.pdf

19. AccountAbility. (2012, January 5). "AccountAbility: Setting the standard for corporate responsibility and sustainable development—Bob Langert." Retrieved from http://www.accountability.org/about-us/news/cr-leaders-corner/bob-langert.html

20. Ibid.

21. Singh, A. (2010, September 10). "At McDonald's, CSR is everybody's business." *Forbes.* Retrieved August 23, 2012, from http://www.forbes.com/sites/csr/2010/09/10/at-mcdonalds-csr-is-everybodys-business

22. Ibid.

23. Ibid.

24. Gunther, M. (2011, December 21). "How McDonald's is mainstreaming sustainability." *GreenBiz.com*. Retrieved August 23, 2012, from http://www.greenbiz.com/blog/2011/12/21/how-mcdonalds-mainstreaming-sustainability

25. Ibid.

26. Baron, D. P. (2005). *Obesity and McLawsuits* (Case P-49, p. 2). (2005, January 25). Stanford, CA: Stanford Graduate School of Business.

27. Carpenter, D. (2004, March 3). "McDonald's to dump supersize portions." *Washington Post*. Retrieved September 6, 2012, from http://www.washingtonpost.com/wp-dyn/articles/A26082-2004Mar3.html

28. Baron, *Obesity and McLawsuits*, p. 3.

29. Patton, "McDonald's new CEO focuses on chicken amid shaky economy."

30. Kliff, S. (2012, September 24). "A Big Mac has 550 calories. McDonald's customers say: So what?" *Washington Post*. Retrieved from http://www.washingtonpost.com/blogs/ezra-klein/wp/2012/09/24/a-big-mac-has-550-calories-mcdonalds-customers-say-so-what

31. McDonald's. (2012). "McDonald's USA nutrition journey: A 2012 progress report." Retrieved from http://www.aboutmcdonalds.com/content/dam/AboutMcDonalds/Newsroom/Electronic%20Press%20Kits/Nutrition%20EPK/McDonaldsNPR.pdf

32. Baron, *Obesity and McLawsuits*.

33. Ibid.

34. Patton, "McDonald's new CEO focuses on chicken amid shaky economy."

35. "Jared's Journey." Subway.com

36. O'Brien, "How McDonald's came back bigger than ever."

37. AccountAbility, "AccountAbility."

38. Ibid.

39. Patton, "McDonald's new CEO focuses on chicken amid shaky economy."

40. Ibid.

41. AccountAbility, "AccountAbility."

42. McDonald's. (n.d.). "Corporate social responsibility and sustainability." Retrieved from http://www.aboutmcdonalds.com/mcd/sustainability/our_focus_areas/nutrition_and_well_being/stories_accomplishments.html

43. Ibid.

44. Aubrey, A. (2011, July 27). "McDonald's courts mom bloggers when changing the menu." *NPR*. Retrieved from http://www.npr.org/blogs/health/2011/07/27/138746335/mcdonalds-courts-mom-bloggers-when-changing-the-menu

45. Ibid.

46. Bhasin, K. (2012, May 7). "McDonald's Has Gained A New Ally By Sucking Up To This Group Of Bloggers." *Business Insider*. Retrieved from http://www.businessinsider.com/how-mcdonalds-works-with-mom-bloggers-2012-5#ixzz3Zx2euw7a

47. Wolfe et al., "Started as crew."

48. O'Brien, "How McDonald's came back bigger than ever."

49. Ibid.

50. Ibid.

51. "How McDonald's makes sure its burgers are safe." (2009, December 29). *USA Today*. Retrieved August 23, 2012, from http://www.usatoday.com/money/industries/food/2009 -12-29-mdonalds-burgers-food-safety_N.htm

52. Galli, C. (2012, August 22). "McDonald's suspends purchases from meat plant shut by USDA." *ABC News*. Retrieved March 11, 2013, from http://abcnews.go.com/Blotter/mcdonalds -suspends-purchases-meat-plant-shut-usda/story?id=17061088

Chapter 6

RESPONSIBLE CORPORATE GOVERNANCE

There is no single definition of corporate governance. In 1992, the Cadbury Commission, a group formed to consider the financial aspects of corporate governance, defined corporate governance in its simplest form as the process and systems by which companies are directed and controlled.[1] However, in light of the high-profile corporate scandals and financial crises in the early 21st century, the growing pressure on businesses to take a more active role in addressing societal issues, and the increasing complexity of international corporations, this definition is both inadequate and obsolete. Corporate governance no longer simply refers to an elite board of directors that meets quarterly to review the performance of C-level executives and discuss the strategic direction of the company.

Rather, the modern era of business demands a more holistic and active role by the individuals who are selected to govern both small and large business organizations, both at the executive management and director levels. As illustrated by the public outcry after the 2010 Upper Big Branch coal mine tragedy in West Virginia, in which 29 miners were killed by a blast resulting from negligence on the part of the mine's owner, Massey Energy, C-level executives and their respective boards are being held responsible by a public that demands answers and accountability from businesses and corporations.[2] This chapter provides an overview of corporate governance with a particular focus on the intersection of corporate governance and corporate social responsibility.

The traditional model of corporate governance was established in the 1919 *Dodge v. Ford Motor Company* decision that established the following:

A business corporation is organized and carried on primarily for the profit of the stockholders. The powers of the directors are to be employed for that end.

The discretion of directors is to be exercised in the choice of means to attain that end and does not extend to a change in the end itself, to the reduction of profits, or to the nondistribution of profits among stockholders in order to devote them to other purposes.[3]

This landmark decision established the foundation for the model of corporate governance that would dominate the business landscape until the start of the 21st century. Managers and directors of corporations were charged with a single goal: maximize the profits of the corporation. This case established the foundation of corporate governance by clearly setting the goal of corporate managers and directors. With the goal set, the debate turned to how corporate governance would achieve the objective of maximizing shareholder value.

In a 1992 article titled "The Corporate Board: Confronting the Paradoxes," Ada Demb and F.-Friedrich Neubauer defined corporate governance as "the process by which corporations are made responsive to the rights and wishes of stakeholders."[4] While this definition is more robust than the initial definition provided at the start of this chapter, it is still not complete and raises the following questions: How are corporations made responsive? And to what rights and wishes is the corporation to be made responsive? And perhaps most important, who are the stakeholders of a business?

Other definitions available in the copious amounts of business literature on the topic attempt to answer these questions and provide a more comprehensive definition of corporate governance. However, what is revealed through a review of current thoughts and opinions on modern corporate governance is that the concept is evolving rapidly. As a result of the corporate scandals in this century and the financial crisis of 2007 in particular, the very foundational goal of corporate governance established in *Dodge v. Ford Motor Company* is under challenge. To understand the evolving nature of corporate governance, it is first necessary to have an understanding of the corporate scandals and financial crisis that gave rise to the movement to rethink the very principal of corporate governance.

THE BOARD OF DIRECTORS

A corporation's board of directors plays an important role in the governance of both small and large companies. This is especially true for publicly traded companies that are required to have an active board of directors. The board of directors, sometimes referred to as the board of governors, board of trustees, or board of managers, but more often simply referred to as "the board," is a body of appointed or elected individuals who cooperatively oversee a company, institution, or organization. An organization or company's bylaws typically establish the specific duties, powers, and responsibilities for a board of directors. The bylaws also detail the size of the board, the selection process for members, and a schedule of required board meetings. In a publicly traded stock company, the members of the board of directors are elected by the shareholders. The board of directors of most companies has the top authority in the strategy of the organization.

To understand the role of the board of directors in corporate governance, it is important first to understand the terminology related to the board. The members of a board of directors are referred to as directors of the corporation. An inside director is a director who is a high-ranking employee, large shareholder, or other individual who is intimately connected to the organization. Inside directors have special knowledge of the inner workings of the firm, including but not limited to financial, marketing, and strategy insights. Typical inside directors include chief executive officers, major shareholders, and representatives of other stakeholders including major lenders.

An outside director is a member of the board who is not employed or engaged with the company. These individuals do not represent stakeholders, but serve as a source of outside counsel on strategy, operations, and performance. Individual directors may serve on multiple boards of other companies, leading to what are referred to as interlocking directorates. Interlocking directorates may result in a small number of individuals having substantial influence over a large number of important organizations. The corporate, social, and legal effects of an interlocking directorate have been debated extensively.

While the specific duties and responsibilities of a board of directors are detailed in an organization's bylaws, there are a consistent set of responsibilities across most boards that can be categorized into three major categories: operational oversight; risk management/accountability; and executive recruitment, performance, and compensation.

Each of these major categories of responsibility has been directly affected by the growing influence of the corporate social responsibility movement. To appreciate the dramatic changes corporate social responsibility has effected on the traditional role of a board of directors, we will examine each board function individually.

Operational Oversight

Since the corporate scandals of the early 2000s, the amount of responsibility placed on a board of directors for the oversight of a publicly traded company has increased dramatically. As seen in the case of Dennis Kozlowski's misdeeds at Tyco, when top executives are able to steal or otherwise misuse large amounts of corporate money, the board is likely to come under intense scrutiny for its lack of oversight. Regarding Tyco, one head of a director search firm asked, "Just how do you hide this much money for so long from your board? It's their job as a director to know what's going on."[5]

There are several issues at play here. One is that board members often have incentives to look the other way when CEOs abuse corporate funds. Executives and directors often sit on each other's boards, creating a symbiotic relationship in which mutual leniency can thrive. And in some cases, directors' firms may be employed by the CEO's company in a consulting capacity, providing added financial incentive not to rock the boat out of concern for losing such lucrative contracts.[6] Both situations make it difficult to ensure proper board oversight; meanwhile, the lack of accountability for board members who foster executive misbehavior limits incentives to blow the whistle.

Risk Management

In a paper on the relationship between risk management and corporate governance, University of New Hampshire Professor of Finance Fred Kaen argues that

> risk management and risk management products help ensure the survival of the firm and thereby support broad public policy objectives—objectives beyond the immediate interests of the owners of the company and a narrow financial objective of shareholder wealth maximization.[7]

As we will see from reading about the corporate scandals outlined later in the chapter, top executives and board members often place immediate gains and individual interests above the overall good of the corporation, with disastrous results.

In a blog post for the Harvard Law School Forum on Corporate Governance and Financial Regulation, Martin Lipton of the New York law firm Wachtell, Lipton, Rosen & Katz argued that the board of directors' responsibility for risk management has never been more important or involved in as many challenges as it is today.[8] He noted that this has been especially true of the financial services sector, where failure to manage risk adequately has resulted in "large-scale bankruptcies, bank failures, government intervention and rapid consolidation."[9]

Such crises in the banking industry have a devastating impact well beyond the industry itself. Companies across a broad spectrum of industries have been affected by credit market paralysis, and the broader economy has suffered. While Lipton acknowledged that the board cannot be involved in day-to-day risk management, fulfilling its responsibility for controlling risk means that directors must ensure that those within the corporation who are tasked with creating and implementing risk management procedures are doing so in line with the board's corporate strategy. Furthermore, it is the board's job to foster an environment where risk management is taken seriously throughout the corporation. Lipton argued:

> Through its oversight role, the board can send a message to the company's management and employees that corporate risk management is not an impediment to the conduct of business nor a mere supplement to a firm's overall compliance program, but is instead an integral component of the firm's corporate strategy, culture and value generation process.[10]

Executive Recruitment, Performance, and Compensation

A critical function of the board of directors with regard to corporate governance is the hiring and performance review of, as well as compensation decisions regarding, the chief executive officer. Recruitment and hiring of the CEO is particularly critical. Typically, a board will engage an executive search firm to assist in the selection of a new CEO. Following the hiring of the CEO, most boards will work closely with the new CEO in the recruitment and hiring decisions for other top executives. The board is also responsible for the annual performance review of a CEO.

For large publicly traded companies, a compensation committee is typically established to review and approve the compensation packages of top executives. In the wake of the 2007 financial crisis, this function of the board came under intense scrutiny, as it was revealed that many top executives were highly compensated even in cases when the executive's company did not perform well financially.

CORPORATE GOVERNANCE IN CRISIS

At the start of the 21st century, the traditional corporate governance model that had dominated the United States business landscape was placed under intense scrutiny due to a succession of highly publicized, dramatic business collapses and scandals. While detailing all the crises that occurred from a corporate governance perspective is beyond the scope of this book,[11] four crises are most important in the evolution of corporate governance: Enron Corporation, Tyco International, Worldcom, and the 2007 financial crisis. These events not only resulted in a focus on the role of corporate governance in ensuring that companies act in the best interests of their financial shareholders, but also increased pressure for corporate governance to consider the interests of a new type of stakeholder, including society at large.

Enron Corporation

On December 2, 2001, Enron Corporation declared bankruptcy as a result of long-standing and methodical accounting fraud that substantially overstated the financial position and earnings of the business. Employing over 20,000 individuals and with claimed revenues of over $100 million, Enron was the largest bankruptcy in the history of the United States as of 2001.[12]

However, Enron Corporation did not fall alone. Arthur Andersen, Enron's accounting auditor and one of the five largest accounting partnerships in the world at the time, dissolved as a result of a dramatic loss of its customers due to its apparent auditing failures. Arthur Andersen was subsequently found guilty in United States District Court for obstruction of justice for intentionally destroying Enron financial documents after being placed on notice by federal investigators.[13] While the company was founded on the principle that an auditor's responsibility is to investors, not company management, Andersen began to relax its standards in the late 20th century, and was eventually in a position where it had lucrative consulting contracts with many of the firm's auditing clients, creating a conflict of interest that incentivized auditors to look the other way regarding accounting issues. In the case of Enron, Andersen was found to be complicit in the company's systematic accounting fraud. Though Andersen's conviction was later overturned because of insufficient jury instruction, Andersen voluntarily surrendered its licenses to practice following the guilty verdict, as the Securities and Exchange Commission (SEC) does not accept audits conducted by convicted felons. This effectively put the firm out of business.

The Enron scandal called into question the effectiveness of the traditional model of corporate governance and the relationship of corporate executives with the board of directors and external auditors. In their analysis of the scandal, titled "The Fall of Enron," Paul Healy and Krishna Palepu wrote in 2003 that a

> well-functioning capital market creates appropriate linkages of information, incentives, and governance between managers and investors. This process is supposed to be carried out through a network of intermediaries that include assurance professionals such as external auditors; and internal governance agents such as corporate boards.[14]

Despite having a board of directors that was deemed to be one of the top five boards in the United States by *Chief Executive* magazine in 2000, Healy and Palepu noted that Enron was still able to "attract large sums of capital to fund a questionable business model, conceal its true performance through a series of accounting and financing maneuvers, and hype its stock to unsustainable levels."[15]

Healy and Palepu concluded that "the governance and incentives that emerged at Enron can also surface at many other firms, and may potentially affect the entire capital market."[16] Robert Jaedicke, former dean of the Stanford Graduate School of Business, was the head of Enron's Audit Committee, drawing confusion from those who knew Jaedicke as an honest and forthright person.[17] According to Arjay Miller, former president of Ford and also a former dean of Stanford GSB, Jaedicke was "a very honest, upright, full-of-integrity individual. If you named the top five academic accountants in the U.S., I feel quite sure he'd make the list."[18] While Jaedicke was not implicated in criminal wrongdoing, his leadership of the committee that oversaw Enron's financial reporting, controls, and compliance raises questions about how the corporation was able to get away with their fraudulent practices.

Tyco International

On January 14, 2002, Tyco International CEO L. Dennis Kozlowski was named one of the top 25 corporate executives of 2001 by *Businessweek* magazine.[19] This award ostensibly recognized Kozlowski's exemplary leadership of Tyco since his being named CEO in 1992. During the late 1990s, Kozlowski led the company through a series of mergers and acquisitions that resulted in the creation of a mega international conglomerate that consistently exceeded Wall Street expectations and enabled the company to achieve the largest earnings and stock prices in the company's history.

However, as 2002 progressed, Tyco International's and Kozlowski's fortunes drastically changed. On January 22, 2002, Kozlowski announced his plans to split Tyco into four independent publicly traded companies, immediately causing Tyco's stock prices to slide downward. One week later, on January 29, 2002, the company's stock price slid even further after an SEC filing revealed that a former Tyco board member, Frank Walsh, had been paid a $10 million fee along with a $10 million charitable donation to the director's charity for assisting in Tyco's 2001 acquisition of CIT Group. Then, on January 30, 2002, *The New York Times* reported that Kozlowski and Tyco's CFO, Mark Swartz, had sold more than $100 million of their Tyco stock the previous year despite public statements to the contrary. In response, Kozlowski and Swartz stated that they would buy 1 million Tyco shares using their own money.

Four months later on June 3, 2002, Kozlowski resigned suddenly as *The New York Times* reported that he was under investigation for tax evasion by the Manhattan district attorney. Both Kozlowski and Swartz were ultimately indicted on multiple charges of fraud and corruption, resulting in a trial that revealed the opulent lifestyle led by company executives, oftentimes funded by company money. Kozlowski in particular was reported to have purchased items including a $15,000 dog umbrella stand and a $6,000 shower curtain.[20] He kept such items in a $25 million New York City apartment paid for by Tyco.[21] In the end, Kozlowski and Swartz were found guilty of stealing more than $150 million from Tyco International and were sentenced to lengthy prison terms. Additionally, Tyco's former board member Frank Walsh pled guilty to charges that he had devised a scheme to hide the fees he received in the CIT Group acquisition.

The trial and Kozlowski's accusation that Tyco's board of directors was aware of his compensation and spending raised questions on the efficacy of the traditional model of board governance. As Gary Strauss commented in his *USA Today* piece titled "Tyco Events Put Spotlight on Directors' Role," "Tyco directors' lack of awareness about events surrounding criminal charges against CEO Dennis Kozlowski underscores the lax oversight of management that plagues many company boards."[22]

WorldCom

Bernard Ebbers was dubbed the "Telecom Cowboy" for his unconventional style, which was reflected by his office attire that included blue jeans and boots.[23] Ebbers also earned a reputation in the 1990s for building one of the largest and most profitable telecommunications companies in the world, WorldCom. In 1983, Ebbers invested alongside several colleagues in Long Distance Discount Services, Inc. (LDDS).[24] In just two years, Ebbers was promoted to chief executive of the company, ultimately leading the corporation through nearly 65 acquisitions of other telecommunications firms over a 10-year period.[25]

In 1995, LDDS changed its name to WorldCom and, one year later, the company completed what was at the time the largest corporate acquisition in U.S. history, a $12 billion acquisition of MFS Communications, Inc. This transaction value record was eclipsed just a year later when WorldCom completed an unsolicited acquisition of MCI Communications for $30 billion.[26] Then, in 1999, MCI WorldCom announced that it would acquire Spring Communications for $115 billion. However, this transaction was deserted after U.S. and European antitrust regulators objected to the acquisition.[27] This failed transaction and a general decline in the telecom market resulted in a decrease in WorldCom stock price.

During WorldCom's remarkable growth during the 1990s, Ebbers had secured loans for substantial personal holdings using his WorldCom stock holdings as collateral. As WorldCom's stock price fell, Ebbers received increasing requests from lenders to provide additional margin calls as additional collateral. From September 2000 to April 2002, WorldCom's board of directors authorized and granted loans and guarantees to ensure that Ebbers would not be forced to sell his shares.[28]

In April 2002, Bernard Ebbers resigned from MCI WorldCom, ultimately leaving the firm with over $350 million in promissory notes.[29] During this time, however, a bigger scandal was brewing. Starting in 1999 and continuing through May 2002, company executives artificially inflated the financial profitability and growth of the company in an effort to increase the price of WorldCom's stock.[30] These executives included Ebbers along with the company's CFO, controller, and director of general accounting. Through the use of devious accounting methods, the executives successfully masked the deteriorating financial position of the company. In the end, the accounting scandal resulted in WorldCom filing for Chapter 11 bankruptcy protection, which at the time was the largest bankruptcy filing in U.S. history.[31] Ebbers was found guilty of fraud, conspiracy, and the filing of false documents with regulators.[32] He was sentenced to 25 years in prison.[33] Incredibly, WorldCom's board was unaware of the company's fraudulent practices, as a result of its extreme passivity. The board is reported to have revered Ebbers, referring to him as "God" or "Superman," and to have allowed him to reign unchecked as a result.[34] Board committees tasked with governance matters, such as the audit and compensation committees, did not engage in their intended roles. The audit committee "rarely scratched below the surface" of financial reports, while compensation matters were usually decided by Ebbers himself rather than the compensation committee.[35]

THE 2007 FINANCIAL CRISIS

To fully describe the scope and scale of the 2007–2012 financial crisis, including a 17-month recessionary period that has come to be known as the Great Recession, would require an entire textbook it its own right.[36] For the purposes of this book, only a cursory review of the crisis is necessary. Considered by many to be the worst financial crisis since the United States' Great Depression during the 1930s, the crisis resulted in the collapse of a major investment bank, mortgage foreclosures on millions of homes, the bailout of banks and insurance companies by national governments, and a severe decline in global stock markets.

The global recession of the early 21st century was kick-started in part by the subprime mortgage crisis, which prompted markets in North America, Europe, and Asia to sink at alarming rates. The turbulence that began in the United States quickly spread around the world, throwing investors and financial analysts into a frenzy. Equity markets both in the United States and abroad tumbled; in January 2008, world equity markets suffered a $5.2 trillion loss, according to Standard & Poor's.[37]

What became known as the Great Recession lasted from October 2007 through March 2009, with the S&P 500's total loss reaching 56.4%. In February 2007, the market had fallen to its lowest level since 1997.[38] The years following the recession did not prove to be the rebound investors were hoping for, with the S&P 500 finishing 2011 exactly flat with a 0.00% change.[39] This brief snapshot has a number of implications for business executives in the current environment, as well as for members of corporate boards. Additionally, corporate governance now has the power to affect events far beyond the corporate boardroom as local markets shift and merge into a global economy and as increased globalization enables one country's recession to initiate a domino effect around the world. As discussed in previous chapters, stakeholders today demand more communication, more transparency, and more access to companies than they have in the past, and the consequences for corporations whose governance-related actions—or inaction—lead to corruption are far greater than ever before.

The Financial Crisis Inquiry Commission issued a report in 2011 that identified governance failures as a principal cause of the 2007 recession, citing "dramatic breakdowns in corporate governance including too many financial firms acting recklessly and taking on too much risk."[40]

GOVERNMENT RESPONSE TO CORPORATE SCANDALS

As a result of the corporate scandals described earlier in the chapter, along with a multitude of others, public trust and confidence in business was greatly diminished. In response to the scandals, and in an effort to restore public and market confidence in businesses, the United States government passed the Sarbanes-Oxley Act of 2002. The act contains 11 titles that were intended to set new standards for U.S. public accounting firms, public company boards, and executive management.

Of special importance to corporate governance is Title III, titled "Corporate Responsibility." The title requires that senior executives take individual responsibility for the completeness and accuracy of corporate financial reports. More specifically, it requires that "principal officers" approve and certify the accuracy and integrity of their company's quarterly financial reports. Additionally, the title outlines the interaction between corporate audit committee members and external auditors, setting civil penalties and forfeiture of benefits for noncompliance.

The efficacy of the law and costs of implementing were immediately debated. Former federal reserve chairman Alan Greenspan commended the act, stating:

> I am surprised that the Sarbanes-Oxley Act, so rapidly developed and enacted, has functioned as well as it has . . . the act importantly reinforced the principle that shareholders own our corporations and that corporate managers should be working on behalf of shareholders to allocate business resources to their optimum use.[41]

Critics of Sarbanes-Oxley, however, contend that the law is both ineffective and too burdensome. A December 2008 *Wall Street Journal* editorial argued, "The new laws and regulations have neither prevented frauds nor instituted fairness. But they have managed to kill the creation of new public companies in the U.S., cripple the venture capital business, and damage entrepreneurship."[42] Regardless of one's position on the Act, there is little disagreement that Sarbanes-Oxley was in direct response to what many individuals considered a failure of corporate governance and that it did not prevent a major meltdown in the financial sector in 2007–2008.

THE EVOLUTION OF CORPORATE GOVERNANCE TO INCLUDE CORPORATE SOCIAL RESPONSIBILITY

As discussed earlier in the chapter, corporate governance began to evolve at the start of the 21st century as a result of a series of high-profile corporate scandals and the 2007 financial crisis. The notion that managers and directors' sole objective and responsibility was to maximize profits came under intense scrutiny as the effects of the scandals and crisis were felt well beyond the walls of corporate boardrooms.

In his book *New Corporate Governance*, corporate governance expert Martin Hilb proposed a new definition of corporate governance. Hilb advocates corporate governance to be redefined as a system "by which companies are strategically directed, integratively managed, and holistically controlled in an entrepreneurial and ethical way and in a manner appropriate to each particular context."[43] Additionally, Hilb argues, "There are just two basic types of corporate governance, the Anglo-American style which focuses on maximizing shareholder value and the relationship-based model which focuses on the interest of all stakeholders."[44] This new definition of corporate governance, which reflects the stakeholder theory of the firm discussed in Chapter 2, considers stakeholders beyond financial shareholders and represents a dramatic shift in the corporate governance role played by managers and directors.

As of September 2012, the Institute of Chartered Secretaries and Administrators, the international qualifying and membership body for the chartered secretary profession and a leading authority on corporate governance and compliance, defined corporate governance as follows:

Corporate governance refers to the way in which companies are governed and to what purpose. It is concerned with practices and procedures for trying to ensure that a company is run in such a way that it achieves its objectives. This could be to maximize the wealth of its owners (the shareholders), subject to various guidelines and constraints and with regard to the other groups with an interest in what the company does. Guidelines and constraints include behaving in an ethical way and in compliance with laws and regulations. From a shareholder's perspective, corporate governance can be defined as a process for monitoring and control to ensure that management runs the company in the interests of the shareholders. Other groups with an interest in how the company acts include employees, customers and, the general public.[45]

This definition again illustrates a shift away from the traditional understanding of corporate governance to a more holistic view of corporate governance that is concerned with ethical behavior, accountability, and stakeholders outside of financial shareholders.

The Corporate Governance Report issued by the United Nations Global Compact stated in 2009 that "[a] new vision of business is emerging—one where a set of core values, encompassing human rights, environmental protection, and anti-corruption measures, guide the board's oversight, relationship with management, and accountability to shareholders."[46] In the same report, the UN included the graphic in Figure 6.1, illustrating how responsible business and sustainable profits are embedded in the function of the board.

In fact, there is a "New Governance" movement that is emerging, as discussed by Amiram Gill in his research on the convergence of corporate governance and social responsibility. Gill writes:

> As corporate governance becomes increasingly driven by ethical norms and the need for accountability, and corporate social responsibility adapts to prevailing business practices, a potential convergence between them surfaces. Where there were once two separate sets of mechanisms, one dealing with "hard core" corporate decision-making and the other with "soft," people-friendly business strategies, scholars now point to a more hybridized, synthesized body of laws and norms regulating corporate practices.[47]

Corporate governance is in a state of transition as it adapts to the growing movement of corporate social responsibility. Effective corporate managers and directors of the future must be able to adapt to their changing roles in business and society.

Executive Compensation

As we will see in the case at the end of this chapter, executive compensation is another crucial element of corporate governance. In the wake of the financial crisis that began in 2007 with the meltdown of the United States housing and mortgage

Figure 6.1 Model illustrating how responsible business and sustainable profits are embedded in the function of the board

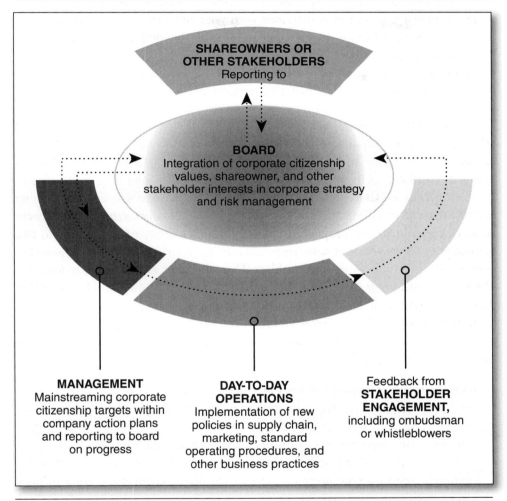

Source: United Nations Global Compact. (2009). *Corporate governance: The foundation for corporate citizenship and sustainable business.* Retrieved August 5, 2014, from http://www.unglobalcompact.org/docs/issues_doc/Corporate_Governance/Corporate_Governance_IFC_UNGC.pdf.

industry, the scale of executive compensation in the United States came under intense scrutiny. In the wake of public bailouts executed for the automotive and financial services industries to stabilize the national and global economies, there was intense public outcry at the compensation received by executives at firms who received bailout funds. As an example, the American Insurance Group (AIG) received $170 billion in taxpayer bailout funds, and in March 2009 it was disclosed that the firm would pay approximately $218 million in bonuses to employees of its financial services division. Government officials, media commentators, and the public unanimously responded with bipartisan outrage. Illustrative of the outrage, commentator Charles Krauthammer stated, "I would deny them the bonuses if possible. I would be for an exemplary hanging or two. Have it in Times Square, invite Madame Defarge. You borrow a guillotine from the French and we could have a party."[48]

In an interview in the wake of the financial crisis, a senior banker at a Wall Street bank stated under anonymity that "the general bias on the Street is if someone unworthy gets paid more than they deserve, then maybe I'll get paid more than I deserve too."[49] This sentiment, however, did not sell well to a public that was outraged in the wake of public taxpayer funds being used to bail out what were seen as greedy and corrupt for-profit corporations. The year 2013 was monumental in terms of CEO pay, as the median pay package rose above eight figures to $10 million. A CEO now makes about 257 times the average worker's salary, which is up sharply from 181 times in 2009.[50] The rationale for such large executive compensation packages is widely debated. A study by the University of Florida found that highly paid CEOs result in higher profitability for their companies as opposed to executives in similar roles paid more modest salaries.[51] On the other side of the debate, a study published in the *Journal of Organizational Behavior* found that highly paid CEOs are more likely to act unethically in their positions.[52]

In the wake of the 2007 financial crisis, the SEC increased its focus on executive compensation. The SEC requested that publicly traded companies disclose information detailing how executives' compensation amounts are decided. Additionally, the SEC began posting compensation amounts on its website for investors and the public. The United States Congress also began to act on executive compensation by including in the stimulus bill of 2009 a specific clause that limited the bonuses of all executives who worked at firms receiving government assistance to no more than one third of the executive's annual compensation. Despite these efforts, the *New York Times* reported in June 2012 that executive pay was still rising, with median pay for the top 200 highest-paid CEOs rising on average 5% from 2010 to 2011.[53]

Golden Parachutes

It is widely believed that the term "golden parachute" was first used in 1961 in reference to an effort by creditors to remove Howard Hughes from control of TWA airlines. From this origin until 2008, the term was used primarily to describe the compensation and benefits received by executives as a result of a merger or takeover. The use of golden parachutes expanded greatly in the 1980s as a result of the significant increase in the number of mergers and acquisitions. However, since 2008 and the global economic crisis, the term has been used to describe excessive executive severance packages, regardless of whether the loss of the executive's employment was the result of a merger or takeover.

A golden parachute is typically a clause in an executive's employment agreement that guarantees the executive significant severance benefits in the event that the executive loses his or her job as a result of termination, firm restructuring, or even planned retirement. The benefits can be in the form of cash, additional equity, the accelerated vesting of stock options, or other benefits, including healthcare and other services. Golden parachutes are typically reserved for only the highest-ranking executives in a company, with the total value of the benefits normally exceeding multiple millions of dollars for executives of large firms. Controversially, golden parachute benefits are not tied to executive performance and have been awarded to executives even in cases when the executive's firm has lost millions of dollars and terminated employees.

Golden parachutes became the topic of national debate as a result of the 2008 financial crisis. According to Google Trends, news headlines referencing golden parachutes spiked in late 2008 as the national dialogue turned to critique of executive compensation in the wake of the financial crisis. Then-candidate President Obama ran a campaign ad in late September 2008 titled "Parachute" that criticized the golden parachutes received by corporate executives despite the financial failing of their firms. The Dodd-Frank Act passed in 2010 contains a clause that mandates a shareholder vote on any future adoptions of golden parachutes for executives of publicly traded firms. As evidence of the increased scrutiny on executive compensation, *USA Today* reported in November 2011 that three executives of Nabors Industries, Google, and IBM were each leaving with golden parachutes worth in excess of $100 million. The newspaper reported that the golden parachutes were "raising eyebrows even among those accustomed to oversized payouts."[54] Despite the negative public reaction to and increased scrutiny on golden parachutes, the professional services firm Alvarez & Marsal reported a 32% increase in the value of golden parachutes awarded to U.S. executives in the two years prior to 2012.[55]

CONCLUSION

Corporate governance is an area of corporate responsibility that has shifted dramatically in recent decades and will continue to evolve as CR becomes more thoroughly integrated with core business strategy across the spectrum of industries. As seen from the examples provided in this chapter, shifts in perspective on corporate governance are especially susceptible to catastrophic events such as corporate scandals and economic downturns.

NOTES

1. Gee & Co. (1992, December 1). "Report of the Committee on the financial aspects of corporate governance." Retrieved August 5, 2014, from http://www.ecgi.org/codes/documents/cadbury.pdf

2. Tavernise, S. (2011, May 19). "Report faults mine owner for explosion that killed 29." Retrieved August 5, 2014, from http://www.nytimes.com/2011/05/20/us/20mine.html?pagewanted=all&_r=0

3. *Dodge v. Ford Motor Company*, 170 N.W. 668 (Mich. 1919).

4. Demb, A., & Neubauer, F. F. (1992). "The corporate board: Confronting the paradoxes," *Long Range Planning, 25*(3), 9–20.

5. Strauss, G. (2002, September 15). "Tyco events put spotlight on directors' role." *USA Today*. Retrieved August 5, 2014, from http://usatoday30.usatoday.com/money/industries/manufacturing/2002-09-15-tyco-direct_x.htm

6. Ibid.

7. Kaen, F. R. "Risk management, corporate governance and the public corporation." University of New Hampshire. Retrieved August 5, 2014.

8. Lipton, M. (2008, November 26). "Risk management and the board of directors." Harvard Law School Forum on Corporate Governance and Financial Regulation. Retrieved August 5, 2014, from http://blogs.law.harvard.edu/corpgov/2008/11/26/risk-management-and-the-board-of-directors

9. Ibid.

10. Ibid.

11. For more on this, see Argenti, P. A. (2012, October 1). *Corporate communication* (6th ed.). McGraw Hill Higher Education.

12. Enron Creditors Recovery Group, http://www.enron.com/ (accessed August 5, 2014).

13. Mears, B. (2005, May 31). "Arthur Andersen conviction overturned." *CNN.com*. Retrieved August 5, 2014, from http://articles.cnn.com/2005-05-31/justice/scotus.arthur.andersen_1_andersen-executives-maureen-mahoney-andersen-officials?_s=PM:LAW

14. Healy, P., & Palepu, K. (2003). "The fall of Enron." Harvard NOM Working Paper No. 03-38.

15. Ibid.

16. Ibid.

17. Pender, K. (2002, February 7). "Ex-dean of Stanford business school led Enron audit panel / Stanford dean's role in Enron." Retrieved August 5, 2014, from http://www.sfgate.com/business/networth/article/Ex-dean-of-Stanford-business-school-led-Enron-2876937.php

18. Ibid.

19. "The top 25 managers of the year." (2002, January 14). *Businessweek*.

20. Kapner, S. (2002, November 10). "Private sector; governance issues take a trip abroad." Retrieved August 5, 2014, from http://www.nytimes.com/2002/11/10/business/private-sector-governance-issue-takes-a-trip-abroad.html

21. Sherman, G. (2004, August 9). "Tyco sells $25 M. apartment where Dennis Kozlowski lived: In contract, but no $6,000 shower curtain." *Observer*. Retrieved August 5, 2014, from http://

observer.com/2004/08/tyco-sells-25-m-apartment-where-dennis-kozlowski-lived-in-contractbut-no-6000-shower-curtain/

22. Strauss, "Tyco events put spotlight on directors' role."

23. Elstrom, P., with Barrett, A., Yang, C., & Flynn, J. (1997, October 13). "The new world order." *Businessweek.* Retrieved August 5, 2014, from http://www.businessweek.com/1997/41/b3548001.htm

24. Ibid.

25. Eichenwald, K. (2002, August 8). "For WorldCom, acquisitions were behind its rise and fall." Retrieved August 5, 2014, from http://www.nytimes.com/2002/08/08/business/for-world-com-acquisitions-were-behind-its-rise-and-fall.html?pagewanted=all&src=pm

26. "WorldCom and MCI: Dial 'M' for merger." (1997, October 1). *PBS NewsHour.* Retrieved August 5, 2014, from http://www.pbs.org/newshour/bb/business/july-dec97/merger_10-1.html

27. Borland, J. (2000, July 13). "Sprint, WorldCom call off $120 billion merger." *CNET.* Retrieved August 5, 2014, from http://news.cnet.com/Sprint,-WorldCom-call-off-120-billion-merger/2100-1033_3-243110.html

28. Beresford, D. R., Katzenbach, N. deB., & Rogers, C. B., Jr. (2003, March 31). "Report of investigation by the Special Investigative Committee of the Board of Directors of WorldCom, Inc." Retrieved March 16, 2015, from http://www.concernedshareholders.com/CCS_WCSpecialReportExc.pdf

29. Blumenstein, R., & Sandberg, J. (2002, April 30). "WorldCom's CEO Ebbers resigns amid board pressure over probe." *Wall Street Journal.* Retrieved August 5, 2014, from http://online.wsj.com/article/SB1020119459695576640.html

30. Beresford et al., "Report of investigation by the Special Investigative Committee of the Board of Directors of WorldCom, Inc."

31. Beltran, L. (2002, July 22). "WorldCom files largest bankruptcy ever." *CNNMoney.* Retrieved August 5, 2014, from http://money.cnn.com/2002/07/19/news/worldcom_bankruptcy

32. Crawford, K. (2005, March 15). "Ex-WorldCom CEO Ebbers guilty." *CNNMoney.* Retrieved August 5, 2014, from http://money.cnn.com/2005/03/15/news/newsmakers/ebbers

33. "Ebbers sentenced to 25 years in prison." (2005, July 13). *NBC News.* Retrieved August 5, 2014, from http://www.msnbc.msn.com/id/8474930/ns/business/t/ebbers-sentenced-years-prison/

34. Hopkins, J. (2003, June 9). "Report: WorldCom board passive." *USA Today.* Retrieved August 5, 2014, from http://usatoday30.usatoday.com/money/industries/telecom/2003-06-09-board_x.htm

35. Ibid.

36. Worstall, T. (2012, November 7). "The Great Recession is just like the Great Depression." *Forbes.* Retrieved August 5, 2014, from http://www.forbes.com/sites/timworstall/2012/11/07/the-great-recession-is-just-like-the-great-depression

37. "World equity markets lost $5.2 trillion in January." (2008, February 8). *CNNMoney.* Retrieved August 5, 2014, from http://money.cnn.com/2008/02/08/news/economy/world_markets

38. "11 historic bear markets." (n.d.). *NBC News.* Retrieved August 5, 2014, from http://www.msnbc.msn.com/id/37740147/ns/business-stocks_and_economy/t/historic-bear-markets/#.TxXfh6US2Hc

39. "S&P perfectly flat for 2011, Dow up 5.5% for year." (2012, January 3). *USA Today.*

40. Financial Crisis Inquiry Commission. (2011)."The financial crisis inquiry report." Retrieved March 16, 2015, from http://www.gpo.gov/fdsys/pkg/GPO-FCIC/pdf/GPO-FCIC.pdf

41. Greenspan, A. (2005, May 15). Commencement address, Wharton School, University of Pennsylvania, Philadelphia. Retrieved August 5, 2014, from http://www.federalreserve.gov/boarddocs/speeches/2005/20050515/default.htm

42. Malone, M. S. (2008, December 22). "Washington is killing Silicon Valley." *Wall Street Journal*. Retrieved August 5, 2014, from http://online.wsj.com/article/SB122990472028925207.html

43. Hilb, M. (2006). *New corporate governance* (2nd ed.). Springer.

44. Ibid.

45. Institute of Chartered Secretaries and Administrators, https://www.icsa.org.uk (accessed August 5, 2014).

46. UN Global Compact. "Corporate governance: The foundation for corporate citizenship and sustainable business." Retrieved August 5, 2014, from http://www.unglobalcompact.org/docs/issues_doc/Corporate_Governance/Corporate_Governance_IFC_UNGC.pdf

47. Gill, A (2008). "Corporate governance as social responsibility: A research agenda." *Berkeley Journal of International Law, 26,* 452.

48. "Krauthammer's take." (2009, March 17). *National Review: The Corner.* Retrieved August 6, 2014, from http://www.nationalreview.com/corner/178923/krauthammers-take-nro-staff

49. Thomas, L., Jr. (2003, August 28). "Big board chief will get a $140 million package. *New York Times*. Retrieved October 12, 2012, from http://www.nytimes.com/2003/08/28/business/big-board-chief-will-get-a-140-million-package.html?pagewanted=all&src=pm

50. Sweet, K. (2014, May 27). "Median CEO pay crosses $10 million in 2013; photos of top 10 highest paid." *Newsday.* Retrieved August 6, 2014, from http://www.newsday.com/business/median-ceo-pay-crosses-10-million-in-2013-photos-of-top-10-highest-paid-1.8191053

51. Keen, C. (2009, December 17). "Paying CEOs more than other CEOs results in stockholder dividends." *University of Florida News.* Retrieved August 6, 2014, from http://news.ufl.edu/2009/12/17/ceo-pay-2

52. "Executive compensation." (n.d.). *Wikipedia.* Retrieved August 6, 2014, from http://en.wikipedia.org/wiki/Executive_pay#cite_note-15

53. Popper, N. (2012, June 17). "CEO pay is rising despite the din." *New York Times*. Retrieved August 6, 2014, from http://www.nytimes.com/2012/06/17/business/executive-pay-still-climbing-despite-a-shareholder-din.html?pagewanted=all&_r=0

54. Strauss, G. (2011, November 7). "CEOs' golden parachute exit packages pass $100 million." *USA Today.* Retrieved August 6, 2014, from http://usatoday30.usatoday.com/money/companies/management/story/2011-11-07/100-million-dollar-chairmen/51116304/1

55. "Golden parachutes on the rise during down economy." (2012, April 5). *Deal Law Wire.* Retrieved August 6, 2014, from http://www.deallawwire.com/2012/04/05/golden-parachutes-on-the-rise-during-down-economy

THE NEW YORK STOCK EXCHANGE AND RICHARD GRASSO: EXCESSIVE COMPENSATION AS A FAILURE OF CORPORATE GOVERNANCE

You can't pay the head of a not-for-profit that much money. The amount paid, close to $200 million US. . . . It's not reasonable.

—Eliot Spitzer, former New York State attorney general[1]

These were honest, diligent, and sound compensation decisions that were thoroughly researched and, most importantly, supported by 100 percent of the board.

—Statement from Kenneth Langone, former NYSE director and chair of the compensation committee[2]

Those who thought they could break me . . . badly underestimated my character and resolve.

—Richard Grasso, former chairman and CEO of the New York Stock Exchange[3]

"Our systems are all go. At 9:30 Monday morning trading will resume on both markets, and the message will be given to the criminals who foisted this on America that they lost," stated Richard Grasso upon announcing the reopening of the New York Stock Exchange (NYSE) after the terrorist attacks on September 11.[4] Trading on the NYSE had been canceled that fateful Tuesday after the second plane crashed into the South Tower, and the Exchange had remained closed for the remainder of the week after the September 11 attacks. In the wake of the tragedy, Mr. Grasso became the public face of the Exchange and was widely praised for enabling the Exchange to return to operations in such a short time, even amid the devastation of lower Manhattan. Rudy Giuliani, the mayor of New York City at the time of the attacks, lauded Mr. Grasso as a hero for his role in reopening the Exchange.[5] Roberta Karmel, a former NYSE director, stated to *The New York Times*, "After 9/11 people couldn't say enough about him."[6]

Yet, just two years after being praised as a hero, Mr. Grasso was asked to step down as the chairman and chief executive officer of the Exchange. How did Mr. Grasso fall so quickly and so hard from an American hero extolled for his leadership to a tarnished executive denigrated as a symbol of corporate greed and crony capitalism? The answer

Source: This case was written by Jonathan Gantt, T'13, under the supervision of Professor Paul A. Argenti at the Tuck School of Business at Dartmouth. This case was prepared with publicly available information. © 2014 Trustees of Dartmouth College. All rights reserved.

to this question involves the ongoing business debate on the scale of executive pay, the appropriate board composition to ensure effective corporate governance, and the controversial dual role of CEO and chairman.

THE NEW YORK STOCK EXCHANGE

The New York Stock Exchange (NYSE) was at the time an iconic landmark of not only the United States but also the global financial system. In a piece titled "Fixing a Tarnished Market," *The New York Times* stated, "There is no more evocative monument to the vibrancy of American capitalism, and to New York City's claim to be the world's financial capital, than the graceful, colonnaded building that houses the New York Stock Exchange on Wall Street."[7] The NYSE was at the time the world's largest stock-trading exchange, with market capitalization of its listed companies at $14.4 trillion as of December 2011 and a daily trading volume of $153 million in 2008.

The NYSE was founded in 1792 by an agreement between 24 stockbrokers in New York City. In 1817, the institution drafted a new constitution and officially adopted the name "New York Stock & Exchange Board." The Exchange grew over the first half of the 19th century and in 1865 moved to its current street, Broad Street in lower Manhattan. Then, in 1903, the current façade and building was constructed along with a new trading floor. From its founding to December 2005, the NYSE was a quasi-public institution, existing as a nonprofit under New York State law, charged with a vital regulatory role. However, in December 2005, with its merger with electronic trading rival, Archipelago, the NYSE officially became a for-profit company.

In March 2006, the NYSE began trading under the name "NYSE Group." Then, in April 2007, NYSE Group merged with Euronext, the European combined stock market, forming the first transatlantic stock exchange, named "NYSE Euronext." Throughout its 220 years of existence, the NYSE faced many trials and challenges, including fires, financial panics, insider trading scandals, and the onset of electronic trading. Despite these challenges, the NYSE endured and remained the symbol of American capitalism.

RICHARD GRASSO

Richard A. "Dick" Grasso's rise was in many ways the classic Horatio Alger story. Born in Jackson Heights, Queens, New York City in 1946, Mr. Grasso was raised by his mother and two aunts after his father left the family when he was just an infant. After graduating from high school, Mr. Grasso attended Pace University for two years prior to enlisting in the Army. In 1968, after leaving the Army, Mr. Grasso was hired as a clerk for the New York Stock Exchange. Over the next 22 years, Mr. Grasso's rise through the ranks of the

New York Stock Exchange would ultimately culminate in his appointment as president in 1988 and chairman in 1995.

Mr. Grasso held the positions of chief executive and chairman of the NYSE until his resignation in 2003. Mr. Grasso was widely accredited with establishing the NYSE as the preeminent stock exchange in United States during his leadership tenure. In the press release announcing his new employment contract, the NYSE Board stated:

> Under Dick's leadership, the NYSE has experienced tremendous growth and success. It has added 1,549 of its 2,800 listed companies, including most of our nearly 500 non-U.S. companies. During this period the market capitalization of the companies listed on the NYSE has more than doubled to $14.8 trillion. In the process, Dick revolutionized the Exchange's technological platform, making it the most efficient and sophisticated in the industry. The value of a seat on the exchange has nearly tripled during his tenure. And throughout his term, Dick has shown an unwavering commitment to regulation and the interests of America's 85 million investors. From his commitment to technology and innovation, which has made the NYSE the world's most efficient and reliable equities market, to leading the securities industry out of the tragedy of 9/11, to his unwavering commitment to investor protection, Dick's leadership has been outstanding.[8]

Yet, this very press release praising Mr. Grasso's outstanding leadership and commitment would result in the compensation scandal that would ultimately end with Mr. Grasso's resignation just one month after its release.

COMPENSATION CONTROVERSY

On August 27, 2003, the board of directors of the New York Stock Exchange circulated a press release detailing the organization's new employment contract with its chairman and chief executive officer, Dick Grasso. This press release was the first time in the NYSE's 200-year history that the Exchange released information regarding the compensation package for its chief executive. What was intended to be an innocuous press release announcing the continued leadership of the Exchange's longtime CEO and chairman in effect resulted in Mr. Grasso resigning as CEO and chairman less than three weeks later. See Exhibit 6.1 for excerpts from the press release.

The press release detailed a compensation package that included $140 million in accrued savings and incentives as well as a $1.5 million salary and a guaranteed bonus of at least $1.0 million. Public reaction to the press release and compensation details was swift and harsh. Charles M. Elson, chairman of the corporate governance program at the University of Delaware, stated:

Exhibit 6.1   Excerpts From Press Release

"The New York Stock Exchange Board of Directors today announced that Dick Grasso, Chairman and Chief Executive Officer, has agreed to a new contract that will run through May 2007. This contract, which was unanimously approved by the Board, replaces his prior contract, signed in 1999, which was set to expire in 2005. Mr. Grasso, 57, has been Chairman since 1995."

***

"As part of his new contract, the NYSE restructured the deferred compensation and savings and retirement plan benefits previously earned by Mr. Grasso . . . and made lump sum distributions to him of his vested account balances. The NYSE for many years has maintained several deferred compensation, retirement and savings plans for its executives, including a Supplemental Executive Retirement Plan ("SE") to supplement benefits under the NYSE Retirement Plan, and a Supplemental Executive Savings Plan ("SE") to provide the executives with the ability to supplement the NYSE Savings Plan and to defer and invest additional compensation. The NYSE distributed to Mr. Grasso his savings account balance of $40.0 million, his previously accrued retirement benefit of $51.6 million and his previously earned account balance of $47.9 million relating to prior incentive awards."

***

"Most recently, the Exchange has been at the forefront of outlining and spearheading corporate governance reform. It is in that spirit that the Board will undertake an annual review of executive compensation and annually disclose, as previously announced, the compensation of the Exchange's five highest paid executives. It is also why we have decided to make this announcement today regarding the details of Dick's new contract. We look forward to his leadership for another four years."

Source: "NYSE announces new contract for Dick Grasso through May 2007." (2003, August 27). NYSE.com. Retrieved March 17, 2014, from http://www.nyse.com/press/1061982038732.html.

This is phenomenal unrisked return for the head of a quasipublic organization. It's really a staggering sum because it's cash that was never at risk. It's mind boggling, more of an entrepreneur's fortune, and may well be more than the earnings of some of the companies that trade on the exchange.[9]

Following up on the public's reaction, Landon Thomas Jr. wrote in *The New York Times*, "Richard A. Grasso has succeeded at what some would consider an impossible task: making Wall Street gasp in astonishment at someone else's compensation."[10]

Mr. Grasso's compensation also caught the attention of regulatory agencies, including the Securities and Exchange Commission (SEC). The SEC sent a letter to the board of the NYSE requesting details on the compensation of Mr. Grasso, including detailed compensation committee meeting minutes as well as broader board meetings. William H.

Donaldson, the SEC chairman at the time and Mr. Grasso's predecessor as chairman of the NYSE board, stated, "In my view, the approval of Mr. Grasso's pay package raises serious questions regarding the effectiveness of the NYSE's current governance structure."[11]

In a response to the request by the SEC for further details regarding Mr. Grasso's compensation, the board revealed that Mr. Grasso was due an additional $48 million of benefits not included in the original $140 million detailed in the press release. Perhaps sensing that this news would be met with an even greater outcry, Mr. Grasso announced the same day that he would forgo the additional $48 million in benefits, stating, "This institution should not be preoccupied about talking about the compensation of its leader. I've put this issue behind me."[12] In the end, in response to inquiries by the SEC, the NYSE board confirmed that Mr. Grasso had received $80.6 million, excluding benefits, in compensation from 1999 to 2002. The $140 million payout detailed in the press release was the result of Mr. Grasso choosing a lump sum payment for deferred compensation in previous years. In his best year, 2001, Mr. Grasso received compensation in the amount of $30.5 million, just shy of his company's total reported earnings for that year, $31.8 million. Mr. Grasso was soon met with widespread calls for his immediate resignation. Investors, the SEC, and public officials representing public pension funds in New York and California demanded that Mr. Grasso step down as the leader of the NYSE.

After publicly denying his intention to resign for three weeks, on September 17, 2003, Mr. Grasso announced that he would immediately resign from his positions as chairman and chief executive of the NYSE. Upon announcing his resignation, Mr. Grasso stated, "I believe this course is in the best interest of both the exchange and myself."[13] He went on to say that he was resigning "with the deepest reluctance."[14]

In fact, Mr. Grasso was not alone in his reluctance regarding his resignation. Seven of the 20 board members of the NYSE voted against accepting Mr. Grasso's resignation. Other observers were wary of the implications to corporate governance caused by the forced resignation of a successful executive simply as a result of negative public and regulatory reaction to compensation. Jeffrey Sonnenfeld, at the time an associate dean of the Yale School of Management, commented, "This will be the first time in American history where someone who is said to have done a good job is being fired because the board is paying him too much. The board's accountability is the second issue to be dealt with."[15]

Indeed, Mr. Grasso's resignation did not end the controversy or the scrutiny of the NYSE's board. Following Mr. Grasso's resignation, additional executives and board members involved in the compensation scandal also resigned or retired, including Frank Ashen, a 25-year veteran of the Exchange; Jurgen Schrempp, chief executive of DaimlerChrysler; and H. Carl McCall, a former politician who as chairman of the Exchange's compensation committee signed Mr. Grasso's contract extension that extended $48 million of additional benefits on top of the $140 million.

Less than a year after his resignation, in May 2004, Mr. Grasso was sued by New York State, demanding repayment of $100 million of his $140 million compensation package. Eliot Spitzer, New York State's attorney general at the time, filed the complaint against Mr. Grasso with the New York State Supreme Court, stating, "There is a simple reality here. Mr. Grasso was paid too much. He has the money in his checking account and he has an obligation to return it."[16] The complaint against Mr. Grasso alleged that Mr. Grasso inflated his pay and intentionally manipulated his board to approve a compensation package that far exceeded the benchmark for comparable executives.

Additionally, Mr. Spitzer had convinced Frank Ashen, the NYSE's internal compensation director and a longtime co-employee with Mr. Grasso, to provide testimony that Mr. Grasso hid $18 million in bonus compensation from the board. Mr. Ashen, who was initially to be named in the lawsuit, agreed to pay back $1.3 million in compensation and provide testimony. The lawsuit painted a picture of a symbiotic relationship between Mr. Grasso and his board, including Mr. Grasso overlooking conflicts of interest for Wall Street research analysts when executives from those firms were authorizing his compensation. In response to the lawsuit, Mr. Grasso stated that he would not repay any of his compensation, commenting, "I'm disappointed that New York's attorney general has chosen to intervene in what amounts to be a commercial dispute between my former employer and me. I look forward to a complete vindication in court."[17] Mr. Grasso filed a countersuit against NYSE and its new chairman, John Reed, claiming "defamation of character."[18] The lawsuits, which would not be fully settled until two years later, placed questions on the scale of executive pay, board composition, and the dual role of CEO and chairman at the forefront of media attention and business debate.

BOARD COMPOSITION

According to the investigative report completed by Winston & Strawan on behalf of the NYSE published on December 15, 2003, Mr. Grasso "had a strong influence in who was selected as members of the Nominating Committee and the Board, and he personally selected which Board members served on the Compensation Committee."[19] This committee was the committee responsible for approving Mr. Grasso's annual compensation. In the wake of the corporate scandals, a renewed interest was placed on the CEO's relationship with the board and the growing trend of an interlocking directorate in the United States: the practice of directors sitting on multiple boards of various companies in different industries.

DUAL ROLE OF CEO AND CHAIRMAN

At the time of the compensation scandal, Mr. Grasso was both the chief executive and chairman of the board of the NYSE. When a chief executive officer also holds the position of chairman of the board, it is commonly referred to as "CEO duality." The effects of CEO duality on the efficacy of boards and firm financial performance have long been debated and studied. The landmark report on corporate governance issued by the Cadbury Commission in 1992, now referred to as the Cadbury Report, recommended that the CEO and chairman roles be separated to ensure effective corporate governance. Specifically, the report dictated as follows:

> Given the importance and particular nature of the chairman's role, it should in principle be separate from that of the chief executive. If the two roles are combined in one person, it represents a considerable concentration of power. We recommend, therefore, that there should be a clearly accepted division of responsibilities at the head of the company, which will ensure a balance of power and authority, such that no one individual has unfettered powers of decision. Where the chairman is also the chief executive, it is essential that there should be a strong and independent element on the board.[20]

Despite this clear recommendation, CEO duality remained commonplace in the United States through the early 2000s. The high-profile corporate scandals of the early 2000s gave birth to renewed focus on ensuring that two separate individuals hold the two most powerful positions within a company. As of 2012, there was no specific law or regulation requiring publicly traded companies to separate the chairman and CEO roles, though many shareholders and investors vocalized a preference for separation.

AN ONGOING DEBATE

The New York State lawsuit and Mr. Grasso's lawsuits moved to trial two years after their initial filings. On October 19, 2006, a New York judge ruled that Mr. Grasso must return a large portion of his compensation. The judge found that Mr. Grasso had deceived his board on details pertaining to his compensation, preventing the board from performing its fiduciary responsibilities, and that he had gained access to retirement funds prematurely. The judge stopped short of stating that Mr. Grasso had committed any illegal activities.

The order that Mr. Grasso return millions in compensation was called "the shot heard round the boardrooms" by *New York Times* journalist Gretchen Morgenson. Writing in *The New York Times*, Morgenson wrote, "The days of pouring other people's money into the pockets of CEO's without justification are over."[21] At the time of the judgment, Mr. Grasso's suit claiming defamation was also dismissed. Mr. Grasso vowed to appeal the decisions, and the legal fight moved to the New York State Court of Appeals. In the appeal, Mr. Grasso's attorney's argued that the judge had "ignored the law and the facts."[22]

On July 1, 2008, the New York State Court of Appeals ruled that Mr. Grasso was entitled to keep his compensation and dismissed all outstanding claims against him. The majority decision cited the fact that NYSE was now a division of a for-profit corporation and that New York had no oversight authority on issues of compensation, ultimately stating that further matters were "not in the public interest." The decision also dismissed outstanding claims Mr. Grasso had against New York and the Exchange. In response to the decision, Mr. Grasso stated, "Right now I'm going to turn to my family and we're going to move on to the next chapter."[23]

The Grasso compensation controversy lasted for more than five years, providing fuel for a national debate on executive compensation, board composition, and the dual role of CEO/chairman. The debate was still ongoing in 2012, and the Grasso controversy was still being referenced as an example of excessive CEO compensation. Sanjay Sangohoee wrote for *Fortune* magazine, in his article titled "We're Having the Wrong Debate on CEO Pay":

> The other big weakness in our system is the propensity of companies and shareholders to accept the "divine right" of CEOs, which elevates them to monarch status and enables them to run their companies like private kingdoms rather than as trusts run for the sake of the owners. Nowhere was this phenomenon more clearly evident than in the case of Dick Grasso, the former head of the New York Stock Exchange, whose disproportionately large $190 million pay package became possible due at least in part to his personally handpicked board, absolute stranglehold over the NYSE's activities, as well as his ability to regulate the very people who were tasked with deciding his compensation.[24]

In many ways, the sentiment expressed by *The New York Times* just days after the now infamous NYSE press release in 2003 captured the essence of the ongoing debate on corporate governance and executive compensation nearly a decade after the start of the Grasso controversy. *The New York Times* stated:

> The recent corporate scandals have taught us, if nothing else, that when reckless chief executives are able to raid their institutions' treasuries at will and enrich themselves beyond reason, it's a sure sign that corporate governance has been corrupted to an alarming degree.[25]

The question remains: Has corporate governance evolved since 2003, or are there still unresolved deficiencies in U.S. corporate governance practices, specifically regarding executive compensation?

Case Questions

1. How is the controversy over Richard Grasso's compensation an example of a failure of governance? Who is more culpable for the executive compensation controversy, Richard Grasso or the NYSE's board of directors?

2. In what ways did Richard Grasso's dual role of chairman and CEO lead to the compensation controversy? In your opinion, was there a conflict of interest? Explain.

3. In what ways did Richard Grasso's involvement in the selection of board members lead to a conflict of interest? Should chief executive officers have any influence on the composition of their company's board of directors when the same board will be responsible for setting the chief executive officer's compensation?

4. Based on the facts presented in the case study, should Richard Grasso have been compelled to return what was considered by many to be "excessive compensation"? Why or why not?

5. Should a CEO's compensation be tied to performance? If yes, should the compensation be tied to short-term or long-term performance? Or both?

NOTES

1. "New York attorney general files suit against former NYSE chairman Grasso." (2004, May 24). *CBC News*. Retrieved March 16, 2015, from http://www.cbc.ca/news/business/story/2004/05/24/spitzer_040524.html

2. "N.Y. attorney general sues ex-NYSE head." (2004, May 24). *Washington Post*. Retrieved October 12, 2012, from http://www.washingtonpost.com/wp-dyn/articles/A52237-2004May24_2.html

3. White, B. (2004, May 25). "Grasso, Spitzer take it personal." *Washington Post*. Retrieved October 12, 2012, from http://www.washingtonpost.com/wp-dyn/articles/A55761-2004May25_2.html

4. FamousQuotes.com, http://www.famousquotes.com/author/grasso

5. "Giuliani: Dick Grasso was a hero." *Fox Business News*. Retrieved October 12, 2012, from http://video.foxbusiness.com/v/1833364294001/giuliani-dick-grasso-was-a-hero

6. Thomas, "Big board chief will get a $140 million package."

7. "Fixing a tarnished market." (2003, September 21). *New York Times*. Retrieved October 12, 2012, from http://www.nytimes.com/2003/09/21/opinion/fixing-a-tarnished-market.html?src=pm

8. "NYSE announces new contract for Dick Grasso through May 2007." (2003, August 27). *NYSE.com*. Retrieved March 16, 2015, from http://www.nyse.com/press/1061982038732.html

9. Thomas, "Big board chief will get a $140 million package."

10. Thomas, L., Jr. (2003, August 29). "A pay package that fat cats call excessive." *New York Times*. Retrieved October 12, 2012, from http://www.nytimes.com/2003/08/29/business/a-pay-package-that-fat-cats-call-excessive.html

11. Countryman, A. (2003, September 3). "Grasso's pay prompts SEC questions." *Chicago Tribune*. Retrieved October 12, 2012, from http://articles.chicagotribune.com/2003-09-03/business/0309030245_1_nyse-compensation-committee-mr-grasso-kenneth-langone

12. Norris, F., & Thomas, L., Jr. (2003, September 10). "Grasso giving up $48 million in benefits." *New York Times*. Retrieved March 16, 2015, from http://www.nytimes.com/2003/09/10/business/grasso-giving-up-48-million-in-benefits.html?ref=richardagrasso

13. "NYSE chairman Grasso resigns." (2003, September 17). *CNN.com*. Retrieved October 12, 2012, from http://articles.cnn.com/2003-09-17/us/wallst.grasso_1_nyse-board-laurence-fink -richard-grasso?_s=PM:US

14. Ibid.

15. "Grasso resigns from New York exchange." (2003, September 18). *Milwaukee Journal Sentinel*. Retrieved March 16, 2015, from http://news.google.com/newspapers?nid=1683&dat=20 030918&id=xHY0AAAAIBAJ&sjid=ho4EAAAAIBAJ&pg=6690,5949373

16. Thomas, L., Jr. (2004, May 24). "New York sues ex-head of big board over pay package." *New York Times*. Retrieved October 12, 2012, from http://www.nytimes.com/2004/05/24/ business/24CND-GRAS.html?pagewanted=all

17. Ibid.

18. Thomas, L., Jr. (2004, July 21). "Grasso sues stock exchange and top officer." *New York Times*. Retrieved October 12, 2012, from http://www.nytimes.com/2004/07/21/business/grasso -sues-stock-exchange-and-top-officer.html

19. Webb, D. K. (2003, December 15). "Report to the New York Stock Exchange on investigation relating to the compensation of Richard A. Grasso." Retrieved March 16, 2015, from http:// www.law.yale.edu/documents/pdf/cbl/5_Webb_Report_to_the_NYSE_.pdf

20. Gee & Co., "Report of the Committee on the financial aspects of corporate governance."

21. Morgenson, G. (2006, October 22). "The shot heard round the boardrooms." *New York Times*. Retrieved October 12, 2012, from http://www.nytimes.com/2006/10/22/business/ yourmoney/22gret.html?pagewanted=all

22. "Grasso to challenge a judge's ruling on compensation." (2006, October 27). *New York Times*. Retrieved October 12, 2012, from http://www.nytimes.com/2006/10/27/business/27grasso .html?ref=richardagrasso&gwh=5BEDF571A41B6C3196152264406FA8C4

23. Anderson, J. (2008, July 2). "Stock exchange's ex-chief wins battle to keep pay." *New York Times*. Retrieved from http://www.nytimes.com/2008/07/02/business/02grasso.html?gwh=C FB8A2F831DDAD49E9120EEC8B46AE6B

24. Sangohee, S. (2012, October 1). "We're having the wrong debate on CEO pay." *Fortune*. Retrieved October 12, 2012, from http://management.fortune.cnn.com/2012/10/01/ceo-pay-2/

25. "Fixing a tarnished market," *New York Times*.

Part III

Corporate Responsibility
in Action

Chapter 7

CORPORATE ETHICS

Writing in the *Financial Times* in October 2012, Michael Woodford, former president and CEO of Olympus Corporation, declared corporate ethics "a matter of life and death."[1] While this may seem hyperbolic, there are indeed many situations in which corporate ethics affect the lives of people around the world. Unsafe conditions along a corporate supply chain as a result of weak or unenforceable labor laws could result in the deaths of factory workers or other laborers. Consider the 2010 crisis at Foxconn facilities in China, a major supplier of Apple's iPads, or the Upper Big Branch coal mine disaster in West Virginia that same year, where the deaths of 29 miners resulted from poor corporate oversight.

In both of these cases, labor law violations occurred, but this is not always the case. As we will discuss later in this chapter, even situations in which no law has been broken can include ethical transgressions. And, even when corporations make smaller ethical decisions that are not a matter of life and death, there are consequences of their actions, some of which can be dire if the wrong decision is made.

Olympus's Woodford speaks from personal experience. As the head of the optical equipment manufacturer, he uncovered accounting fraud in the amount of $1.7 billion dollars, which he exposed after being forced to leave the company.[2] While he received considerable positive press for his actions, Woodford denied that anything he did should be viewed as extraordinary, stating that "such action should be the norm, not the exception." Regarding ethical violations by corporations, he wrote:

> It is not acceptable to sit back and allow abuses to be committed in your name. Companies have a responsibility to the societies they feed and that feed them. Like people, these corporate citizens must hold fast to the values of integrity, honesty and altruism. To eschew these values is toxic.[3]

To ensure adherence to such values, organizations must integrate them into corporate culture. In this chapter, we will discuss the history and evolution of business ethics, the role of ethics in business decision-making, and how to create and implement an enforceable code of ethics. We begin by defining corporate ethics.

DEFINITION OF CORPORATE ETHICS

Corporate ethics, also called business ethics, is a subset of applied ethics dealing with the ethical issues facing corporations and their officers.[4] Like individuals, corporations must face decisions about what is right versus wrong daily. Sometimes such decisions are made easier because of laws or internal policies, but other times companies have to make decisions that are beyond the scope of written rules. Therefore, corporations' ethical responsibilities stretch beyond what is legally mandated into voluntary actions and behaviors that may be seen as representative of corporate culture or values.

In Chapter 3, we discussed how corporations that opted for a proactive approach to environmental regulations by adjusting their practices before laws went into effect positioned themselves for competitive advantages over companies that waited to make changes until legally required to do so. Similarly, corporations that codify their ethical values and standards, share them throughout the organization, and integrate them into corporate culture across business units will be better protected from the potential risk associated with ethical scandals.

Some consider corporate responsibility to be a subcategory of corporate ethics. In their book *Ethics for the Real World: Creating a Personal Code to Guide Decisions in Work and Life,* Stanford management professor and ethicist Ronald A. Howard and entrepreneur Clinton D. Korver identify three categories of issues to which corporate ethics apply—deception, theft, and harm—explaining that "no matter what [their] religion or culture, [people] will consider these three central to ethical behavior."[5]

The first category, *deception*, refers to situations in which corporations mislead stakeholders through their words or actions. In the summer of 2012, Peregrine Financial Group CEO Russ Wasendorf Sr. was indicted on charges related to a $200 million fraud scheme at the company he had founded.[6] While his primary sin was theft, after stealing or embezzling customer funds, Wasendorf covered his tracks by supplying his accounting department with falsified financial statements, resulting in the deception not only of company employees but external stakeholders as well.[7] In the end, 24,000 of Peregrine's customers were found to be missing money, and the damage to Wasendorf's personal reputation was immense, with prosecutors in the case proclaiming, "He has gone from being a hero in his community to a villain . . . the perpetrator of one of the most lengthy and egregious frauds in the history of this district."[8]

Theft deals with the appropriation of others' property for personal use without the owners' permission. In the case of corporate theft, this may involve the misuse of money or other resources. Much of the attention paid to corporate theft over the past few years has pertained to the abuse of corporate funds by top executives. For example, in Chapter 6, we discussed Tyco CEO Dennis Kozlowski's alleged use of corporate funds to buy a $15,000 umbrella stand and other extravagant items. While such egregious cases of reallocating corporate money for personal use are most likely to be reported in the mainstream press, theft-related offenses occur on a smaller scale as well, such as using corporate resources for personal tasks such as phone calls and web surfing.

Harm includes anything that negatively affects the well-being of corporate stakeholders. For example, in 2011, ExxonMobil was sued by Indonesian villagers who claimed that the company enabled the commission of murder, torture, and sexual assault by its security forces in their country's Aceh province.[9] At first, ExxonMobil was able to have the case thrown out because the villagers were not allowed to use U.S. courts to sue over alleged actions that took place in Indonesia and involved the Indonesian military during a period of martial law, though the suit was later reinstated. These circumstances make the Exxon situation a good example of how being ethical does not always mean simply following the letter of the law. Corporations that follow laws, whether home country or local, in the overseas markets in which they operate may nonetheless be committing ethical violations if their practices or those along their supply chain result in harm.

THE EVOLUTION OF CORPORATE ETHICS

In his 2005 paper titled "A History of Ethics," ethicist Richard T. DeGeorge, a professor of philosophy at the University of Kansas, discussed the understanding of business ethics based on three different definitions:[10]

- The usage of the term "business ethics" since the 1970s in academia—in other words, the emergence of corporate ethics as an area of academic study and research.
- The association of business ethics with business scandals or, more broadly, the role of ethics within business; this prong, DeGeorge explains, is as old as business itself.
- "A movement within business or the movement to explicitly build ethics into the structures of corporations in the form of ethics codes, ethics officers, ethics committees and ethics training."[11]

Together, these three definitions outline a short, but robust view of how the term "business ethics" has emerged and developed over the past few decades, and interestingly enough, all these definitions are applicable today depending on the context or situation.

Earlier in this book, we looked at University of Chicago economist Milton Friedman's view of corporate responsibility. It is no surprise that Friedman's views on CR are also applicable to business ethics. We can examine competing perspectives on ethics in business through the lenses of Friedman and Charles Handy's views of CR. As Friedman wrote, "Few trends could so thoroughly undermine the very foundations of our free society as the acceptance by corporate officials of a social responsibility other than to make as much money for their stockholders as possible."[12] Alternatively, as briefly discussed in Chapter 1, Handy believes that companies want to exist in the long term and therefore that they must be part of a sustainable planet to protect their own future business.[13] From these insights, we can conclude that Friedman was somewhat unconcerned with business ethics (other than abiding by the law), as the sole goal of a business was to be profitable. Handy, however, likely believed that business ethics was important to protect the reputation and, by default, the future of the corporation. While profit may be the most important goal of a corporation, the economic events of the early 21st century have made it clear that corporate ethics has a direct effect on the ability of a business to generate and hold on to its profits, because many different stakeholders care about business ethics. Throughout this chapter, we will look at the relationship between corporate ethics and business activity, and how business value is generated by ethics much in the same way that CR activities create shared value.

CORPORATE ETHICS IN THE MODERN ERA

The economic events of the early 21st century brought corporate ethics into the forefront of the public conversation about business decision-making. With capital markets in North America, Europe, and Asia plummeting, it was unsurprising that the ethical values and principles of top executives came under public scrutiny.[14] Grassroots movement Occupy Wall Street became a global force for change, using social media channels such as Twitter and Tumblr to organize protestors against corporate greed.

Whole Foods co-CEO John Mackey and Raj Sisodia, a thought-leader in business ethics and co-founder of Conscious Capitalism, a nonprofit that helps businesses tie together purpose, culture, leadership, and their stakeholders, outline in their HBR blog how approaching business from an ethical standpoint generates value for stakeholders:

"Conscious Capitalism" is a way of thinking about capitalism and business that better reflects where we are in the human journey, the state of our world today, and the innate potential of business to make a positive impact on the world. Conscious businesses are galvanized by higher purposes that serve, align and integrate the interests of all their major stakeholders. Their higher state of consciousness makes visible to them the interdependencies that exist across all stakeholders, allowing them to discover and harvest synergies from situations that otherwise seem replete with trade-offs.[15]

While right now the number of Conscious Capitalism chapters is limited to several major cities and a few international locations, the movement is expected to grow as the scrutiny of businesses' actions continues to increase.

Another development related to business ethics that has grown in popularity over the last few years is the ranking of the most ethical corporations. The Ethisphere Institute is an organization that publishes a list of the world's most ethical companies each year. Ethisphere began publishing this list in 2006. A *Forbes* article about the list says:

To earn a spot on the list, explains Ethisphere's general counsel Michael Byrne, companies must have robust corporate compliance programs, strong corporate social responsibility policies, they need to comply with federal sentencing guidelines, they should be abiding by international labor, anti-trust and trade laws and they should be monitoring their supply chain to make sure that companies they contract with are also sticking to international law and labor standards. Ethisphere nixes companies that have legal charges pending and it won't consider firms that deal in alcohol, tobacco or firearms.[16]

The 2014 list of the "World's Most Reputable Companies" includes 3M, Ford Motor Company, and Thomson Reuters. Other lists that are published that consider similar business characteristics include the "World's Most Trustworthy Companies," by GMI Ratings and the "World's Most Reputable Companies," by Reputation Institute.[17] With these types of rankings published, consumers can be more informed about the companies they do business with and firms can get a leg up on their competitors.

How to Create a Corporate Code of Ethics

So how does your company get on the "World's Most Reputable Companies" list? Creating a corporate code of ethics would be a great first step. In *Ethics for the Real World*, Ronald A. Howard and Clinton D. Korver outline the process of developing an individual ethical code.[18] Their advice is easily adaptable for businesses looking to create a corporate code of ethics that fits with their companies' values, vision, and mission. Howard and Korver recommend a three-step process (see Figure 7.1).

Drafting Standards. The first step to creating a corporate code of ethics is to determine what ethical dilemmas employees may face and then how, in an ideal world, employees should think about and approach these situations when they arise. Howard and Korver suggest beginning this phase of the process by focusing on three categories of ethical wrongdoing: "deceiving, stealing, and harming."[19] They emphasize that it is often small ethical dilemmas, rather than major quandaries, that tend to create challenges throughout the day. Similarly, according to William Shaw in his textbook *Business Ethics*:

> Stories of business corruption and of greed and wrongdoing in high places have always fascinated the popular press, and media interest in business ethics has never been higher. But one should not be misled by the headlines and news reports. Not all moral issues in business involve giant corporations and their well-heeled executives, and few cases of business ethics are widely publicized. The vast majority of them involve the mundane, uncelebrated moral challenges that working men and women meet daily.[20]

By understanding the types of challenges that employees may face, a firm can outline realistic expectations for its workers that they can relate to and actively pursue in their day-to-day work.

Testing the Code. This is the phase in which corporations determine whether the code established in Phase 1 meets their own requirements. Howard and Korver

Figure 7.1 Howard and Korver's three-step process for creating a corporate code of ethics

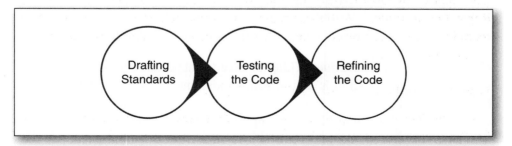

Source: Howard, R. A., & Korver, C. D. (2008). *Ethics for the real world: Creating a personal code to guide decisions in work and life.* Boston, MA: Harvard Business Review Press.

recommend using a three-step process to evaluate whether the ethical standards drafted in Phase 1 are appropriate and comprehensive.

Check the logic. First, look at the standards through the lenses of universality and reciprocity. Ask whether you would want others (such as corporate competitors) to follow the rules, and whether you would be comfortable with others applying the rules to your company.

Check for focus. While it may seem counterintuitive to cut items from what is designed to be a comprehensive corporate code of ethics, the truth is that eliminating ethical statements that are irrelevant to a corporation's line of business or unlikely to arise will make it easier to create a code of ethics that provides guidance for the types of issues that employees will deal with regularly. Howard and Korver advise removing prudential issues from the code of ethics; while it is important, for example, to stress the importance of keeping up with industry-related news and knowledge, this particular conversation has no place in an ethical code.

The authors also recommend avoiding vague words (such as "respect") that are laudable pursuits but provide little concrete guidance on behavior. Additionally, while positive ethics (goals such as honesty and charity) are important, they are also limitless; as a result, corporations may choose to leave these out of ethical codes and instead leave them to values statements. New York Life Insurance Company, for example, identifies its core values as Humanity, Integrity, and Financial Strength.[21] These positive elements know no upper bounds, so it would be difficult to incorporate them into a code of ethics.

Test-drive for usefulness. This is the step of the testing process in which corporations determine the practicality of proposed ethical standards. Howard and Korver suggest asking, "How well do our standards operate in everyday life? Are they practical? Do we really mean them?" Think about whether there are times when a particular ethical statement need not hold true.

Refining the Code. The final step requires thinking about the nuances of the ethical code. Again, Howard and Korver recommend a three-step process:

Clarify degrees of separation. While it's nice to think that ethical questions can be cut-and-dried, the truth is that in many situations, the standards drafted may bend slightly. It's essential, then, for corporations to determine "how close is too close" to unethical action.[22] One example is the decision made by a consulting firm as to whether to take on clients whose businesses they find unethical, such as tobacco companies. Does taking on a contract make the consultancy complicit in the firm's dealings?

Draw sharper lines. As noted above, positive ethics can be challenging to codify because they lack upper bounds. This is the step in which the scope of positive ethics should be refined, making them more actionable.

Consider a hierarchy. It's likely that, at some point, a corporation will find itself in the position of having to choose between two conflicting values. This is the step in which priorities are delineated, so that the path through such a conflict will be clear. Corporations that operate in markets throughout the world are likely to see clashes between cultural values.

Howard and Korver also warn to watch out for several failure factors when drafting an ethical code. In Figure 7.2, we include those most relevant to developing a corporate code of ethics.

THE RELATIONSHIP BETWEEN ETHICS AND OTHER AREAS OF CR

How does the establishment of a corporate code of ethics relate to the other CR topics we have discussed in this book? In Chapter 3, we discussed corporate environmental responsibility and sustainability issues. As you may recall, one area of

Figure 7.2 Failure factors

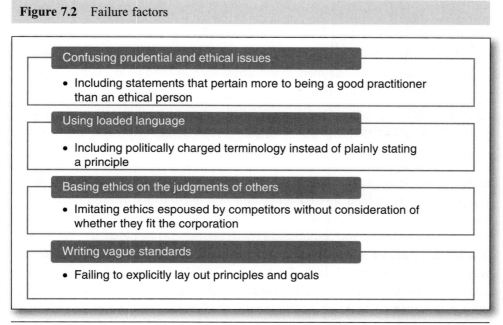

- Confusing prudential and ethical issues
  - Including statements that pertain more to being a good practitioner than an ethical person
- Using loaded language
  - Including politically charged terminology instead of plainly stating a principle
- Basing ethics on the judgments of others
  - Imitating ethics espoused by competitors without consideration of whether they fit the corporation
- Writing vague standards
  - Failing to explicitly lay out principles and goals

Source: Adapted from Howard, R. A., & Korver, C. D. (2008). *Ethics for the real world: Creating a personal code to guide decisions in work and life.* Boston, MA: Harvard Business Review Press.

discussion was the difference between regulatory compliance and taking voluntary action to improve a corporation's environmental impact and limit negative externalities such as pollution or the decimation of natural resources used in production. In the same vein, if a company follows the local laws, then it is technically in compliance with all rules and regulations. However, if a company takes it a step further and also follows its code of ethics, then the firm is not just doing business, but doing business while working to make a positive impact on the communities where business is done.

With regard to human rights and labor issues, discussed in Chapter 4, ethics can fill gaps when a multinational corporation is looking at differences between its home country's laws and those in the geographical areas in which it does business. It's easy for companies to fall into the trap of ethical relativism, allowing themselves to believe that their behavior abroad is acceptable as long as it adheres to the legal standards and norms of the country in which a particular aspect of their business is located. By having a standard code of ethics that the company agrees to apply under all circumstances, a corporation can protect itself from potential scandals that can arise when citizens in its home country learn of nefarious activities abroad. Nike, for example, as discussed in Chapter 4, came under scrutiny for labor violations along its supply chain, as did Apple. Had the Nike and Apple factories been in the U.S., these labor violations would likely have never occurred. A stronger culture of business ethics at headquarters and with suppliers may have prevented the PR scandals that negatively affected both companies.

Consumer responsibility is another area in which ethical decision-making plays an important role. In Chapter 5, we looked at the division of responsibility between corporations and their consumers in industries such as food production and healthcare. The responsibility of corporations to consumers is a perfect example of an ethical dilemma because there are many situations in which correctly manufactured products have negative effects on human health due to long-term use.

As the public's expectations of corporations has shifted to include social and environmental responsibility, there has been much discussion about where consumer responsibility ends and corporate responsibility begins, especially in the industries we examined in Chapter 5: food production and healthcare. As consumer expectations of corporations change in the coming years, the ethics of personal versus corporate responsibility will continue to be debated.

Corporate governance, covered in Chapter 6, is an area in which ethical dilemmas arise on a daily basis. In the wake of multiple corporate scandals during the early 21st century, many of which were found to have resulted at least in part from poor corporate oversight, the role of the board of directors has come under greater scrutiny—and harsher criticism for lack of attention paid to the activities of top executives. One challenge in encouraging board members to monitor and speak out against executive misdeeds is that directors are often incentivized to stay silent. Executives and directors may have seats on each other's boards—or board members' companies may have lucrative consulting contracts with the firm that they wish to protect by not rocking the boat. For this reason, ethics is more important than ever to the topic of corporate governance.

Corporate ethics is an integral part of any corporate responsibility strategy. A corporate code of ethics can help a firm decide how to approach environmental and sustainability issues and human rights and labor laws. A firm with an ethical compass will also be better equipped to navigate the complex nature of consumer responsibility and corporate governance. Overall, a business code of ethics can help a company to make a positive and lasting impact on all its key stakeholders.

HOW ETHICS INFORMS BUSINESS DECISION-MAKING

Like CR values and vision, ethics should trickle down from the top of an organization, but CE leadership is needed at all tiers to ensure integration throughout the company. Writing in the *Journal of Business Ethics*, Adam Lindgreen et al. outline the role of future leaders within an organization—whom they term "high-potentials"—to promote CR values and vision at all levels of the company.[23] Similarly, high-potentials can provide ethical leadership across organizational tiers, for the same reasons that they make excellent CR stewards. One, high-potentials are skilled at persuading others to adopt their points of view, which positions them as champions for an issue and catalysts for organizational change.[24] Two, high-potentials

> possess strong personal and business competencies, such as self-confidence and awareness, ambition, clear objectives, dedication and motivation, communication and social skills, leadership, analytic and problem-solving skills, teamwork and team building, creativity and flexibility, the ability to organize and manage, independence and autonomy, and prioritization of improvement and innovation.[25]

The combination of these qualities makes them ideal candidates to create buy-in around an ethical code.

The future leaders of corporations will come from many different paths and backgrounds, and therefore it is difficult to universally prepare them for their roles in management. While their personality traits and innate skills allow them to be capable champions of corporate responsibility programs and codes of ethics, instilling these values early on would help these individuals to be that much more successful. Not all high-potentials will earn their MBA; however, ethics has become a hot topic in many MBA programs over the past few years, given the number of executive scandals that have been in the news. A debate (which will be discussed later in the chapter) concerning whether ethics should be part of the MBA curriculum is ongoing, but today many MBA programs have courses dedicated to the study and understanding of corporate ethics. From one of the best business school programs in the country comes the MBA Oath. The MBA Oath is one effort designed to prepare future high-potentials early in their careers. The Oath was started by a group of 2009 graduates of the Harvard Business School who were concerned about the events of the financial crisis and began questioning its roots:

> The global financial crisis of this past year has prompted many in the public and in the press to question whether business schools are successfully executing their missions of educating leaders for society. How did we get into this crisis? Why didn't business school professors sound the alarms in advance of the meltdown? Why were so many MBAs involved in the decisions leading up to the crisis? Are MBAs so concerned with increasing their personal wealth that they ignore ethics and their responsibilities to society?

Similar to the Hippocratic Oath undertaken by medical doctors, the MBA Oath asks MBAs to agree to a list of goals and principles pertaining to their roles as business leaders and their responsibility to society. The text of the Oath can be seen in Figure 7.3.

A 2008 *Harvard Business Review* article compliments the Oath, advocating making management a "true profession" in the way that medicine and law already are:

> The claim that managers are professionals does not withstand scrutiny when you compare management with true professions such as medicine and law. Unlike doctors and lawyers, managers don't need a formal education, let alone a license, to practice. Nor do they adhere to a universal and enforceable code of conduct. Individual companies may write and enforce corporate codes or value statements, but there's no universally accepted set of professional values backed up by a governing body with the power to censure managers who deviate from the code.[26]

The MBA Oath filled this void, but then faced the challenge of how to keep the new standards at the front of the minds of business leaders. As we will see in Chapter 10, when Chiquita introduced its new Core Values to employees, one challenge was ensuring that they stayed in the forefront of employees' minds.

Figure 7.3 The MBA Oath

THE MBA OATH

As a business leader I recognize my role in society.

My purpose is to lead people and manage resources to create value that no single individual can create alone.

- My decisions affect the well-being of individuals inside and outside my enterprise, today and tomorrow.

Therefore, I promise that:

- I will manage my enterprise with loyalty and care, and will not advance my personal interests at the expense of my enterprise or society.

- I will understand and uphold, in letter and spirit, the laws and contracts governing my conduct and that of my enterprise.

- I will refrain from corruption, unfair competition, or business practices harmful to society.

- I will protect the human rights and dignity of all people affected by my enterprise, and I will oppose discrimination and exploitation.

- I will protect the right of future generations to advance their standard of living and enjoy a healthy planet.

- I will report the performance and risks of my enterprise accurately and honestly.

- I will invest in developing myself and others, helping the management profession continue to advance and create sustainable and inclusive prosperity.

In exercising my professional duties according to these principles, I recognize that my behavior must set an example of integrity, eliciting trust and esteem from those I serve. I will remain accountable to my peers and to society for my actions and for upholding these standards.

This oath I make freely, and upon my honor.

Source: MBA Oath, http://mbaoath.org/about/the-mba-oath/ (accessed August 29, 2014).

Chiquita accomplished this by distributing Core Values wallet cards.[27] Similarly, the creators of the MBA Oath print both wallet cards and small buttons with the values listed, to be used as constant reminders to fulfill the oath. In response to the MBA Oath, a conversation began over whether it is even appropriate for business to have an oath. Other criticisms suggested that it is not enforceable.

In recent years, there have been many examples reported of situations where holes in corporate codes of ethics led to crises. *Forbes* magazine, citing research from executive outplacement firm Challenger, Gray & Christmas, reported that during 2011, 42 CEOs were forced out as a result of ethical violations.[28] There is both good news and bad news related to this. The good news is that corporate boards are becoming more stringent about scrutinizing executive activity, possibly driven by the numerous scandals in recent years, especially those where board apathy was an issue (see Chapter 6 for more on this). As the *Forbes* article explained:

> Shareholders and employers are demanding—or finding, due to social media and increasing media scrutiny—the information un-ethical executives have formerly been more easily able to hide. Increasingly strict disclosure rules and public scrutiny are forcing more executives to behave in a way that is ethical or to face the increasing reality of being removed from their jobs.[29]

The bad news is that despite these events, dishonorable behavior by top managers is increasing. The results are devastating and include "rapid disintegration, destruction and loss of relationships, corporations and personal lives."[30]

In the absence of a code of ethics and an appropriate system for evaluating and making ethical decisions, a situation can occur in which organization members, particularly younger employees who report to others in a hierarchy, make decisions that are out of line with personal or corporate ethics because they are simply following orders from above. A famous example of this is the results of the Milgram experiment of 1961, which measured the willingness of participants to submit to the demands of an authority figure, even when such demands led them to commit acts in violation of their personal ethics. The experiment found that people are susceptible to developing a mindset that they are "just following orders" and bear no personal responsibility or guilt for unethical actions.

How does this relate to business? According to Aine Donovan, director of the Ethics Institute at Dartmouth College and a professor at the Tuck School of Business:

> Once MBAs get into the mechanics of business—particularly if they wind up in finance—it's easier for them to compromise their values, or overlook the bad behavior of their peers or bosses with a wink and nod. It becomes easier to slide.[31]

For a company to have a strong ethical culture, C-suite executives and all other levels of management must fully believe in the ethical mission of the company. Management should use the code of ethics as a guide in every decision that is made and instill the firm's ethical compass in each of their employees. The MBA Oath is one way of impressing the importance of ethical values on future leaders. However, firms must be careful who they hire in the first place, because without a good example of what ethical management is, employees will struggle to follow even the most clear and concise code of ethics.

THE ROLE OF ETHICS IN MBA CURRICULA

In addition to the MBA Oath, creating or expanding the ethics curriculum at schools that offer MBA programs is another way that future leaders could be taught how to make ethical decisions and how to create an ethical business environment at the firms they eventually work for. However, while people understand the importance and need for business ethics, there is some disagreement about where ethics should be taught. Both academics and business practitioners have differing opinions about the role of ethics in schools. Some feel that MBA programs are an appropriate venue in which to educate future business leaders about how to approach the moral decisions they will make during their careers; however, others take a different view, claiming that ethics cannot be taught the same way as other classroom disciplines such as marketing or finance. We will hear from both sides of the debate in this section.

Writing in *Businessweek*, Jennifer Merritt advocates MBA programs that integrate ethical teachings into the curriculum, suggesting that business schools do three things: "make bigger investments in ethics research, do a better job of screening MBA applicants, and put pressure on corporate partners to support long-term efforts in ethics."[32] But, as Professor Donovan explains, schools must take an MBA-appropriate approach:

> MBA students don't necessarily care about Kant's third formulation of the categorical imperative—they need a simple values toolkit that they can understand and have at the ready, not an impression that all ethics are relative, or just intellectual chewing-gum.[33]

It's also important to focus not just on scandals but also on positive examples of ethical behavior from executives and other organization members. More business cases that focus on ethics are needed, as are more financial investment and encouragement for academics to pursue ethics as a primary academic track.

Screening prospective MBAs is also important. In the early 21st century, several top schools rescinded offers of admission or expelled enrolled students upon finding that candidates had falsified information on their MBA applications. As a result, top MBA programs have begun employing third-party services such as Kroll to vet candidates. By signing off on MBAs who later commit ethical breaches, business schools not only put corporations in peril but also risk their own reputations. For example, several Wharton and Harvard MBAs were embroiled in an insider trading scandal in 2011;[34] Raj Rajaratnam, the mastermind behind it all, is currently serving an 11-year prison sentence.[35] This type of news reflects poorly on the schools these individuals received their MBAs from and brings into question what they learned while earning their degrees.

Putting pressure on corporate partners to support ethics-related efforts may be the most challenging aspect of integrating ethics into MBA programs. Until corporations fully understand the negative repercussions of having unethical people within their ranks, they will have little incentive. Additionally, business schools—especially top business schools that need recruiting relationships with blue-chip companies to ensure they hold onto their rankings—are in a difficult position in terms of their ability to put pressure on corporations.

Different MBA programs take different approaches to CR and ethics issues, with many establishing separate programs to tackle these concerns. Similar to how many corporations continue to keep their corporate responsibility departments separate from the rest of their business activities, the existence of niches for CR or ethics concerns within MBA programs suggests that there is still much progress to be made at business schools in terms of the understanding of the relationship between CR and more traditional business disciplines.

Prospective MBAs have several tools at their disposal for evaluating the role of CR and ethics within the curricula of different business schools. Net Impact, a nonprofit whose members leverage business skills toward social and environmental gains, publishes an annual "Business as UNusual" report in which it reviews MBA programs from around the world and provides data on their engagement around CR issues (see Figure 7.4). Schools achieve Gold or Silver accreditation by meeting Net Impact membership quotas and offering activities related to social and environmental impact.

Another ranking is the Aspen Institute Center for Business Education's annual report, "Beyond Grey Pinstripes," also known as BGP.[36] The Institute, a DC-based educational and policy studies organization, uses BGP to spotlight "innovative full-time MBA programs leading the way in the integration of issues concerning social and environmental stewardship into the curriculum."[37] The report ranks programs around the world on factors including relevant coursework, student exposure to CR issues, business impact, and faculty research. Of course, the information in such reports is valuable only if MBAs believe in the importance of corporate responsibility. It's telling that traditional MBA rankings such as the lists published by *U.S. News* and *Businessweek* fail to take into account the role of CR and ethics in their methodology. As a result, they reinforce the increasingly outdated notion that business value—and by extension, the disciplines learned in business schools—is a separate issue from corporate responsibility.

Figure 7.4 An excerpt from Yale SOM's 2014 Business as UNusual scorecard

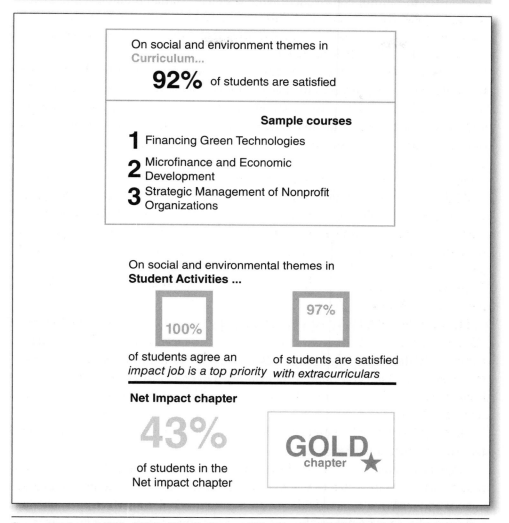

On social and environment themes in
Curriculum...

92% of students are satisfied

Sample courses

1 Financing Green Technologies

2 Microfinance and Economic Development

3 Strategic Management of Nonprofit Organizations

On social and environmental themes in
Student Activities ...

100%
of students agree an
impact job is a top priority

97%
of students are satisfied
with extracurriculars

Net Impact chapter

43%
of students in the
Net impact chapter

GOLD
chapter ★

In the other camp are those individuals who believe that ethics cannot and should not be taught in an MBA program. In a 1992 letter to the editor of *Businessweek*, Wallace F. Smith, professor of business administration at the University of California, Berkeley, wrote:

Teaching ethics is certainly an oxymoron. Ethics is the inherent inner voice, the source of self-control in the absence of external pressure or compulsion.

Teaching about ethics is something else, something that should never be entrusted to a professional school. That is a clear conflict of interest—unethical, if you please.[38]

If ethics are not to be taught in a school setting, the obvious next question is, where should ethics be taught? As of now, the critics have not offered an answer. Meanwhile, the focus on how to educate students about ethics has increased over the past few years. Melissa Korn, a reporter from *The Wall Street Journal*, wrote about what schools are doing to beef up their coursework and curriculum to focus on ethical issues. She says:

Schools admit that they are not going to change someone who is a fundamentally bad person into a good person . . . but what they can do is teach the people around that bad person to see signs of that bad behavior and learn to gain a voice to speak up when they are seeing those bad things happen.[39]

The debate of how and where to teach ethics continues, but it's clear that schools, students, and consumers all believe in the value of a strong, ethical conscience.

ETHICS AS A CREATOR OF SHARED VALUE

As we have discussed throughout this book, there is a strong business case for engaging in strategic corporate responsibility. Given that some consider CR to be a subset of business ethics, it makes sense that ethics creates shared value in much the same way that CR does.

Michael Porter and Mark Kramer defined shared value as "policies and operating practices that enhance the competitiveness of a company while simultaneously advancing the economic and social conditions in the communities in which it operates."[40] Ethics contributes to shared value creation because creating a corporate code of ethics allows organizations to protect themselves from the future potential costs associated with unethical business decisions and can also lower the likelihood of unethical behavior by employees at all levels. A corporate code of ethics serves as a road map for companies when making business decisions. The road map can help companies stick to their core competencies by offering services and products that make sense for that company, given their business model, operating environment, and corporate strengths and weaknesses. A code of ethics helps employees to focus on the business and their customers without being distracted by competitors, get-rich-quick schemes or fast tracks to a promotion. In addition to providing guidance and direction, a corporate code of ethics helps a firm to do the right thing in terms of treating its workers well, respecting the environment in which it operates, and helping to improve the communities that the firm interacts with. While a code of ethics will not automatically allow a company to fully capitalize the concept of shared value, it will certainly help the firm to start thinking about its long-term strategy and business decisions in a different manner, which will hopefully lead to changes that make the company more profitable and more competitive and leave its employees, consumers, and other stakeholders more satisfied.

How Ethics Creates Value for Stakeholders

Like corporate responsibility, corporate ethics generates value for a variety of internal and external stakeholders. For current and potential employees, a corporation's reputation as an ethical business can serve as a powerful means of attracting and retaining top talent. As seen from the Edelman goodpurpose® survey, consumers are also swayed by companies that engage in business practices that do good; 87% of global consumers surveyed believed that business should place at least the same weight on societal interests as business interests.[41]

Projecting an image of ethical responsibility is an opportunity for corporations to increase profits, as 73% of global consumers surveyed expressed willingness to switch brands if a different brand of similar quality supported a good cause.[42] Consumers will feel better about the purchases they make, while corporations will benefit from increased profits by unlocking consumer demand for more ethically produced products and services.

Investors are another stakeholder group who benefit from corporate ethics—and not just those engaged in socially responsible investing (SRI). A corporation's adherence to ethical principles is also important in terms of risk management, as seen in the financial crisis. The Peregrine Financial Group story from the beginning of this chapter is one example of a situation in which the ethical failures of top management put investor funds at grave risk. Unethical corporate behavior can destroy shareholder value by causing stocks to plummet. While creating a corporate code of ethics may take some work, especially in large, complex organizations, it's difficult to understand why a company wouldn't invest the resources in creating such a document, given the numerous benefits it provides to all its key stakeholders and to the business itself.

CONCLUSION

Ethics is a crucial component not only of any CR strategy, but of any corporate strategy in general. Without an ethical code of conduct that is put in writing, disseminated throughout the company, and integrated into corporate culture, a corporation is in greater danger of ethical scandals that could lead to a tainted corporate reputation, legal consequences, loss of license to operate, dampened profits, and decreased shareholder value. Ethics education must begin in schools but continue throughout peoples' careers. For this to happen, there must be equal buy-in from both business schools and corporations, and pressure from each group onto the other. The most ethical firms will have a clear, concise, and applicable code of ethics that senior management will stand behind and instill in their employees. These firms will understand that creating and maintaining an ethical culture is a constant process that takes dedication, commitment, and resources, but that the benefits to the firm and all its stakeholders are well worth the effort and that the alternative is no longer an option.

NOTES

1. Woodford, M. (2012, October 21). "Corporate ethics are a matter of life and death." *Financial Times*. Retrieved August 29, 2014, from http://www.ft.com/cms/s/0/6cca2bec-19d6-11e2-a379-00144feabdc0.html#axzz2IA0jpOWE

2. Soble, J. (2012, September 5). Former Olympus executives plead guilty. *Financial Times*. Retrieved August 29, 2014, from http://www.ft.com/intl/cms/s/0/7fb1e160-06c0-11e2-abdb-00144 feabdc0.html#axzz2IA0jpOWE

3. Ibid.

4. Blowfield, M., & Murray, A. (2011). *Corporate responsibility* (2nd ed., p. 376). New York, NY: Oxford University Press.

5. Howard, R. A., & Korver, C. D. (2008). *Ethics for the real world: Creating a personal code to guide decisions in work and life*. Boston, MA: Harvard Business Review Press.

6. Foley, R. J. (2012, August 13). "Iowa brokerage CEO indicted in $200M fraud scheme." *Yahoo! News*. Retrieved April 1, 2015, from http://news.yahoo.com/iowa-brokerage-ceo-indicted -200m-fraud-scheme-225744552--finance.html

7. Foley, R. J. (2012, September 17). "Feds appeal ruling that would free Peregrine CEO." *Yahoo! Finance*. Retrieved April 1, 2015, from http://finance.yahoo.com/news/feds-appeal-ruling -free-peregrine-ceo-152248284--finance.html

8. Ibid.

9. "Exxon Mobil to face Indonesia human rights suit, court says." (2011, July 8). *Bloomberg News*. Retrieved August 29, 2014, from http://www.bloomberg.com/news/2011-07-08/exxon -mobil-to-face-indonesia-human-rights-claims-court-rules.html

10. De George, R. T. (n.d.). "A history of business ethics." Santa Clara University. Retrieved August 29, 2014, from http://www.scu.edu/ethics/practicing/focusareas/business/conference/ presentations/business-ethics-history.html

11. Ibid.

12. Friedman, M. (1970, September 13). "The social responsibility of business is to increase its profits." *New York Times Magazine*.

13. Handy, C. (2002, December). "What's a business for?" *Harvard Business Review.*

14. "World equity markets lost $5.2 trillion in January." (2008, February 8). Retrieved August 28, 2014, from http://money.cnn.com/2008/02/08/news/economy/world_markets

15. Mackey, J., & Sisodia, R. (2014, August 29). "'Conscious Capitalism' is not an oxymoron." Retrieved August 29, 2014, from http://blogs.hbr.org/cs/2013/01/cultivating_a_higher_conscious .html

16. "The world's most ethical companies 2014." (2014, March 20). *Forbes.* Retrieved August 27, 2014, from http://www.forbes.com/sites/susanadams/2014/03/20/the-worlds-most-ethical-companies/

17. Ibid.

18. Howard & Korver, "Ethics for the real world."

19. Ibid., p. 73.

20. Shaw, W. H. (2013). *Business ethics: A textbook with cases.* Cengage Learning.

21. http://www.newyorklife.com (accessed August 29, 2014).

22. Howard & Korver, "Ethics for the real world," p. 82.

23. Lindgreen, A., Swaen, V., Harness, D., & Hoffmann, M. (2011). "The role of 'high potentials' in integrating and implementing corporate social responsibility." *Journal of Business Ethics, 99*(S1): 73–91.

24. Ibid.

25. Ibid.

26. Khurana, R., & Nohria, N. (2008, October). "It's time to make management a true profession." *Harvard Business Review.* Retrieved August 29, 2014, from http://hbr.org/2008/10/its-time -to-make-management-a-true-profession/ar/1

27. Ibid.

28. Hall, A. (2012, June 5). "Good news or bad: Ethics causing a rise in CEO exits." *Forbes.* Retrieved August 29, 2014, from http://www.forbes.com/sites/alanhall/2012/06/05/good-news-or -bad-ethics-causing-a-rise-in-ceo-exits/

29. Ibid.

30. Ibid.

31. Donovan, A. (2009, April 14). "Can ethics classes cure cheating?" *Harvard Business Review.* Retrieved August 29, 2014, from http://blogs.hbr.org/how-to-fix-business-schools/2009/04/ can-ethics-classes-cure-cheati.html

32. "Ethics is also B-school business." (2003, January 16). *Bloomberg Business.* Retrieved August 29, 2014, from http://www.businessweek.com/stories/2003-01-16/ethics-is-also-b-school -business

33. Donovan, "Can ethics classes cure cheating?"

34. Byrne, J. A. (2011, May 11). "Wharton MBA guilty of insider trading." Retrieved August 29, 2014, from http://poetsandquants.com/2011/05/11/wharton-mba-convicted-of-insider-trading/

35. Hurtado, P. (2013, March 21). "Raj Rajartnam's brother charged with insider trading." *Bloomberg Business.* Retrieved August 29, 2014, from http://www.bloomberg.com/news/2013 -03-21/raj-rajaratnam-s-brother-charged-with-insider-trading.html

36. http://www.beyondgreypinstripes.org/ (accessed August 29, 2014).

37. http://www.beyondgreypinstripes.org/content/about-us (accessed August 29, 2014).

38. Smith, W. F. (1992, May 3). "Teaching ethics is an oxymoron." *Bloomberg Business.* Retrieved August 29, 2014, from http://www.businessweek.com/stories/1992-05-03/teaching-ethics-is-dot-dot-dot-an-oxymoron

39. Korn, M. (2013, February 6). "Does an 'A' in ethics have any value?" *Wall Street Journal.* Retrieved August 29, 2014, from http://online.wsj.com/news/articles/SB10001424127887324761004578286102004694378

40. Porter, M. E., & Kramer, M. R. (2011, January/February). Creating shared value (p. 6). *Harvard Business Review.* Retrieved from https://hbr.org/2011/01/the-big-idea-creating-shared-value

41. Edelman. (2012). "2012 Edelman goodpurpose study." Retrieved August 29, 2014, from http://purpose.edelman.com/

42. Ibid.

IL MARE'S OCULARE

Anna Rose was a newly minted MBA from the Tuck School of Business who had just completed her first year on the job at Il Mare, a small, high-end, Italian skin care company that had been acquired recently by a large, British cosmetics firm just after she was hired in 2015. Il Mare's products were the most expensive on the market, but according to the well-heeled women who used them, they possessed almost magical powers and were capable of making users appear 10 years younger.

Anna progressed rapidly at the company and found herself the product manager for the company's new Oculare line. The company had invested millions of dollars developing a new eye cream and conducting clinical testing to try to substantiate its product benefit claims. Anna Rose's pre-business-school background as a microbiologist with a PhD from Oxford made her the perfect candidate for the product manager position.

Dr. Rose's trained research eye and preliminary testing on the Oculare eye cream indicated that the product was both safe (even for the most highly sensitive skin) and efficacious. The company had committed millions of British pounds to advertising and promotional support for the launch and was forecasting strong sales. As Anna's boss at Il Mare, Michael Kaye, had told her, the parent company's fourth quarter results depended almost exclusively on the success of this product launch.

As she sat at her desk in London working with her team on the final presentation for the product launch and press conference which was to take place at One Aldwych Hotel, Anna received a call from her boss, Michael, telling her that she was to be rewarded for her hard work by making the presentation to senior managers and the media the next day. Her job was to present the results of the clinical testing she had commissioned, which showed that Oculare significantly outperformed the leading competitive products in reducing the visible signs of aging. Upon application, the eye area became dramatically brighter and smoother. With repeated use, fine lines and wrinkles noticeably decreased. Test participants had indicated a 98% purchase intent. Anna knew she had a home run on her hands. Once older women realized that they could virtually reverse the aging process with the Oculare eye cream, they would gladly pay the luxury price.

As Anna was about to leave to go home to practice her presentation, a scientist from the company's lab came to see her with some startling news. An ongoing safety study with over 500 participants now showed that the Oculare eye cream had caused skin cancer in the eye area in a very small percentage (less than 1%) of the women using the product over a six-month period. Michael Kaye had told her earlier that the study had already been completed and confirmed product safety; this was the first time she was hearing otherwise.

Source: This case was written by Professor Paul A. Argenti with help from Joanie Taylor, T'11, and Dartmouth Professor Aine Donovan.

Anna couldn't believe what she was hearing. "What should I do?" she asked slowly, in disbelief. The researcher shrugged his shoulders and said, "It's your call. We don't know for sure that the Oculare causes the cancer in this small population and I would proceed with extreme caution here. The whole company is depending on this product to meet analysts' expectations in the next quarter."

The presentation and press conference was the next morning at 8 a.m., following a 7:30 a.m. breakfast. Anna reached for her mobile phone only to find a text message from her boss: "This is a great opportunity for you and Il Mare tomorrow, Anna. Don't let me down; I'm counting on you!"

Anna sighed and pondered what to do. Was this one of those dilemmas her professor for Tuck's Corporate Responsibility class had talked about? Or was she making a big deal out of nothing? After all, 1% was pretty small and the study was inconclusive. Given the potential for this product launch, she wondered if she should proceed tomorrow with the press conference and then ask for more research going forward. "I wish I were in class again rather than trying to come up with an answer on my own." Anna poured herself a cup of tea and decided to give it all some thought.

Case Questions

1. What is the moral dilemma in this case?

2. Based on what you read in this chapter, what would you recommend to Anna if you could give her advice?

Chapter 8

CORPORATE PHILANTHROPY

C orporate philanthropy (CP) is at the root of what has grown into broader CR strategy during the late 20th and early 21st centuries, and includes donations of money, employee time, and gifts in kind. Historically, there have been several motivations behind a corporation's decision to initiate a philanthropic program, ranging from the desire to be a good corporate citizen to reputation and relationship building. However, these approaches to CP have also been consistently criticized as PR efforts at best, making them not as transformative as other potential social investments, and in some cases a waste of shareholder money.

Historically, there has been a great deal of argument about the role of business in society. In Chapter 2, we explored University of Chicago economist Milton Friedman's view that the social responsibility of a business is to maximize its profits. The other side of the argument, reflected in an article by David Chandler and William Werther in *Ethical Corporation Magazine*, is that business has a moral obligation to contribute to society. Chandler and Werther argued that business is about more than profits, stating that "corporations should act with greater responsibility toward all their constituents."[1] While Friedman's words in 1970 espoused a strong divergence from this view, an article by Archie Carroll and Kareem Shabana in the *International Journal of Management Reviews* notes, "The idea that business enterprises have some responsibilities to society beyond that of making profits for the shareholders has been around for centuries," adding, however, that the wide popularity of such a stance is a more recent development: "largely a post-World War II phenomenon [that] did not surge in importance until the 1960s and beyond."[2]

MOTIVATIONS BEHIND AND CRITIQUES AGAINST CP

The belief in corporate responsibility beyond profit generation was the genesis for corporate philanthropy, which was one of the first components of early CR programs.

During the 1950s, there were three core ideas at the forefront of conversations about corporate responsibility.[3] The first was the idea of the manager as public trustee, the second was the balancing of competing claims to corporate resources, and the third was the subject of this chapter, corporate philanthropy.[4]

Philip Kotler and Nancy Lee define CP as "a direct contribution by a corporation to a charity or cause, most often in the form of cash grants, donations, and/or in-kind services."[5] Of the various corporate social initiatives that exist, CP is the most traditional form, and has long been crucial to the operating budgets of nonprofit organizations.[6]

These types of corporate contributions to charities and other worthy causes would today be termed "community obligation," and still comprise a large portion of most companies' CP portfolios. Such gifts are often the result of a corporation's desire to deliver on feelings of duty to the communities in which it operates, as well as a belief in the importance of being a good corporate citizen.[7] As we have discussed in previous chapters, many early philanthropic initiatives focused solely on making a good social contribution, never expecting or calculating a return. This focus was enhanced by the nature of the times, in which social responsibility was not only recognized, but made a priority by many.

At the same time, the 1950s saw limited discussion of the relationship between CR programs and business benefits. Instead, CR initiatives focused mainly on corporations' responsibilities to society and doing good works as a matter of altruism[8]—a very different perspective from Porter and Kramer's shared value creation framework, discussed in detail in Chapter 2. The 1960s and 1970s, meanwhile, were the "awareness" and "issue" eras of CR.[9] During these decades, there were shifts in social consciousness and recognition of overall responsibility; nonetheless, the focus on philanthropy within CR programs continued.[10] According to Carroll and Shabana, the lack of connection between CR and financial gains persisted:

> Another characteristic of the 1960s was an absence of any coupling of social responsibility with financial performance. In other words, social responsibility was driven primarily by external, socially conscious motivations, and businesses were not looking for anything specific in return.[11]

Without metrics for measuring the return on investment of corporate responsibility programs—or even voiced beliefs that such metrics could or should exist—it makes sense that Milton Friedman entered the conversation with his belief that an efficiently operating corporation, in and of itself, was the best possible contribution to society. The notion that any diversion of corporate funds away from this goal is stealing from shareholders can perhaps be applied most precisely to traditional CP—in other words, direct corporate donations without any economic returns to the firm.

Whereas traditional CP views included the notion of manager as public trustee, Friedman felt that "a corporate executive . . . has direct responsibility to his employers. That responsibility is to conduct business in accordance with their desires, which generally will be to make as much money as possible."[12] Friedman took a harsh view of managers who sought to effect social impact in addition to economic impact, stating, "Managers who sacrifice profit for the common good also are in effect imposing a tax on their shareholders and arbitrarily deciding how that money should be spent."[13] Additionally, he outlined what he viewed as the inevitable consequences of a management approach that did attempt to integrate CR principles:

> Executives are hired to maximize profits; that is their responsibility to their company's shareholders. Even if executives wanted to forgo some profit to benefit society, they could expect to lose their jobs if they tried—and be replaced by managers who would restore profit as the top priority.[14]

Porter and Kramer, however, argue that the kind of business Friedman abhors has long been the backbone of a healthy and growing society, calling into question the relevance of Friedman's views even at the time they were made: "In the old, narrow view of capitalism, business contributes to society by making a profit, which supports employment, wages, purchases, investments, and taxes. Conducting business as usual is sufficient social benefit."[15]

It is arguable that capitalistic pursuit of profit and social progress go hand in hand. One benefit of capitalism is that it spurs innovation as a means of increasing profits; meanwhile, innovation is often a major catalyst of social and environmental gains.[16] And without the profits generated by corporations, there would be insufficient tax and charity dollars for government programs and nonprofit organizations.[17]

In lockstep with changes in societal views of corporate responsibility overall, corporations began to see further motivations to begin or expand their CP programs over time. As CP programs gained publicity, corporations began to see philanthropy as a means of enhancing their reputations and legitimizing their practices. Nowadays, corporate responsibility is given considerable attention, to the degree that corporations must prioritize CR initiatives and integrate them into core business strategy. As Porter and Kramer explained:

> Myriad organizations rank companies on the performance of their corporate social responsibility (CSR), and, despite sometimes questionable methodologies, these rankings attract considerable publicity. As a result, CSR has emerged as an inescapable priority for business leaders in every country.[18]

Where does corporate philanthropy fit into the larger CR picture? It is a piece of the CR puzzle that contributes to the legitimacy and reputation of a corporation. Corporations that are criticized for failure to deliver on environmental responsibility or product safety (i.e., responsibility to consumers) may find that charitable contributions are a relatively risk-free means of boosting legitimacy and strengthening corporate reputation.[19] Such companies may also find philanthropy to be a useful means of fostering trust.[20]

Consulting firm FSG terms this concept "reputation and relationship building philanthropy," defining it as follows:

> This giving cluster reflects a conscious effort to secure the goodwill of critical stakeholders—such as employees, channel partners, customers, community leaders, or other funders—by supporting causes that they favor. More broadly, these gifts seek to improve the organization's external and internal image. These kinds of gifts can take many forms from employee matching gifts, to sponsoring a high-profile arts organization or the pet project of an important community leader.[21]

Corporations' use of CP to enhance their reputation and legitimacy is a tactic aimed not only at customers, but also at shareholders, employees, and other important stakeholders. Looking at corporate philanthropy within the context of society's changing values, CP could now be framed as a marketing activity, which could help build a business case to appease shareholders. While Milton Friedman argued in 1970 that engaging in CR activities was unfair to shareholders, a recent article in *The Wall Street Journal* took a different view of the relationship between shareholders and philanthropy:

> Shareholders tolerate a certain amount of what looks like corporate philanthropy because some customers like to see it, and so become more inclined to buy the company's products. Used in this way, philanthropy is simply part of a firm's marketing.[22]

Additionally, studies have shown that growth in a consumer product corporation's charitable contributions is positively correlated with future revenue growth.[23] Meanwhile, revenue growth is not necessarily an indicator of future charitable giving, suggesting that corporate philanthropy is actually a contributor to financial performance—rather than an indicator that a corporation is giving more money to charitable causes simply because it is earning greater revenues.[24] The explanation for this is that consumer satisfaction increases as a result of CP, and happier customers are likely to spend more money, generating greater revenues for the corporation.[25]

As discussed in Chapter 1, there are benefits to employee recruitment and retention from corporate responsibility, and CP is no exception. CP, particularly the donation of employee hours, raises employee satisfaction, with current employees reporting higher job satisfaction and commitment and potential employees being more attracted to companies with robust community involvement.[26] There are other, business-related benefits of corporate philanthropy in the form of volunteer hours, as volunteer opportunities can enhance employee's leadership skills.[27] Meanwhile, the impact of corporate volunteer programs on employee morale is measurable. After Microsoft announced a volunteer program in Egypt, the corporation's employee satisfaction saw an increase of 30 percentage points, from 61% to 91%.[28]

There are other business benefits of engaging in philanthropic programs. CP is often a means of mending damaged relationships between a corporation and community leaders or other stakeholders.[29] CP has also been increasingly pursued as preemptive compliance with regulation by government and other external stakeholders, who, according to Porter and Kramer, "are seeking to hold companies accountable for social issues and highlight the potentially large financial risks for any firm whose conduct is deemed unacceptable."[30]

It is in businesses' self-interest to behave responsibly,[31] with CP as a means of protecting a corporation's license to operate. Porter and Kramer note that government regulation has been trending toward mandating social responsibility reporting,[32] while activist groups have become increasingly aggressive and effective in their attempts to incite public pressure on corporations to behave responsibly.[33] Strategically, "activists may target the most visible or successful companies merely to draw attention to an issue, even if those corporations actually have had little impact on the problem at hand."[34] Corporations, therefore, must be proactive in identifying potential threats, and corporate philanthropy is a relatively safe way of hedging against reputational risk.

At the same time, despite the increase in the justifications for pursuing CP programs, there were still a number of critiques of the practice when approached in this manner, namely, that using CP as a response to or means of preventing negative attention amounts to putting out fires and provides no real benefits to society. This perspective echoes Friedman's view, under which this kind of CP would be deemed simply marketing or PR efforts, and a waste of shareholder money. Consequently, Porter and Kramer agree that when CP is used as nothing more than a PR campaign to generate goodwill, Milton Friedman is validated in his view that CP is a misallocation of shareholders' money.[35] Another fairly cynical view of corporate philanthropy was described by Matteo Tonello in a blog post for Harvard Law School:

Compared to other social initiatives . . . it is relatively easy for companies to open or close the corporate checkbook in a given year, which makes contributions more variable over time and more subject to criticism that they are simply a waste of shareholder money.[36]

As reported in *The Wall Street Journal*, "some naysayers insist that corporate philanthropy is a distraction from some of the more nefarious practices in which a business may engage."[37] Porter and Kramer argue, however, that viewing CP and business gains as competing rather than harmonious entities is a grave mistake on the part of corporations, and note that this perspective has not always been dominant:

> The best companies once took on a broad range of roles in meeting the needs of workers, communities, and supporting businesses. As other social institutions appeared on the scene, however, these roles fell away or were delegated . . . outsourcing and offshoring weakened the connection between firm and their communities.[38]

This approach to CP is not strategic and therefore holds no long-term benefits for either the business or society. And one consequence of failure to recognize the connection between CP and good business is that companies often engage in CP initiatives that are too aligned with executives' personal gains—and not enough with their core business strategies. A McKinsey study surveyed 721 companies and found that 45% of respondents believed that "personal interests of CEO/board members" held the most weight in determining the focus of the corporate philanthropy program.[39] There are several reasons why executives are personally invested in corporations' CP decisions, including status increase, the advancement of pet projects, and the opportunity to curry favor among corporate board members. Meanwhile, companies feel obliged to engage in CP activities to appease stakeholders, but this kind of reactive, shortsighted approach can do more long-term harm than good to the business. CP is an area in which "managers often have discretion to use a company's slack resources independent of business objectives," and because good causes benefit from corporate giving, there is reluctance among top managers to question how charitable dollars are spent—potentially resulting in less oversight of charitable contributions relative to other business activities.[40]

On the other hand, relinquishing decisions about CP spending to stakeholders is also a mistake. While stakeholders' views are important, their understanding of a corporation's inner workings is limited,[41] so corporations that yield to pressure from outsiders are likely to find themselves with a CP program that amounts to a series of defensive reactions, versus a long-term strategic approach to philanthropic initiatives that creates shared value.[42] As Porter and Kramer point out, beyond failure to provide tangible gains, such programs may not even have positive effects on reputation: "Studies of the effect of a company's social reputation on consumer purchasing preferences or on stock market performance have been inconclusive at best."[43]

THE STRATEGIC APPROACH TO CP

What *does* an effective corporate philanthropy program look like, then? GE, for example, selects underperforming high schools near several U.S. facilities and contributes between $250,000 and $1 million to each school over a five-year period, as well as in-kind donations. How is this different from pure charity? In addition to tangible resources, GE offers the schools access to its managers and employees, who partner with school administrators to identify areas of need and provide mentorship to students. On the corporate level, GE's program creates goodwill, enhances relationships with local stakeholders such as government officials, and increases morale among participating employees. Participating schools, meanwhile, have shown significant improvement nearly across the board.[44]

One criticism of GE's approach is that its school program has not had a major impact on the company's employee recruitment and retention efforts. There is new potential for both impact and competitive positioning through strategic CR. For the purposes of this chapter, we will focus on how strategic giving offers corporations an opportunity to combine philanthropic efforts with a means of solving business problems. As defined by FSG, strategic giving is "giving that simultaneously advances critical social and business objectives, thereby improving a company's business context while creating social value."[45] The concept of strategic giving is a good fit with Porter and Kramer's framework, as they argue that strategic CR, which leads to shared value creation, is generated "when a company adds a social dimension to its value proposition, making social impact integral to the overall strategy."[46]

An example of FSG's strategic giving concept in action is an initiative at Microsoft called Working Connections. During the 2000s, the corporation partnered with the American Association of Community Colleges as a means of addressing a business problem—namely, the dearth of IT workers, which is a major hindrance to Microsoft's growth. As of 2006, there were more than 450,000 unfilled IT positions in the United States, whereas community colleges in the U.S. had a total enrollment of 11.6 million students, or 45% of all U.S. undergraduates. While this situation seemed symbiotic—Microsoft needed workers, and the students sought employment opportunities after graduation—the corporation realized that community colleges were not perfectly equipped to train a future IT workforce because of issues with curricula and technology, as well as a lack of professional development programs for faculty.[47]

In response to these concerns, Microsoft created a $50 million, five-year initiative in which, in a similar vein to GE's school program, the corporation donated money and products as well as employee time. But in Microsoft's program, the employees volunteered their time using professional skills directly related to their jobs, offering them an opportunity for further professional development while volunteering—and the corporation addressed a crucial need by training a workforce in a skill set that was both scarce and critical to the corporation's future. Porter and Kramer identify this as an impressive example of shared value creation through philanthropy: "Microsoft has achieved results that have benefited many communities while having a direct—and potentially significant—impact on the company."[48]

THE BUSINESS CASE AND VALUE CREATION

Critiques of traditional corporate philanthropy programs as purely opportunistic and a waste of shareholders' money have created a shift toward a strategic approach to CP. This kind of focus can provide both a competitive advantage for the company and a great benefit to society, especially when the focus is on shared value creation.

The focus of CP has recently shifted to necessitate a strategic alignment with business objectives to justify expenditures. Corporate philanthropy has changed over the past few decades, but particularly during the late 20th and early 21st centuries, in response to growing pressure to deliver on traditional expectations of shareholder value while giving back to the community in which a corporation operates.[49]

A McKinsey study found that CP is a way for corporations to fulfill consumer expectations of the role of business in society. At the same time, however, only one-fifth of the survey's respondents believed that their companies' philanthropic programs were meeting CR goals and stakeholder expectations. As summarized by McKinsey, "at these companies, philanthropy programs are more likely to address social and political issues relevant to the business, to be collaborative, and to meet any business goals companies have for them."[50] Other respondents to the survey stated an intention for their companies' philanthropic programs to address business goals in addition to creating social good.

Business engagement with society is shifting from traditional measures, which were disconnected and mainly compliance measures to minimize harm, to shared value creation, which is integrated into the overall company strategy and can "strengthen competitiveness through reduced cost, increased productivity, (and) increased revenue/profits."[51] The reasoning behind the shift toward the creation of a business case for CP is twofold. First, being able to argue a business case for philanthropic activity will help corporations appease concerned shareholders by using their funds in a strategic manner to generate both social *and* economic returns. The long-term sustainability of corporate giving depends on its ability to provide a financial return on investment;[52] the days in which it was sufficient for CP to deliver a "good feeling" are over, as CP will not continue over the long run if it cannot prove its financial worth.[53] Echoing Porter and Kramer's views on CR, Matteo Tonello argues, "A well-designed corporate giving program clearly articulates a congruence between the company's philanthropic activities and its other business activities."[54]

Second, the business case for CP is a means of using corporate giving to produce a true competitive advantage for the corporation. When corporations have well-designed, carefully executed CP programs, they can provide a competitive advantage in the form of increased recognition of a brand or company, improved quality of life in the community or communities in which a corporation does business, and improved economic conditions in developing areas of the world that could someday become new market opportunities.[55] Additionally, such programs enable corporations to recruit and retain talent and stimulate innovation.

For example, MasterCard's CR initiatives focusing on financial inclusion include a CP-heavy component, incorporating monetary donations to existing, relevant organizations, and a considerable amount of employee volunteer time. As noted in *Forbes*, "MasterCard's strategy engages the company's entire network— monetary resources, employee time and expertise and cardholders—to create social value."[56] In turn, the company gains new and devoted customers.

Based on the results of a survey conducted by McKinsey and the Committee Encouraging Corporate Philanthropy (CECP), there are four strategic pathways by which philanthropic initiatives can contribute to business value: (1) enhancing employee engagement, (2) building customer loyalty, (3) managing downside risks to the company's reputation, and (4) contributing to business innovation and growth opportunities.[57] See Figure 8.1 for further information.

However, many scholarly arguments claim that truly strategic philanthropy is possible only when the focus is on maximizing both economic and social results.[58] This kind of CP is both more effective and minimizes the existence of more traditional, opportunistic approaches. To engage in or shift to strategic CP, companies must ensure that their philanthropic initiatives are aligned with their business activities. When a corporation's philanthropic activities are aligned with its business goals, it is easier to ensure that the organization has the necessary resources and capabilities to make a meaningful social or environmental impact.[59] As discussed in Chapter 2, Porter and Kramer recommend focusing on shared value creation in CSR to maximize both social

Figure 8.1 Strategic pathways by which CP contributes to business value

Enhance employee engagement

- Group volunteer programs and awareness of philanthropic initiatives engage employees by increasing their motivation, productivity, and sense of identification with the company

Build customer loyalty

- An organization's commitment to communities and philanthropic causes can enhance brand perception, customer loyalty, repeat business, and word-of-mouth promotion

Manage downside risks to the company's reputation

- Philanthropic initiatives are an opportunity to prioritize and address ways in which the company may not be meeting public expectations

Contribute to business innovation and growth opportunities

- CP also provides access to new relationships and opportunities whereby the company can find, test, and demonstrate new ideas, technologies, and products

Source: Adapted from Lim, T. (2010). "Measuring the value of corporate philanthropy: Social impact, business benefits, and investor return." Committee Encouraging Corporate Philanthropy.

and economic results, and the same holds true for CP. Shared value is effectively social impact that creates business impact[60] and results in intentionally targeted, highest-priority outcomes. Here, we use the term "business impact" to refer only to directly measurable economic business value—not indirect effects such as reputation boosts. According to FSG, "shared value opportunities exist at the intersection of social need, business context, and unique corporate assets."[61] And according to Terrence Lim of the Committee Encouraging Corporate Philanthropy:

> Companies who find natural, innovative opportunities to commit a broad array of company product, expertise, and capabilities beyond cash grants can multiply the business and social returns that their philanthropic initiatives achieve. These opportunities are more likely to arise when companies establish meaningful, long-term relationships with nonprofit partners aligned with the company's priority areas. When corporate donations are disbursed without strategy, the benefits will be greatly limited.[62]

As covered in Chapter 2, there are three main ways in which companies are creating shared value: (1) reconceiving products and services, (2) redefining productivity in the value chain, and (3) strengthening clusters and frameworks.[63] The recommended approach for CP addresses the last sphere of shared value creation, strengthening clusters and frameworks. Porter and Kramer term it context-focused philanthropy—that is, improvement and enhancement of, as well as increased engagement in, the environment in which the company operates. If this approach is used to maximize value, it allows corporations to tap into "a new set of competitive tools that well justifies the investment of resources" while delivering tangible social and environmental impact.[64]

Additionally, this approach is not only strategic, but cost-effective as well. Philanthropy is often the most cost-effective means of creating shared value toward competitive advantage. It positions corporations to make the most of their own resources while leveraging the existing efforts of their philanthropic beneficiaries.[65] As explained by Porter and Kramer, "true strategic giving . . . addresses important social and economic goals simultaneously, targeting areas of competitive context where the company and society both benefit because the firm brings unique assets and expertise."[66]

Strengthening clusters as a means of giving strategically is also progressively becoming both more relevant and more effective. Corporate success is becoming increasingly intertwined with contextual conditions because of changes in the competitive environment; namely, competitive advantage is now driven more by increasing productivity than by saving costs on inputs.[67] Logically, social and economic objectives are inherently connected because a company's ability to compete depends "heavily on the circumstances of the locations in where they operate."[68]

How can context-focused philanthropy address competitive issues? By addressing issues such as factor conditions, demand conditions, the context for strategy and rivalry, and related and supporting industries, this type of strategic CP allows corporations to contribute to causes in ways that ultimately strengthen competitive advantage as well.[69] *Factor conditions* include necessary resources such as trained workers, appropriate infrastructure, and natural resources. The Microsoft program cited in the first section of this chapter is an example of how strategic giving can positively affect factor conditions—in this case, by providing a trained workforce.

Demand conditions relate to the size and quality of a corporation's local market. Apple has addressed this need by donating computers to schools as a means of introducing students to the company's technology products. Beyond generating goodwill associated with the charitable gifts, Apple fosters comfort with and loyalty to its product line. The *context for strategy and rivalry* refers to the environment in which an organization competes. Here, companies can create a better competitive environment through increased transparency and productivity. Finally, thinking about corporate giving within the context of *related and supporting industries* allows companies to develop local clusters and strengthen complementary industries.

In terms of associations with nonprofit, governmental, and community organizations, this kind of engagement inherently promotes longer-term relationships that look more like partnerships.[70] Corporations will also find added benefit from partnering with other companies who share their competitive context, forming "clusters," which Porter and Kramer define as "geographic concentration of interconnected companies, suppliers, related industries, and specialized institutions in a particular field."[71] The power of clusters is that a philanthropic investment by one member of a cluster can have tangible benefits for all, enhancing the cluster's ability to compete both as a group and individually.[72]

Ideally, good CP strategy should result in sufficient business value that a corporation would engage in the same philanthropic practices even without the added benefit of positive publicity and goodwill.[73] The next steps in shifting to a truly strategic CP program involve creating an internal organizational infrastructure that will support the company's philanthropic goals and initiatives to ensure that they are sustainable over the long term. Corporations must clarify executive and board roles in their corporate giving decisions and engage the highest levels of management; buy-in at the top of an organization is key to ensuring that the commitment to strategic CP is spread and understood throughout the company.[74]

Additionally, there must be internal controls in place to define which causes are to benefit from the company's philanthropy program and the amount of money and other resources to be contributed, as well as to prevent top executives from receiving benefits in exchange for donating to certain organizations.[75] It is also crucial to establish standards of independence from board members, which ensures that philanthropy initiatives are not pet projects of specific directors. Finally, good CP is measurable, and corporations must evaluate results by measuring social and financial performance and readjusting, as is done with any business process to optimize outcomes.[76] The process by which corporations can measure and evaluate the progress toward business and social goals will be discussed in more detail in the next section of this chapter.

MEASURING PROGRESS AND IMPROVING OUTCOMES

To test and demonstrate the value of their CP programs and ensure their long-term sustainability, companies must develop systems to consistently track metrics on the resulting financial and social progress. Measurement is as important to CR programs such as philanthropy as it is to more traditional business processes. Companies need to track results to ensure that their investments are creating the intended progress. These metrics can prove the business case surrounding their CP programs, which is necessary to justify their existence and ensure their long-term success. In response to skepticism of the value of CP programs, organizations must demonstrate that their philanthropic initiatives are strategic and cost-effective.[77] Continually measuring and evaluating the progress made by CP programs is necessary to provide tangible evidence that corporate giving creates value for stakeholders.

Measurement and reporting on CP programs can do more than support the business case; it can also provide credibility for the company and prove good management to investors. Companies that are able to show that they have had significant positive effects on social and environmental problems are in a better position to establish credibility among the public than are those that simply write checks.[78] In a report for the Committee Encouraging Corporate Philanthropy, Terrance Lim notes, "There is a significant opportunity for companies to lead the industry in developing standards or differentiating themselves to the investor community through their disclosures about philanthropic efforts."[79] Interestingly, financial personnel including chief financial officers and professional investors often consider ESG program performance to be a stand-in for managerial effectiveness.[80]

Why is this? The fact is that environmental, social, and governance programs affect areas deemed important by investors: leadership quality, adaptability, and balancing short-term needs with long-term, strategic vision.[81] According to Lim, "investors increasingly esteem companies that demonstrate strong social performance, believing that this represents management quality and valuable intangibles."[82]

Perhaps most crucially, creating a measurement and reporting system for corporate philanthropy programs legitimizes them and puts them on par with other business activities, helping to ensure their integration and long-term success. This, in turn, promises a continued and sustainable benefit to society. Reporting is a critical piece of the puzzle, as keeping records of a corporation's CP measurement process will be helpful in establishing standards and disclosures.[83] An efficient, detailed measurement process is necessary to ensure effective management. According to Lim, it also shows that a corporation understands how CP strategy can contribute to long-term business value.[84]

Additionally, without tracking process on social impact goals, a corporation will not be able to assess whether it is creating shared value through its CP initiatives. Failure to adequately measure and review CP metrics comes at a cost: "When companies do not understand or rigorously track the interdependency between social and business results, they miss important opportunities for innovation, growth, and social impact at scale."[85] Thinking strategically is crucial to the development of a robust, effective CP program. Porter and Kramer argue that corporations should think about shared value creation as being similar to research and development functions—in other words, as long-term investments that are likely to produce sizable future gains in the competitive landscape, instead of short-term, isolated investments.[86]

As is the case in other business decisions, data-based evidence of the impact of corporate philanthropy is crucial. Qualitative information about a CP program can be useful in gaining positive publicity and enhancing corporate reputation, but hard numbers make it easier to assess the positive effects of corporate giving, bolstering the case for why companies should engage in CP. According to Lim at the CECP:

> If corporate philanthropy is to make progress in meeting these challenges, the industry must meaningfully assess current practices and measurement trends, clarify precisely what is needed in terms of impact evidence, and then identify the most promising and practical steps forward.[87]

With such obvious benefits of measurement and reporting, why don't all companies maintain hard data on the results of their CP programs? The reason why many corporations fail to measure and evaluate the progress of their CP programs is that measurement is not always easy. The challenges inherent to CP progress measurement have been described in a variety of literature, including papers by Porter and Kramer, McKinsey, and the CECP. According to Porter and Kramer, "corporate philanthropy is in decline," with executives finding it difficult "to justify charitable expenses in terms of bottom-line benefit."[88]

Many executives recognize strategic CP as an opportunity to deliver both business and social value by strengthening their businesses at the same time that they are contributing to social and environmental causes. Unfortunately, such executives often find that coming up with an approach to corporate philanthropy that serves both of these needs is challenging.[89] Despite the necessity of CP programs to both business and society, there is increasing pressure for corporations' CP professionals to produce tangible evidence that such programs are both cost-effective and relevant to business goals. Accordingly, many CP professionals identify measurement as their primary management challenge.[90]

Why is measurement so difficult? One reason is that results and impact are often long term or intangible. Given that CP should involve a strategic, visionary approach, it is often difficult to demonstrate the value of CP programs in the short term. Social change rarely, if ever, happens overnight, and trying to track and measure slow, gradual change can be challenging.[91]

It is also difficult for CP professionals to acquire the necessary data—and especially to ensure that the data they do collect are reliable. This is true not only for corporations that are just beginning their CR or CP programs, but also for companies that have long been involved in such initiatives and have an advanced, experienced view of shared value creation through corporate giving. This lack of data makes optimization of results extremely challenging, if not downright impossible.[92]

At the same time, the consequences for corporate-giving professionals who fail to gather necessary, reliable data can be dire. Without hard evidence of the effectiveness of CP programs, both in terms of their social impact and their contribution to a business's financial bottom line, it is difficult to justify the continued existence of philanthropic investments. For there to be buy-in among top corporate decision-makers, CP professionals must be able to illustrate how their work relates to a company's core business—and how it contributes to shareholder value.[93] Another issue is that corporate giving is often fragmented.[94] This is true not only in terms of where the corporate dollars used to fund philanthropic gifts are sourced within an organization, but also with regard to how gifts are distributed among nonprofit organizations and other worthy causes. As a result, many corporations do not have a clear, comprehensive understanding of how their many philanthropic gifts piece together. This makes it easier for individual gifts to slip through the cracks: some donations are unrecorded or not appropriately vetted, while others are not assessed for effectiveness after the fact.[95]

Such failures are indicative that significant improvements must be made to an organization's measurement systems and procedures to ensure that gifts are effectively measured and categorized throughout an organization.[96] At the same time, even highly organized systems for measuring and reporting philanthropic gifts sometimes produce unreliable data. This happens because ratings often rely on surveys with statistically insignificant response rates, or on self-reported company data without third-party verification.[97] Unsurprisingly, companies with something to hide are less likely to respond, resulting in the collection of data that are largely meaningless.[98]

What kinds of CP information are typically measured? One standard measurement technique is outcomes reporting. Traditionally, most tracking has been done in a very basic way, measuring simply outputs and outcomes but not actual social impact. In this type of measurement approach, CP is evaluated in simple, quantifiable terms such as dollars spent or volunteer hours contributed.[99] The problem with this approach is that it fails to consider the impact of such donations.

Impact assessments, meanwhile, look at how contributions of money or volunteer hours have positively affected the recipients of such gifts, creating benefits for communities. Tracking this information serves to validate CP initiatives in the eyes of stakeholders by demonstrating such programs' social, environmental, and economic results as well as changes over time.[100] The challenge of using this type of measurement method is that it relies on more resources than outcomes reporting, as impact assessments often require historical data or involve complicated, expensive evaluation processes. Meanwhile, such assessments also tend not to examine or illustrate the relationship between the impacts and corporate performance.[101]

Another challenge is that when there is sufficient focus on social impact reporting, the tracking tools used have usually been developed by the social sector. This means there is a lack of standardization, and also no alignment with the companies' standard business analytics. Meanwhile, there are difficulties in establishing the financial value of intangible benefits of CP such as reputational boosts or employee morale and development. This makes it hard to incorporate such benefits into the bottom-line profits resulting from strategic CP.[102] According to Lim at the CECP:

> The nonprofit sector employs a broad range of frameworks, tools, and methodologies to measure the social impact of programs and grants. Many of these approaches have evolved through application by sophisticated private foundations and government agencies, reflecting these organizations' own unique preferences, priorities, and social values.[103]

While there are benefits to standardization, particularly in terms of CP professionals' ability to demonstrate bottom-line impact to stakeholders, there are also needs that must be addressed according to the unique environment of each organization.

Activities and output metrics and targets are the most basic set of trackable performance measures. In programs comprising short-term, one-off grants, such metrics may very well be the only trackable measures. By themselves, however, output metrics offer little indication that social change is being achieved or unintended harm caused.[104] While formal evaluations, such as those provided by social-impact consultancy FSG, have the potential to prove impact, very few companies engage in them. Such evaluations are crucial for providing links between CP initiatives and social impacts,[105] and yet only a small number of corporations undergo them. Subjecting a company's CP portfolio to a strategic review can help a business categorize types of corporate giving, establish consistent internal policies, and match philanthropic spending to objectives. Even fewer firms systematically analyze the ways they can use corporate resources and expertise to leverage the impact of their cash contributions.[106]

There are some attempts to tie social goals to financial reporting,[107] but these are often problematic because the valuation methods can be extremely subjective. ROI methods for calculating the social returns of corporate-giving programs are appealing because they use traditional business frameworks to assess the effectiveness of such programs.[108] But such methods rely heavily on data collection, assumptions, and value judgments: "Funders must assemble data and calculations on the program's monetary benefits and make subjective judgments on the relative value of different types of social changes."[109]

One ROI method for calculating social returns is SROI, or social return on investment. SROI is a means of calculating the total value created by investments in social and environmental causes. SROI assigns a financial value to social and environmental outcomes, so that it can be considered as a concrete piece of a corporation's financial picture when combined with economic value.[110] While presenting social value in quantifiable terms should make it more attractive to investors, the SROI methodology actually has its own set of problems—namely, that it combines notional and actual economic value and includes subjective information in the form of assigning a monetary value of social change.[111]

A more holistic approach, argued by Michael Porter et al. in a paper for FSG, is one capable of measuring the shared value of CP programs. Standard methods of outcome or even impact measurement still do not include metrics that will demonstrate any shared value created. What is needed is a system to track the mutual benefits gained through CP initiatives, which can then be used to communicate both the social and business value to the investment community in terms they understand.

So far, a framework that connects social progress and business success has not been established.[112] But Porter and Kramer argue that if businesses approached CR opportunities the way they consider traditional business decisions, they would unlock greater business potential from CR:

> If, instead, corporations were to analyze their prospects for social responsibility using the same frameworks that guide their core business choices, they would discover that CSR can be much more than a cost, a constraint, or a charitable deed—it can be a source of opportunity, innovation, and competitive advantage.[113]

It is essential not only to determine how substantial the relationship is between a corporation's social performance and its financial success but also to demonstrate how the former affects the latter.[114] To adequately quantify the impact of CP, it is essential to measure and understand the operational drivers of business value, particularly how it is derived from intangible benefits such as employee morale and engagement, consumer loyalty, and corporate reputation—in other words, benefits often created through corporate-giving programs.

To ensure that their successes are valued by investment professionals and others in more traditional areas of business, CP personnel must connect philanthropic activities to business metrics including revenue growth, cost reduction, and profitability.[115] So far, attempts to prove that social programs create economic value have been largely unsuccessful because of the difficulty of identifying the specific drivers of such value. As Porter et al. explain, "shared value measurement, however, through directly linking social and business results, provides investors a direct line of sight between achieving social results and business performance."[116] It is only through shared value measurement that CP professionals can accurately assess "progress and results, generating actionable data and insights to refine shared value strategies." Additionally:

> Data and insights from measuring shared value enable companies to scale shared value initiatives while also providing an indispensable basis for effective communication with the investment community. By illuminating the direct connection between tackling social issues and achieving economic value creation, shared value measurement will diminish investor skepticism.[117]

Porter et al. identify several key ideas behind measuring the shared value of CP programs. The first is that it is important to be specific, measuring only select metrics with the greatest potential. Measuring value is an endeavor separate from measuring impact. "Companies . . . need to identify and prioritize the set of highest potential social results that they are targeting and resist measuring every possible benefit for every possible social dimension affected by their efforts."[118]

The process of tracking shared value creation can be informed by measurements of outcomes and impacts, but it should use separate metrics. This can be daunting, but is necessary to create transformative progress. Shared value measurement uses existing measurement systems as a jumping-off point, but focuses on points at which business and social value intersect.[119] According to Porter et al., "shared value measurement is distinct from other existing measurement approaches, is practical and achievable, and powerfully informs improvement and innovation in shared value strategies."[120] While there may be reluctance to introduce a new measurement system, a corporation that is committed to unlocking the true potential of shared value must adopt the shared value measurement methodology.[121]

Another key component of shared value measurement is setting targets. It is important to set goals related to both business and social impact and track progress against projections, because it is easier to make a persuasive business case for CP if corporate-giving professionals can articulate their strategies for using philanthropic activities to reach strategic business goals.[122]

Where possible, corporations should also try to use preexisting business techniques or concepts to track and evaluate results. Lim identifies relevant processes:

Related business disciplines have developed a body of evidence and measurement approaches that can be applied. When benefits to the business are long-term or intangible, modeling approaches for valuing future cash flows, analyzing scenarios, and calibrating expected monetary profits linked to the behaviors of loyal customers and engaged employees can be used to estimate financial value as well as to clarify assumptions. Intermediate metrics can help programs deliver those business benefits by enabling managers to make mid-course adjustments as necessary.[123]

Given the power of strategic corporate philanthropy to unlock competitive advantages, it is no surprise that competitive and strategic analysis tools are also useful in assessing the interdependence of a company and society to create a CP plan that maximizes both social and business benefits.[124] Finally, a McKinsey report recommends taking a quantifiable value approach, stating that the best programs "create financial value in ways the market already assesses—growth, return on capital, risk management, and quality of management. Programs that don't create value in one of these ways should be reexamined."[125] See Figure 8.2 for more details on quantifiable value.

It is also essential to integrate shared value management into existing management processes as well as incentive structures to align strategy and indicate executive support. As discussed earlier in the chapter, the long-term, strategic nature of CP progress means that timelines may vary, and it is important to measure intermediate progress when necessary. As Porter et al. explain, "effective shared value measurement must address the fact that business results and social results can have different time horizons. Measurement of intermediate outcomes allows early insights into social results to refine the strategy."[126] It is also crucial that corporations not try to aggregate results, as different social dimensions should be measured separately to account for differences in how they are measured. At the same time, it is appropriate to compare programs and investments that share the same type of outcome.[127]

Once results have been assessed, how should the information be used? One use is targeted communication to the investment community, which "remains the ultimate lever for encouraging shared value adoption at scale,"[128] along with other external stakeholders. Investors need to see evidence of economic value directly generated by corporations' philanthropic investments.[129] Corporations can also use results to grow the total shared value created. Once this process is put in place, the results can prove efficiency and contribute to a virtuous cycle, increasing value on both ends and validating the link between social and business results.[130]

Figure 8.2   Quantifiable value

		Value in environmental, social, and governance (ESG) programs	
Quantifiable value The best environmental, social, and governance programs create financial value for a company in ways that the market already assesses.	**Growth**	New markets	• Access to new markets through exposure from ESG programs
		New products	• Offerings to meet unmet social needs and increase differentiation
		New customers/market share	• Engagement with consumers, familiarity with their expectations and behavior
		Innovation	• Cutting-edge technology and innovative products/ services for unmet social or environmental needs; possibility of using these products/services for business purposes—e.g., patents, proprietary knowledge
		Reputation/ differentiation	• Higher brand loyalty, reputation, and goodwill with stakeholders
	Returns on capital	Operational efficiency	• Bottom-line cost savings through environmental operations and practices—e.g., energy and water efficiency, reduced need for raw materials
		Workforce efficiency	• Higher employee morale through ESG; lower costs related to turnover or recruitment
		Reputation/price premium	• Better workforce skills and increased productivity through participation in ESG activities • Improved reputation that makes customers more willing to pay price increase or premium

	Risk management	Regulatory risk	• Lower level of risk by complying with regulatory requirements, industry standards, and demands of nongovernmental organizations
		Public support	• Ability to conduct operations, enter new markets, reduce local resistance
		Supply chain	• Ability to secure consistent, long-term, and sustainable access to safe, high-quality raw materials/products by engaging in community welfare and development
		Risk to reputation	• Avoidance of negative publicity and boycotts
	Management quality	Leadership development	• Development of employees' quality and leadership skills through participation in ESG programs
		Adaptability	• Ability to adapt to changing political and social situations by engaging local communities
		Long-term strategic view	• Long-term strategy encompassing ESG issues

Source: Exhibit from "Valuing social responsibility programs," July 2009, *McKinsey Quarterly*, http//www.mckinsey.com/insights/mckinsey_quarterly. Copyright (c) 2009 McKinsey & Company. All rights reserved. Reprinted by permission.

CONCLUSION

Similar to broader corporate responsibility, corporate philanthropy has evolved from a series of charitable donations unconnected to core business goals into a long-term, strategic program designed to maximize both social impact and bottom-line contribution. While many practitioners of traditional business remain skeptical of the ability of CP to generate business value, shifts toward shared value measurement systems for corporate-giving programs present an opportunity to demonstrate the economic value derived from strategic corporate philanthropy.

NOTES

1. Chandler, D., & Werther, W. (2006, April). "Why corporate social responsibility matters." *Ethical Corporation Magazine.*

2. Carroll, A. B., & Shabana, K. M. (2010). "The business case for corporate social responsibility: A review of concepts, research and practice." *International Journal of Management Reviews, British Academy of Management.*

3. Ibid.

4. Ibid.

5. Kotler, P., & Lee, N. (2005). *Corporate social responsibility: Doing the most good for your company and your cause.* Hoboken, NJ: John Wiley.

6. Ibid.

7. Kania, J. V., & Oakley, M. W. (2003, Winter). "Design for giving: Understanding what motivates CP." *Perspectives on Corporate Philanthropy.*

8. Carroll & Shabana, "The business case for corporate social responsibility."

9. Ibid.

10. Ibid.

11. Ibid.

12. Friedman, M. (1970, September 13). "The social responsibility of business is to increase its profits." *New York Times Magazine.*

13. Karnani, A. (2010, August 23). "The case against corporate social responsibility." *Wall Street Journal.*

14. Ibid.

15. Porter, M. E., & Kramer, M. R. (2011, January/February). "Creating shared value." *Harvard Business Review.*

16. Chandler, D., & Werther, W. (2006, April). "Why corporate social responsibility matters." *Ethical Corporation Magazine.*

17. Ibid.

18. Porter, M. E., & Kramer, M. R. (2006, December). "Strategy and society: The link between competitive advantage and CSR." *Harvard Business Review.*

19. Carroll & Shabana, "The business case for corporate social responsibility."

20. Ibid.

21. Kania & Oakley, "Design for giving."

22. Whyte, J. (2010, July 21). "When corporate theft is good." *Wall Street Journal.*

23. Tonello, M. (2011, August 20). "Making the business case for corporate philanthropy." Harvard Law School Forum on Corporate Governance and Financial Regulation.

24. Ibid.

25. Ibid.

26. Ibid.

27. Ibid.

28. Ibid.

29. Ibid.

30. Porter & Kramer, "Strategy and society."

31. Carroll & Shabana, "The business case for corporate social responsibility."

32. Porter & Kramer, "Strategy and society."

33. Ibid.

34. Ibid.

35. Porter, M. E., & Kramer, M. R. (2002, December). "The competitive advantage of corporate philanthropy." *Harvard Business Review.*

36. Tonello, "Making the business case for corporate philanthropy."

37. Whyte, J. (2010, July 21). "When corporate theft is good." *Wall Street Journal*; Karnani, "The case against corporate social responsibility."

38. Porter & Kramer, "Creating shared value."

39. *McKinsey Quarterly.* (2007, January). "The state of corporate philanthropy: A McKinsey global survey." Retrieved March 20, 2015, from http://www.mckinsey.it/storage/first/uploadfile/attach/139974/file/stof08.pdf

40. Tonello, "Making the business case for corporate philanthropy."

41. Porter & Kramer, "Strategy and society."

42. Ibid.

43. Ibid.

44. Ibid.

45. Kania & Oakley, "Design for giving."

46. Porter & Kramer, "Strategy and society."

47. Ibid.

48. Ibid.

49. Kotler & Lee, *Corporate social responsibility.*

50. *McKinsey Quarterly*, "The state of corporate philanthropy: A McKinsey global survey."

51. "Making the case to the C suite: How good philanthropy aligns with good business." (2012, September). FSG presentation, Corporate Philanthropy Conference.

52. Tonello, "Making the business case for corporate philanthropy."

53. Ibid.

54. Ibid.

55. Ibid.

56. "Corporate philanthropy—The new paradigm: Volunteerism. Competence. Results." (2011, December). *Forbes,* pp. 14–15.

57. Lim, T. (2010). "Measuring the value of corporate philanthropy: Social impact, business benefits, and investor return." Committee Encouraging Corporate Philanthropy.

58. Porter & Kramer, "The competitive advantage of corporate philanthropy."

59. Tonello, "Making the business case for corporate philanthropy."

60. "Making the case to the C suite," FSG presentation.

61. Ibid.

62. Lim, "Measuring the value of corporate philanthropy."

63. "Making the case to the C suite," FSG presentation.

64. Porter & Kramer, "The competitive advantage of corporate philanthropy."

65. Ibid.

66. Ibid.

67. Ibid.

68. Ibid.

69. Ibid.

70. Kotler & Lee, *Corporate social responsibility.*

71. Porter & Kramer, "The competitive advantage of corporate philanthropy."

72. Ibid.

73. Ibid.

74. Tonello, "Making the business case for corporate philanthropy."

75. Ibid.

76. Ibid.

77. Lim, "Measuring the value of corporate philanthropy."

78. Porter & Kramer, "The competitive advantage of corporate philanthropy."

79. Lim, "Measuring the value of corporate philanthropy."

80. Bonini, S., Koller, T. M., & Mirvis, P. H. (2009). "Valuing social responsibility programs." *McKinsey Quarterly.*

81. Ibid.

82. Lim, "Measuring the value of corporate philanthropy."

83. Ibid.

84. Ibid.

85. Porter, M. E., Hills, G., Pfitzer, M., Patscheke, S., & Hawkins, E. (2012). "Measuring shared value: How to unlock value by linking social and business results." FSG.

86. Porter & Kramer, "Strategy and society."

87. Lim, "Measuring the value of corporate philanthropy."

88. Porter & Kramer, "The competitive advantage of corporate philanthropy."

89. "Making the most of corporate social responsibility." (2009, December). *McKinsey Quarterly.*

90. Lim, "Measuring the value of corporate philanthropy."

91. Ibid.

92. Porter et al., "Measuring shared value."

93. Bonini et al., "Valuing social responsibility programs."

94. Kania & Oakley, "Design for giving."

95. Ibid.

96. Ibid.

97. Porter & Kramer, "Strategy and society."

98. Ibid.

99. Ibid.
100. Porter et al., "Measuring shared value."
101. Ibid.
102. Lim, "Measuring the value of corporate philanthropy."
103. Ibid.
104. Ibid.
105. Ibid.
106. Hanleybrown, F., & Oakley, M. (2003). "Communicating the value of corporate philanthropy: Bringing focus to social investment."
107. Porter et al., "Measuring shared value."
108. Lim, "Measuring the value of corporate philanthropy."
109. Ibid.
110. Porter et al., "Measuring shared value."
111. Ibid.
112. Ibid.
113. Porter & Kramer, "Strategy and society."
114. Lim, "Measuring the value of corporate philanthropy."
115. Porter et al., "Measuring shared value."
116. Ibid.
117. Ibid.
118. Ibid.
119. Ibid.
120. Ibid.
121. Ibid.
122. Lim, "Measuring the value of corporate philanthropy."
123. Ibid.
124. Porter & Kramer, "Strategy and society."
125. Bonini et al., "Valuing social responsibility programs."
126. Porter et al., "Measuring shared value."
127. Ibid.
128. Ibid.
129. Ibid.
130. Ibid.

CORPORATE PHILANTHROPY AT GOLDMAN SACHS: 10,000 SMALL BUSINESSES

The year 2008 had been hard on the U.S. economy: the housing bubble had burst, the value of securities had plummeted, credit had evaporated, and thousands of jobs had vanished. Americans were deeply concerned about the bleak economic picture, with the expectation that job losses and declines in the value of investment portfolios would continue. Two storied financial institutions, Bear Stearns and Lehman Brothers, had collapsed, resulting in an environment of fear and uncertainty.

Meanwhile, 2008 had arguably been a much kinder year to Goldman Sachs, the multinational investment-banking firm headquartered in New York City. While the bank had certainly been affected by the macroeconomic downturn, it had also rebounded in a much shorter time than the rest of the country. Some believed that Goldman Sachs had even prospered during this period, a perception that fueled public animosity toward the firm. A *Vanity Fair* article described the ethos of the time:

> In a weird way, what happened at the start of the subprime crisis confirmed to people at Goldman Sachs what they fundamentally believed about themselves—that they really are better than everybody else on Wall Street. But, for many on the outside, it offered proof instead that Goldman put protecting its own interests ahead of protecting the interests of clients.[1]

This external perception of greed and selfishness led to a fairly strong public outcry against Goldman Sachs. The handful of public relations missteps its executives made served only to strengthen public resentment toward the company. Consequently, in 2009, it was clear to Goldman Sachs that the company needed to make efforts to amend its relationship with the American public. At the end of that year, the firm launched its 10,000 Small Businesses initiative, a philanthropic program designed to help small business owners manage and grow their companies. While Goldman Sachs never acknowledged a connection between the program and its faltering public image, there was much speculation that the company intended for the initiative to help mend its relationship with the public.[2]

THE 2008–2009 FINANCIAL CRISIS

At the time of the 2007–2008 financial crisis, there was strong debate over the causes of the economic downturn. Frequently, fingers pointed toward the actions of the country's

Source: This case was written by Lauren Hirsch, T'12, under the supervision of Professor Paul A. Argenti at the Tuck School of Business at Dartmouth. This case was prepared with publicly available information. © 2014 Trustees of Dartmouth College. All rights reserved.

largest banks. Most of these banks had eagerly packaged and sold two types of securities products, collateralized debt obligations (CDOs) and mortgage-backed securities (MBS), which had fizzled and left investors with quicksand balance sheets. In addition, the banks' payment structures, which awarded large bonuses to bankers who brought in large returns, had encouraged risk-taking.

Adding to public resentment of the banks, the U.S. government had publicly and controversially given financial aid to the banks as the crisis struck, arguing that if it did not do so, the banks' subsequent failure would result in catastrophic economic issues. In this vein, the government passed the Emergency Economic Stabilization Act of 2008, which authorized the United States Treasury to funnel money back into the banks. As part of the Act, Goldman Sachs received $10 billion from the federal government, in addition to the money it received from the government's bailout of the insurance corporation AIG. Goldman Sachs was also one of the major banks that was allowed to issue debt cheaply through the support of the Federal Deposit Insurance Company (FDIC).[3]

Goldman Sachs was not unique in its initial fiscal suffering nor in the aid the company received from the U.S. government. It did, however, contrast with other large banks in several notable ways. First, Goldman had long been lauded as the "savviest and most admired firm among the ranks,"[4] possessing a "much-celebrated culture and superior ability to manage risk."[5] The firm was also arguably the most politically intertwined. Among the many Goldman Sachs alumni who had made their way to high-ranking government positions was treasury secretary Hank Paulson. For this reason, the nickname "Government Sachs" soon became common parlance.

Through a combination of the above factors, the bank did not take long to find its footing. By the second quarter of 2009, Goldman was able to post the company's greatest profit in its 140 years of business. In the same year, the bank also set aside $5.35 billion for compensation and benefits, an increase of 94% over the year prior.[6]

SMALL BUSINESS WOES

Goldman Sachs generally rebounded faster than other large banks, but the most notable contrast drawn at the time was that between the firm's success and the struggles of private citizens at large. By the time the firm appeared to have rebounded, the country had already shed 2.5 million jobs[7] and private industry salary growth was declining at an alarming rate.[8]

A notably visible victim of the troubled economy was small business. The crisis had created a credit squeeze, and many small businesses were struggling to maintain the cash flow necessary to sustain themselves. That Goldman Sachs had received federal money while small business owners were struggling to make payments did not go unnoticed. As small business owner Carl Hawkins explained, "I can tell you point blank that getting money out of banks for anything these days is extremely difficult for small businesses. You name it, it's hard."[9] Small businesses were equally unable to find relief from the government: in 2009, the Small Business Administration (SBA), a U.S. government agency that provides support to entrepreneurs and small businesses, approved 36% fewer government-guaranteed loans, or $3.4 billion less, than the $9.3 billion it had approved during 2010.[10]

The contrast between Goldman Sachs's success, which had been aided in part by the government, and the struggles faced by small businesses in the wake of the economic downturn was striking, leading to further negative press for Goldman. In a *New York Times* op-ed piece, columnist Frank Rich wrote:

> Most Americans know all too well that only the intervention of billions of dollars in taxpayer bailout money saved Goldman from the dire fate of its less well-connected competitors. The growing ranks of under-and-unemployed Americans, meanwhile, are waiting with increasing desperation for a recovery of their own.[11]

Juxtaposed with the dire circumstances of many Americans, including small-business owners, Goldman Sachs's success was all the more glaring.

GOLDMAN SACHS'S PUBLIC RELATIONS CRISIS

The firm quickly realized the threat to its reputation from op-ed pieces such as Rich's, and as the gap between Goldman Sachs's rebound and the difficulties of the American public widened, Goldman Sachs made steps to rectify the situation. Unfortunately for the bank, many of the decisions it made with the goal of mending its image served only to further public anger.

In October 2009, alongside its strong earnings and bonus announcements, the firm declared its intention to double the size of its charitable foundation, focused on educational programs, by $200 million. Perhaps because education was an initiative not directly related to the current crisis, or perhaps because the amount offered was not particularly large compared with Goldman's earnings, the gesture was largely interpreted as a move designed purely to hush criticism.[12] As *New York Times* columnist Rich wrote, "In Goldman dollars, that largess is roughly comparable to the nickels John D. [Rockefeller] handed out to children a century ago."[13]

To make matters worse for Goldman, the company's CEO, Lloyd Blankfein, gave an interview with the *Times of London* in which he was quoted as saying he was doing "God's work."[14] Blankfein tried to quell the controversy by explaining that he had been joking, but it was too late: in a world where Internet access ensured that the word of corporate blunders moved quickly around the world, Blankfein's hastened apology was insufficient to reverse the damage done by his off-the-cuff remark. As Fox Business Network journalist Charles Gasparino, generally thought of as a supporter of the bank, wrote in *The Huffington Post*:

> There is something truly unsettling about the new message coming from the firm, honed I hear from a phalanx of image consultants who are literally trying to re-write history as the firm gets ready to dole out its enormous bonus pool. And that's what all this spinning is about. For the record Goldman Sachs didn't take down the financial system last year—Citigroup, Merrill, Lehman or Bear are much more responsible for that. And for the record every firm spins—its [*sic*] called public relations, and Goldman will need all the PR it can muster as it decides in the coming weeks how much of the $20 billion it will hand out to its executives.[15]

Perhaps both more succinctly and more bitingly, *Rolling Stone*'s Matt Taibi wrote in his exposé on Goldman Sachs, "The Great American Bubble Machine," that the firm was a "great vampire squid wrapped around the face of humanity, relentlessly jamming its blood funnel into anything that smells like money."[16] At a time when many Americans were looking for parties to blame for the dire financial straits in which they found themselves, the press did an excellent job of portraying Goldman Sachs as the obvious culprit.

THE LAUNCH OF AN INITIATIVE

Unsurprisingly, Goldman knew that it needed to act swiftly to stem the stream of negative press around its corporate activities, and on November 17, 2009, the firm announced a new philanthropic initiative designed to deal with the issues that many Americans believed were at least in part attributable to Goldman's reign of greed. This time, Goldman took a more strategic approach to corporate responsibility, launching a massive project designed to leverage the company's resources toward aiding the success of small businesses. Called 10,000 Small Businesses, this new program was based on the firm's successful 10,000 Women initiative, which it had launched in 2008. The goal of the original program was to train and educate 10,000 women in developing countries on the principles of business and management. While the timing of the new initiative's launch was suspicious, the firm maintained that its reincarnation of the program had been in the works since a year prior—though the program's potential to double as an olive branch was obvious.

To support the 10,000 Small Businesses project, the firm set aside $500 million and established a three-pronged approach. The first prong was business and management education for small-business owners, to which Goldman Sachs allotted $200 million. The second prong was loans and grants to small businesses, to which Goldman Sachs allotted

$300 million; to extend these loans, Goldman Sachs partnered with community development financial institutions (CDFIs), which provide credit and financial services to underserved markets and populations. The third prong involved an outlay of human capital: a mentoring and networking program, in which Goldman offered its employees and partners as guides to the small business owners. The program itself would sit under the umbrella of the Goldman Sachs Foundation, the corporation's philanthropic arm, which was one of the largest corporate foundations in the world.[17]

To take part in the program, small businesses had to fulfill certain criteria. They were required to have had a minimum of four full-time employees and earned revenues between $150,000 and $4 million in the most recent fiscal year. The businesses also had to have been in business for at least two years and were required to operate predominantly in underserved markets.

Dina Powell managed the program. Ms. Powell had joined Goldman Sachs in 2007 as head of global corporate engagement and had previously managed the 10,000 Women initiative. Prior to Goldman, she had worked for the State Department under the George W. Bush administration on cultural and education issues.

The immediate reaction following Goldman's announcement was strong, if not positive. *The New York Times* set up a forum on the subject, in which readers could discuss possible implications of the project; the website received so many questions from small-business owners about the initiative that it eventually posted a link to an email address where it could email its questions to Goldman Sachs directly.[18] *The Wall Street Journal* wrote a laudatory article on the effort, describing Goldman Sachs as the "'Dear Abby' of small business woes."[19] Throughout the country, small-business owners were calling one of the most powerful bankers in the U.S., Lloyd Blankfein, with their personal small-business questions. On the receiving end of these calls was an automated recording from Lloyd Blankfein himself, asking callers to send an email for further information.

RISKS ASSOCIATED WITH THE INITIATIVE

Despite Goldman's standout success rate in the world of banking, it was unclear whether the firm's accomplishments would translate to the world of small business. Without intervention, the failure rate for small businesses is extremely high at 75%,[20] and larger corporations that attempt to step in and assist small business owners are not always successful in preventing such failures. One potential problem is the reallocation of valuable man-hours at small firms that have a limited number of employees to share the workload: some studies argue that training small-business owners hurts them by replacing valuable management hours with training hours.

Nicholas Bloom, an economist at Stanford University, explained, "It all sounds very inspiring and fantastic, but it turns out that the evidence from large samples [of aid to small business] is less encouraging."[21] Goldman Sachs faced its own unique challenges in this realm, given the differences between its core business and the line of work of the small businesses it sought to advise. As pointed out in *The New York Times*, "the types of things a pie baking shop needs to know are either very detailed skills the Goldman Sachs guy won't know about, or very basic things like how to keep accounts in Excel, which they typically already know."[22]

Fortunately, Goldman Sachs was aware of the challenges and risks confronting the firm, and leveraged the competencies of external partners to give 10,000 Small Businesses a better chance of success. To help oversee the program, it recruited some of its smartest and most influential friends, including Warren Buffett and famed business strategist Michael Porter. To help design its management curriculum, Goldman enlisted the help of experts from the Wharton School of the University of Pennsylvania and the F. W. Olin Graduate School of Business at Babson College.

THE PROGRAM IN ACTION

The program inducted its first class of small-business owners in April 2010, with 23 business owners meeting every other Saturday from 8:30 a.m. until 6 p.m. The courses, taught by professors from Wharton, Babson, and LaGuardia Community College, covered topics including accounting, hiring practices, and legal issues. Each student was asked to devise a "growth plan" for his or her business; for homework, students were asked to prepare financials or perform a supply chain analysis to support this plan. Before each session, students met with their "growth group," groups of four to six who ran complementary businesses. In addition to peer-to-peer learning, these groups were meant to foster leads and referrals.[23]

One student described his experience as follows:

We meet as our full class, and we have a small group within that class. It is extremely interactive and engaging—this is not a lecture hall where we sit and take notes. We are fully engaged in rolling up our sleeves and working together and sometimes independently on our business. No two sessions have been the same, there have been some amazing business professionals that have been brought to us in the form of a panel discussion.[24]

FEEDBACK

Feedback from program participants was largely positive. Jessica Johnson, owner of Johnson Security Bureau, a company that offered security services, took part in the program in 2010 and discussed her experience with a journalist from *The New York Times*.

Johnson found value in many aspects of the program, but identified the peer-to-peer education in her growth group as one of the most valuable components. One challenge Johnson had been grappling with prior to starting 10,000 Small Businesses was difficulty bidding on construction projects, largely because she had been unable to project her costs beyond 18 months out. Fortunately, Leo Fabio, who owned a construction service company, was in her growth group. Mr. Fabio suggested that Ms. Johnson break out her costs rather than be overwhelmed by the variables, and as Ms. Johnson told *The New York Times*, "it made me stop and think about how I was estimating. Everything I'd learned about it, I'd learned from my dad and grandmother." The construction industry soon became her company's greatest growth sector.[25]

Other cited benefits of program alumni included the building of confidence, enhancement of negotiation skills, and a stronger network. Ms. Johnson summed up her experience this way: "Before, we were like a 10-year-old girl, cute and a little awkward. Now we're more like a 15-year-old—not quite as awkward, with a better idea of where we want to go."[26]

According to Margaret Spellings, who was both a member of the 10,000 Small Businesses Advisory Council and a former U.S. education secretary, as of 2012 the program had a 99% retention rate across all sites, 75% of the participants were seeing an increase in their revenues, more than half were creating new jobs, and the participants were developing a strong network between small-businesses owners.[27]

The program has also earned accolades from government officials. Chicago's Democratic mayor, Rahm Emmanuel, lauded Goldman's program as a complement to his plan to revamp his city's community colleges and focus on training in fields that will likely lead students to jobs in the future, including information technology, hospitality, and healthcare. Emmanuel even expressed interest in making the program permanent.[28]

Mr. Buffett gave his own positive perspective on the program's success, telling *Businessweek*:

I talked to a number of graduates who told me they were able to renegotiate leases or franchise fees—they really put it to use, having someone there who is like an outside investor, but isn't. There's no question that it will work.[29]

GOING FORWARD

In an interview Ms. Powell gave to *Businessweek* in 2012, she maintained that Goldman Sachs's commitment to the project had not wavered and would remain firm in the future, saying, "Even though we began this work in 2007, when the downturn hit, we stayed fully committed. We did not decrease by one penny the commitment of the firm, even through the difficult economic times."[30] As of 2012, the program was present in six U.S. cities (New York, New Orleans, Houston, Los Angeles, Chicago, and Long Beach, New York) as well as four cities in the United Kingdom (London, Manchester, Leeds, and Birmingham).[31] Its UK expansion had begun in 2010 in Yorkshire, with a UK-tailored program.[32]

The firm continued to maintain and grow partnerships with local community business schools to host the programs, leading business schools Babson and Wharton to develop curriculum and access faculty; nonprofit organizations such as the Initiative for a Competitive Inner City and the National Urban League to develop its area expertise; and CDFIs including Seedco Financial Services, Inc., and Valley Economic Development Center, Inc., to provide capital.[33]

Criticisms of the program seemed to rest on its slow rate of growth. As of 2012, the program had helped 300 small business owners, a mere 3% of its goal of 10,000 small businesses. The aid these owners had received was largely in the form of training; only $15 million in loans had been closed or approved by Goldman Sachs's community development financial institution (CDFI) partners.[34]

Despite the shortcomings of the 10,000 Small Businesses program, it was an important step for Goldman Sachs toward the establishment of meaningful corporate responsibility initiatives, with social goals that aligned with the bank's business mission. While skepticism of the role of ethics in the company's business dealings continued in the years after the program's launch, the positive press and public reception of 10,000 Small Businesses mitigated some of the damage done to Goldman's corporate reputation during the financial crisis.

Case Questions

1. How is Goldman Sachs's 10,000 Small Businesses program an example of strategic corporate philanthropy?

2. What are some shortcomings of the program in terms of shared value creation? How could the program be improved to better serve its beneficiaries and Goldman personnel involved as mentors and advisers?

3. Was 10,000 Small Businesses a successful initiative for Goldman in terms of its ability to mend the company's public reputation?

4. What are some metrics Goldman could use to assess whether the program has been successful in terms of the results it delivers for its participants?

5. Based on the information in the chapter, how can Goldman measure the results of 10,000 Small Businesses and use this data to improve the program going forward?

NOTES

1. McLean, B. (2009, December). "The bank job." *Vanity Fair.* Retrieved March 21, 2015, from http://www.vanityfair.com/business/features/2010/01/goldman-sachs-200101

2. McGill Murphy, R. (2011, January 18). "Goldman Sachs's gift to 10,000 small businesses." *Fortune.* Retrieved March 21, 2015, from http://archive.fortune.com/2011/01/17/small business/goldman_sachs_entrepreneurs.fortune/index.htm

3. Bowley, G., & Saltmarsh, M. (2009). "Goldman earns $3.19 billion, beating estimates." *New York Times.* http://www.nytimes.com/2009/10/16/business/16goldman.html

4. Creswell, J., & White, B. "The guys from 'Government Sachs.'" *New York Times.* Retrieved March 21, 2015, from http://www.nytimes.com/2008/10/19/business/19gold .html?pagewanted=all&_r=0

5. McLean, "The bank job."

6. Bowley & Saltmarsh, "Goldman earns $3.19 billion, beating estimates."

7. Rampell, C. (2009, January). "Layoffs spread to more sectors of the economy." *New York Times.* Retrieved March 21, 2015, from http://www.nytimes.com/2009/01/27/business/ economy/27layoffs.html

8. "Economic crisis brings job losses, delayed retirement, benefit reductions and stagnant pay." Towers Watson. Retrieved from http://www.towerswatson.com/en/Insights/Newsletters/ Americas/insider/2009/economic-crisis-brings-job-losses-delayed-retirement-benefit-reductions- and-stagnant-pay

9. Spector, M. (2009, November 19). "Small businesses turn to Goldman." *Wall Street Journal.* Retrieved March 21, 2015, from http://online.wsj.com/article/SB1000142405274870453 3904574544202372453482.html

10. Ibid.

11. Rich, F. (2009, October 17). "Goldman can spare you a dime." *New York Times.* Retrieved March 21, 2015.

12. Bowley, G. (2009, November 17). "$500 million and apology from Goldman." *New York Times.* Retrieved March 21, 2015, from http://www.nytimes.com/2009/11/18/business/18goldman .html

13. Rich, "Goldman can spare you a dime."

14. Gasparino, C. (2010, March 18). "Goldman Sachs doing God's work?" *Huffington Post.* Retrieved March 21, 2015, from http://www.huffingtonpost.com/charles-gasparino/ post_439_b_351116.html

15. Gasparino, "Goldman Sachs doing God's work?"

16. Taibbi, M. (2010, April 5). "The Great American Bubble Machine." *Rolling Stone Magazine.* Retrieved March 21, 2015, from http://www.rollingstone.com/politics/news/the-great -american-bubble-machine-20100405

17. Kolhatkar, S. (2012, May 24). "Goldman's job act." *Bloomberg Business.* Retrieved March 21, 2015, from http://www.bloomberg.com/bw/articles/2012-05-24/goldmans-jobs-act

18. "What will the Goldman Sachs plan mean to you?" (2009, November 18). *New York Times*. Retrieved March 21, 2015, from http://boss.blogs.nytimes.com/2009/11/18/what-will-the-goldman-sachs-plan-mean-to-you

19. Spector, "Small businesses turn to Goldman."

20. Kolhatkar, "Goldman's job act."

21. Rampell, C. (2013, February 13). "Small businesses still struggle, and that's impeding a recovery." *New York Times*. Retrieved April 1, 2015, from http://www.nytimes.com/2013/02/14/business/smallbusiness/small-businesses-struggle-impeding-a-recovery.html

22. Kolhatkar, "Goldman's job act."

23. Gardella, A. "One of Goldman's small businesses." *New York Times*. Retrieved March 21, 2015, from http://boss.blogs.nytimes.com/2012/01/11/one-of-goldman-sachss-10000-small-businesses/

24. "Entrepreneurial growth powered by Goldman Sachs 10,000 Small Businesses Program." (n.d.). Total Event Resources. Retrieved March 21, 2015, from http://www.total-event.com/whats-new/entrepreneurial-growth-powered-by-goldman-sachs-10000-small-businesses-program/

25. Gardella, "One of Goldman's small businesses."

26. Kolhatkar, "Goldman's job act."

27. Times Staff. (2012, June 5). "Goldman Sachs initiative yields results for small businesses." *Community College Daily*. Retrieved March 21, 2015, from http://www.ccdaily.com/Pages/Workforce-Development/Goldman-Sachs-initiative-yields-results-for-small-businesses.aspx

28. Kolhatkar, "Goldman's job act."

29. Ibid.

30. Ibid.

31. Ibid.

32 Goldman Sachs. (2012, November 9). "Goldman Sachs announces 10,000 Small Businesses UK National Alumni Network" [Press release]. Retrieved April 1, 2015, from http://www.goldmansachs.com/media-relations/press-releases/archived/2012/10ksb-uk-alumni-network.html

33. Goldman Sachs, 10,000 Small Businesses, http://www.goldmansachs.com/citizenship/10000-small-businesses/about-the-program-us/partners.html (accessed March 21, 2014).

34. Baram, M. (2011, June 8). "Goldman Sachs's small business program off to a slow start despite praise." *Huffington Post*. Retrieved March 21, 2015, from http://www.huffingtonpost.com/2011/06/08/goldman-sachs-small-business_n_873452.html

Chapter 9

COMMUNICATING CORPORATE RESPONSIBILITY

In this chapter, we look at why a robust communications strategy is a necessary component of any strategic corporate responsibility program. In addition to establishing the case for deftly communicating a company's commitment to responsible business, we will offer relevant advice about what to communicate and best practices for relaying messages about CR programs to constituents. Effective communication is essential for engaging stakeholders, which, in turn, will be crucial for restoring trust in business and driving positive corporate reputation.

Throughout the chapter, we will look at how CR communication fits into the current environment, key factors to consider in developing a CR communication strategy, how CR-related messaging influences corporate reputation, and the impact of technology on communication strategy, particularly with regard to crisis situations. We begin by exploring the strategic relevance of CR communication.

THE STRATEGIC IMPORTANCE OF COMMUNICATING CR

What does it mean to communicate CR, and why is it important? Even the strongest of CR strategies are lacking if they do not include a clear communications component. By clearly communicating their commitment to corporate responsibility, organizations stand to reap a host of benefits and competitive advantages.

In a blog post for the Harvard Law School website, Matteo Tonello explains the link between corporate responsibility and consumer engagement: "A company's positive record of CSR fosters consumer loyalty and, in some cases, can turn customers into brand ambassadors and advocates who may be willing to even pay a premium to support the company's social policies."[1] Of course, for consumers to develop CR-based brand loyalty, they must first be aware of what corporations are doing to optimize their social and environmental impact.

There are several key ways in which strategic CR communication enables corporations to create competitive advantage. Over the past few decades, there has been a rapid increase in the number of brands for whom CR is a primary business strategy. Such companies, which include Tom's of Maine and Ben & Jerry's, among others, have benefited from their ability to establish an industry leadership position and leapfrog over competitors. The Ben & Jerry's website (www.benjerry.com) makes it clear that CR is a part of the company's core business strategy, including "Values" as a header on the site menu alongside more traditional components such as company and product information. Because Ben and Jerry's is explicit about the role of social and environmental impact in its business strategy, consumers who value CR (a growing group, as seen from the Edelman goodpurpose® 2012 study) are more likely to gravitate toward the company's products versus those of competitors who either pay less attention to CR issues or simply fail to communicate their own CR practices adequately.

IBM's Smarter Planet is another corporate example of business strategy that is fused with CR. In Chapter 3, we discussed how companies that are proactive in adapting to environmental standards unlock competitive advantages. IBM's approach echoes this wisdom; on its website, the company states its intention to "change the paradigm from react to anticipate.[2] IBM also lays out the fundamental needs of performing on a smarter planet, as seen in Figure 9.1.

In addition to helping corporations promote existing brands or lines of business, communicating CR can also help companies launch new brands, as sustainability is a known driver of innovation. This strategy has been especially effective in the automotive industry. In November 2012, BMW debuted its newest electric car, the i3, at the Los Angeles Auto Show.[3] The i3, which was launched in major cities globally between 2013 and 2014,[4] is

> powered by huge lithium-ion batteries positioned under the floorboards (a distribution of weight that eases handling) with a drive system, chassis and energy storage unit all incorporated into a body module made of aluminum. There are three driving modes and an electric range of 100 miles to a full charge.[5]

The i3 delivers an optimal driving experience for consumers while having minimal negative effects on the environment.

Toyota's hybrid car, the Prius, which was introduced worldwide in 2000 following its success in Japan, is another product that thrived because of its positive environmental impact. Toyota's "Harmony" advertisement for the 2010 Prius, which featured the car driving up a mountain and leaving a sea of

Figure 9.1   IBM's Smarter Planet

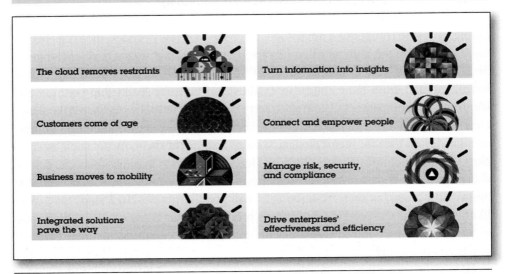

The cloud removes restraints

Turn information into insights

Customers come of age

Connect and empower people

Business moves to mobility

Manage risk, security, and compliance

Integrated solutions pave the way

Drive enterprises' effectiveness and efficiency

Source: "IBM Smarter Planet overview." Smarter Planet®. Retrieved August 12, 2014, from http://www.ibm .com/smarterplanet/us/en/overview/ideas/index.html?lnk=ussph1.16.

green trees and flowers in its wake, topped Nielsen's Top 10 Most-Liked New Ads list upon its release.[6]

Communicating with stakeholders about CR initiatives allows the corporation to profile a new product, or penetrate a new market and convert stakeholders. It is also an opportunity to connect and engage with stakeholders, and engender customer loyalty. As demonstrated by the results of the Edelman goodpurpose® 2012 survey and other consumer opinion polls, CR is a powerful driver of consumer demand for products and services.

As discussed in prior chapters, CR is also a valuable means of generating employee commitment. CR can help corporations recruit and retain new employees. A 2010 study revealed that an estimated 34% of employees said that they would take a pay cut to work for a socially responsible firm.[7] CR initiatives can also improve relationships with existing employees who partake in fundraising or community volunteer activities, or who work directly on shaping the company's CR strategy. Dailah Nihot, global head of sustainability at ING, explains how CR can help shape corporate culture in a positive way:

> Employees should know what's happening with regard to social or environmental topics, so they can feel proud, become part of the programs, or tell the story to their peers and customers. In that perspective, CR can provide

valuable content to the communications teams, and communications can help the CR team in developing messaging and accessing important "channels" to tell the message.[8]

In Chapter 3, we discussed the role of high-potential individuals at all levels of an organization in creating buy-in around a company's CR goals and vision. To engage such employees, it is essential for CR values to be codified and distributed throughout the company. One means of securing internal buy-in around these values is to solicit input from employees in the planning stages, through surveys.

Given that a CR program should be part of a company's business strategy, it should also be part of the communications strategy. When the two are integrated, companies can embed values across the organization and enhance both internal and external communications. From a practical standpoint, one of the easiest ways to integrate Communications and CR is by integrating calendars. Advises Nihot:

> Set the CR agenda for the year taking into consideration the scope of the team (which may include only philanthropy, or also issue management and business advisory), then work on an integrated story. Use general communications products, tools and plans, including quarterly results, CEO messaging, investor road shows, branding campaigns, talent acquisition campaigns, and product advertising, to tell the company's overall, integrated, story—including the company's vision and plans with regard to social and environmentally sound behavior.[9]

Determining where to place CR in relation to Communications is another corporate challenge worth examining. The answer depends on a number of factors, including industry, function, how the company or organization defines CR, and what kind of other specialist departments the company or organization has in its structure. Many companies situate CR within Communications, allowing collaboration on a host of activities including developing and publishing annual nonfinancial reports; servicing the socially responsible investing community and conducting road shows together with Investor Relations; researching market trends; monitoring the company's overall CR performance data and setting targets; supporting the CEO and board in overall positioning; and developing employee volunteer programs.[10]

Other companies view all activities that are related to the business as best positioned outside Communications. Given that Communications is focused on developing parts of a company's overall strategy and positioning, "the greening of the shop" is not its core task. In that sense, innovation and adjusting business models should be the responsibility of the people that know most about their specific fields. CR can support the relevant departments with knowledge and share the company's overall ambition levels, but allow the particular groups to build the product. Furthermore, a CR team that is part of a communications department may be taken less seriously by the outside world, primarily NGOs and analysts, because it is considered to be responsible only for messaging and public relations, not for change in the business—and can therefore be a reputation risk in itself. Unless there is a strategic approach to actually innovating core processes as well, and there are specialist teams responsible for that (preferably reporting to board level), CR in communications can be considered to be greenwashing.[11]

As seen from above, CR has a huge impact on a company's reputation. Thus, corporate communicators must be actively engaged in CR messaging to ensure consistency and integration with the overall communication and reputation management strategy. Communicators can and should play a role in CR strategy and tactics from their inception.

THE CURRENT ENVIRONMENT FOR PROMOTING RESPONSIBLE BUSINESS PRACTICES

The paradigm shift that we have seen in attitudes to business, and their responsibility to contribute to a sustainable society, is unprecedented. The climate for promoting responsible business could not be better or the need stronger, given the considerable decline in public trust of corporations over the past few years, as demonstrated by the Edelman Trust Barometer.[12] According to the 2014 report, fewer than one in five members of the general public trust business leaders to tell the truth when confronted with a difficult issue, as seen in Figure 9.2.

Another catalyst for changes in consumer attitudes toward CR has been the global financial crisis. Arguably, companies that were worst affected by the financial crisis are those that most need to assert their commitment to corporate responsibility. As we saw in the Goldman Sachs case at the end of Chapter 8, the events surrounding the economic downturn offered corporations an opportunity to repair their public image by devising creative CR initiatives designed to mitigate the negative consequences of their business dealings on society. The crisis stemmed from considerable corporate irresponsibility at many top financial institutions, and public confidence in the responsibility of business has been seriously shaken.[13] The rise of digital platforms, which has facilitated the rapid dissemination of information and provided consumers with a forum in which they have loudspeakers online, is another reason why consumer attitudes around corporate responsibility have shifted.[14]

The new expectations of the millennial generation are another driver of changes in expectations of corporations. The evidence suggests that the next generation will have even higher expectations of corporate behavior—and an even lower tolerance threshold for anything that appears to be insincere or spin. Transparency

Figure 9.2 Levels of trust in business leaders

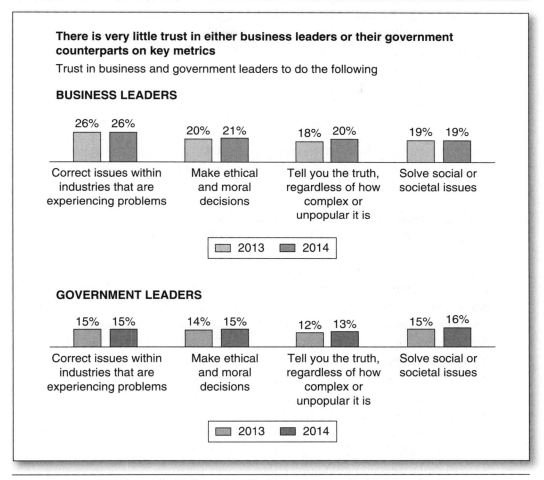

There is very little trust in either business leaders or their government counterparts on key metrics

Trust in business and government leaders to do the following

BUSINESS LEADERS

26% 26%   20% 21%   18% 20%   19% 19%

Correct issues within industries that are experiencing problems | Make ethical and moral decisions | Tell you the truth, regardless of how complex or unpopular it is | Solve social or societal issues

☐ 2013   ■ 2014

GOVERNMENT LEADERS

15% 15%   14% 15%   12% 13%   15% 16%

Correct issues within industries that are experiencing problems | Make ethical and moral decisions | Tell you the truth, regardless of how complex or unpopular it is | Solve social or societal issues

☐ 2013   ■ 2014

Source: Edelman. "Global results" slideshow (slide 22). Retrieved August 12, 2014, from http://www.edelman.com/insights/intellectual-property/2014-edelman-trust-barometer/about-trust/global-results.

and authenticity will be vital ingredients for all organizations—and it follows, therefore, that this will be particularly important for a business trying to explain its understanding of what it means to be responsible and sustainable.[15]

Meanwhile, sustainability-focused shoppers are a growing trend with powerful wallets. Throughout the earlier chapters in this book, we have looked at examples of how consumers' desire for socially and environmentally responsible products and services continues to increase, with many shoppers reporting that they would switch brands if another brand of similar quality contributed to social or environmental causes.[16]

Global environmental and socioeconomic trends are another driver for increased conversation around CR issues, between rapid globalization, population growth, and global warming. The imperative to stretch resources ever further will make sustainability a central design principle for the winning corporations of the future (as discussed in depth in Chapter 3).

HOW TO EFFECTIVELY COMMUNICATE YOUR COMPANY'S CR STRATEGY

For corporations of the 21st century, the question is not whether to put resources behind communicating CR strategy to constituents, but *how* to communicate CR, both internally and externally, in a way that demonstrates how a company's CR programs relate to its business mission and values. Below, we lay out the key areas that help create a workable model for communicating CR inside and outside an organization.

Determine Your Communication Channels

Determine how to disseminate the messages and through which channels. Options may include brochures, mailing lists, labels and packaging, events, websites, traditional advertisements, newsletters, reports, press releases, social media, or interviews.

Identify Content

Establish what it is you want to communicate to stakeholders. This can include the following:

Marketplace Content

Marketplace-related communications should illustrate how your business has integrated responsible entrepreneurship into practice. Examples may include your company's efforts to improve its support of local suppliers and timely payment of bills, customer retention and satisfaction, product safety, and the quality of its products and services.

Marketplace content communication also involves the disclosure of pertinent information to consumers (such as through product labeling and packaging), offering fair pricing, adhering to marketing and advertising ethics, and giving attention to consumer rights. It can also include after-sales service and consumer education, a company's criteria for selecting business partners, and how the business affects working and living conditions and human rights issues in developing countries where it sources raw materials or employs labor forces.

Workplace Content

Workplace-related communications should center on new or innovative actions taken by the company to enhance the employee experience, such as the improvement of working conditions, pay, benefits, or increased job creation. Some ways that corporations can communicate workplace-related content include reporting on actions to improve job satisfaction, employee health and safety, and staff training and development, as well as publicizing efforts to ensure equal opportunity employment and workplace diversity. Work–life balance—including flexible hours and other opportunities for workers to balance family and work obligations—is another crucial piece of communication around the workplace environment. Building upon corporate reputation through workplace-related communications is a key means for corporations to attract and retain top talent.

Community Content

Community-related communications should concentrate on any company-supported volunteer activities by owners or employees, as well as charitable donations or sponsorships and ways in which the company promotes economic regeneration. As discussed in Chapter 8, decisions pertaining to corporate philanthropy, which includes donations of both corporate dollars and manpower, should be made with an eye toward creating shared value. Other examples of community content that is relevant to stakeholders can include the corporation's efforts to improve social integration (ethnic tolerance and social cohesion), community healthcare or education, quality of life (through initiatives related to sporting or cultural events), the local infrastructure, or security.

Environment Content

Environment-related communications should demonstrate ways in which your company takes actions to protect the natural environment. Examples include initiatives that increase energy or water conservation, reduce air or water pollution, reduce use of hazardous chemicals, maintain biodiversity, or reduce waste generation or hazardous waste.

The Dangers of Empty Boasting

It is essential to focus on authenticity when communicating about CR activities. Trumpet your actions, but make sure they are backed by substance. Make sure it is part of your business planning process and that you have a team dedicated to it. In Chapter 3, we looked at greenwashing—the practice of disingenuously spinning products or policies as environmentally friendly or beneficial. Greenwashing is little more than slick advertising, and has been divided into seven categories (or "sins") by environmental marketing agency TerraChoice (you can read more on this in Chapter 3).

While some corporations may feel that greenwashing is a clever means of using purported environmental friendliness to swindle eco-minded consumers, many savvy consumers have become wise to greenwashing tactics. The Greenwashing Index, a website with the tagline "Help keep advertising honest," allows consumers to rate advertising campaigns on the basis of the truth behind their green marketing tactics, using a scale of 1 to 5, where lower scores correspond to greater authenticity.[17] Some of the ads deemed most egregious include those for BMW in South Africa, the Malaysian Palm Oil Council, and FIJI Water.

Match Rhetoric With Action

As demonstrated by the increased popularity of greenwashing, there is a lot of rhetoric around the idea of going green, and it can be difficult for companies with a real commitment to social impact and environmental sustainability to differentiate themselves from those whose motives are less than pure. As consumers have started to place a higher premium on companies' CR practices in their purchasing decisions, the amount of CR chatter has increased, and corporations that focus on speaking the truth will separate themselves from the pack. It is important not to make empty promises, according to David Pearson, global sustainability leader of Deloitte Touche Tohmatsu Limited, who offers the following advice to companies: "Be perceived at the same level you are performing."[18]

The Transparency Initiative

To ensure a commitment to truth in CR communication, it is essential to be self-critical and transparent. The prevalence of social media means that corporations have to reveal both their good news and their bad news. Being transparent with consumers and others about less-than-positive news allows companies to build trust with stakeholders. Furthermore, taking a proactive approach to reporting negative news allows a corporation to manage the conversation around the situation and control the potential reputational damage. When communicating about CR issues with stakeholders, it is also imperative that corporations not cloud their reports with confusing language. Simple, direct communication is more effective than verbose prose, and will seem more authentic to constituents.

Know Your Audience

It is also important to identify your stakeholders and engage them by focusing on the issues most relevant to the company's business. The relevant receivers of the communication must be identified, and therefore it is crucial for a company to fully understand the concept of and be aware of stakeholders.

Create an Ongoing Dialogue

CR communications should be a two-way street, with corporations reporting to consumers and other stakeholders on their progress and goals but also listening to constituents for suggestions as to how to improve their track records. Listening to and understanding the expectations of its constituency enables a company to stay ahead of the changing ethos and strengthen its reputation. Corporations must foster ongoing dialogue with their constituents to understand their expectations and concerns.

Collaborate With Friends and Foes

Not only do corporations need to know who they are communicating with, but they also need to stay aware of who is talking about them and their CR activities. Partnering with an NGO whose mission complements the company's business practices is one means of strengthening corporate reputation and protecting the company from risk.

While NGOs evolved to influence governments, many such organizations now realize that targeting corporations, and key corporate constituents such as investors and customers, can be an even more powerful way to effect change. Simon Heap argues in his book *NGOs Engaging With Business: A World of Difference and a Difference to the World* that as the balance of power shifted from governments to multinational corporations, NGOs had no choice but to change their approach to social problems.[19]

In some ways, these two agents—corporations and NGOs—now control much of the agenda formerly dictated by governments. Peter Sutherland, chairman of Goldman Sachs and former chairman of BP, states, "The only organizations now capable of global thought and action—the ones who will conduct the most important dialogues of the 21st century—are the multinational corporations and the NGOs."[20] For this reason, companies that think strategically about corporate reputation with regard to CR issues must engage with NGOs, both as a protective measure and as a means of developing competitive advantage in the CR space.

As we saw in Chapter 4, Shell missed an opportunity to partner with Greenpeace on issues related to the Brent Spar disposal, and taking a proactive approach to potential crises related to environmental and human rights violations may have prevented reputational damage. Beyond exploring potential partnerships with NGOs, corporations need to monitor and stay ahead of current and potential antagonists. In the Greenpeace situation, these two pieces of advice were two sides of the same coin: Greenpeace became an antagonist, but might have become an ally had the corporation exercised more foresight.

Focus on Employee Engagement

Employee engagement is of vital importance to any strategic CR program and requires thoughtful internal communications. The connection between CR and engaged employees continues to grow, as demonstrated by the results of various reports, including a Hewitt & Associates study that looked at nearly 300 workplaces with more than 100,000 employees and found that the more a company actively pursues worthy environmental and social efforts, the more engaged its employees are.[21]

The Society for Human Resources Management compared companies that have strong sustainability programs with companies that have poor ones and found that in the former morale was 55% better, business processes were 43% more efficient, public image was 43% stronger, and employee loyalty was 38% higher.[22] Add to all that the fact that companies with highly engaged employees have three times the operating margin[23] and four times the earnings per share[24] of companies with low engagement, and we have a compelling business case for this trend to continue into the future.

Be Consistently Credible

Don't ignore your mistakes. Know when to say too much, and too little.

Know How to Communicate Your Successes, and to Whom

It is important to talk about your successes and develop relationships with the media.

The Corporate Communication Strategy Framework presented in Figure 9.3 incorporates these and other communication models to provide a valuable framework for effectively analyzing corporate communications.[25]

Looking at the framework, one can easily visualize the connections between each component. As communication theorist Annette Shelby states, "the unique interrelationships of these variables determine which messages will be effective and which will not."[26] These interrelationships will also determine the most effective tools for communicating the message. In addition, this framework is circular

Figure 9.3 The consolidated Corporate Communication Strategy Framework

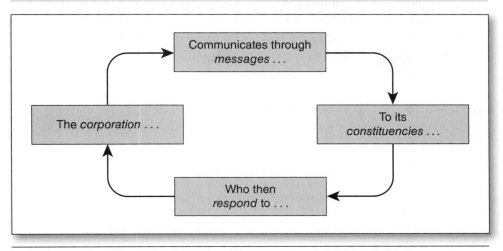

Source: Argenti, P. A. (2012). *Corporate communication* (6th ed., p. 31). McGraw-Hill/Irwin.

rather than linear, which reflects the reality that communication of any kind is an ongoing process rather than one with a beginning and an end. Whether an organization is trying to enhance its reputation through social media, to communicate a new healthcare plan to employees, or to convince shareholders that the company is still worth investing in, it is critical to use a coherent communication strategy. An effective strategy should take into account the impact that the message will likely have on its audience.

THE CONNECTION BETWEEN COMMUNICATING CR AND CORPORATE REPUTATION

A 2011 *California Management Review* article noted that in establishing its CR reputation, a corporation has two levers at its disposal: the positive CR lever and the negative CR lever.[27] The positive lever involves the corporation's participation in "activities that contribute to the sense the firm 'does the right thing.'" Examples of this are everything from investing in local community services to treating employees extraordinarily well. The second lever, avoiding negative CR, can include

> employing (or buying from a supplier who employs) slave labor, engaging in farming or mining in an environmentally unfriendly way, or driving impossibly hard bargains with suppliers or workers that leave it impossible for them to earn a living wage.[28]

One of the key outcomes of successful CR and CR communication is an enhanced understanding of company values and responsibilities, which in turn can enhance the company's reputation in the eyes of the its stakeholders—including customers, shareholders, existing and future employees, suppliers, the financial community, and the media.

Like CR, reputation strategy is a critical part of a company's bottom line and yields a host of benefits. Meanwhile, CR is itself critical to a company's perceived reputation. The average consumer is not likely to put sufficient time and effort into researching a corporation's responsibility programs or social and environmental impact, but instead to make decisions based on a general sense of whether the company engages in good business practices from an ESG standpoint. For this reason, corporate reputation, as much as the actual impact of a business's practices on society, is a major indicator of CR success or failure. For savvier consumers, there are multiple means of gaining access to information about a corporation's practices relative to those of its competitors. The numerous CR ratings, together with data from the Reputation Institute's 2011 "Pulse Survey," which indicate that CR is responsible for more than 40% of a company's reputation, lay the basis for CR competition.[29] *Fortune*'s list of the World's Most Admired Companies is another driver of reputation—and uses CR as a key measure in its methodology.[30]

The beauty industry has long come under fire for promoting unrealistic standards for people (especially women) to aspire to, and is in many ways another perfect example of the consumer responsibility issues discussed with regard to the food and healthcare industries in Chapter 5. Dove's successful Real Beauty campaign turned many of the industry's tactics on their heads in its advertising, positioning the brand as a leading advocate for better body image for women among its skin care competitors. The campaign's print advertisements used images of women with ostensible flaws such as wrinkles and freckles and asked potential consumers to rethink their perceptions of the women pictured, as seen from one example in Figure 9.4.

Dove's approach not only allowed the brand to differentiate itself from competitors, whose advertising often highlights women's physical flaws to sell products designed to mask or eliminate such imperfections, but also to use advertising to improve body image for women and girls. Dove also introduced a series of "Self-Esteem Fund" events for preteen girls around the world. As reported by Brandchannel .com, "rather than prey on [girls'] lack of confidence by offering beauty 'solutions' and use that info to their marketing advantage, Dove is actually trying to get at the root of the problem and boost girls' confidence and self-esteem."[31]

However, as we have seen in previous chapters, using CR in public relations strategy has inherent risks, and Dove's celebration of real beauty drew not only positive press but also greater scrutiny. In a 2008 *Businessweek* article, Burt Helm pointed out that the Campaign for Real Beauty actually used retouched images of the women in its advertisements, despite "Dove and Ogilvy's righteous noise about the practice" elsewhere.[32]

The unfortunate truth is that while it can take years to build a positive corporate reputation, it only takes days or months of negative activities to wipe out this progress. According to *California Management Review*:

> "Bad" activities are going downhill in their effect of reputation erosion, whereas "good" activities are going uphill to build reputation. Thus, a firm seeking only a neutral reputation (i.e., by trying to limit negative events and activities) may in the end fare better than the firm that instead commits the same

Figure 9.4 Dove's Real Beauty campaign

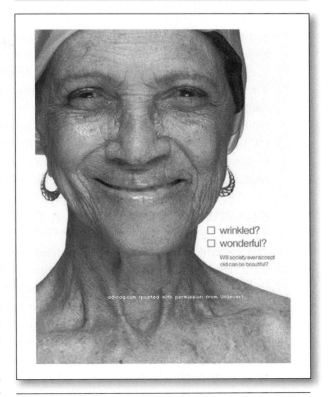

Source: The Dove® Campaign for Real Beauty.

resources to "doing good" while neglecting the "avoiding harm" lever. In fact, as firms are increasingly involved in some "good" activities in building positive CSR, the value of doing so diminishes.[33]

CR REPORTING

The role of corporate responsibility in management is becoming more central than ever before, as is evident from the fact that approximately 90% of large companies worldwide have published their CSR reports.[34] One of the key aspects of good CSR practices involves effective and transparent communication channels with internal and external stakeholders. This process is key to identifying issues of concern that the company should address and, after these have been addressed, informing about the ensuing performance.

Consequently, there is an increased demand for establishing an appropriate communication strategy that helps identify proper communication tools and ensures that the right information is collected and disseminated. Studies have shown that despite this growing importance of CR communication, organizations have yet to learn how to communicate their CR.

Stakeholders are now paying closer attention than ever to how CR is reported. The current CR landscape is a metrics-conscious environment, so it is essential for corporations not only to positively affect social and environmental issues through their responsibility programs, but also to be able to demonstrate the impact of their CR initiatives in quantifiable terms. It is important for companies to choose where to report their CR results and how to present their view of CR. A corporation's CR objectives and results show who its stakeholders are.[35]

COMMUNICATING CR IN A DIGITAL WORLD

The incredible rise of digital communications platforms over the past decade has significant implications for any company determining its CR communication strategy. Social media's ability to disseminate information and connect stakeholders has necessitated a shift in thinking on the part of CR executives. We now live in a world in which corporate communications is no longer a one-way push of messaging from the boardroom to a passive audience, but instead a two-way conversation where individuals and groups are empowered to talk back—in many cases over public forums.

This new reality presents a host of opportunities for CR professionals looking to connect with their constituencies in new and meaningful ways. The web's ability to deliver corporate messages directly to targeted groups of consumers without the bloated budgets of traditional marketing is just one advantage. TOMS is one such company that has consistently implemented brilliant marketing that leverages its community and current web applications to make an impact without shelling out larger amounts of money.

In 2012, TOMS launched its "Ticket to Give" campaign, where it randomly picked one customer each week throughout the year to send to one of the 40 countries where TOMS shoes are donated. The project created firsthand customer stories that highlighted TOMS' mission, which then became video assets that TOMS could use in its social media platforms. The campaign brought together the brand, its customers, and the communities in which it operated in an innovative way, for a fraction of the cost of advertising spend.

Perhaps even more impactful is social media's ability to build relationships with existing consumers and to reach new ones. Best-in-class CR-focused companies know that they can lure potential buyers by embracing digital domains and campaigns. PepsiCo, for example, was one of the first to use crowdsourcing as a means of building an online CSR campaign. Its Pepsi Refresh Project was philanthropic in nature, but put the Pepsi brand in front of consumers who were not necessarily customers—yet.

Launched in 2010, the Project was created to award $20 million in grants to individuals, businesses, and nonprofits that promoted new ideas that had a positive impact on their community, their state, or the nation. Members of the public would then vote for their favorite project online. As a sign of its commitment to the Project and hopes for its success, Pepsi launched Refresh in January, and in February opted out of traditional advertising during the Super Bowl for the first time in 23 years.

Measuring the campaign from a social media perspective, it was a tremendous success: in its first year, the Project received over 61 million responses, 5 million site registrations, and a tenfold increase in the number of Pepsi Fans on Facebook. Because voters could only do so via their Facebook pages, interacting with these consumers via the competition also gave Pepsi access to millions of new Facebook profiles and potential leads in the future. Whether the campaign can be linked to higher sales is still an issue of debate, but the campaign yielded the intangible: extraordinary levels of engagement between the brand and consumers and social ROI, which amounted to a smart long-term equity play for Pepsi.[36]

What best-in-class companies like TOMS and PepsiCo demonstrate is a willingness to embrace social media as a means of communicating their commitment to CR-focused initiatives. Doing the right thing needs to be noticed by people, and the web is a powerful means of communicating a company's success. How do companies get noticed online and which social platforms work best when delivering CSR? The answer depends largely on the purpose behind the message, and the target audience. Although Facebook and LinkedIn offer conversation possibilities, nothing reaches shareholders as quickly and efficiently as Twitter.

Companies are learning that in a crisis, Twitter is a vital link between them and their customers. In many world crises to hit global headlines over the past few years, including natural disasters like 2012's Hurricane Sandy and political uprisings such as the 2011 movement known as Arab Spring, Twitter has played a role. As a digital tool, Twitter is also core to CR strategy at America's leading companies, including FedEx, HP, Microsoft, and Intel.

Facebook is an essential communication tool for any serious CSR program as well, but is more business-to-consumer focused. Without the word limitations of Twitter, companies can build an entire CSR campaign on Facebook, and follow people who are interested in their CSR performance while keeping tabs on stakeholder sentiment on emerging issues. Regardless of the tool chosen, CR professionals must remember that social media is an always "on" platform. Companies must be present to the ongoing conversation, ready to engage and respond.

Much as digital platforms allow consumers to experience the good in a company's business practices, they can also discover less flattering results. News that an organization is not living up to social or environmental standards can spread like wildfire thanks to digital platforms, and potentially precipitate a crisis. The Susan G. Komen Foundation learned this lesson in 2012, when it announced in a press release that it would be pulling funding targeted to Planned Parenthood for political reasons. Komen faced a massive social media backlash after announcing the decision, with angry people flocking to its message boards and Facebook wall to state that they would no longer donate to the breast cancer charity, driving and inflaming national debate about Komen's decision.

Critically, organizations must be able to identify who is doing the talking, and have existing relationships with the right watchdogs. Tracking and developing relationships with influential bloggers not only in the CR universe, but in a particular industry, can be the difference between an under-control and a viral crisis. NGOs also enjoy a prominent role in our increasingly globalized economy and bear strong influence over companies, online and off. To manage the increased pressure and scrutiny from NGOs, many companies forge partnerships with organizations whose supported causes align with their own. There are a number of benefits to this strategy: support from a third-party lends credibility to CR initiatives, having allies in the nonprofit sector enhances corporate reputation, participating with NGOs often results in positive media coverage, and corporate partnerships provide ways for a company to market its support of good causes.

CONCLUSION

A strategic corporate responsibility program is only as strong as a company's ability to communicate its strengths and value to both internal and external stakeholders. When constructing a CR communications plan, it is essential not only to identify what to communicate, but also to know one's audience and its priorities and expectations. A bolstered corporate reputation stemming from robust CR communications can mitigate potential risk from CR crises, especially in this age of rapid globalization and instantaneous dissemination of information.

NOTES

1. Tonello, M. (2011, April 26). "What board members should know about communicating corporate social responsibility." Retrieved March 22, 2015, from http://blogs.law.harvard.edu/corpgov/2011/04/26/what-board-members-should-know-about-communicating-corporate-social-responsibility

2. "IBM Smarter Planet overview." Smarter Planet®. Retrieved August 12, 2014, from http://www.ibm.com/smarterplanet/us/en/overview/ideas/index.html?lnk=ussph1.16

3. Elliott, H. (2012, November 30). "World debut: BMW i3 electric car." *Forbes*. Retrieved August 12, 2014, from http://www.forbes.com/sites/hannahelliott/2012/11/30/world-debut-bmw-i3-electric-car

4. "BMW i3 availability." (n.d.). Retrieved August 12, 2014, from http://www.mybmwi3.com/availability

5. Elliott, "World debut."

6. Korzeniewski, J. (2009, June 23). "Toyota Prius ad campaign most liked by TV viewers." *AutoBlog*. Retrieved August 12, 2014, from http://green.autoblog.com/2009/06/23/toyota-prius-ad-campaign-most-liked-by-tv-viewers-w-video

7. Argenti, P. A. (2012, October 1). *Corporate communication* (6th ed., p. 119). McGraw Hill Higher Education.

8. Personal interview with Dailah Nihot, February 27, 2013.

9. Ibid.

10. Ibid.

11. Ibid.

12. "2014 Edelman Trust Barometer: Global results." Retrieved August 12, 2014, from http://www.edelman.com/insights/intellectual-property/2014-edelman-trust-barometer/about-trust/global-results/

13. http://www.ogilvypr.com/files/CSR-chap1-7.pdf (accessed August 12, 2014).

14. Argenti, P. A., & Barnes, C. (2009). *Digital strategies for powerful corporate communications* (p. 172). McGraw-Hill.

15. http://www.ogilvypr.com/files/CSR-chap1-7.pdf

16. Edelman. (2012). "2012 Edelman goodpurpose study." Retrieved August 12, 2014, from http://purpose.edelman.com

17. Greenwashing Index, http://www.greenwashingindex.com/ (accessed August 12, 2014).

18. Frampton, J., & Pearson, D. (2012). "Best global green brands 2012" [Video file]. Retrieved August 12, 2014, from http://www.bestglobalbrands.com/previous-years/2012

19. Argenti, P. A. (2004, Fall). "Collaborating with activists: How Starbucks works with NGOs." *California Management Review, 47*(1).

20. Ibid.

21. Aon Hewitt. (2014, May 9). "Aon Hewitt's 2014 'Green 30' study highlights Canada's environmentally and socially responsible organizations—as decided by employees." Retrieved August 12, 2014, from http://www.marketwired.com/press-release/aon-hewitts-2014-green-30-study-highlights-canadas-environmentally-socially-responsible-1908466.htm

22. Society for Human Resource Management, BSR, & Aurosoorya. (2011, April 10). "Advancing sustainability: HR's role survey report." Retrieved August 12, 2014, from http://www.shrm.org/Research/SurveyFindings/Articles/Pages/AdvancingSustainabilityHR%E2%80%99sRole.aspx

23. http://www.towerswatson.com/en-US/Insights/Newsletters/Global/strategy-at-work/2011/Viewpoints-QA-Employee-Engagement-to-the-Power-of-Three (accessed August 12, 2014).

24. Gallup.com. Employee Engagement. (accessed August 12, 2014).

25. Argenti, *Corporate communication*, p. 31.

26. Ibid.

27. Minor, D., & Morgan, J. (2011, Spring). "CSR as reputation insurance: *Primum non nocere.*" *California Management Review, 53*(3).

28. Ibid.

29. Reputation Institute, http://www.reputationinstitute.com/ (accessed August 12, 2014).

30. *Fortune*, World's Most Admired Companies, http://money.cnn.com/magazines/fortune/most-admired/ (accessed August 12, 2014).

31. Miller, M. J. (2012, October 18). "Dove takes real beauty campaign to girls." Retrieved August 12, 2014, from http://www.brandchannel.com/home/post/2012/10/18/Dove-Real-Beauty-Girls-101812.aspx

32. Helm, B. (2008, May 7). "Surprise! Dove's 'Campaign for Real Beauty' ads actually kind of fake." *Bloomberg Business.* Retrieved August 12, 2014, from http://www.businessweek.com/the_thread/brandnewday/archives/2008/05/surprise_doves.html

33. Minor & Morgan, "CSR as reputation insurance."

34. Randles, G. (2013, October 4). "Do CSR reports really tell us anything about businesses' social impact?" *The Guardian.* Retrieved August 12, 2014, from http://www.theguardian.com/voluntary-sector-network/2013/oct/04/corporate-social-responsibility-reports-impact

35. Kingma, K. (2009, March 25). "Four important insights for communicating CSR online." *Jungle Minds.* Retrieved August 12, 2014, from http://www.jungleminds.com/our-publications/article/four-important-insights-for-communicating-csr-online

36. Zmuda, N. (2012, October 8). "A teaching moment: Professors evaluate Pepsi Refresh Project." *Advertising Age.* Retrieved March 22, 2014, from http://adage.com/article/viewpoint/a-teaching-moment-professors-evaluate-pepsi-refresh-project/237629

FIJI WATER: GOING GREEN OR GREENWASHING?

Having an accurate account of our carbon footprint and ensuring transparency by reporting it annually to the Carbon Disclosure Project (CDP) are important steps to enable us to understand where to focus resources to reduce carbon emissions. We are very proud to be the first bottled water brand to pioneer carbon disclosure of our products.[1]

Thomas Mooney, senior vice president of Sustainability for FIJI Water, called Rob Six, vice president of corporate communications, into his office for their last meeting before that afternoon's press release on joining the Carbon Disclosure Project (CDP) and the launch of the company's new website, FIJIGreen.com. As part of a successful, privately held company, FIJI Water (FIJI) was a powerful brand that had experienced tremendous growth in the United States since its debut in late 1997. But now, in April 2008, the entire bottled water industry had been taken to task with debate about the negative environmental impact of the business, and FIJI had experienced perhaps the largest backlash in the press and from environmental groups.

Therefore, it was critical that this press release highlight the positive environmental initiatives already under way and the future plans of the company to be more environmentally friendly. More important, however, and a potential sticking point with the media, would be the bold claim that FIJI would become carbon negative, offsetting its total carbon footprint by 120%.[2] Mooney believed that this assertion would once again demonstrate to consumers why they should not only buy FIJI water, but also act as brand ambassadors for the product and encourage others to drink the brand to do something good for the environment.

FIJI WATER BACKGROUND

FIJI Water was founded in 1996 by David Gilmour, a wealthy Canadian financier.[3] Gilmour made millions from his investments in real estate, gold mining, and hotels. Amongst these hotels was an exclusive resort he established on his own island in Fiji, which allowed him to establish a relationship with the Fijian government.

In the early 1990s, Gilmour had leveraged these relationships to secure from the Fijian government the lease rights to tap the aquifer discovered by government-contracted geologists for 99 years, and the FIJI Water brand was born.[4] In late 1997, the first bottles

Source: This case was sponsored by the Allwin Initiative for Corporate Citizenship and prepared by Kristin Gaudino, T'09, and Kathleen O'Leary, T'12, under the direction of Professor Paul A. Argenti. © 2012 Trustees of Dartmouth College. All rights reserved. For permission to reprint, contact the Tuck School of Business at 603-646-3176.

of water were shipped to the United States.[5] FIJI Water later became available at retail locations throughout North America, the United Kingdom, France, Spain, Australia, the Caribbean, Mexico, and Germany.

From its inception, Gilmour saw the marketing potential for FIJI Water. Gilmour planned to stress the superior taste that occurred due to the secluded source that was "untouched by man" and to position the product as super premium.[6] To execute this strategy, Gilmour used his contacts in the hotel industry to pitch his product to luxury hotels, resorts, and restaurants. Furthermore, FIJI placed the product in leading Hollywood movies and other high-profile events to attract attention and create buzz around the water as a product with a taste worthy of trendsetters and movie stars.

In November 2004, shortly after being honored by Colin Powell for his work in Fiji with the Secretary of State's Award for Corporate Excellence, Gilmour sold FIJI Water to Roll International, a privately held company owned by agribusiness billionaires Stewart and Lynda Resnick.[7] In addition to being the largest growers of citrus in the U.S. and having large shares of the almond and pistachio market, the Resnicks owned the flower delivery service Teleflora, the Franklin Mint collectibles company, and POM Wonderful, which started a pomegranate fad and allowed the couple to further capitalize on another one of their crops. In 2007, FIJI Water had sales of $150 million.[8]

CSR AT FIJI WATER

One way in which FIJI differentiated itself was with its CSR efforts. As Anna Lenzer noted in *Mother Jones*, FIJI "has spent millions pushing not only the seemingly life-changing properties of the product itself, but also the company's green cred and its charity work."[9] Following the lead of the philanthropic owners, FIJI donated money to many conservation groups, including the Waterkeeper Alliance and the Nature Conservancy. In terms of the good works FIJI performed in its native country, FIJI and Mooney boasted about a "strong net positive for the economy of Fiji"[10] in terms of providing 350 jobs and engaging the FIJI Water Foundation in many charitable initiatives, including providing potable water throughout the island and paying to help build schools. The company strongly promoted their charitable donations and in 2008 gave $1.3 million to support schools, health clinics, and clean water supplies in Fiji. As Mooney said, "if we did . . . cease to exist, a big chunk of the economy would be gone, the schools that we built would go away, and the water access projects would go away."[11]

In 2002, FIJI Water created the Vatukaloko Trust Fund, a charity focused on a few villages surrounding its plant.[12] The company agreed to donate 0.15% of its Fijian operation's net revenues, which was about $100,000 in 2007.[13] Although a step in the right direction, the effort seemed fairly minor in light of FIJI's 2008 marketing budget of

$10 million and the company's recent investment of $250,000 to become a founding partner of the new Salt Lake City soccer stadium.[14]

Additionally, the company's water constituted as much as 15% to 30% of the small nation's exports, according to different sources. This could be viewed as helping the overall economy; however, there were still areas of concern over the actual good the company was doing. The company had an arrangement under which it would avoid paying taxes in Fiji until 2009; however, during 2007 and 2008, disputes arose between FIJI Water and the government over export duties, namely a 20-cent-per-liter tax. This resulted in litigation, impounded shipments, and a self-imposed industry-wide shutdown of Fijian water bottlers. The Fijian government eventually backed off.[15]

In January 2008, there was also an issue around FIJI's use of transfer pricing. The government suspected that Fiji was being hurt by the practice of selling FIJI Water produced in the country by the U.S.-owned Fijian subsidiary for low prices to the U.S. parent company, which in turn sold the water for more than 10 times the price.[16] Although the company was quickly exonerated of any wrongdoing and it was deemed logical that a multinational company would shift most of its profits and assets to the low-tax, stable, and safe countries, very little export earnings came into Fiji and most of the profits were pocketed by the U.S. parent. Nevertheless, Mooney contended that "when someone buys a bottle of FIJI, they're buying prosperity for the country."[17]

ENVIRONMENTAL BACKLASH OVER BOTTLED WATER AND INDUSTRY RESPONSE

In the 1970s, bottled water barely existed as an industry in the United States. By 2006, Americans were spending more than $15 billion on Poland Spring, FIJI Water, Evian, Aquafina, and Dasani bottled water products, which was more than what was spent on Apple iPods or movie tickets.[18] More staggering, worldwide, consumers spent five times more on bottled water annually than it would cost "to eradicate the 1.8 million deaths of children attributable to waterborne illness each year."[19] Globally, the bottled water market was estimated to be around $77 billion by 2008. It was estimated that this business would grow to approximately $26.5 billion by 2013. The business was solid, with profit margins estimated in the range of 25% to 30%, with 90% of the costs coming from everything else besides the actual water.[20]

In the early 21st century, the bottled water industry had come under attack as an industry with highly negative effects on the environment. The major issue that environmentalists had with this industry was the packaging and the high percentage of plastic water bottles that went into landfills. While recycling was not just an issue with the bottled water industry, it was hard to dispute that 85% of plastic water bottles went to landfills.[21]

The industry responded by reducing the amount of plastic used to make the bottles and encouraging recycling legislation in the United States. Most of the key players in the bottled water industry made efforts to be environmentally friendly. The industry leader in the U.S., Nestlé Waters North America, reduced packaging in 2007 by 15%, which saved over 65 million pounds of plastic in 2008.[22] More recently, the Eco-Shape bottle claimed to use 30% less plastic[23] and also encouraged recycling on its packaging.

CARBON FOOTPRINTS

Additionally, environmentalists took issue with the carbon emissions that occurred during the manufacturing and transportation and distribution of bottled water. Carbon footprints were measured as the total amount of carbon dioxide (CO_2) and other greenhouse gases released into the environment over the full life cycle of a product or service. The carbon footprint to produce and ship a bottle of water from a spring in the U.S. emitted 50 times as much CO_2 and greenhouse gases as tap water run through municipal pipes, and this number doubled when the bottled water came from France.[24]

The bottled water industry had not been the only business criticized for high carbon emissions. This focus around the carbon footprint of a manufactured product or a car or an airplane had led to an entire market for carbon credits and offsets. In general terms, carbon offsets allowed people or companies to mitigate their environmental impact by paying to plant trees or support renewable energy projects. In the U.S., the Chicago Climate Exchange allowed certified farmers and forest owners to sell carbon credits bought by companies that wanted to offset their emissions, possibly because the company was over the government-restricted limit for emissions.

Critics found the carbon footprint of bottled water so disturbing because they focused on the comparison to tap water, assuming that bottled water was an unnecessary substitute for tap water in developed countries. Lynda Resnick for one did not find the comparison to tap water valid, claiming that tap water was "not a real or viable alternative"[25] due to tap water contaminants. Additionally, the bottled water industry preferred that consumers think about the bigger picture. For example, the 1-liter bottle of water manufactured and shipped from France emitted as much carbon dioxide as an average car emits in about half a mile.[26]

Furthermore, Jane Lazgin, a Nestlé Waters North America spokeswoman, claimed that with water, a consumer was actually "choosing a bottle with the least environmental footprint"[27] when compared to other bottled and canned food and beverage products that required more processing or farming. Additionally, 75% of bottled water was produced and distributed regionally, which limited transportation during distribution.[28] As John Mackey, CEO and cofounder of Whole Foods Market, explained:

You can compare bottled water to tap water and reach one set of conclusions. But if you compare it with other packaged beverages, you reach another set of conclusions. It's unfair to say bottled water is causing extra plastic in landfills and it's using energy transporting it. There's a substitution effect.[29]

Regardless of the industry efforts to curb this attack, many municipal office buildings, including those in San Francisco and New York City, stopped supplying bottled water to government employees, and many cities put forth campaigns to encourage drinking tap water.[30]

Further threats to the bottled water industry came from companies like Nalgene, Klean Kanteen, Sigg, and Brita, which took advantage of the backlash to sell their refillable bottles and home filters as the responsible options.[31] The recession of 2008 also affected the bottled water industry and Americans drank less bottled water in 2008 than in 2007, which was the first drop in six years.[32]

IT'S HIP TO BE "GREEN"

These attacks on the bottled water industry were just one by-product of the growing consciousness of American's to carbon footprints, sustainability, and recycling. As a response to this undercurrent of environmentalism, many companies focused marketing efforts around "green" initiatives. From CPG companies like Clorox flaunting "green" products to conglomerates like General Electric highlighting its "Ecomagination" capabilities in wind energy and fuel-efficient locomotives, green marketing campaigns proliferated to the point where they were no longer unique and differentiated. To be viewed as a forward-thinking company by the trendsetters, a green campaign was an imperative.

Some of the most interesting and most effective green marketing campaigns were for companies in industries that had typically been viewed as highly harmful to the environment, such as the airline industry and the automotive and petroleum industries. To bolster the reputation of their corporations in response to environmental criticism, automotive companies like Toyota made the general public believe in hybrid cars through the Prius campaigns highlighting the happy flora and fauna that sang and danced as the car drove by. Additionally, notorious polluters like British Petroleum, Shell, and ExxonMobil put forth campaigns that demonstrated the steps they were taking to reduce their environmental impact. Finally, the airline industry publicized its attempts to reduce fuel consumption and its carbon footprint, with one campaign coming from American Airlines.[33]

Unfortunately, the sincerity of many of these campaigns was called into question, and many environmentalists and consumers were jaded by results that fell below planned goals. Some even accused several of these companies of "greenwashing," a term coined to describe misleading or deceptive information disseminated by an organization to present an environmentally responsible image. (See Chapter 3 for a deeper discussion of the greenwashing phenomenon.)

"GREEN" MARKETING OF FIJI WATER

FIJI Water was criticized for the environmental costs embedded in each bottle. In fact, even though FIJI was a small bottler compared to others in the industry, it was targeted as "one of the worst carbon offenders."[34] The production plant operated 24 hours a day using diesel fuel. The high-grade plastic materials used to make the bottles were shipped from China to Fiji, and full bottles were subsequently shipped around the world to markets in North America and Europe. FIJI Water traveled approximately 5,470 miles to West Coast markets in the United States.[35] This travel distance was similar to that of other imported water, but was staggering when compared with local bottled water traveling a mere 20 to 250 miles. On average, a 1-liter bottle of FIJI Water contaminated 6.74 liters of water to stretch-blow-mold the plastic, burned fossil fuel to transport plastic pellets from China to Fiji, distributed full bottles to the country of sale, and produced 0.25 kg of greenhouse emissions if the United States was the final country of sale.[36]

In response to criticism and perhaps to alleviate consumer guilt while also bolstering its own image, FIJI Water announced an aggressive sustainable growth program in November 2007.[37] At the time, Mooney told the press that the environmental plans had been under way long before the announcement, but that the "media environment" of environmental attacks on the industry and company had "prompted FIJI to 'rethink the value' of publicizing its efforts," since announcing the efforts prior to the attacks would have just showed FIJI "solving a problem no one in [the] industry thought existed."[38]

Mooney's blog on the *Huffington Post* in November 2007 (see Exhibit 9.1) outlined FIJI's environmental goals.[39] The program included a commitment to become carbon negative beginning in 2008. FIJI Water pledged to reduce actual greenhouse gas emissions 25% by 2010 by reducing packaging 20%, supplying at least 50% of the energy used at its bottling facility with renewable energy, and optimizing logistics to take advantage of more carbon-efficient modes of transportation.[40]

The April 2008 launch of FIJI Green was the latest CSR effort by FIJI Water.[41] Building on the promises to reduce packaging and shipping emissions in November 2007, the company invested heavily in this new initiative. However, for as much as FIJI Green could be viewed as an indicator of the company's desire to be more environmentally responsible, it could also be seen as another genius marketing strategy meant to elevate and further differentiate the brand in the eyes of consumers, which could open the company up to accusations of greenwashing.

It was hard to deny that FIJI was using a green product strategy to build the brand and grow the business in the future, especially with a $5 million marketing budget the company placed around promotion of the FIJI Green initiative.[42] The campaign brazenly urged consumers to drink imported water to fight climate change with the tagline "Every drop is green" printed on all the bottles. The FIJI Green website claimed that because of the 120% carbon offset, buying a big bottle of FIJI Water created the same carbon reduction as walking five blocks instead of driving.[43] Mooney noted in his *Huffington Post* blog post that "we'd be happy if anyone chose to drink nothing but Fiji Water as a means to keep the sea levels down."[44]

To achieve the carbon-negative goals, FIJI Water used a "forward-crediting" model where the company purchased verified carbon offsets related to reforestation, land preservation, and renewable energy projects to cover the emissions it could eliminate.[45] However, many of the purchased reductions would happen over a period of a few decades, even though FIJI could take the offsets at the time of purchase.[46]

However, forward crediting did not stop FIJI Water from touting its carbon-negative product on its packaging (beyond "Every drop is green," others included "Carbon negative, globally positive" and "A Convenient Truth") as well as in print ads, including *Elle*, *Esquire*, and *Vanity Fair* magazines.[47] The full-page ad in the *Vanity Fair* 2007 green issue was perhaps the most indicative of how serious FIJI was about its green campaign.

ENVIRONMENTAL PARTNERSHIPS

As part of FIJI's green product strategy, the company decided to partner with several environmental organizations, which also gave the company some credibility for its environmental efforts. With its April 2008 press release, FIJI could tout being one of the first privately owned companies to disclose its carbon footprint and join the Supply Chain Leadership Collaboration of the Carbon Disclosure Project (CDP).[48] The CDP was the world's largest investor coalition on climate change and an independent not-for-profit organization established in 2000 "to facilitate dialogue between companies and investors to encourage a rational response to climate change."[49] As part of the FIJI Green press release, Mooney expressed the importance of measuring the company's carbon footprint, stating:

> FIJI Water believes that consumers will make environmentally responsible purchasing decisions if they have the information they need. . . . [T]he only way consumers can turn their good environmental intentions into good decisions is to give them the information they need regarding the emissions associated with the products they buy. We sincerely hope that other companies, in our industry and beyond, will follow in providing comparable product lifecycle emissions data for all of their products.[50]

To this end, FIJI also partnered with ICF to have an independent emissions analysis (see FIJIGreen.com). FIJI Water's total annual carbon footprint for the year ending June 30, 2007, was 85,396 CO_2eq.[51]

Additionally, FIJI partnered with Conservation International (CI) to achieve its carbon-negative goal as well as to protect the Sovi Basin rainforest and the Yaqara Valley watershed in Fiji, the main source of FIJI Water.[52] The preservation of the rainforest was the most effective carbon offset for the company in terms of truly helping the environment and was also crucial to the long-term sustainability of the company and its product. According to the company website, the Sovi Basin project was extremely important to the company and would protect 50,000 acres of the last remaining lowland rainforest in the South Pacific. This project would pay local villagers to prevent them from selling their timber rights to logging companies, which would offset deforestation, ensuring one of the largest sources offsetting carbon emissions, the equivalent of removing 2 million cars from the highway.[53] Additionally, the company would replant native tree species in the rainforest as part of the carbon offset project.

The partnership with CI puts FIJI Water on the same "green" ground as companies like Starbucks and Wal-Mart, to name just a couple of the more than 1,000 corporate partnerships that CI had developed since 1987. "Building upon a strong foundation of science, partnership, and field demonstration, CI empowered societies to responsibly and sustainably care for nature for the well-being of humanity."[54] Stewart Resnick sat on the board of directors at that time for CI; Lynda Resnick was also listed as an emeritus member of the board.

THE BOLD NEW STRATEGY

The new strategy to position FIJI Water squarely as a green product was definitely bold for a brand that had made its name on premium taste and celebrity cache and in an environment where competitors were quietly making their products more environmentally friendly without a lot of fanfare. Although Mooney was entirely confident that FIJI's target audience would respond positively to this new spin, there were some lingering thoughts in his mind about whether the company should be so visibly touting these initiatives that had not yet come to fruition even after nearly six months since the initial announcement that the company would reduce packaging and shipping carbon emissions. Was this campaign opening the company up to further attacks from environmentalists? Would environmental groups and possibly even some consumers view these initiatives as purely greenwashing to capitalize on the green movement to sell more FIJI Water?

Case Questions

1. Has there been backlash toward FIJI due to the green positioning of the product? Google can provide some articles with interesting reactions, especially on treehugger.com.

2. Is FIJI Water a leader in the "green" movement? Compare/contrast with other bottled water companies.

3. Evaluate the methods that FIJI Water is using to measure their carbon footprint as well as their strategy for reducing their carbon footprint. Is FIJI Water truly a carbon-negative company?

4. Is the FIJI Green marketing campaign proactive or reactive? The years preceding the launch of FIJIGreen.com and the "green" initiatives (2007 and 2008) were years where the bottled water industry had been under attack for selling an unnecessary product at a high environmental cost.

5. Are these sustainability initiatives sincere on the part of FIJI Water, or is going "green" the company's next big brand-building activity that keeps the brand relevant for target consumers?

6. What has been the true impact of the other FIJI Water CSR and charitable efforts?

7. Are there conflicts of interest with third-party conservation organizations? Who are some other organizations FIJI Water should consider partnering with?

Exhibit 9.1 FIJI Water Goes Green

This week, FIJI Water announced a major sustainability initiative that we're calling "FIJI Green," which was highlighted in the *New York Times*. FIJI Green is all about our path to sustainability and it's a comprehensive approach—cradle-to-cradle—to lessen our environmental impact and actually reduce the amount of carbon in the atmosphere.

Bottled water has taken hits from the media and environmental groups of late, and many may think we have launched this initiative solely in response to their criticism. Not so. Our industry's growth remains strong as consumers continue to turn away from sugary drinks, and FIJI Water continues to grow even faster than our industry.

Personally, I believe the environmental spotlight belongs on sodas and other manufactured beverages that outsell bottled water and may also contribute to the obesity problem. To put things in perspective, bottled water accounts for only 0.02% (two-hundredths of one percent) of America's oil consumption, and plastic water bottles contribute only one-third of 1 percent to the municipal waste stream.

Ironically, we have much in common with the very groups who have been so critical. From the start, FIJI Water has been an environmental leader in Fiji and in our industry. We have never bottled our water in glass, which consumes more energy, emits more carbon, and generates more waste than our PET plastic bottles. We made our bottles square because this reduces shipping volume by 10% compared to traditional bottles. And we make our own bottles in Fiji to avoid needless transportation of bottles into the country.

The heart and soul of our brand and the quality of our water depend upon our Yaqara source and the pristine ecosystem that surrounds it. Our water is not only the finest in the

(Continued)

Exhibit 9.1   (Continued)

world; it is also a sustainable, renewable resource that we cherish. We have saved the Sovi Basin, Fiji's largest lowland rainforest, through a partnership with Conservation International and with the people of Fiji that has been in the works for several years now. In addition, our success with FIJI Water has allowed us to give back to Fiji in so many ways, from water access projects in over 100 towns, to schools we have built and help to support, to some of the best paying jobs in Fiji.

So why launch FIJI Green now? We're a small company and represent only about 1 percent of the entire bottled water industry, but we are also very visible and believe we can raise the expectations consumers have of our industry. We also think that people who love FIJI Water deserve to know everything we're doing for the environment and for the people of Fiji. By drinking our water they become a part of these efforts.

FIJI Green includes:

Becoming Carbon Negative in 2008 – We're cutting carbon emissions by 25% across our product lifecycle by 2010. And, working with Conservation International, we will invest in reforestation and other projects that take carbon out of the atmosphere; these will add up to at least 120 percent of our remaining carbon emissions starting in 2008. Also, 50% of the energy needed to power our bottling facility will come from renewable sources, such as wind, by 2010.

Saving the Fijian Rainforest – We are partnering with Conservation International and with the people of Fiji to protect and preserve the Sovi Basin, the largest rainforest in Fiji. This effort will keep 10 million tons of carbon out of the atmosphere for perpetuity, the equivalent of removing about 2 million passenger cars from the road for an entire year.

Reducing Packaging – We will reduce the amount of packaging in our products by at least 20% over the next three years, and we will increase the use of recycled inputs.

Expanding the Charge for Recycling Programs – We are advocating for expanded curbside recycling and consumer incentive programs.

On that last point, recycling is one of the best ways for all of us to have a positive and immediate impact on the world in which we live. About 70 percent of the beverages we drink come in packages, and we need to give all consumers the tools and incentives they need to recycle. It makes a difference. The 11 states that have container deposit laws account for 60% of recycled bottles in the U.S., even though only 3 of these include bottled water. Oregon is about to include bottled water in its program, but the remaining 46 states must address this issue.

Bottled water is here to stay, and the industry will continue to grow. Consumers simply do not want to go back to a time when soda and other sugary drinks were the only convenient choice they had. But consumers also expect us to be environmentally sustainable, and that is what we intend to do.

Source: Mooney, T. (2007, November 13). "FIJI Water goes green." *Huffington Post blog.* Retrieved from http://www .huffingtonpost.com/thomas-mooney/fiji-water-goes-green_b_72406.html.

NOTES

1. "FIJI Water becomes first bottled water company to release carbon footprint of its products: Unveils FIJIGreen.com to report progress on its carbon negative commitment" [Press release]. (2008, April 9.) *PR Newswire*. Retrieved March 22, 2015, from http://www.prnewswire.com/news-releases/fiji-water-becomes-first-bottled-water-company-to-release-carbon-footprint-of-its-products-57319297.html

2. Ibid.

3. FIJI Water. (n.d.). "Company history." Retrieved from http://www.fijiwater.com/company/company-timeline

4. Lenzer, A. (2009, September 1). "Spin the bottle: Obama sips it. Paris Hilton loves it. Mary J. Blige won't sing without it. How did a plastic water bottle, imported from a military dictatorship thousands of miles away, become the epitome of cool?" *Mother Jones*.

5. FIJI Water, "Company history."

6. FIJI Water. (n.d.). "Untouched by man." Retrieved from http://www.fijiwater.com/water/untouched-by-man

7. FIJI Water, "Company history."

8. Deutsch, C. (2007, November 7). "For FIJI Water, a big list of green goals." *New York Times*.

9. Lenzer, "Spin the bottle."

10. Deutsch, "For FIJI Water, a big list of green goals."

11. Lenzer, "Spin the bottle."

12. Deutsch, "For FIJI Water, a big list of green goals."

13. Lenzer, "Spin the bottle."

14. Hein, K. (2008, April 14). "Advertising: FIJI Water ups ad spend, pours forth 'eco' message: premium water boosts budget to $10M to tout environmental actions." *Brandweek*.

15. Bolwig, C. (2008, July 26). "Fiji government yields to bottled water company pressure." *Ice News*. Retrieved March 22, 2015, from http://www.icenews.is/2008/07/26/fiji-government-yields-to-bottled-water-company-pressure/

16. Field, M. (2008, January 21). "Fiji–US row brews over water exports." *Dominion Post*.

17. Lenzer, "Spin the bottle."

18. Fishman, C. (2007, July/August). "Message in a bottle" (p. 110). *Fast Company, 117*.

19. Siegle, L. (2008, February 10). "It's just water, right? Wrong. Bottled water is set to be the latest battleground in the eco war." *The Observer*.

20. Ferrier, C. (2001, April). "Bottled water: Understanding a social phenomenon." Discussion paper commissioned by WWF.

21. Container Recycling Institute. (n.d.). "Plastic facts & statistics." Retrieved from http://www.container-recycling.org/index.php/factsstatistics/plastic

22. Boslet, M. (2007, December 16). "Our guilty gallons: Bottled water's impact on environment." *San Jose Mercury News*.

23. Siegle, "It's just water, right?"

24. Boslet, "Our guilty gallons."

25. Lenzer, "Spin the bottle."

26. Boslet, "Our guilty gallons."

27. Ibid.

28. Ferrier, "Bottled water."

29. Fishman, "Message in a bottle," p. 110.

30. Lee, J. 8. (2008, June 17). "City council shuns bottles in favor of water from tap." *New York Times.* Retrieved March 22, 2015, from http://www.nytimes.com/2008/06/17/nyregion/17water.html

31. Siegelbaum, H. (2008, June 6). "FIJI Water by the Numbers." Retrieved March 22, 2015, from http://www.marketplace.org/topics/sustainability/greenwash-brigade/fiji-water-numbers

32. Mui, Y. Q. (2009, August 13). "Bottled water boom appears tapped out." *Washington Post.* Retrieved March 22, 2015, from http://articles.washingtonpost.com/2009-08-13/business/36772525_1_ bottled-water-capita-consumption-deer-park

33. "American airlines plans green marketing campaign." (2007, July 19).

34. "Observer: Guilt free?" (2007, November 9). *Financial Times.* Retrieved March 22, 2015, from http://www.ft.com/intl/cms/s/0/292efb74-8e67-11dc-8591-0000779fd2ac.html#axzz3VAZuTIDh

35. Bibo, T. (2009, August 18). "Kicking the bottle will save you big, water experts say." *Journal Star.* Retrieved from http://www.pjstar.com/article/20090818/News/308189885

36. Alter, L. (2007, February 6). "Pablo calculates the true cost of bottled water." Treehugger. Retrieved March 22, 2015, from www.treehugger.com/files/2007/02/pablo_calculate.php

37. Deutsch, "For FIJI Water, a big list of green goals."

38. Ibid.

39. Mooney, T. (2007, November 13). "FIJI Water goes green." *Huffington Post blog.* Retrieved from http://www.huffingtonpost.com/thomas-mooney/fiji-water-goes-green_b_72406.html

40. Ibid.

41. "FIJI Water becomes first bottled water company to release carbon footprint of its products," *PR Newswire.*

42. Lenzer, "Spin the bottle."

43. FIJIGreen.com.

44. Ibid.

45. Deutsch, "For FIJI Water, a big list of green goals."

46. Lenzer, "Spin the bottle."

47. Hein, "Advertising."

48. "FIJI Water becomes first bottled water company to release carbon footprint of its products," *PR Newswire.*

49. Ibid.

50. Ibid.

51. Ibid.

52. "Corporate partners: FIJI Water Company LLC." Retrieved from http://www.conservation .org/how/partnership/corporate/Pages/fiji_water.aspx

53. FijiWater.com.

54. Conservation International, http://www.conservation.org/about/Pages/default.aspx (accessed October 14, 2009).

Chapter 10

IMPLEMENTING A CR STRATEGY

As we have discovered throughout the preceding chapters of this book, identifying corporate responsibility initiatives that will align with a corporation's business strategy and create shared value is a significant challenge for companies across all industries. For decades, companies have struggled with how to allocate resources to CR activities that will not only produce social and environmental results but also contribute to a firm's financial bottom line in a meaningful way.

Throughout the cases in this book, we have seen firms from McDonald's to Walmart to Goldman Sachs successfully devise a CR strategy and sustainability programs that create value for a variety of stakeholders. Once a corporation has successfully addressed this problem, however, there is still a major challenge ahead: how to execute its CR strategy successfully.

CURRENT APPROACHES TO CR IMPLEMENTATION

While Michael Porter and Mark Kramer's *Harvard Business Review* article "Strategy and Society" has been cited frequently for its discussion of the connection between corporate responsibility and competitive advantage, one piece of the puzzle that is missing from the article is an actionable, step-by-step process for implementing a CR program.[1] Porter and Kramer understand the difficulties in taking a CR program from idea to action. They state, "Integrating business and social needs takes more than good intentions and strong leadership. It requires adjustments in organization, reporting relationships, and incentives," and advise that "companies must shift from a fragmented, defensive posture to an integrated, affirmative approach."[2]

Fortunately, a number of other researchers have stepped into the conversation where Porter and Kramer left off, proposing frameworks for implementation of the type of strategic corporate responsibility programs Porter and Kramer recommended in HBR. Writing in *The Journal of Global Business Issues*, John Milliman, Jeffery Ferguson, and Ken Sylvester introduced a five-step process for corporations to use in implementing a strategic CR program (see Figure 10.1).[3]

First, Milliman, Ferguson, and Sylvester recommend identifying societal issues that affect the firm and ways to address them that will translate such issues into a corporate advantage. Second, they advise preparing a menu of CR program options that could be used to create opportunities associated with the issues identified in the first step. Third, the firm should perform an analysis of the program options identified in Step 2, considering both economic and societal impacts, along with other variables specific to the corporation. The fourth step is implementing the best CR program based on the analysis in Step 3; this step may involve coordination with other entities, such as outside organizations or complementary sectors. Finally, the firm must measure financial and social outcomes and report the program's results to both internal and external stakeholders.[4]

Writing in the *Journal of Business Ethics*, Marco Werre takes a slightly different approach to CR program implementation, identifying four necessary steps (see Figure 10.2).[5]

Werre's approach begins by engaging corporate leaders. First, he recommends increasing awareness at the top of the organization. Second, it is essential for an organization to create a vision for its corporate responsibility program and identify

Figure 10.1   Implementing strategic CR

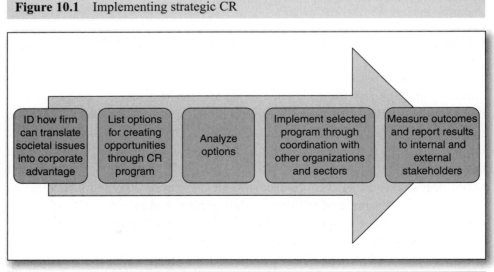

Source: Adapted from Milliman, J., Ferguson, J., & Sylvester, K. (2008). "Implementation of Michael Porter's strategic corporate social responsibility model." *Journal of Global Business Issues, Conference Edition.*

Figure 10.2 Implementing CR

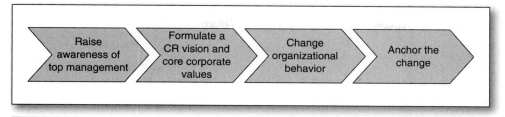

Source: Werre, M. (2003, May). "Implementing corporate responsibility: The Chiquita case." *Journal of Business Ethics, 44*(2/3), 247–260.

core corporate values that will drive the program to success. Third, the corporation must set about changing behavior within the organization to bring it in line with the new CR strategy. Finally, the company must anchor the change.

A third set of researchers, Francois Maon, Adam Lindgreen, and Valerie Swaen, used Kurt Lewin's force field model of organizational change as the basis for their own CR implementation framework (see Figure 10.3). Lewin's model includes three phases: unfreezing, moving, and refreezing.[6] *Unfreezing* means unlearning practices associated with the status quo to make way for new processes. *Moving* refers to pushing the organization toward a new set of assumptions, and *refreezing* means setting these new assumptions in place to replace the previously unlearned practices. Maon et al. added a fourth stage in their own research: *sensitizing*, which precedes the unfreezing stage and is defined as raising top management's awareness of the importance of CR issues.

The researchers propose implementing strategic CR initiatives via a nine-step process to accomplish the four stages in Figure 10.3:[7]

Figure 10.3 Force field model

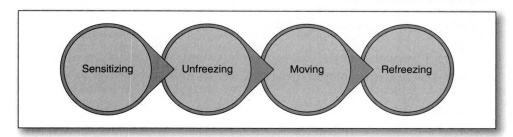

Source: Maon, F., Lindgreen, A., & Swaen, V. (2008, September). "Designing and implementing corporate social responsibility: An integrative framework grounded in theory and practice." *Journal of Business Ethics, 87,* 71–89.

1. Raising CSR awareness inside the organization

2. Assessing corporate purpose in a societal context

3. Establishing a working definition and vision for CSR

4. Assessing current CSR status

5. Developing an integrated CSR strategic plan

6. Implementing the CSR integrated strategic plan

7. Maintaining internal and external communication

8. Evaluating CSR-related strategies and communication

9. Institutionalizing CSR policy

In a separate paper, Lindgreen and Swaen partnered with David Harness and Marieke Hoffmann to outline a slightly different approach to CR implementation.[8] This approach includes a different set of steps toward creating a strategic CR program:

1. Conduct "zero-assessment"

2. Develop CSR goals within the organization's mission, vision, and strategy

3. Gain top management support

4. Gain employee support to ensure they own CSR as part of their work life activities

5. Gain support from external stakeholders

6. Prioritize change effort and focus on achieving goals

7. Measure progress and fine-tune the process

8. Anchor change

9. Reorder the implementation system

The implementation of CR strategy also draws often on general project management strategies used in other areas of business. As Werre explains:

The implementation of CR can be viewed as a specific case of an organizational change process. Therefore, we can draw from the vast experience and literature on organizational change in general to determine the critical implementation-aspects and build a CR implementation-model taking these into account.[9]

OUR APPROACH

We will use the implementation frameworks described above as a jumping-off point for our own recommendations around embedding a CR program into an existing corporate structure. While we will touch on many of the steps listed above, for the purposes of this book, we have divided the process into four key implementation sections (see Figure 10.4).

We defined the four steps as such:

1. **CR strategy definition:** In the first step, a corporation decides where to focus its CR efforts, how to refine this to specific areas, and how to drive engagement at the top levels of the organization.

2. **Driving internal change:** The second step involves figuring out how to rally employees effectively to support these efforts and to institutionalize the focus into decision-making.

3. **Partnering with external parties:** The third step is deciding which external organizations to collaborate with, figuring out how to form agreements, determining how such partnerships will help, and identifying pitfalls to avoid.

4. **Measuring and reacting:** The final step of the process is developing a robust system for monitoring performance and determining how to leverage positive results and adapt when targets are not met.

HOW CR STRATEGY RELATES TO IMPLEMENTATION

As discussed throughout the previous chapters, there are a wide range of reasons why companies engage in corporate responsibility programs. Here, we will look

Figure 10.4   Driving change through CR

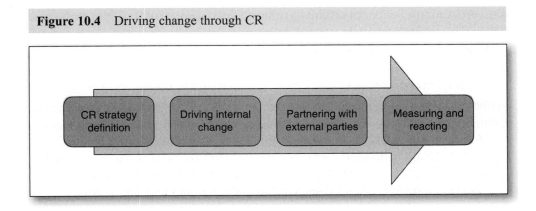

at the motivations from a slightly different perspective as a means of understanding how they relate to CR implementation. Academic reviews use a number of different ways to categorize the different motivations behind CR programs. The simplest of these categories is between *proactive* and *reactive* companies, which can also be further broken down into proactive from the start, proactive as a change, reactive ahead of a crisis, and reactive in a crisis.

When thinking about implementation, the reasons why a company has developed a CR strategy and the stage at which the company is operating at are especially important in terms of their sizable impact on the implementation approach. A company that proactively decides to implement a CR program from the start of the firm's history is likely to hire more like-minded employees and design their products or services to demonstrate their social or environmental friendliness. On the other hand, a long-standing company that is implementing a CR strategy for the first time in the face of a crisis may have more inertia within the organization and experience greater resistance to implementing the change. As we explore the various steps to implementation, we will call out the different approaches required for each of the situations.

As explained by Milliman et al.:

> The CSR literature identifies a number of reasons why firms engage in CSR practices. These include to (a) bolster the organization public image, (b) meet needs or pressures from key external stakeholders, (c) be in alignment with industry or community expectations, (d) protect itself from legal threats, (e) provide a source of motivation for employees, and (f) achieve a marketing advantage or other direct economic impacts.[10]

As Werre points out, corporations often ramp up their corporate responsibility efforts because of heightened awareness among top management of how changes in the environment affect the organization.[11] Such a change in executive awareness can either take a proactive or a reactive approach, with the former allowing the corporation a better opportunity to control the trajectory of its CR response and effectiveness, while the latter leaves much up to chance.

Werre cites the case of Chiquita Brands International, Inc. The company is an international food manufacturer, with much of its revenue coming from its banana business. In 1992, Chiquita joined the Better Banana Project of the Rainforest Alliance, a U.S.-based nonprofit designed to advance the goal of sustainable agriculture, particularly in the areas of tropical agriculture and forestry, but it was not until 1998, in response to negative publicity, that the company began to fully integrate CR into its business. Chiquita found itself depicted in the press as a corporation that was exploitative both of the environment and human labor, and the company's management knew it had to respond.

As Werre explains:

> The [negative] articles led Chiquita's senior management to reconsider the personality of their company. At the time, corporate responsibility was not part of company policy and different locations showed substantial variability in their operations. . . . A need arose to have a uniform standard of corporate responsibility and the systems in place to consistently be able to demonstrate Chiquita's quality and trustworthiness with regard to CR.[12]

As we have seen in earlier chapters, there is great threat of danger to corporate reputation and other assets including license to operate for those organizations that fail to meet standards of environmental, social, and governance (ESG) responsibility. Shell and Nike are two such examples, the former coming under intense scrutiny for its dealings in the UK with Brent Spar and in Nigeria with the Ogoni (see the case at the end of Chapter 4 for additional information). Nike, on the other hand, was attacked by a wide range of activists including Global Exchange as a result of its outsourced manufacturing in developing nations. Meanwhile, other corporations were founded on ESG principles; for example, both The Body Shop and Ben & Jerry's are known for developing business models built on ethical foundations.[13]

A change in how management views CR can be driven by circumstances seemingly beyond a corporation's control—such as negative publicity, pressure applied by NGOs, or protests or boycotts led by activists.[14] For example, during the 1990s, Swedish furniture manufacturer and retailer IKEA came under scrutiny for child labor issues after the media brought attention to the company's practices. Other situations are proactive, with internal stakeholders demonstrating a personal commitment to CR. For instance, when more stakeholders identify with the personal values of a powerful individual or groups inside the organization, CSR is driven by a sense of personal morality, inspired by managers' or employees' socially oriented personal values.

As we will see in the Timberland case at the end of this chapter, social responsibility had long played a prominent role in the company's activities. Indeed, the integration of business and social responsibility—or, as former CEO Jeff Swartz described it, "commerce and justice"—was not simply an aspect of the company's mission but an integrated component of its strategy.[15]

WHERE DO CSR STRATEGIES USUALLY COME FROM?

When a company decides to focus on CSR, the most common theme is the importance of having top leadership drive the change. While some articles look at bottom-up generation of ideas, where employee values influence the CR strategy, there are few examples of successful CR strategy implementation without CEO support and a strong supporting organizational infrastructure.

There are also a number of instances where a change in CEO leadership sparked new attention to developing a CR strategy, particularly after a crisis. More often than not, corporate responsibility becomes a strategic theme within an organization only when top management deems it to be important. According to Werre, the motivation to begin a CR program is dependent on the values and priorities of top executives, and "the particular forms of CR suited for the specific organization will also differ with the dominant values."[16]

In many cases, there is a champion for a particular CR project or goal within an organization—for example, a top manager whose personal values align with the goals of the chosen initiative, or who simply views environmental and social impact, generally, as important. In the case of Chiquita, a major driver of motivation among the lower ranks was the CEO's vested interest in and passion for improving the company's CR results.

During the initial stages of establishing a strategic CR program, the firm should look at how its activities affect society in order to identify potential threats to the organization should its business be perceived to have a negative impact on the environment or society.[17] To ensure that all potential threats are accounted for, it is crucial to engage key operational managers who are familiar with the company's impact across the breadth of corporate activities, as well as employees of departments that work closely with new products or customers.

HOW DO YOU SELECT AND REFINE YOUR CSR FOCUS?

Porter and Kramer's philosophy of strategic corporate responsibility has dominated much of the recent dialogue about how to refine organizational CR focus. Much of the additional research has elaborated on how to identify the strategic CR initiatives. Porter and Kramer define three categories of CR issues: generic social issues, value chain social impacts, and social dimensions of competitiveness.[18] They view the value chain as looking from inside the company outward, and define it as incorporating "all of the activities a company engages in while doing business."[19] The value chain "can be used as a framework to identify the positive and negative social impact of those activities."[20]

Social dimensions of competitiveness, on the other hand, involve looking from outside the corporation inward. To establish and maintain an effective, strategic CR program, the firm must understand its competitive context, namely, the social dimensions of the environment in which it competes. In Chapter 8, we looked at these dimensions, as defined by Porter and Kramer, in depth: (1) the context for

Figure 10.5 Value chain framework

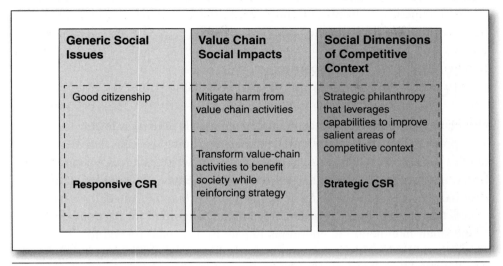

Source: Porter, M., & Kramer, M. (2006, December). "Strategy and society: The link between competitive advantage and corporate social responsibility." *Harvard Business Review.* Retrieved from https://hbr.org/2006/12/strategy-and-society-the-link-between-competitive-advantage-and-corporate-social-responsibility.

strategy and rivalry, (2) factor conditions, (3) local demand conditions, and (4) related and supporting industries.

In response to Porter and Kramer's work, Milliman et al. outlined a process for corporations to use in implementing CR programs:

1. "Scoping the organization's environment for ways the firm can translate societal issues which impact it into some type of a corporate advantage.

2. "Development of an expanded menu of CSR program options to create corporate opportunities associated with these societal issues.

3. "Careful analysis of strategic CSR program options based on consideration of economic and societal impacts as well as other relevant organizational variables."[21]

Echoing Milliman's recommendations, Werre recommends beginning with a scenario analysis that will allow corporations to "identify and prioritise the trends . . . shaping the future of the organization."[22] He recommends this be done through internal and external interviews and conferences incorporating stakeholders both within and outside the firm. The trends, which he calls "driving forces," should be ranked according to their effect on the organization and their likelihood of occurring.[23]

Benchmarking a firm's CR practices against those of competitors is another crucial step, one that will allow corporations to determine the best means of maintaining competitive advantage through CR while also realizing which CR activities constitute an inappropriate use of resources.[24]

HOW SHOULD A CORPORATION EVALUATE CR STRATEGIES/OPPORTUNITIES?

One challenge corporations face in implementing CR initiatives is how to evaluate and approve CR strategy decisions. One school of thought argues that these opportunities should be evaluated using traditional frameworks, such as discounted cash flows, net present value, or internal return on revenue, and only be approved if they pass these hurdles. Meanwhile, others argue that CR strategies have larger effects that are less easily measured but are still important for the company (such as the small likelihood but enormous impact of a scandal related to CR failure). Those on this side of the conversation argue that you should use traditional tools, but that the intangibles should also be considered. As Porter and Kramer state, "The interdependence of a company and society can be analyzed with the same tools used to analyze competitive position and develop strategy."[25]

Therefore, companies that are truly serious about making an impact through corporate responsibility programs should approach CR with the same rigor they bring to more traditional business decisions. This means considering the opportunity costs associated with not engaging in a strategic CR program, but also considering how implementing such a program will affect other important organizational goals such as public relations, regulatory enforcements, employee morale and motivation, and so forth. In addition, the organization should assess whether the proposed alternative is consistent with the company's core values and culture.[26]

DRIVING INTERNAL CHANGE

Introduction to Internal Change

Implementing a CSR strategy begins internally, and it is essential for corporations to have internal buy-in around their CR plans to ensure their success. Effective change management requires organizational changes, dialogue with and motivation of employees, and realignment of incentives around the new goals. It is crucial for an organization to have sufficient infrastructure in place to support its CR initiatives. As Porter and Kramer put it, "Integrating business and social needs takes more than good intentions and strong leadership. It requires adjustments in organization, reporting relationships, and incentives."[27]

Werre echoes this sentiment, describing corporate vision and values as "conscious, shared and lived within the organization."[28] For this reason, the corporate value and values as they pertain to corporate responsibility must be fully integrated into corporate culture. A mere decree from top management will be insufficient to create the degree of buy-in necessary to ensure internal alignment with the company's CR mission and goals.

How can corporations ensure that sufficient steps have been taken to create a CR strategy that can be incorporated throughout the organization in a meaningful way? One way is to introduce a central CR function, with a senior manager given the role of chief sustainability officer (CSO), or a similar title, put in charge of implementing the CR program. Additionally, the firm should identify an external measurement standard that it can use, under the guidance of the top CR manager, to develop a code of conduct and a basis for benchmarking the firm's CR performance. While installing a top manager such as a CSO to oversee the CR program is a necessary part of the process, it is insufficient without buy-in at other levels of the organization. For this reason, educating employees about CR concepts is crucial as they relate to the firm's business practices and stakeholders. Across all levels of the company, employees must understand the vision, core values, and code of conduct associated with the CR initiative.[29]

To ensure that employees understand the relationship between the corporation's responsibility programs and its core business mission and strategy, Werre explains, CR training must "connect to the values and day-to-day experiences of the employees, making the vision and core values come to life for each employee."[30] This way, employees across different business units will understand how to replicate the CR vision and values in their daily actions, "helping to build a conviction within each employee that he or she can in fact make a difference."[31] Similarly, it is crucial for managers to be trained to incorporate CR criteria into their decision-making process—especially those managers who serve as mentors or coaches to other employees.

A major difficulty in developing a business strategy that considers ESG issues is how to plan for both the short term and long term simultaneously. Writing in the *European Management Journal*, Francisco Szekely and Marianna Knirsch explain that this is challenging because

> the adoption of a sustainable approach requires a much longer timeframe and perspective than the short- to medium-term planning horizon most business leaders use. The market's short-term evaluation is a major impediment to businesses that are trying to align performance with sustainable development. Embarking on sustainable performance entails long-term scenario planning and risk management to secure future business success.[32]

For this reason, corporations must see CR as a strategic issue and that CR programs have the vocal support of senior executives, who should encourage employees throughout the organization to work cross-functionally to develop innovative products and business models to support the company's CR goals.

ESTABLISHING A CHANGE MANAGEMENT ORGANIZATION

Many companies institute formal organizational changes to reflect the increased focus on CR, echoing the Lewin model discussed above. According to Ed Williams, head of corporate social responsibility for British retailer Marks & Spencer, one key component is the establishment of a connection between those making CR decisions and those responsible for traditional business decisions.

As you will see from the case at the close of this chapter, Timberland was wise enough to support its CR plans with infrastructure changes. In 2007, the company had launched the Four Pillars program, a reorganization of its formerly disparate corporate social responsibility activities. Despite the lack of a formal structure for organizing its CR initiatives, Timberland had long taken a proactive approach to social and environmental responsibility. While Global Exchange's activism compelled Nike to launch a much-needed supply chain compliance department in 1996 and corporate responsibility department in 1998, Timberland had launched a supplier Code of Conduct in 1994 and instituted several programs and NGO collaborations to address social injustices. By 2009, roughly 15% of public companies (including Timberland) had a CSR committee on their board of directors, with Timberland's early CR actions putting them ahead of the curve. Gordon Peterson, formerly the head of CSR at Timberland, described the genesis of Timberland's new approach to CSR:

> How do you prioritize when CSR's in three different departments? You're not operating together in an integrated way. Now it's completely different—you have everyone together physically, but also in terms of establishing and executing priorities. You can put money against the most important activity. . . . This is what made sense for us to better utilize the resources we have and at the same time make a statement about where we wanted to go as a company.[33]

Peterson's words illustrate the necessity of having a cohesive CR strategy that relates closely to core business goals.

Starbucks is another corporation that made organizational changes to support CR strategy, with the establishment of a central CSR function. The purpose of the company's CSR department, according to its senior vice president of corporate social responsibility, was twofold. First, it communicated across departments to ensure that social and environmental concerns were being considered during decision-making processes at different business units. Second, Starbucks' CSR function helped the company ensure that it followed through on promises, holding employees across departments responsible for fulfilling CR goals.[34]

Over the past decades, it has become increasingly common for corporations, particularly multinationals, to establish dedicated CR departments inside their organizations. But as discussed in Chapter 2, the CR function can be structured in different ways, and some companies may assign CR issues to their public relations or corporate communications departments, or spread the duties associated with CR across different business units instead of having a single CR department. And as we have discussed earlier in this book, as CR matures as a business function, more and more corporations are beginning to eliminate the concept of CR as a separate area of the company, instead choosing to integrate CR goals and strategies into all areas of business.

GAINING THE SUPPORT OF THE TOP MANAGEMENT TEAM

As discussed earlier in this chapter, a necessary component for the successful implementation of a strategic corporate responsibility program is buy-in from top managers who can inspire those below them in the organization to commit to the CR vision and values. One way to recruit top executives to the cause is by holding a team meeting focusing on values, at which several key topics can be discussed: (1) the personal values of the managers in attendance, (2) how these personal values compare with the current organization culture (including how things are done in the boardroom), (3) whether the current culture is sufficient to ensure that the organization functions effectively in the context of its current and future surroundings, and (4) how bringing top managers' personal values into the organization could benefit the company's future.[35]

For CR to be truly integrated throughout an organization, there must be cultural change driven by top management and others who have the ability to spread CR principles throughout the company. Beyond those already in top managerial positions, Lindgreen et al. emphasize the role of "high potentials," which they define as individuals within an organization "who have been selected for the fast track into senior management."[36] High-potentials make excellent ambassadors for the company's CR goals and values for several key reasons. First, they tend to be gifted in both persuasion and vigilance, both of which enable them to serve as champions for an issue and be catalysts for organizational change.[37] Second, high-potentials possess strong personal and business competencies, such as self-confidence and awareness, ambition, clear objectives, dedication and motivation, communication and social skills, leadership, analytic and problem-solving skills, teamwork and team building, creativity and flexibility, the ability to organize and manage, independence and autonomy, and prioritization of improvement and innovation.[38]

Successful CR implementation must involve not only recruiting top management as champions of the company's CR goals, but also incentivizing leaders at all levels of the organization who encourage others to become more CR-minded.[39]

ESTABLISHING ORGANIZATIONAL MOMENTUM

Still, recruiting managers and future managers to drive others toward more sustainable practices is only a first step. There are many barriers to the implementation of a strategic CR program that is integrated throughout all levels and functions of an organization. Some commonly cited obstacles are as follows:[40]

- Threats to stability
- Fear of change
- Belief that CR is an inappropriate usage of corporate resources
- Concern that a focus on CR will cause the company to lose sight of core business values

These issues highlight why it is especially important for corporations to introduce CR initiatives that align with corporate goals and strategies: "so that taking CSR considerations into account becomes as natural as taking customer perspectives into account."[41]

Returning to the Chiquita example from earlier in the chapter, Chiquita was able to unite its employees toward CR goals through the establishment of four core values that would guide its CR efforts going forward.[42] The corporation ensured that these core values reflected its employees' individual beliefs and goals by incorporating the views of nearly 1,000 employees at all levels of the organization. Top management spent a year discussing the values before publishing the final list. The next challenge was to determine how to ensure that the core values stayed in the forefront of employees' minds. Chiquita accomplished this by distributing the list of values on wallet-sized cards and by hanging up posters with the values at the main entrance of each facility.[43]

The process by which Chiquita established and publicized its core values is an excellent example of how corporations can establish internal support for CR programs before communicating their missions and goals to outside stakeholders such as consumers and investors. Internal marketing programs, such as the poster and wallet card campaign used at Chiquita, are a crucial investment of CR dollars and time because they educate employees throughout the organization about the goals and impact of CR efforts.[44]

To support internal marketing programs, it is important for human resources control systems to be reconfigured in such a way that they reinforce the messaging around CR within a corporation. According to Lindgreen, internal buy-in is also a means of protecting an organization: "By embedding CSR into policies and everyday business practices, the firm reduces the potential that CSR comes decoupled from decision making when the organization confronts economic challenges."[45]

REINFORCING THROUGH INCENTIVES

Once the CR vision and values have been communicated throughout an organization, there needs to be sufficient corporate infrastructure in place to ensure that the commitment to executing CR plans does not wane with the initial excitement. One way to ensure sustained commitment to CR is to incentivize managers and other employees to deliver CR results. As Porter and Kramer recommend, "value chain and competitive-context investments in CSR need to be incorporated into the performance measures of managers with P&L responsibility."[46]

Werre, meanwhile, advocates anchoring CR in existing management systems.[47] He gives several examples of how this can be done:

- "Provide regular management information on environmental and social aspects.
- "Incorporate CR criteria in the pay-related objectives of all managers; recognize and reward people creating CR-successes.
- Create a full set of CR-procedures (e.g. conforming to external measurement standards) at each business location."[48]

In addition to benchmarking the progress of CR initiatives against stated objectives, providing routine updates on CR results can help companies continue to motivate employees toward CR goals by perpetuating enthusiasm about CR programs.[49] Meanwhile, creating a reward system that incentivizes employees to contribute suggestions for improving social or environmental impact and evaluates performance partially on adherence to CR principles is a practical way to encourage individuals throughout an organization to think about CR on a daily basis.

PARTNERING WITH EXTERNAL PARTIES

Corporations have a tradition of partnering with external organizations such as NGOs on their corporate responsibility programs as a means of taking advantage of such organizations' knowledge and positive reputations. In this section, we will examine why companies should consider getting outside help with their CR initiatives and goals, and how to do identify appropriate external partners and joint ventures.

Why Should You Worry About External Parties?

Notions of fairness in business are highly subjective and often controversial—expect to be scrutinized and criticized as a company or leader when making efforts to "do the right thing."[50] NGOs, the media, and public opinion can be more forceful than written laws in affecting decision-making.

Since 1990, over 100,000 new citizens' groups have been established worldwide, and small single-issue groups with Internet access have become powerful enough to take on large corporations.[51] As we have seen from previous chapters, this trend prompted companies to create CR programs as a means of proactively managing their relationships within their broader social context. Given the widespread supplier base of multinational apparel and footwear companies (The Gap, for example, had over 10,000 suppliers), footwear companies increasingly pursued a socially responsible supplier base.

How Should You Approach External Partnerships?

When trying to identify appropriate external partners for CR projects, it is essential that corporations realize that socially and environmentally responsible companies are likely targets for PR crises—but also attractive candidates for collaboration.[52] The corporations best equipped to deal with a crisis, should one arise, are those that take a proactive approach to CR partnerships with external organizations such as NGOs that combat social or environmental issues that arise as a by-product of a company's business dealings. Smart companies don't wait for a crisis to collaborate, but instead think strategically about their relationships with NGOs and industry peers. It is important to recognize that collaboration involves some compromise and that building relationships with NGOs takes time and effort.

Partnerships with NGOs are also an opportunity for businesses to learn from NGOs; specifically, they can think more like an NGO by using communication strategically. It is also important to recognize that business is not a zero-sum game—reaching goals may involve collaborating with adversaries or competitors. Think back to the Shell case at the end of Chapter 4—had Shell thought more strategically about the Brent Spar situation, the corporation might have identified an opportunity to work with Greenpeace on its environmental initiatives, instead of being portrayed in the press as a villain.

As we have discussed throughout this book, CR initiatives are most successful when they are in line with core business strategy. Identifying potential collaborators for a joint CR project is no different. Corporations looking to work with outside organizations have an opportunity to leverage the partner organization's knowledge and experience to fill in gaps in their own backgrounds. But to do this effectively, businesses must work with NGOs whose missions and goals relate to their practices. Corporations considering collaborating with an external partner should start by identifying several appropriate possibilities, performing a detailed assessment of each, and then developing an approach in conjunction with the partner organization or organizations it has selected.[53]

While the ideal approach to external partnerships is a proactive one, such partnerships can be useful to corporations even if entered only after a crisis. When lobby groups or NGOs challenge an organization on the social or environmental impact of their business practices, companies can use external partners as allies in improving their public image.[54] For example, when Starbucks came under fire for resource decimation, the company opted to partner with the nonprofit Conservation International to promote water and soil conservation, crop diversification, and chemical fertilizer reduction. Nike, meanwhile, had initially denied claims that it had issues adhering to labor regulations along its supply chain, but ultimately made concessions to human rights activists.[55]

How Should Partnerships Be Structured?

Timberland, which will be discussed in greater depth in the case at the end of this chapter, built its CR program on the foundation of the ad hoc initiatives it had launched previously. Timberland's partnership with City Year, an organization that sent volunteers to areas of need, not only served as an oft-referenced model of public–private partnership, but also laid the foundation for a more formalized program by providing Timberland experience in engaging with diverse stakeholders to pursue a common goal. It also gave Timberland exposure to effective models of community engagement, leading them to launch their own community service programs, including the "Path of Service" program, which enabled all employees to take 40 hours of paid leave per year to perform community service. As one Timberland insider explained, "we simply could not engage purposefully in the community without City Year's guidance and expertise."[56]

Examples of Successful Partnerships

Chiquita's work with the Rainforest Alliance is one example of successful partnership between a corporation and an NGO with a complementary mission. One of the benefits of this collaboration was a shift in Chiquita management's view on the issues the corporation's practices affected.[57] Second, the introduction of third-party audits of farms along Chiquita's supply chain was a major catalyst of changes in the organization's culture—namely, a shift toward greater transparency and openness. Third, the project educated Chiquita on how external standards and verification can benefit a corporation by increasing internal commitment to higher levels of performance.

MEASURING AND REACTING

Why Is Measurement Important?

Measurement is crucial to the success of CR initiatives, as we discussed in Chapter 3. Having a reliable measurement and reporting system is essential to identifying and making necessary improvements to a CR program, as it allows a corporation to keep track of what works well and why, as well as areas in which corporate responsibility programs are coming up short of their stated goals.[58] This allows businesses to develop better strategies and processes for the future by identifying obstacles and ways of overcoming them, while refining their CR goals as new information comes in.

Companies tend to rely on lagging indicators (which reflect changes and confirm long-term changes) when evaluating the effects of their businesses on social and environmental issues, failing to consider leading indicators (which predict or signal future events).[59] While lagging indicators are a useful tool in evaluating outcomes of business practices in terms of their social and environmental impact, neglecting leading indicators limits corporations' ability to track activities in real time. This could result in failure to predict and prevent risk associated with CR issues. Only by using both lagging and leading indicators will companies ensure that they have a complete picture of the relationship between corporate activity and ESG results, through which they can mitigate risk and improve performance.

What and How to Measure

Now that we know why measurement is important in implementing a strategic CR program, the obvious next question is how businesses should decide what to measure and how to track the necessary information. Again, it is crucial to focus on impact rather than mere effort; for example, the number of students receiving degrees through corporate funding is a better indicator of success than the amount of scholarship donations received.[60] According to Szekely:

> A variety of management measures need to be taken and supported by top management, not only the establishment of management systems, but also the introduction of incentives and training on sustainability issues that drive performance on non-financial issues. These measures must also include product and process innovations that improve sustainability performance.[61]

Companies have their choice of a wide variety of approaches to evaluating progress on social and environmental issues. Some means of measuring, tracking, and evaluation this progress are discussed below (see also Figure 10.6).

Figure 10.6 Measuring CR progress

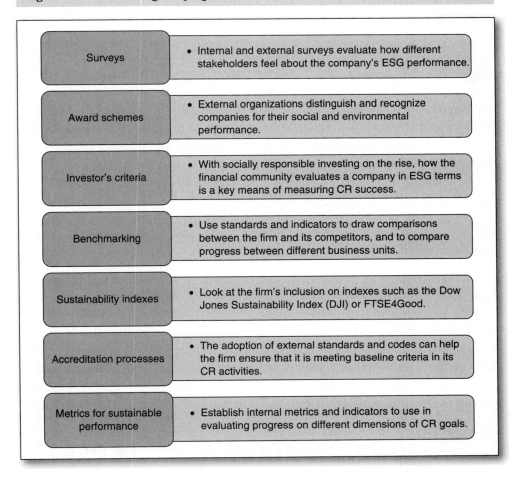

| Surveys | • Internal and external surveys evaluate how different stakeholders feel about the company's ESG performance. |

| Award schemes | • External organizations distinguish and recognize companies for their social and environmental performance. |

| Investor's criteria | • With socially responsible investing on the rise, how the financial community evaluates a company in ESG terms is a key means of measuring CR success. |

| Benchmarking | • Use standards and indicators to draw comparisons between the firm and its competitors, and to compare progress between different business units. |

| Sustainability indexes | • Look at the firm's inclusion on indexes such as the Dow Jones Sustainability Index (DJI) or FTSE4Good. |

| Accreditation processes | • The adoption of external standards and codes can help the firm ensure that it is meeting baseline criteria in its CR activities. |

| Metrics for sustainable performance | • Establish internal metrics and indicators to use in evaluating progress on different dimensions of CR goals. |

Sustainability indicators are another means of measuring and evaluating CR progress. The Global Reporting Initiative, a nonprofit organization promoting economic, environmental, and social sustainability, divides sustainability indicators into three different categories: (1) productivity/efficiency ratios, (2) intensity ratios, and (3) percentages.[62]

Productivity/efficiency ratios relate value to impact.[63] These ratios are often used to measure financial results. Corporations can use productivity/efficiency ratios to measure several different types of social and environmental results. Such ratios help firms evaluate labor productivity (output per employee), resource productivity (how the consumption of a particular resource relates to business results; e.g., sales per unit of energy consumption), process eco-efficiency (how environmental externalities relate to business results; e.g., sales per unit of greenhouse gas emissions), and the functional eco-efficiency of the firm's products or services (e.g., the fuel efficiency of transportation methods used by the corporation).[64]

Intensity ratios measure impact per unit of activity or unit of value. A corporation should aim to see smaller and smaller intensity ratios over time, indicating that performance is improving. Intensity ratios can help a firm measure and track its environmental performance. Some valuable intensity ratios include emission intensity (the amount of CO_2 emissions per unit of electricity generated), waste intensity (the amount of waste per production volume), and resource intensity (for example, energy consumption per activity).

Percentages look at the relationship between two like issues, where the issues are expressed as ratios with the same unit in the numerator and denominator. They are useful for evaluating a variety of different social, environmental, and economic performance indicators, as seen in Table 10.1.

SOCIAL SUSTAINABILITY

Social sustainability metrics look at a variety of important issues not always captured by the metrics above—and some of which can be difficult to quantify in the way that environmental or financial results are. They measure corporate performance on human rights issues, labor issues, supplier relationships, community initiatives, and corporate philanthropy.[65] Many of these concerns were discussed in depth in Chapter 4. Human rights issues have become an increasingly important component of CR with the rise of globalization, as have labor issues—many major

Table 10.1 Evaluating performance indicators

Percentage type	Example
Input/output ratios	Process yields
Losses	Unusable output per material input
Recycling percentages	Percentage of total waste that is recycled
Fractions	Percentage of renewable energy
Quotas	Women in upper management as a percentage of total top managers
Financial performance ratios	Return on equity

Source: Adapted from Szekely, F., & Knirsch, M. (2005). "Responsible leadership and corporate social responsibility: Metrics for sustainable performance." *European Management Journal, 23*(6), 628–647.

corporations including Nike (in the 1990s) and Apple (more recently) have come under intense scrutiny for human rights violations along their supply chains.

According to Szekely, successful social sustainability metrics must fulfill the following criteria:

- Used throughout the company
- Measured frequently, with adjustments made as necessary
- Performance tracked based on starting points
- Audited externally
- Capable of being benchmarked internally and externally
- User-friendly and meaningful
- Balanced cost/benefits in measuring/reporting/achieving results

As one CSR manager explained:

Awareness is a step-by-step process that takes time, and we are not done yet. I think that everybody at Bank 1 knows that we are involved in CSR, that about 25% of the employees understand what our choices are in CSR, but a large group does not yet know. People feel a certain involvement with the issues in society that they see in the media and think what it means for them in work life.[66]

CR implementation is a continuous, iterative process; as a result, Lindgreen states, "critical markers may provide a good means to assess both the extent of change in the culture and the evolution of the organization as a whole."[67]

CONCLUSION

Implementing a corporate responsibility program can be nearly as challenging as designing the program in the first place. To ensure that CR initiatives are aligned with overall corporate strategy, corporations must clearly define their CR strategy, determine how best to drive internal change, identify appropriate external partners, and measure and react to the results of CR activities, making changes as necessary.

NOTES

1. Porter, M., & Kramer, M. (2006, December). "Strategy and society: The link between competitive advantage and corporate social responsibility." *Harvard Business Review.* Retrieved from https://hbr.org/2006/12/strategy-and-society-the-link-between-competitive-advantage-and-corporate-social-responsibility

2. Ibid.

3. Milliman, J., Ferguson, J., & Sylvester, K. (2008). "Implementation of Michael Porter's strategic corporate social responsibility model." *Journal of Global Business Issues, Conference Edition.*

4. Ibid.

5. Werre, M. (2003, May). "Implementing corporate responsibility: The Chiquita case." *Journal of Business Ethics, 44*(2/3), 247–260.

6. Maon, F., Lindgreen, A., & Swaen, V. (2008, September). "Designing and implementing corporate social responsibility: An integrative framework grounded in theory and practice." *Journal of Business Ethics, 87,* 71–89.

7. Ibid.

8. Lindgreen, A., Swaen, V., Harness, D., & Hoffmann, M. (2011, February). "The role of 'high potentials' in integrating and implementing corporate social responsibility." *Journal of Business Ethics, 99,* 73–91.

9. Werre, "Implementing corporate responsibility."

10. Milliman et al., "Implementation of Michael Porter's strategic corporate social responsibility model."

11. Werre, "Implementing corporate responsibility."

12. Ibid.

13. Maon et al., "Designing and implementing corporate social responsibility."

14. Ibid.

15. Argenti, P. A. "The Timberland company: Managing a socially responsible supply chain." (See the end of this chapter.)

16. Werre, "Implementing corporate responsibility."

17. Milliman et al., "Implementation of Michael Porter's strategic corporate social responsibility model."

18. Porter & Kramer, "Strategy and society."

19. Ibid.

20. Ibid.

21. Milliman et al., "Implementation of Michael Porter's strategic corporate social responsibility model."

22. Werre, "Implementing corporate responsibility."

23. Ibid.

24. Maon et al., "Designing and implementing corporate social responsibility."

25. Porter & Kramer, "Strategy and society."

26. Milliman et al., "Implementation of Michael Porter's strategic corporate social responsibility model."

27. Porter & Kramer, "Strategy and society."

28. Werre, "Implementing corporate responsibility."

29. Ibid.

30. Ibid.

31. Ibid.

32. Szekely, F., & Knirsch, M. (2005). "Responsible leadership and corporate social responsibility: Metrics for sustainable performance." *European Management Journal, 23*(6), 628–647.

33. Personal interview.

34. Liu, S., & Liu, L. (2009). "Implementing corporate external social responsibility strategies through organizational design and operation." *Journal of International Business Ethics, 2,* 79–83,119.

35. Werre, "Implementing corporate responsibility."

36. Lindgreen et al., "The role of 'high potentials' in integrating and implementing corporate social responsibility."

37. Ibid.

38. Ibid.

39. Ibid.

40. Maon et al., "Designing and implementing corporate social responsibility."

41. Ibid.

42. Werre, "Implementing corporate responsibility."

43. Ibid.

44. Maon et al., "Designing and implementing corporate social responsibility."

45. Lindgreen et al., "The role of 'high potentials' in integrating and implementing corporate social responsibility."

46. Porter & Kramer, "Strategy and society."

47. Werre, "Implementing corporate responsibility."

48. Ibid.

49. Maon et al., "Designing and implementing corporate social responsibility."

50. Argenti. P. "CR Class 9 Wrap 2012.pptx." Unpublished PowerPoint.

51. Argenti, "The Timberland Company."

52. Argenti, P. (2004, November 1). "Collaborating with activists: How Starbucks works with NGOs." California Management Review.

53. Milliman et al., "Implementation of Michael Porter's strategic corporate social responsibility model."

54. Liu & Liu, "Implementing corporate social responsibility strategies through organizational design and operation."

55. Ibid.

56. Argenti, "The Timberland Company."

57. Werre, "Implementing corporate responsibility."

58. Maon et al., "Designing and implementing corporate social responsibility."

59. Szekely & Knirsch, "Responsible leadership and corporate social responsibility."

60. Milliman et al., "Implementation of Michael Porter's strategic corporate social responsibility model."

61. Szekely & Knirsch, "Responsible leadership and corporate social responsibility."

62. Global Reporting Initiative, http://www.globalreporting.org (accessed August 15, 2014).

63. Szekely & Knirsch, "Responsible leadership and corporate social responsibility."

64. Ibid.

65. Ibid.

66. Lindgreen et al., "The role of 'high potentials' in integrating and implementing corporate social responsibility."

67. Ibid.

THE TIMBERLAND COMPANY: MANAGING A SOCIALLY RESPONSIBLE SUPPLY CHAIN

At Timberland we act on the belief that doing well and doing good are not separate activities. In fact, our commitment to social justice is a part of how we can earn our living. It's how we provide distinction for our customers. It's how we recruit top talent. Finally, it's how we create real, sustainable change in our communities and choose to compete in the world.[1]

Timberland CEO Jeffrey Swartz was discussing the importance of maintaining safe working conditions throughout the company's supply chain via teleconference with a diverse set of stakeholders, much as he might discuss financial performance. In 2007, the company had launched the Four Pillars program, a reorganization of what were disparate corporate social responsibility (CSR) activities at the time. The program was embraced internally as a manifestation of the value the company placed on social responsibility and received accolades in the industry and the media. The Workplaces pillar would be home to Timberland's ambitious activities to provide not only a safe workplace for the manufacturers of their shoes, but also opportunities for those workers to thrive "beyond factory walls."

But in 2009, a recession and an unusually rainy summer brought storm clouds over Timberland's Stratham, New Hampshire, headquarters. Jeff Swartz, who had received his MBA from Dartmouth's Tuck School of Business before becoming Timberland's director of international sales in 1986, its chief operating officer in 1991, and its chief executive officer in 1998, faced a dilemma. Sales were down 13% over the past two years. The board of directors was anxious to see Timberland's investment—both financial and in terms of brand identity and employee focus—in its new CSR program, and in its Workplaces pillar specifically, pay off. However, Swartz could not demonstrate that there was a positive financial return on their CSR investment. More fundamentally, it seemed that the consumer just didn't care how industry-leading Timberland's treatment of its global workforce was.

As Jeff Swartz reviewed a pared-down CSR budget for the upcoming year, he pondered, how could he reconcile his long-term goal to improve the lives of workers worldwide with the short-term realities of budget constraints, financial performance, and a consumer base unresponsive to Timberland's Workplaces efforts? Where were the limits of Timberland's responsibilities to the global worker? Most importantly, Swartz asked himself, how could upholding this responsibility "help us sell more

Source: This case was prepared by Dan Galemba, T'09, under the supervision of Professor Paul A. Argenti, with sponsorship from the Allwin Initiative for Corporate Citizenship and the cooperation of The Timberland Company. © 2009 Trustees of Dartmouth College. All rights reserved. For permission to reprint, contact the Tuck School of Business at 603-646-3176.

boots"? Finding the answer was not simply the right thing to do for the over 250,000 workers worldwide manufacturing Timberland products; it could unlock a tremendous business opportunity.

TIMBERLAND HISTORY

Despite Timberland's changes over time, its values of humanity, humility, integrity, and excellence had remained a point of unwavering consistency since the company's humble beginnings as the Abington Show Company in 1952. Social responsibility had long played a prominent if not explicit role in company activities. Indeed, the integration of business and social responsibility—or, as Jeff Swartz described it, "commerce and justice"—was not simply an aspect of the company's mission but an integrated component of its strategy. According to Timberland, "our mission is to equip people to make a difference in their world. We do this by creating outstanding products and by trying to make a difference in the communities where we live and work."

While outdoors enthusiasts were Timberland's core customers, Timberland was active in a variety of markets. And as the company gained increasing recognition for quality and became the brand of the American outdoors, it generated international demand.

Consequently, the diversified apparel and footwear company went global in 1980. By 2009, Timberland was deriving close to 52% of its sales internationally. By the end of the year, the company was employing 5,400 people, in roughly 200 stores in the U.S., Europe, and Asia, as well as in multiple domestic and international distribution centers, and in a manufacturing facility in the Dominican Republic.

The retailer had an extensive supply chain that began with the sourcing of raw materials like cotton and leather. Intermediate suppliers (e.g., leather tanneries) would use these raw materials to produce leather and fabric, which they then sold to manufacturing facilities. These facilities (one of which was owned by Timberland) produced the final product, which was sent to Timberland-owned distribution facilities before being shipped out to Timberland-owned or other retail or wholesale outlets. By 2009, Timberland was sourcing supplies from over 300 suppliers in 38 countries; about 250,000 workers manufactured Timberland products throughout this supply.[2]

THE RISE OF CSR IN THE FOOTWEAR INDUSTRY

With the dawn of the new millennium and widely publicized accounting scandals at companies like Enron and WorldCom, CSR gained an increasing level of visibility. In the footwear industry specifically, the nongovernmental organization (NGO) Global Exchange made social responsibility a top-of-mind concern in the 1990s with its campaign against Nike's use of sweatshop labor. The footwear industry responded by collaborating with

NGOs and other brands to create monitoring groups like the Fair Labor Association (FLA) in attempts to identify and redress human rights violations abroad.[3]

Since 1990, over 100,000 new citizens' groups have been established worldwide, and small single-issue groups with Internet access could become powerful enough to take on large corporations.[4] This trend prompted companies to create CSR programs to proactively manage their relationships within their broader social context. Given the widespread supplier base of multinational apparel and footwear companies (The Gap, for example, had over 10,000 suppliers[5]), footwear companies became increasingly sensitive to managing as socially responsible a supplier base as possible.

Global Exchange's activism compelled Nike to take great strides in social responsibility—they launched a supply chain compliance department in 1996 and a corporate responsibility department in 1998. Timberland launched a supplier Code of Conduct in 1994 and instituted several programs and NGO collaborations to address social injustices. By 2009, roughly 15% of public companies (including Timberland) had a CSR committee on their board of directors.[6]

TIMBERLAND'S CORPORATE SOCIAL RESPONSIBILITY PROGRAM PRE-2007

While social responsibility has long been an implicit tenet of Timberland's mission, Timberland did not have an official CSR department prior to 2007. Instead, it had an assortment of initiatives designed to accomplish different social goals under different management. Despite this apparent lack of organization, organizations ranging from nonprofits to popular magazines consistently recognized Timberland as being at the forefront of social responsibility.[7]

Having grown up in a Timberland family with a belief system rooted in having a positive impact on the community, Jeff Swartz wanted Timberland to be a force for good. In 1989, Alan Khazei and Michael Brown approached him to request 50 pairs of boots. Khazei and Brown were co-founders of an upstart nonprofit called City Year, which aimed to create a "powerful national youth corps as a sustainable force for community change."[8] Swartz's decision to support City Year was ultimately premised on the similarities he perceived in the values of the two organizations. He saw City Year as the vehicle through which his own ambition to "save lives" could come to fruition. According to Gordon Peterson, director of CSR, when Swartz went on a service project with City Year to learn more about the organization, it was "a truly transformational day for him. And he brought that back to our company."[9]

Twenty years later, Timberland was one of nine City Year National Leadership Sponsor corporations; the company had outfitted all 1,500 City Year staff and corps members; and Jeff Swartz had served as chair of City Year's national board of trustees from 1994 to 2002.[10] Timberland even housed the headquarters of City Year New Hampshire within its corporate headquarters. As ad hoc as the City Year relationship began, it not only served as an oft-referenced model of public–private partnership,[11] but also laid the foundation for a more formalized program by providing Timberland experience in engaging with diverse stakeholders pursuing a common goal. It also gave Timberland exposure to effective models of community engagement, leading them to launch their own community service programs, including the "Path of Service" program, which enabled all employees to take 40 hours of paid leave per year to perform community service. According to Swartz, "we simply could not engage purposefully in the community without City Year's guidance and expertise."[12]

Timberland's foray into CSR did not stop with City Year. Timberland launched its first supplier Code of Conduct in 1994 (see Exhibit 10.1), representing its long-held belief in the importance of managing workplace safety and providing the guidelines for supplier audits, whereby auditors would visit a factory to monitor compliance with the Code. In 2003, Timberland also became a member of Social Accountability International (SAI), which promotes human rights globally by using and verifying compliance with an ethical sourcing standard. In 2005, Timberland switched to a consultative assessment program to assist supplier management in creating sustainable workplace change (discussed below).

Meanwhile, recognizing the footwear value chain's impact on the environment, Timberland joined Business for Innovative Climate and Energy Policy, an association of companies eager to limit business's impact on the environment. Timberland also was a founding member of the Leather Working Group (LWG), whose mission was "to develop and maintain a protocol that assesses the compliance and environmental performance of tanners and promotes sustainable and appropriate environmental business practices within the footwear leather industry."[13] Leather had the biggest environmental impact of any aspect of Timberland's value chain (70% of emissions in Timberland's value chain came from raw materials, and the biggest contributor was leather). By 2009, the LWG involved nine brands, including competitors like Adidas, Nike, New Balance, North Face, and Wolverine, and many more tanners and suppliers. Timberland collaborated with these companies to improve measurement and management of emissions resulting from manufacturing leather.

Timberland also took advantage of the natural resources present at its large facilities. By 2002, its distribution center in Holland was powered entirely by wind, and in 2006, the company had built one of California's largest solar arrays at its Ontario distribution center. Timberland also took steps to make its products more environmentally friendly, such as sourcing for organic cotton in 2000 and switching to water-based adhesives, which are far less damaging to the environment than traditional glues, in 2002. Timberland also made its face to the world—its retail stores—reflect its values by using recycled materials, glass, and low-electricity lighting, thus solidifying social responsibility as a core component of the brand image.

Timberland thus had a rich history of social responsibility, but its activities were diverse and managed in correspondingly different areas of the organization. While it was clear that Timberland was doing good, it was not clear that its CSR initiatives were being as effectively managed as possible, and Timberland might have been leaving opportunities to "make a difference in the communities where we live and work" on the table.

CSR EVOLVED: TIMBERLAND'S FOUR PILLARS PROGRAM

In 2007, Timberland set about creating a unified program that would encompass its broad array of social endeavors and more strategically integrate these activities with corporate strategy. Gordon Peterson described the genesis of Timberland's new approach to CSR:

> How do you prioritize when CSR's in three different departments? You're not operating together in an integrated way. Now it's completely different—you have everyone together physically, but also in terms of establishing and executing priorities. You can put money against the most important activity. . . . This is what made sense for us to better utilize the resources we have and at the same time make a statement about where we wanted to go as a company.

Timberland reorganized its existing CSR programs into one integrated CSR department, led by Peterson, a 20-year veteran of Timberland who was previously director of Code of Conduct. Peterson reported directly to the executive committee, giving the CSR department an opportunity to both observe and influence corporate strategy. Reporting to Peterson were the managers of Timberland's "Four Pillars," each of which encompassed a largely discrete aspect of Timberland's social involvement. In addition, Beth Holzman was hired with responsibilities over reporting, stakeholder engagement, and execution of CSR strategy.

The Four Pillars program was an opportunity to move CSR forward both in terms of visibility—within and outside the organization—and activism. Timberland's Four Pillars, and their taglines as of 2009, were:[14]

- *Service*: Community greening
- *Energy*: Become carbon neutral by 2010
- *Product*: Design recyclable products
- *Workplaces*: Fair, safe, and nondiscriminatory workplaces

Timberland introduced detailed metrics for each pillar, as well as a dashboard summarizing performance on the 15 most important metrics (Exhibit 10.2), to assess progress and next steps. Timberland's annual CSR expenditures dropped in half from 2005 to 2009, due partly to cost-cutting across the business, but primarily due to elimination of redundancy.

Timberland had published annual CSR reports since 2000, long before most of its competitors; its 2007 report won an award for "Best Sustainability Reporting."[15] However, no sooner had the company won the award than Timberland announced it would begin publishing quarterly reports, recognizing that the CSR environment, and the corresponding metrics, were constantly shifting. The reports would be released online and followed by a stakeholder call led by Jeff Swartz, mirroring Timberland's financial reporting schedule and emphasizing the central role CSR played at the company.[16] In 2009, Timberland further revamped its reporting by shortening the CSR report and adding pillar-specific "Dig Deeper" papers that highlighted detailed success stories and progress left to attain.

Timberland also pursued a Web 2.0 platform, partnering with JustMeans, a CSR consultancy focused on stakeholder engagement.[17] Timberland created its own online community called Earthkeepers™, co-branded with a new line of environmentally friendly footwear, aimed at recruiting 1 million people to pledge to lessen their impact on the earth. The Earthkeeper community was even linked to the online social networking tool Facebook, as Timberland attempted to gain more visibility for its CSR initiatives among a young, activist-oriented population. One Earthbook/Facebook initiative was called "Virtual Forest": by installing a Facebook "app" a user could "plant a virtual tree and [give] seeds to friends." When the virtual tree grew, Timberland would plant a real tree in a deforested part of the world.[18]

Perhaps most notably, the Four Pillars made CSR at Timberland more visible and structured and thus enhanced CSR's role in driving action. With a more integrated CSR program, Timberland could better deploy CSR, as Michael Porter suggested, as "a source of opportunity, innovation, and competitive advantage," not simply as "a cost, a constraint, or a charitable deed" required by the market.[19] Skeptics noted that "Jeff can scream from the woods and say that this is actually helping his numbers, but the fact is we don't have those metrics yet."[20] Still, with few companies taking decisive action in CSR, Swartz took a stand and increased his commitment: "When you hear 'after you, after you,' and nobody moves, eventually you've got to close your eyes and jump."[21]

Pillar 1: Service

Timberland had a long history of community involvement; the Path of Service program had existed since shortly after the City Year relationship began, and an annual service day called Serv-a-palooza, in which thousands of Timberland employees and suppliers worldwide used working hours for as many as 170 community service projects, had been in place since 1997.[22] However, Timberland lacked the tracking mechanisms to ensure employee accountability for quantity and quality of service events. Timberland therefore introduced the Global Stewards program in 2006. Being a Global Steward was a highly coveted opportunity; the 28 international Stewards were responsible for driving employee engagement in the Path of Service program and to communicate Timberland's CSR messages more broadly to its offices.

The Four Pillars program added new opportunities for employees who were passionate about service but unable to become Stewards. Timberland even rolled out its culture of service to its value chain, launching the Community Stewards program in 2009 to help distributors and suppliers organize their own service activities. In 2008, Timberland created the GREEN standard, a rigorous framework for assessing the value of service opportunities to ensure that the company's "commitment to excellence and environmental sustainability are infused in the review, planning, and implementation of every project."[23] Timberland's commitment to engage employees in service was credited with increasing retention[24] and for consistently putting Timberland in *Forbes* magazine's "Top 100 Companies to Work For."[25]

Pillar 2: Energy

The Energy pillar unified many existing Timberland activities under a consistent strategy. The top priorities of the Energy pillar were (1) reducing emissions, (2) expanding use of renewable energy, and (3) purchasing carbon offsets. Achieving carbon neutrality by 2010 was a "way station" of sorts as the company pursued these goals.

Timberland partnered with third-party reporting agencies specializing in tracking carbon emissions, a notoriously complicated and imperfect process. The company used the World Resources Institute protocol for GHG emission measurement, partnered with Clean Air–Cool Planet and Forum for the Future for third-party verification, and reported emissions with the Climate Registry to make the results public.[26] Timberland set a goal of reducing company emissions 50% by 2010 over a 2006 baseline; it would make up the difference by purchasing carbon offsets to achieve carbon neutrality. The company set targets for renewable energy (60% of total energy usage by 2015) and energy reduction by facility and updated its progress every quarter.

In addition to encouraging employees to carpool, teleconference instead of travel, and work from home, Timberland offered a $3,000 credit for employees to buy fuel-efficient vehicles. By 2009, its Ontario, California, solar array provided 60% of the energy requirements of the facility, even though it might take 20 years to show a positive return,[27] and 100% of energy needs at Timberland's distribution center in the Netherlands came from wind power. In 2009, Timberland painted the roof of its headquarters white, which would cut energy costs by an estimated 20%.[28] Carbon offsets were used to finance renewable energy projects where Timberland had facilities but renewable energy was not offered by local utilities (wind energy in Colorado and hydroelectricity in Kentucky), reflecting its goal of using offsets only when doing so would invest in potential renewable energy sources for the company.[29] Timberland even supported the adoption of hydroelectric power when it became available in the heart of Kentucky coal country, despite a 25% increase in electricity costs.[30] In 2008, Timberland's retail stores in Salem, New Hampshire, and Peabody, Massachusetts, received LEED Silver and Gold awards, respectively, for environmentally friendly design; in fact, Timberland was the first company to receive awards under the LEED retail certification.[31] Carbon emissions in these stores declined 30%.[32]

Finally, while Timberland fell far short of its goal of 22% renewable energy usage for 2008, achieving only 7% largely due to lack of progress in the Dominican Republic,[33] it invested in carbon offsets and other renewable energy research in the Dominican Republic. In 2005, Timberland built a wind turbine at the facility as a demonstration project. As of mid-2009, Timberland had reduced its carbon emissions by 27% since 2006 and was on track to achieve its goal of carbon neutrality by 2010.

Importantly, Timberland's carbon neutrality goal applied only to company-controlled facilities and activities, accounting for only 4% of the total carbon emissions from its supply chain.[34] The other 96% was primarily incurred in developing countries where alternative sources of energy were limited, and even within the 4% of the supply chain controlled by Timberland, the Dominican Republic represented the biggest challenge in achieving the goals the company had set.[35] Timberland used the Green Index (described below) to communicate the environmental impact of its products; tracked environmental performance of suppliers as part of its Code of Conduct; and joined the Clean Cargo Working Group to measure logistics emissions against industry standards.[36] However, no industry standard or third-party organization existed to measure or verify total supply chain emissions. While Timberland attempted to measure direct emissions from its suppliers, 70% of supply chain emissions came from raw materials sourcing, even further removed from Timberland's control. Because of these complications, Timberland had no set goal for emissions reductions elsewhere in the supply chain.

Pillar 3: Product

Timberland's goals for the Product pillar were to design environmental harms out of products and empower the consumer to make eco-friendly purchasing decisions. The Earthkeeper™ line of shoes, co-branded with Timberland's stakeholder engagement platform, testified to these goals. Earthkeepers were "cradle-to-cradle" products—they were designed to be recycled into new footwear. Earthkeeper shoes used 30% recycled rubber, biodegradable lining, organically tanned leather, and hemp. The line was introduced in 2007, and increased from 1.5% to 5% of Timberland's footwear volume between year-end 2008 and July 2009.[37] In late 2009, Timberland introduced Earthkeepers 2.0, with 15% less environmental impact than the original Earthkeepers. This was due in part to an exclusive partnership with Green Rubber to make outsoles with 42% recycled tire rubber[38] and designing the shoes to be more recyclable. Timberland planned to take the concept of easy disassembly for recycling to its other shoes in 2010.[39] Timberland had sourced organic cotton since 2000 (in 2009, it accounted for 26% of cotton usage); used recycled PET plastic (e.g., from drink bottles) for shoe lining; and used 100% post-consumer cardboard and soy-based inks for packaging. Timberland was also replacing environmentally hazardous PVC (polyvinyl chloride)–based adhesives with water-based adhesives (WBAs).[40]

Leather consumed more resources than any other input in a Timberland shoe. In 2005, four years before Greenpeace called broader attention to the issue, Timberland banded with Nike and the UK-based BLC Leather Technology Center to create the LWG. The LWG aimed to improve tannery management and to motivate multinational brands to further this process by working only with tanneries that performed up to set environmental standards. Accordingly, the LWG developed a tannery rating system, and the British Leather Center performed audits on the LWG's behalf. This rating system became an industry-wide standard; with common metrics, performance could be assessed and improved. By 2010, Timberland intended to source all its leather from tanneries with at least a Silver rating. Meanwhile, Beth Holzman acknowledged, "we've got to get leather out of there" to make a significant impact in supply chain emissions. Earthkeepers were already being designed with less leather.

In 2006, Timberland first experimented with placing "nutrition labels" on its footwear boxes, which listed the "environmental statistics" of the company. Realizing that most consumers never looked at the box when making a purchase decision, Timberland revamped the label and in 2007 launched the "Green Index." The Green Index label was stuck directly to a shoe and scored an individual shoe's environmental impact on a scale of 1 to 10 on three dimensions: climate impact, chemical use, and resource consumption. The total score was an average of these three scores. As of mid-2009, only 5% of Timberland's footwear offerings were scored—the process was labor intensive and required collecting data that most suppliers did not track—but Timberland strove to have all its footwear scored by 2011.[41] Additionally, by helping suppliers track these metrics, Timberland gathered data to design shoes with reduced environmental impact before they went to production.[42]

Jeff Swartz hoped that "like-minded companies will join us in developing an industry-wide rating system for comparing the environmental impacts of our design choices";[43] even with 100% of their footwear scored, Timberland might not benefit if consumers could not compare the impact of a Timberland shoe to a competitor's shoe. Timberland invested in measurement systems at the supplier level that were integrated with standard business processes and in further rolling out the Green Index in the hope that, if and when such a label was expected by the consumer, the company would be ahead of the competition. For this goal to be viable, the entire industry would have to adopt a standard set of metrics that consumers understood; thus, Timberland worked with the Outdoor Industry Association to convene 40 footwear brands to establish these metrics. Jeff Swartz described his commitment to making Timberland products resonate with consumers and generate momentum for broader change:

If 30 million consumers say "I get it" then we win because then there'll be demand, there'll be pressure on the [footwear industry] ecosystem. . . . If someone picks up a Timberland boot and it says 5% of the energy used to make it is renewable, that seems like a very low number. But in this case 5% only matters in relative terms. What if it's 0%? Consumers need to say, "if they can do 5%, why can't you do 5%?" And then innovation will follow, and all the pressure won't just be coming from us.

Pillar 4: Workplaces

While Timberland was not the first company to launch a "code of conduct" for its global supplier network, it was ahead of the industry in engaging with suppliers to improve working conditions. Timberland's Code of Conduct was launched in 1994 and outlined contractual obligations of suppliers; for example, Timberland refused to use a supplier that had employees under age 16 or that worked employees over 60 hours a week. The original Code focused on human rights and was enforced by auditors who would visit a facility on average once a year. Suppliers in violation were given probationary periods to improve their conditions and would be audited more frequently. Timberland's Code of Conduct also enabled the company to proactively get ahead of industry backlash for employment conditions in the developing world.

However, concerned that audits did little to fundamentally change supplier behavior, in 2005 Timberland shifted from an "audit" to an "assessment" system. Under the new system, as opposed to "compliance police" checking off factory conditions over half a day, an assessor spent two to five days collaborating with factory management to instill and monitor management systems to ensure ongoing enforcement of the Code of Conduct. Timberland added an "Environment" section to the Code, and a new supplier scorecard tracked progress on eight social criteria (immediate actions, leading practices, supplier commitment, risk profile, progress profile, systems profile, worker needs assessment, and collaboration profile) and seven environmental metrics (systems, compliance, water, use of water-based adhesives, chemicals, energy, and waste). Assessor manuals detailed the scoring system to ensure standardization.

An assessment started with 70 points; points were added or subtracted based on performance on the eight social metrics. Factories with scores below 60 were "High Priority"; assessors were given latitude in devoting resources to boost working conditions. Factories scoring below 50 were "high risk" and were required to undergo more frequent assessments. By 2008, Timberland had reduced its High Priority suppliers to 38% of the supplier base from 50% in 2006. Scores of 60 to 80 were "Acceptable"; no immediate action was required but improvement was still warranted. Scores above 80, with minimum required scores on each of the eight metrics, qualified a supplier for "Partner" status. Sustained partnership status could qualify a supplier as a Partner of

Excellence. Partners of Excellence, 10% of Timberland's supplier base in 2008, were subject to less frequent assessments. Timberland instituted the Environmental component of the Code and assessment to identify ways to reduce suppliers' environmental impact, but given the inability of many suppliers to measure environmental performance and Timberland's historic focus on working conditions, only the Social aspect was adjudicated.

Assessors built trust with workers to encourage them to offer their own ideas for improving factory conditions. Among the tactics employed to encourage two-way dialogue were:[44]

- *Opening and closing meetings:* Assessors convened meetings announcing the reason for their visit and ensuring mutual understanding, and invited all employees, not just management.
- *Group discussions:* Assessors used participatory discussions to enhance workers' awareness and confidence and empower them to speak up and take action.
- *Training sessions:* Assessors trained workers about the Code of Conduct, their rights under it, and their responsibility in identifying, addressing, and seeking resolution.
- *Community engagement:* Assessors used Timberland's service toolkit to assist factories in organizing service events and engage workers in local service projects.

Timberland partnered with Verité, a nonprofit organization that monitors and addresses labor abuses worldwide, to establish pilot Worker Code Committees in China whereby workers conducted their own assessments and could therefore identify and resolve issues when assessors were not present. Timberland encouraged engagement beyond assessments by requiring factories to have new-hire training sessions on the Code of Conduct and performing annual employee surveys.

Finally, Timberland broached the subject of "sustainable living wage," a wage that enables a worker to meet his or her basic requirements in his or her local context. This wage was typically far higher than the legally mandated minimum wage in the countries in which Timberland's suppliers did business. A major problem with the sustainable living wage, however, was that in many communities, workers had no access to basic necessities regardless of pay. Timberland created its own program, Sustainable Living Environments, to address this issue. Through working with local NGOs, studying local social problems, and listening to the needs of factory workers, Timberland attempted to identify basic needs in a community and empower workers to devise the means to resolve them. In 2008, Timberland added questions focusing on Sustainable Living Environments to the assessment process. This gave the company insight into community needs and provided the basis for discussions about potential projects. By mid-2009, Timberland had completed or was undergoing four Sustainable Living Environment initiatives.

FROM AUDIT TO ASSESSMENT AND BEYOND

Timberland's shift from "audit" to "assessment" in 2005, and the subsequent creation of the Workplaces pillar, highlighted the supply chain as one large, complex improvement opportunity. With 13 assessors verifying Code compliance and consulting with factory management to facilitate ongoing improvement, Workplaces was the second-most-expensive pillar. It accounted for 37% of an annual CSR budget that typically fell in the $2 to $3 million range. (Service accounted for 48% of CSR expenditure in 2009, due primarily to outfitting City Year; Energy and Product made up the final 15%.) The move from audit to assessment came about because of Timberland's desire to achieve sustainable improvement in workers' lives. Colleen Von Haden, who joined Timberland as an assessor in 2005 and became senior manager of Code of Conduct when Gordon Peterson became head of the CSR department, explained the benefit to suppliers and their employees:

> [Consultative assessments] gain us room at the table with factory managers more than if we were just in the factory telling them what they're doing wrong. Then they start seeing that we're really there to help and to see how we can make the lives of workers better, and by doing so you should see more loyalty, less turnover, more productivity. That gives us a way to get managers to think about compliance in a different way, and that's through your bottom line.

Beth Holzman explained the decision from Timberland's business perspective as well:

> The biggest way we see return [on investment] on the social side is in terms of "license to operate." Our Code was developed when a lot of footwear brands were under scrutiny, and to compete we needed to have our Code. . . . Without having suppliers be on board with our Code program and be producing at the quality we need we wouldn't have the business we have. . . . We work on sustained improvement so that our license to operate continues to exist.

While competitors in the footwear industry were increasingly cognizant of human rights issues in their supply chain and all major global brands had developed compliance systems, Timberland's assessment program was unique in its engagement with factory employees and management, its organizational visibility, and its record of environmental and social impact according to assessment metrics. According to Gordon Peterson, "the assessment process for some [brands] is, 'Is Timberland there [in the factory]?'" Colleen Von Haden added:

> A big distinction between our program and others is the debate about whether or not you should even be in a [low-scoring] factory. Part of our mission is that if we are

going to be in a factory we think we can have positive change. There are a lot of other companies that would say that's too much risk, or we'll get publicly scrutinized, but then it creates a vicious cycle where they're in and out of factories and . . . the workers are the ones that suffer. And the reality is that if we pull out someone else is going to come in to pick up that extra capacity and they might come in with no Code at all, so we'd much rather stay in and make change.

Timberland partnered with 10 brands in 25 factories to develop assessment and compliance synergies. Most notably, the company worked with Levi's to conduct joint assessments and remediation plans, thus more effectively deploying the resources of its assessors as well as avoiding "audit fatigue" from factory managers having to undergo assessments multiple times a year from multiple companies. At General Shoes, a supplier in Vietnam, Timberland collaborated with several brands not only to conduct assessments and remediation plans but also to roll out a joint Sustainable Living Environment project. These partnerships enabled Timberland to leverage scale to achieve a broader impact than it would have been able to achieve alone, while mitigating its burden to improve workplace conditions only so other brands could benefit. Additionally, these initiatives positioned Timberland as a leader in changing the terms by which international brands worked with suppliers. Still, Timberland conducted assessments and remediation plans on its own in 90% of the factories it sourced from, and was still responsible for assessments that complied with the Code in the factories in which it conducted joint assessments. Von Haden recognized Timberland's role as an industry leader whose transparent assessments bought the company credibility but further obligated it to "dive deeper into underlying root causes."

In the long term, for supplier development to be sustainable, it had to be a part of not just Timberland's DNA but of other brands and of the suppliers themselves. The Fair Factories Clearinghouse, created in 2004 by Reebok and several nonprofits, aimed to make factories more sustainable from a human rights perspective by enabling companies to input data about human rights abuses at their suppliers into a software program. Timberland was an early member and one of a handful of footwear companies to contribute supplier data. By doing so, Timberland lowered the cost of creating and managing compliance programs for other companies, reduced audit fatigue, and facilitated collaboration to create compliance standards.[45]

Ultimately, despite the emphasis Timberland put on the Code both internally and externally and the investment that went into it, it was only one of several factors deciding where Timberland did business. The Value Chain division made decisions about suppliers based on quality, reliability, cost, and other business factors, and while the Code was part of the Balanced Scorecard, Timberland still had about 30% supplier turnover annually for reasons not typically related to human rights.

While Value Chain was responsible for supplier footprint, a repeatedly poor assessment trumped the business case for working with a supplier. In 2006, Timberland fired Kingmaker, a Chinese supplier that had accounted for 17% of Timberland's production but consistently performed poorly on audits. This was the first (and only) supplier to be fired solely for Code violations.[46] Timberland devoted extensive resources to getting the facility up to code for both business and human rights reasons. However, conditions stagnated, and Timberland even became the subject of an attack from a human rights advocacy group called China Labor Watch.[47] Timberland finally had to let go.

The move cost Timberland $1 million as it transitioned production to other suppliers. Timberland considered the experience a failure not because of the expense, however, but because, according to Von Haden, "we thought to ourselves, 'if we leave, who does the worker have?'" Moreover, Timberland's withdrawal had little impact on Kingmaker. Jeff Swartz commented:

> When we left Kingmaker . . . the right outcome should have been that no one else went in. And yet good brands piled in, and the consumer's take was, "Don't ask, don't tell." And that is hard for me to live with.[48]

Jeff Swartz himself often asked, "What is the role of the brand—does it stop at the factory floor?"[49] Timberland became more active outside factory walls under the assessment program with Sustainable Living Environments (SLEs). The company did not view SLEs as "international development" but as a more effective means of compensating workers. Timberland's factory in the Dominican Republic was key to experimenting with solutions to the needs expressed by workers. According to Beth Holzman:

> We're really unique among footwear companies in that we actually do have our own wholly-owned factory in the developing world. We can treat the Dominican Republic as a learning lab for different approaches to social and environmental initiatives. . . . A lot of our basis to build a business case for our Workplace initiatives comes from what we do there.

As early as 1999, factory management, and workers themselves, noted that a sustainable living wage was insufficient to provide for their basic needs and suggested that they would take advantage of access to healthcare and education if it were available. Accordingly, management launched a literacy program whereby local teachers taught classes after working hours and workers could study toward completion of a high school equivalency exam. By the end of 2008, 120 employees were participating. Similarly, factory management worked with other factories in their export processing zone to launch a co-op program to purchase healthy food at lower prices. Approximately 40% of the workforce participated in this program, which filled a need employees were not having met outside of work.[50]

Timberland next took the concept of Sustainable Living Environments to their suppliers. Since 2000, Timberland had sourced from a factory in Bangladesh that employed 5,600 workers, 85% of whom were migrant women. The assessment process made clear that these and other women in the export processing zone lacked basic health awareness and services. Timberland collaborated with CARE, an international humanitarian organization, on improving awareness of and access to health services for the 24,000 garment workers in the export processing zone. The company set out an ambitious agenda of education, access to basic medical needs, and a microfinance program. Timberland extended the partnership to provide discounted medicine for 3,000 children.

The most successful and innovative aspect of the program was the microfinance program, which allowed workers to take out loans averaging $95 at a favorable interest rate. By 2008, the program had 18,000 participants, a 99% payback rate, and was self-sustaining. Monte Allen, CARE's executive director, pointed out that "the fact that Timberland was broad-minded enough to open the project to workers from other factories—even if they did not produce Timberland products—dramatically magnified the benefits of the program."[51]

Timberland also worked with Business for Social Responsibility (BSR) in Vietnam and China. BSR created Health Enables Return projects (HERprojects) to improve health awareness among female workers. Timberland partnered with them for three pilot projects. Initial responses to the programs, launched in 2007–2008, were positive, with factory managers stating they would continue the programs with their own funding. A BSR study on a non-Timberland HERproject showed that for every $1 invested in health training, there was a $3 return through reduced absenteeism, higher productivity, and lower turnover.[52]

Despite the success of these projects from a humanitarian standpoint, Von Haden said that the cost ($500,000 for the Bangladesh/CARE project alone) was too high. Peterson added:

> How do you define return [on human rights investments]? . . . We can't accurately measure or even quantify the impact. . . . But we're choosing factories that provide a better workplace, which improves retention, productivity, and consistency in our supplier network, so clearly we're getting strategic benefits for the company.

Holzman noted, "We have very limited resources, so embedded in the 'where do we go from here' thought process is 'how do we allocate our resources to have the biggest impact?'" Timberland's SLE projects as of 2009 had been ad hoc combinations of NGOs approaching Timberland and assessments revealing basic needs to satisfy.

Thus, while Timberland had spent almost $1 million on four SLEs by 2009, there was no standardized system for identifying them, approving them, prioritizing them, measuring their success, determining a budget, or identifying how best to work with NGOs. Still, Timberland was committed to refining its approach to make the initiative sustainable and to have a lasting impact that could be scaled. After all, according to Jeff Swartz, "No one believes in [Timberland's slogan: 'Boots, Brand, Belief'] more than we do, and that is our competitive advantage."[53]

LOOKING TO THE FUTURE: WHERE SHOULD TIMBERLAND CSR GO NEXT?

With suppliers throughout the developing world, Timberland had the potential to alleviate social problems in communities worldwide, and the SLE program in effect made Timberland a player in international development. Given the scope of the corresponding challenges Timberland faced, Jeff Swartz had to ask himself and his CSR team: if this is a business we should be in, how can we do it sustainably, and how can we make it resonate with consumers? He voiced the dilemma:

> [NGOs] had a 3-year debate with Nike to tell them the names of their factories and Nike said no. So we put the names of our factories right on the shoe label and thought something would come of it. Nothing. One-handed applause. Dead silence. . . . And so the concern I have about Workplaces is: a lot of energy from us, and we're not going away from it; some energy from activists; but until there's another crisis in human rights I see the issue receding in the minds of the people who have the power to cause change.

As a reference brand in CSR, Timberland had many eyes on them, but as a relatively small player in the global footwear market, Timberland had limited resources to pursue its lofty human rights agenda. From a broader perspective, Timberland had taken the public stance that it intended to address some of the most challenging problems facing business. As the company drew up its CSR budget amid two years of declining sales, it had to weigh the value of investing in parts of the CSR agenda that had a less clear link to consumer behavior—for example, factory workers' welfare—against the value of spending directly on more overtly consumer-oriented initiatives, like the Green Index. Budget cuts had already stripped the Workplaces pillar primarily to assessments until the business case existed for additional projects "beyond factory walls." The Four Pillars program had given structure to Timberland's long-term vision of social responsibility, including an implicit promise to factory workers that Timberland would strive to improve their lives; however, long-term CSR goals had to mesh with short-term budget realities and obligations for financial performance. Jeff Swartz had in the back of his mind with each decision, "How does this help us sell more boots?"

Timberland had made impressive strides in developing and honing an industry-leading integrated CSR organization, and by introducing the assessment process it launched a superior way of having an impact on workers' lives. But with each new step a new challenge emerged, and with each challenge a new set of increasingly ambitious goals for overcoming them. Swartz had to decide how far down the road to keep running. And he knew that if the decision was wrong, "you will die on the battlefield of 'I can solve this problem.'"[54]

EPILOGUE

In September 2011, Timberland was acquired by VF Corporation, a "leader in branded lifestyle apparel" and owner of The North Face and Wrangler brands, among others.[55] Jeff Swartz was replaced as president of Timberland by Patrik Frisk, a senior executive at VF.[56]

Following the acquisition, Timberland substituted its Code of Conduct with VF's Terms of Engagement (TOE) and Global Compliance Principles. The VF audit team has assumed responsibility for reviewing factory compliance with VF's Terms of Engagement, allowing the Timberland team to focus on "beyond compliance" efforts. Colleen Von Haden explains: "We've shifted the process to a more collaborative approach. . . . VF has a strong inspection team, which then allows the Timberland team to take the next step and drive change." Von Haden is optimistic that the collaboration with VF will continue to prove successful, and that this will allow [Timberland] to "influence other VF brands."[57]

Case Questions

1. How does Timberland's CSR strategy fit into its overall corporate strategy and culture?

2. What are the key reasons for Timberland's success to date? Could its strategy have worked at a company like Nike?

3. What is Timberland doing right in terms of managing its suppliers? What are its biggest threats, challenges, and opportunities to address among its supplier base?

4. What responsibility, if any, does Timberland have for driving its industry, and corporations in general, forward in terms of CSR? What responsibility, if any, does it have to global workers?

5. Timberland states in its "Dig Deeper" paper on its Workplaces pillar that "as a consequence [of our goal to strengthen communities and workers' lives], we end up in conversations of social policy that we never imagined as a simple boot maker from New England. Yet here we are." Should they be there?

Exhibit 10.1 Timberland Code of Conduct (as of 2009)

We believe in the power of an individual to make a difference in the world where we live and work. One voice can and must make a difference. We believe that speaking up for a courageous idea or voicing a grievance strengthens Timberland and builds our community.

We respect and promote the Universal Declaration of Human Rights and the International Labor Organization (ILO) conventions that establish international human and labor rights. Timberland strives to provide the opportunity for all employees to work in fair, safe and non-discriminatory environments, and we define "employee" as any individual working in an enterprise. We believe that companies must provide opportunities for employee development. We seek to apply both the letter and the spirit of all applicable local laws and to promote continuous improvement in our operations. We hold our business partners to these same standards and actively seek partners who share our beliefs. The following requirements are meant to ensure that these standards are maintained.

Human Rights

Voluntary Employment: *Each employee's presence must be voluntary. This specifically prohibits all forms of prison labor, indentured labor, slave labor, or any other forms of compulsory labor. Employees must have the option to leave employment.*

Freedom of Association: *Employees must be given the right to decide how their best interests will be represented in the workplace. This includes the right to freely associate and bargain collectively. Where the right to freedom of association is restricted under law, there must be an equivalent means of independent representation for employees.*

Fair and Equal Treatment: *Work environments must be free of intolerance, harassment, abuse, retribution for grievances, and corporal punishment. There cannot be discrimination based on race, color, sex, religion, political opinion, nationality, social origin, social status, indigenous heritage, disability, age, marital status, capacity to bear children, pregnancy, sexual orientation, genetic features, or other status of the individual unrelated to the ability to perform the job.*

Child Labor: *The labor of children cannot be used. We define "child" as younger than 16 years of age or the compulsory age for school attendance, whichever is greater. Laws on restrictions for employees of certain ages must be followed.*

Compensation: *For regular work hours, employees must receive wages and benefits that at a minimum meet all applicable laws governing minimum wage and mandated benefits. For overtime hours, employees must receive a premium rate, which must be no lower than local law. Wages must be paid on a regular schedule and employees must receive an understandable payslip that shows how wages are calculated. There cannot be conditional employment practices, such as training or apprenticeship wages, pre-employment fees, deposits, or other practices that effectively lower an employee's pay below the legal minimum wage.*

Working Hours: *The regular work schedule (excluding appropriately compensated overtime) must not exceed 48 hours per six day period. Total working hours (including overtime) cannot exceed 60 hours in a given week or 12 hours in a given day. Employees shall receive at least 1 day off of rest after working 6 consecutive days. All overtime must be voluntary.*

Health and Safety: *The workplace must be safe and healthy based on the recognized standards of the ILO and national laws. This requirement applies to any residential facilities provided. Employees must receive training on workplace safety practices.*

Environment

We expect a strong environmental commitment and aggressive efforts to protect and restore the natural environment. We will favor partners who: 1) have a management system demonstrating environmental commitment; 2) publicly disclose environmental impacts and activities through regular reporting; 3) eliminate toxic and hazardous substances from products and operations; 4) increase efficiency and thereby minimize pollution and waste; 5) reduce use of natural resources including raw materials, energy and water; 6) take responsibility for proper waste management and any environmental problems associated with disposal of wastes. We require a continuous effort to improve environmental performance along a defined path towards clean production.

Right of Review

To measure our compliance and the compliance of our business partners, we conduct ongoing audits and reviews of facilities. We require full and open access (for our staff and representatives) to the facilities and operations involved in our business. Employees must have the opportunity to notify us anonymously on any violations of standards at a workplace, and they must not receive any retribution for this action. We will make information on our compliance program available publicly.

Source: "Key Performance Indicators" exhibit. The Timerbland Company. Used with permission of The Timberland Company, 2009.

Exhibit 10.2 CSR Key Performance Indicators (the "Dashboard") as of September 2009

KEY PERFORMANCE INDICATORS

FOCUS	CATEGORY	INDICATOR	ANNUAL PERFORMANCE			TARGETS	
			2006	2007	2008	2010	2015
Climate and Energy	Footprint	Metric Tons Carbon Emissions[1]	25,559	23,037	18,781	12,800	6,400
	Renewable Energy	Renewable Energy as Percentage of Total Energy Use[1]	5.73%	4.99%	6.67%	39%	60%
	Supply Chain	Metric Tons of Emissions for Footwear Factories	New metric in '07	116,760	104,887	Baseline	NT
Cradle-to-Cradle Product	Green Index®	Average Green Index® Source (weighted by production of scored shoes)	New metric in '07	6.31	6.13	TBD[2]	NT
	Chemicals	Average Grams/Pair of Volatile Organic Compounds (VOCs)	New metric in '08		74.9	71.2[3]	NT
	Raw Materials	Percentage of Total Cotton Sourced that is Organic[4]	5.70%	7.35%	N/A	TBD[2]	NT
Fair, State and Non-Discriminatory Workplaces	Purchasing Practices	Percentage of footwear production in "High Risk" factories	New metric in '07	34%	1%	0%	0%
	Scoring	Percentage of "High Priority" factories	50%	38%	38%	30%	20%
	Improvement	Average Assessment Score	57.0	61.9	62.0	70.0	75.0
		Average Environmental Score (not including tanneries)	2.12	1.88	2.10	2.75	3.00
		Average Environmental Score (including tanneries)	2.53	2.53	3.17	4.00	NT
		Percentage of Continued Factory Partners with Improved Score	55%	51%	69%	70%	70%

KEY PERFORMANCE INDICATORS

FOCUS	CATEGORY	INDICATOR	ANNUAL PERFORMANCE			TARGETS	
			2006	2007	2008	2010	2015
Community Service	General Service Statistics	Hours Utilization Rate (HUR)	39%	40%	38.8%	41%	45%
		Hours Spent Serving the Community	80,632	86,037	79,018	80,262	87,784
		Benefit Utilization Rate (BUR)	71%	76%	77%	80%	84%

Source: "Key Performance Indicators" exhibit. The Timberland Company. Used with permission of The Timberland Company, 2009.

[1]Timberland's carbon footprint includes emissions from facilities we own and operate (such as offices, distribution centers, our manufacturing facility in the Dominican Republic and retail locations) and emissions from employee air travel. These emissions represent approximately 4% of Timberland's influence in the value chain. The other 96% of our carbon footprint comes from emissions from inbound transportation, emissions from finished product footwear factories and emissions embedded in the raw materials of our product. We have yet to determine adequate measurement and tracking of emissions from apparel factories licensees, or the IPATH® and howies® brands.

As of December 2008, we revised historical data from 2006 (our current baseline) through year end 2008 to account for updated emissions factors provided by the World Resources Institute (WRI)/World Business Council on Sustainable Development (WBCSD) Greenhouse Gas (GHG) Protocol. In this process, we also discovered historical accounting errors in our 2006, 2007 and 2008 and data, mostly due to better record-keeping and improved understanding of energy consumption. As a result, we have restated our 2006 baseline, and 2007 and 2008 performance accordingly. Please note we are also restating our long-term emissions reductions goals in order to maintain our absolute emissions reductions targets of 24% in 2008 and 50% in 2010 (over the 2006 baseline). We are on track to have our GHG Inventory verified by a third party by 2010.

[2]TBD targets are those that we plan to disclose in late 2009 after we have verified data quality for internal calculation purposes.

[3]Target for new metric of Average grams/pair of Volatile Organic Compounds (VOCs) is for 2009 rather than 2010 because this is the first year we are disclosing this data.

[4]We do not have 2008 year-end data for percentage of total cotton sourced that is organic because we began licensing apparel during 2008. As a result, mid-2008 performance is not directly comparable to other data points, as of 2009, this metric includes licensee data and is a global metric.

NT stands for No Target. We will set long-term targets in 2010 for these metrics.

NOTES

1. City Year, http://www.cityyear.org (accessed August 15, 2009).

2. While Timberland designates intermediate processers of raw materials as "suppliers" and manufacturers of finished products as "manufacturing facilities," this case uses "suppliers" to refer to all suppliers and manufacturers that are not owned by Timberland.

3. Massing, M. (2001, July 1). "From protest to program." *American Prospect*. Retrieved August 15, 2009, from http://www.prospect.org/cs/articles?article=from_protest_to_program

4. Bonini, S., Mendonca, L., & Oppenheimer, J. (2006, Spring). "When social issues become strategic." *McKinsey Quarterly*, p. 21.

5. Massing, "From protest to program."

6. 2008 Ceres/Riskmetrics survey.

7. Publications and organizations including *Fortune*, Business for Social Responsibility, Points of Light, Businesses Strengthening America, America's Promise, and Commitment to Encourage Corporate Philanthropy have all cited Timberland as an example of exceptional social responsibility in business.

8. City Year. (2006). "Timberland and City Year: Celebrating 15 years of doing well by doing good." Retrieved August 15, 2009, from http://www.cityyear.org

9. Many of the quotations in this case were obtained from personal interviews.

10. Battistelli, M. (2008, August 1). "City stories." *Fundraising Success Magazine*. Retrieved September 1, 2009, from http://www.fundraisingsuccessmag.com/article/114000-114999/114448.html

11. Arena, C. (2004). Cause for success: 10 companies that put profits second and came in first (p. 79). New World Library.

12. Ibid.

13. Leather Working Group, http://www.leatherworkinggroup.com

14. Timberland. (n.d.). "Timberland responsibility." Retrieved July 27, 2012, from http://responsibility.timberland.com

15. "Ford, Timberland win Ceres-ACCA sustainability reporting awards." (2008, May 1). *Environmental Leader*. Retrieved August 20, 2009, from http://www.environmentalleader.com/2008/05/01/ford-timberland-win-ceres-acca-sustainability-reporting-awards/

16. "Timberland to release quarterly CSR data." (2008, May 5). *Environmental Leader*. Retrieved August 20, 2009, from http://www.environmentalleader.com/2008/05/05/timberland-to-release-quarterly-csr-data

17. Just Means, http://timberland.justmeans.com (accessed August 20, 2009).

18. http://apps.facebook.com/earthkeepers (accessed August 20, 2009). This link is no longer active.

19. Porter, M., & Kramer, M. (2006, December). "Strategy and society: The link between competitive advantage and corporate social responsibility" (p. 80). *Harvard Business Review*. Retrieved from https://hbr.org/2006/12/strategy-and-society-the-link-between-competitive-advantage-and-corporate-social-responsibility

20. Reingold, J. (2005, November). "Walking the walk" (p. 84). *Fast Company*.

21. Borden, M., & Kamenetz, A. (2008, September). "The Prophet CEO" (p. 128). *Fast Company*.

22. Feldman, A. (2008, February 15). "Fast 50 2008: Timberland." *Fast Company*. Retrieved September 1, 2009, from http://www.fastcompany.com/fast50_08/timberland.html

23. Timberland Company. (2009). "Engaging employees: Timberland's Global Steward's program."

24. Cone, C., Feldman, M., & DaSilva, A. (2003, July). "Causes and effects" (p. 99). *Harvard Business Review*; McCormick, H. (2007, November 6). "Sprucing up CSR with Timberland" (p. 24). *Personnel Today*.

25. "100 Best Companies to Work For." *Forbes*. Retrieved August 25, 2009, from http://money.cnn.com/magazines/fortune/bestcompanies/2007

26. California Climate Action Registry, http://www.climateregistry.org (accessed August 20, 2009).

27. Timberland Company. (2009). "Timberland corporate social responsibility report 2008."

28. Arena, C. (2009, August 10). "At Timberland, candor moves the dial." *Fast Company*. Retrieved August 20, 2009, from http://www.fastcompany.com/blog/christine-arena/case-point/timberland-candor-moves-dial

29. Timberland Company, "Timberland corporate social responsibility report 2008."

30. Timberland Company. (2009). "Timberland climate strategy, 2009."

31. Buell, A. (2009, July 1). "An environmental statement: Timberland store earns LEED Gold certification for retail interior." *Environmental Design and Construction*. Retrieved August 25, 2009.

32. Timberland Company, "Timberland corporate social responsibility report 2008."

33. Timberland Company, "Timberland climate strategy, 2009."

34. Timberland Company, "Timberland corporate social responsibility report 2008."

35. Ibid.

36. Business for Social Responsibility, http://www.bsr.org/consulting/working-groups/clean-cargo.cfm (accessed September 1, 2009).

37. Timberland Company. (2009). "Timberland's Green Index strategy."

38. Bouchard, N. P. (2009, February). "There's hope ahead" (p. 42). *Sporting Goods Business*.

39. Schwartz, A. (2009, July 8). "The Earthkeepers 2.0 boot: Timberland's attempt at closing the loop." *Fast Company*. Retrieved August 20, 2009, from http://www.fastcompany.com/blog/ariel-schwartz/sustainability/earthkeeper-20-boot-timberlands-attempt-closing-loop

40. Timberland Company, "Timberland corporate social responsibility report 2008."

41. Ibid.

42. Ernst, J. (2007, December 3). "Green days." *Footwear News*, p. 44.

43. Timberland Company, "Timberland's Green Index strategy."

44. Timberland Company. (2009). "Responsibility beyond factory walls."

45. http://www.fairfactories.org/what-we-do/History.aspx (accessed September 10, 2009).

46. Timberland Company. (2007). "Timberland corporate social responsibility report 2006" (p. 21).

47. China Labor Watch. (2004, December 18). "Kingmaker footwear (Timberland made in China)." Retrieved August 25, 2009, from http://www.chinalaborwatch.org/report/11

48. Borden & Kamenetz, "The Prophet CEO," pp. 128–129.

49. Ibid.

50. Timberland Company, "Responsibility beyond factory walls," p. 17.

51. Ibid., p. 22.

52. Ibid., p. 23.

53. Reingold, J. (2005, November). "Walking the walk" (p. 80). *Fast Company*.

54. Timberland Company. (2008, October 29). "Responsible sourcing" (CSR quarterly conference call). Podcast retrieved from http://responsibility.timberland.com/stakeholder-engagement -calls/

55. Greensboro, N. C., & Stratham, N. H. (2011, June 13). "VF to acquire the Timberland Company for $43 per share" [Press release]. Retrieved August 1, 2012, from http://www.vfc.com/ index.php/news/press-releases?nws_id=A59704D6-E939-704E-E043-A740E3EA704E

56. Greensboro, N. C. (2011, September 13). "VF completes acquisition of the Timberland Company" [Press release]. Retrieved August 1, 2012, from http://www.vfc.com/index.php/news/ press-releases?nws_id=ACD3A724-6461-2098-E043-A740E3EA2098

57. Timberland Company. "Collaborating to improve workers' lives." Retrieved August 1, 2012, from http://responsibility.timberland.com/wp-content/uploads/report-builder/singles/collaborating -to-improve-workers-lives.pdf

INDEX